T0219702

The Blockchain Developer

A Practical Guide for Designing, Implementing, Publishing, Testing, and Securing Distributed Blockchain-based Projects

Elad Elrom

Apress®

The Blockchain Developer

Elad Elrom
New York, NY, USA

ISBN-13 (pbk): 978-1-4842-4846-1   ISBN-13 (electronic): 978-1-4842-4847-8
https://doi.org/10.1007/978-1-4842-4847-8

Copyright © 2019 by Elad Elrom

Managing Director, Apress media LLC: Welmoed Spahr
Acquisitions Editor: Louise Corrigan
Development Editor: James Markham
Coordinating Editor: Nancy Chen

Cover designed by eStudioCalamar

Cover image designed by Chris Barbalis on Unsplash

Distributed to the book trade worldwide by Springer Science+Business Media New York, 233 Spring Street, 6th Floor, New York, NY 10013. Phone 1-800-SPRINGER, fax (201) 348-4505, e-mail orders-ny@springer-sbm.com, or visit www.springeronline.com. Apress Media, LLC is a California LLC and the sole member (owner) is Springer Science + Business Media Finance Inc (SSBM Finance Inc). SSBM Finance Inc is a **Delaware** corporation.

For information on translations, please e-mail rights@apress.com, or visit www.apress.com/rights-permissions.

Apress titles may be purchased in bulk for academic, corporate, or promotional use. eBook versions and licenses are also available for most titles. For more information, reference our Print and eBook Bulk Sales web page at www.apress.com/bulk-sales.

Any source code or other supplementary material referenced by the author in this book is available to readers on GitHub via the book's product page, located at www.apress.com/9781484248461. For more detailed information, please visit www.apress.com/source-code.

Printed on acid-free paper

I would like to dedicate this book to my children, Romi Scarlett Elrom and Ariel Rocco Elrom. Have solid boundaries, and don't allow anyone to dictate what you cannot achieve or cannot do. I love you very much and will always be there for you.

Table of Contents

About the Author

 **Elad Elrom** is a coder, technical lead, and technical writer. As a writer, he has co-authored four technical books. Elad has consulted for a variety of clients, from large corporations, such as HBO, Viacom, NBC Universal, and Weight Watchers, to smaller startups. Aside from coding, Elad is a certified PADI dive instructor and an accomplished certified pilot. You can contact him at `elad.ny@gmail.com`.

About the Technical Reviewer

**Nishith Pathak** is India's first Artificial Intelligence (AI) Most Valuable Professional (MVP), a Microsoft Regional Director (RD), a lead architect, a speaker, an AI thinker, an innovator, and a strategist. Nishith's expertise lies in helping Fortune 100 companies design and architect next-generation solutions that incorporate AI, machine learning, cognitive services, blockchain, and many more. He sits on several technical advisory boards across the globe and is the author of multiple books on AI and blockchain. Nishith has played a PAN account enterprise architect role where he was responsible for everything from the overall architecture to the design in multiple projects. He is an internationally acclaimed speaker on technologies such as AI and blockchain and regularly speaks at various technical conferences.

For his expertise on artificial intelligence, Microsoft awarded him the first Most Valuable Professional in the Artificial Intelligence category. Globally, he is among 19 MVPs on AI, recognized by Microsoft for their sheer expertise in AI. He has also been awarded the Microsoft Regional Director award, bestowed upon 150 of the world's top technology visionaries chosen specifically for their proven cross-platform expertise. Nishith is currently working on key areas such as artificial intelligence, machine learning, cognitive computing, blockchain, Internet of Things, and cloud computing; he helps companies architect solutions based on these technologies.

He can be contacted at NisPathak@GMail.com or found on LinkedIn (https://www.linkedin.com/in/nishithpathak/), Twitter (http://twitter.com/nispathak), or Microsoft (https://rd.microsoft.com/en-us/nishith-pathak).

CHAPTER 1

Blockchain Basics

This chapter will serve as your ground school before you "take off" toward development. It will introduce basic concepts that will help you to understand the blockchain technology. This chapter is split into four parts.

- Introduction to Cryptoeconomics
- Blockchain Explained
- Cryptocurrencies Overload
- Blockchain P2P Network

To understand cryptoeconomics, you first need to understand concepts such as encryption and decryption, private-public keys, cryptography, digital assets, cryptography, and cryptocurrency.

Once you understand these basic concepts, I will cover blockchain. I will cover the pieces that make up an individual blockchain, such as blocks, and how the blocks are linked together, as well as the problems with blockchain such as double spending. I will also explain cryptomining, cryptominers, and cryptocurrency wallets.

Then, I will cover the different types of cryptocurrencies: bitcoin, tokens, and alternative cryptocurrency coins (altcoins).

Last, I will cover the P2P network that is used with the blockchain technology and the different layers that make up the network: consensus layer, miner layer, propagation layer, semantic layer, and application layer.

© Elad Elrom 2019
E. Elrom, *The Blockchain Developer*, https://doi.org/10.1007/978-1-4842-4847-8_1

Introduction to Cryptoeconomics

The world of crypto is full of technical jargon that can confuse even the savviest technology ninja. Bitcoin introduced the concept of cryptoeconomics and paved the way for the creation of many blockchain platforms. Before we dive deep into how a blockchain works, let's understand what cryptoeconomics is and the underlying concepts behind a blockchain.

Verbal communication is based on selecting words to describe a message you want to convey. However, sometimes you want to communicate with only certain people while excluding others. A good example is during wartime; a commander communicates with soldiers stationed on the front line while ensuring the enemy is unable to listen. The commander could use encryption for this communication.

Electronically speaking, today all shopping sites offer their merchandise over an encryption protocol, called Secure Sockets Layer (SSL), that can protect your personal information from hackers. Video encryption and decryption are common to ensure the delivery of video to authorized members only, and on personal computers, people often use encryption to back up and protect files and passwords.

Moreover, as a developer, you likely sent encrypted messages and also decrypt incoming messages with the help of libraries as all programming languages offer string encryption and decryption functions.

So, let's look at some definitions:

- *Encryption*: Encryption is a process of converting your message into code so that only authorized parties can access it.

- *Decryption*: Decryption is reversing the encryption process so that the message can be converted to the original message.

- *Cryptography*: This is using the techniques of encryption and decryption to send and receive messages.

- *Cryptocurrency*: This is using cryptography the same way as the earlier SSL or video example but specifically to fit the needs of a digital asset.

Note   A *digital asset* can be anything of value, such as the combination to your home safe, a secret password, a list, a message, electronic cash, a document, a photo, and so on.

- *Cryptoeconomics*: This is the combination of cryptography and economics to provide a platform to pass digital assets.

For further clarification, let's look at these terms in more detail and apply them to the topics I will be covering in this book.

Ig-pay Atin-lay

To begin, let's go back in time. Have you ever spoken as a child in Pig Latin? The secret Pig Latin language is simple. You take off the first letter of the word you want to say and then move the letter to the end of the word, as well as add the sound "ay."

For example:

- "Pig" become "ig-pay."

- "Latin" becomes "atin-lay."

What we just have done is encryption. Then to understand the words we have encrypted, we need to work backward.

–   "Ig-pay" becomes "pig" by removing "ay" from the end
     and taking the last letter and putting it as the first letter.

–   Similarly, "atin-lay" becomes "Latin."

What we have just done is decryption. Children are able to use these
techniques to encrypt and decrypt words in a simple form of cryptography.

Encryption/Decryption

Encryption enables you to pass messages between specific parties in a
secure manner so excluded parties will not understand them. Throughout
history, there was a need to be able to send secret messages between
parties. One party sends an encrypted message at one place, and then the
other party is able to receive and decrypt the message elsewhere.

In fact, encryption was used a lot during World War I (WWI) and World
War II (WWII). The Nazis used a machine called Enigma to encrypt and
decrypt messages (see Figure 1-1). The Allies figured out a way to break
the Nazi Enigma machine's secret code and decrypt the messages. This is
believed to have shortened WWII by years.

Figure 1-1. Enigma machine. Photo credit: wikimedia.org.

Encryption and decryption went from pure Army usage to public usage by way of the development of the Data Encryption Standard (DES) by IBM in 1970 and the invention of key cryptography in 1976. In fact, in the past, cryptography and encryption were synonymous.

Encryption + Decryption = Cryptography

As mentioned, cryptography is the process of using the techniques of encryption and decryption. The word *cryptography* came from the Greek word *kryptos*, which means hidden or secret.

In the Pig Latin language example, I described how you can encrypt and decrypt words. That technique of removing the first letter and adding it to the end with "ay," and then vice versa, is cryptography. Without knowledge of the technique, you wouldn't be able to understand the Pig Latin language.

Most people are probably smart enough to figure out the secret Pig Latin language as it's simple in nature; however, a complex encryption example would be a different story.

For instance, going back to the WWII Enigma machine, the Nazis were passing messages over the air. The Allies were capable of receiving these messages (the messages were the "public keys"), but without a way to decode them (the "private keys"), it was not enough. It took a scientist named Turing and others five-and-a-half months to decrypt the Nazi's secret messages.

Note   A cryptographic *key* can be used to encrypt a message. The encrypted message can then be decrypted only by using the second key (a private key) that is known only to the recipient.

5

Turing's contribution was to automate a machine that was capable of figuring out different settings the Nazis made in their Enigma machine so they could decrypt messages In other words, it automated the process of searching for the private key. That machine was called *bombe*.

Digital Assets + Cryptography = Cryptocurrency

Cryptocurrency is a digital asset designed so that electronic cash is able to be exchanged using strong cryptography (encryption and decryption) to ensure the security of funds, transactions, and the creation of new funds.

The cryptography's private key mechanism must be strong enough that it would be almost impossible (in other words, take too much time and effort) to figure out. Otherwise, all users could potentially lose their electronic cash if the cryptography could be figured out within a few months such as with the Enigma machine.

An example of cryptocurrency is bitcoin. Although bitcoin was not the first cryptocurrency invented, it's generally considered the first successful cryptocurrency.

Bitcoin's success is attributed to the following characteristics: no one can break the public-private key, it's distributed without a controlled government, it's publicly available, and it's published as open source code.

Note   Bitcoin was invented in 2008 by Satoshi Nakamotoi with the publication of a white paper called "Bitcoin: A Peer-to-Peer Electronic Cash System" (`https://bitcoin.org/bitcoin.pdf`). The actual complete open source software was released a year later in 2009 (`https://github.com/bitcoin/bitcoin`).

Cryptography + Economics = Cryptoeconomics

Cryptoeconomics is the combination of cryptography and economics to provide a platform that gives an incentive to maintain the platform, its scalability, and its security; in addition, it is absent of central or local government control. In other words, it's *decentralized*. The network is made up of a collection of multiple computers instead of one central computer.

Note   Decentralized is the opposite of central control; it means without central or local government control.

Bitcoin is able to achieve cryptoeconomics' goals by using the private-public key concepts; cryptography and cryptographic hashing functions are used indirectly. In fact, the relation between cryptography and cryptocurrency is indirect not just for bitcoin but for most cryptocurrency out there.

For instance, cryptography is used in bitcoin in other ways such as the following:

- Bitcoin uses private keys (bitcoin calls these *digital signatures*) with the help of an algorithm function (called the ECDSA elliptic curve) to prove ownership.

- Hashing algorithms are used for holding the structure of the database ledger data (or blockchain) via a hash generator called SHA256.

- The hashing algorithms are used to generate math puzzles that a computer tries to solve for a prize. Once the puzzle is solved, the computer is selected to help handle the transactions.

- Hashing algorithms are also used to generate account addresses.

- There is the concept of Merkle trees (covered in the next chapter), which use the hashing keys of large data in small pieces. This is useful for lightweight wallets that are needed on constrained hardware devices such as mobile devices.

Bitcoin does not gather identity information for its users; however, the transactions are public, meaning that all the information is transmitted and available online. Think of the Enigma example again; this means that anyone can intercept the messages transmitted. However, without the private key, no one can decrypt the messages.

Since the release of bitcoin in 2009, there are many other platforms that use different types of privacy for sending information in a secure manner and that use encryption for more portions of the process so that less information is public. Platforms such as Monero and Zcash use anonymity via cryptography even for messaging a transaction's details.

Blockchain Explained

As I mentioned, bitcoin was the first successful open source digital cash. Blockchain is the core technology, or the heart behind bitcoin and in fact behind all cryptocurrency platforms.

But what is blockchain?

In short, a *blockchain* is a shared digital ledger. Think of a database that instead of storing all the database entries on one computer it stores the data on multiple computers. A fancier definition would be that a blockchain is a decentralized and distributed global ledger.

Blocks + Chain = Blockchain

Each block contains records and transactions; these blocks are shared across multiple computers and should not be altered absent an agreement (consensus) of the entire network. The network is ruled according to a specific policy. The computers are connected on one network and called *peers* or *nodes*.

Note   What is blockchain? A *blockchain* is a digital decentralized (no financial institutions involved) and distributed ledger. In layperson's terms, it is a database that stores records and transactions on multiple computers without one controlling party and according to an agreed policy. The data that is stored is a block, and the blocks are linked (chained) together to form a blockchain.

Linked Blocks

A blockchain consists of a collection of data (a *block*) linked to the previous block. How are they linked? A block contains data, and each block references the block preceding it, so they are linked just as a chain link would be connected to the chain link before it. Take a look at Figure 1-2; as you can see, each block is referencing the previous block.

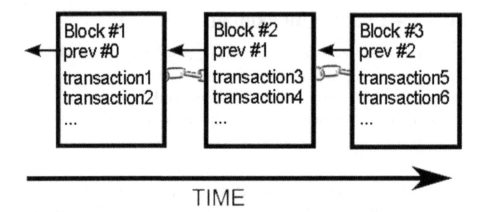

Figure 1-2. *Blocks chained together*

So, a blockchain contains blocks, which hold records of transactions. The private keys are held by the owner to show proof of ownership (this is the digital signature), so no one without the private key can decrypt the string and claim ownership. This combination of public keys and private keys represents the electronic cash.

Note   Peers form a network of nodes, so throughout this book, you may see the word *peer* or *node*. These words are synonymous for the purpose of this book.

As I said, digital assets can be anything—a music file, video file, electronic document, and so on. In cryptocurrency, a digital asset is represented as electronic cash; you can think of the public key as your bank account and routing number and the private key as the actual cash in your account. Yes, you can share your bank's information with others, but the funds will stay in your account. To claim your cash, you need to prove ownership. You go to the bank and show a form of ID and prove it's you by a way of signature; only then can you get your money out of your account. A similar process happens with cryptocurrency. There is a public address that represents your account, and only the owner holds the private key to prove ownership.

Double Spending Problem

A digital signature (public keys and private keys) securely ensures a party's identity is kept private and electronic cash is stored.

This concept of a private-public key combo enables you to encrypt and decrypt strings and keep a string safe, just as you saw with the Enigma machine. However, it is still not enough to solve the biggest problem of digital currency—double spending.

When you use fiat money (a paper money made legal by a government) such as U.S. dollars or euros, the paper is inconvertible, which means that once you gave the paper away, you cannot spend it again. In cryptocurrency, what happens if you prove ownership and send your digital asset twice at the exact same time? This could lead to *double spending*.

Hackers can try to reproduce digital assets as well as potentially double spend them, which cryptocurrency had to solve before it could be used as a digital currency.

Note   *Double spending* is the risk that digital currency can be spent twice because the digital signature could be reproduced and one could prove ownership and send a digital asset twice at the same time.

Blocks that hold keys are not enough to provide security and solve the double-spending potential issue to form a digital currency.

Bitcoin solves this problem by creating a network of computers and proving that no attempts of double spending have occurred. This is done by having all the computers on the network aware of every transaction. All the transactions are shared with all the computers in the network.

Double Spending Solution: P2P Network

In cryptocurrency, using a peer-to-peer network provided the solution to solve the double-spending problem.

Note *P2P networking* is a distributed application architecture that splits the tasks that need to be performed between different peers, with each peer having the same privilege. Together the peers create a P2P network of nodes.

Any computer that is connected on the network is called a *peer*. The peer can be any computer that meets the network requirements such as a laptop, mobile device, or server. The computers are connected to each other on the Internet via a P2P network protocol and form a network of nodes.

The P2P network protocol is not new. It has been used extensively on the Web for years now, from downloading files via Kazaa or LimeWire networks to having video chats via Skype.

As I mentioned, bitcoin was the first viable cryptocurrency, and it solved the double spending issue as well as allows electronic cash to be stored without going through financial institutions by utilizing P2P to form the blockchain protocol.

> *"A purely peer-to-peer version of electronic cash would allow online payments to be sent directly from one party to another without going through a financial institution."*
>
> —Satoshi Nakamoto, *Bitcoin: A Peer-to-Peer Electronic Cash System*

Cryptomining by Cryptominers

As noted, each computer that holds a copy of the shared ledger and is connected to the P2P network is a peer. A peer can help to add records and verify transactions. The process is called *cryptocurrency mining* or *cryptomining*, and the peer that helps record and verify the transactions is called a *cryptominer* or a *miner* for short.

Each miner helps to verify and add transactions to the blockchain digital ledger. The miners are often rewarded with a fee for the work, and to stay competitive with other miners, the miner usually needs a computer with specialized hardware.

Cryptocurrency Wallet

I covered what the public keys and private keys are and how they are used to encrypt and decrypt strings. The strings are digital currency or cryptocurrency, and the keys represent digital money.

A *cryptocurrency wallet* stores one or multiple public key and private key combinations and is used to receive or spend cryptocurrency.

A good analogy is to think of a wallet like your bank account. Cryptocurrency can be created by getting a reward by doing the miner work, or it can be purchased. I will expand on wallets later in the book.

Cryptocurrencies Overload

Before diving deeper into the blockchain P2P network, you should know that another concept that can cause confusion is the difference between coins and tokens. According to Coinmarketcap.com, at the time of writing, there are 1,833 listed cryptocurrencies with a market cap of $200 billion.

Many of these coins will surely disappear in the years to come as they offer little value, and these projects will be terminated because of a lack of interest or being a scam.

This can be confusing and intimidating, and most people don't understand the concept of bitcoin, let alone the large number of coins and tokens out there. To help understand these concepts, let's break down cryptocurrencies into three types: bitcoin, tokens, and alternative cryptocurrency coins (altcoins). See Figure 1-3.

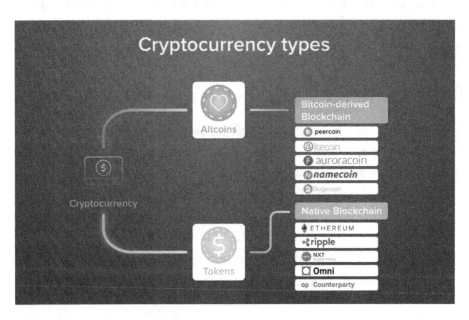

Figure 1-3. *Cryptocurrency coins and tokens. Photo credit: blog. citowise.com.*

Bitcoin Digital Cash

Bitcoin was the first successful implementation of a decentralized distributed digital currency. There are 21 million coins in total. The coins replace a traditional fiat currency.

Tokens

Tokens are a decentralized product offering. It is another option similar to an initial public offering (IPO) or crowdfunding. The tokens can be created anywhere in the world and delivered via Ethereum, EOS, or another capable blockchain platform. Tokens are usually created and distributed to the public via an initial coin offering (ICO).

Tokens stand for a utility or an asset that usually sits on top of a native blockchain. It can represent any digital asset including loyalty points, cryptocurrencies, or any good or commodity with individual units that are an interchangeable, fungible, or tradable asset. You can create a token using an existing blockchain template such as the Ethereum platform, or you can create your own tokens on an existing native blockchain and issue your own tokens. You can utilize smart contracts to simplify the process of creating tokens, as will be discussed in later chapters.

Note   Smart contracts are programmable code that runs on its own without the need for third parties. For instance, Solidity is a contact-oriented programming language and can be deployed on multiple blockchains.

Alternative Cryptocurrency Coins (Altcoins)

Alternative cryptocurrency coins (*altcoins* for short) are coins that are derived from bitcoin core source code by forking it (soft fork or hard fork). Examples are litecoin (which was a fork of the bitcoin core client), dogecoin (dogecoin 1.10 is a complete rebuild based on the bitcoin 0.11 build), bitcoinX, bitcoin cash, and bitcoin gold. In fact, at the time of writing, there are 26 altcoins.

Note   Hard forks are backward incompatible because the changes split the network code into two—the P2P network with the original code and the new P2P network running the new code. Soft forks are backward compatible, meaning that previously valid blocks/transactions become invalid, and old nodes recognize new blocks as valid. This forking happens often when there is a disagreement of developers regarding a direction. For instance, some developers would like to implement changes that other developers disagree with or a major fix is needed to be implemented.

Litecoin was a fork of the bitcoin's core client. Litecoin changed the time of blocks being sent from 10 minutes to 2.5 minutes, enabling transactions to be transferred quickly and more efficiently than bitcoin. Litecoin can then continue and add features as it's not relying on bitcoin's code anymore. For instance, in the future, litecoin will enable atomic swap, allowing people to convert Litecoin to bitcoin via smart contracts without involving an exchange. However, changes in the bitcoin core will require manual implementation to have these changes included in litecoin.

With that said, many will argue that Litecoin and many of these altcoins don't offer enough value to survive and are made with the purpose of enriching the developers who created the fork. Only time will tell.

EOS is another good example of altcoins. This time, the altcoin is turning into a token, as upon its release the EOS company issued Ethereum tokens, but as EOS is building its own blockchain platform, it is replacing the Ethereum token with its own EOS tokens.

In a nutshell, the main difference between altcoins and tokens is in their structure. An altcoin is its own currency like bitcoin or Litecoin, with its own dedicated network blockchain and need for miners. Tokens such as Ethereum tokens operate on top of an existing blockchain, which provides the token and the infrastructure (such as Ethereum) for the creation of a decentralized application (dapp). An example of an Ethereum token is the binance token (BNB).

In regard to Ethereum tokens, Ethereum offers the creation of different token standards or Ethereum Request for Comments (ERCs) such as ERC-20, ERC-223, or ERC-777. In the BNB token example, ERC-20 was used. These standards differ and will be discussed in more detail in later chapters.

Blockchain P2P Network

Now that you have a better understanding of the key concepts, you can dive deeper into understanding how a blockchain uses a P2P network to solve the double spending issue as well as exclude financial institutions.

In this section, you will see how the cryptocurrency P2P network works. You will explore different blockchains policies specifically and the P2P network in general by breaking the P2P network into five layers.

- Consensus layer

- Miner layer

- Propagation layer

- Semantic layer

- Application layer

The overview here will pave the way for the next chapters where you will be utilizing the bitcoin core API to configure and run a peer. This fundamental understanding can help you understand how any blockchain network works by utilizing different policies such as NEO and EOS.

Consensus Mechanism

In a traditional centralized system such as a bank, there is a master computer that is trusted with the ledger of transactions. The bank can obviously trust its own computer, and therefore it has no problem being the one responsible for the security and integrity of the master computer.

When you are dealing with untrusted peers sharing a ledger, there is a need to place rules that will ensure security and provide integrity of the ledger to prevent double spending and other potential hacker attacks. These rules and agreements are called a *consensus mechanism.*

Note   A consensus mechanism is an agreement needed for the network to operate properly even in the event of a failure. It needs to be able to achieve agreement on the data of the network within the distributed P2P network.

The blockchain is not just one master computer and aims to work globally. It achieves integrity with a consensus of the data by all the computers connected on the network. A distributed consensus means that a pool of peers, geographically apart, agree in a decentralized manner, instead of one master computer (centralized). Instead of regulations, there are rules that are usually set in an open source environment instead of being set by a government entity.

The P2P network enables a ledger. To achieve this goal in a secure way, the P2P network stores the digital ledger rules and security. The consensus mechanism provides not only the rules but also the incentives to do the work of storing the data and creating transactions by giving the reward to miners.

The P2P network works globally using an Internet connection and is able to provide a platform to achieve a globally distributed consensus mechanism. In cryptocurrencies, the consensus/agreement is on whether the blocks are valid or not. If a block is valid, the block will be added to the blockchain. If a block is invalid, it will be rejected from being added to the blockchain.

That's where a consensus policy comes into play. Most of the peers in the network hold the same blocks in their validated best blockchain and follow the same rules (consensus rules); that's how blockchain ensures security. The most difficult to re-create chain is known as the *best blockchain* (more about this concept later in the chapter).

Proof of Work, Proof of Stake, and Delegated Proof of Stake

As the blockchain gained popularity, many consensus mechanisms policies were created. The first one was created by bitcoin, and many others were built to solve problems that exist in other mechanisms. In the following sections, I will discuss a few popular ones.

- Proof of work (PoW)

- Proof of stake (PoS)

- Delegated proof of stake (DPoS)

In addition to these three, there are many other consensus mechanisms that are not covered in this book, such as proof of importance, proof of elapsed time (PoET), proof of authority (PoA), proof of burn, proof of capacity, proof of activity, and so on. Feel free to explore these on your own; each has its pros and cons and fits different needs.

Proof of Work

PoW is the first and most popular mechanism; it's used by bitcoin and Ethereum, which are the most popular cryptocurrencies at the time of writing. PoW is achieved by having a network of miners and presenting the miners with a mathematical problem. When miners solve a problem, they are rewarded with a cryptocurrency. The reward is the proof of the "work" done, and that's where the name comes from.

Note   Ethereum's development community is looking to move from PoW to PoS or ProgPoW (reduced ASICs' hash rate benefit mechanism).

PoW determines what peer does the work by the amount of computer power (*hash rate*) and allocates the work as a percentage so it's fair. PoW does not trust any peer on the network individually, but the network trusts all of them as a collective network.

This does not mean that one miner competes against another miner. A network of miners (called a *pool*) can compete against another pool of miners for the job. The higher hash rate the pool has, the more chances it has to get the "work."

As covered previously, cryptocurrencies are decentralized and work without one trusted computer in charge of the ledger. The PoW is the mechanism that ensures data integrity and discourages malicious attacks.

The proof of work (PoW) is the mathematical puzzle the miner needs to solve. A miner needs to find a solution to a complex mathematical problem to become the leader and be able to create the next best block to be added to the blockchain. The more miners that exist in the network, the more complex the mathematical difficulty that needs to be solved. For bitcoin, only one block is added every ten minutes with only one winner, so the competition is fierce. Solving a problem puts the chips in the computer to work, which consume electricity and produce heat. Think of your computer running an intensive video game that includes lots of media or your computer processing a video for production.

You can also use this online resource, which connects to a bitcoin peer and does all sort of calculations to figure out the next difficulty: https:// bitcoinwisdom.com/bitcoin/difficulty.

This information is useful for figuring out mining profitability. At the time of writing, bitcoin shows 5 trillion as the difficulty rate, with an estimated next difficulty increase of +3.74% and a total hash rate of 43 trillion GH/s. It also shows that one block takes 9.9 minutes to create, and it generates about 25 bitcoins. A quick calculation shows that if every 10 minutes we get a block the data size of 4.2 MB per year, then 80 bytes of data per block $*$ 6 hours $*$ 24 hours $*$ 365 days = 4.2 MB of data per year.

Having a block created every ten minutes is a limiting factor, and the number of transactions that can be included in each block is limited. That creates a scalability issue that other consensus mechanisms tried to improve on.

To summarize, each miner is racing to solve the same problem; once the problem is solved, the process restarts. This problem is a mathematical puzzle known as the *proof-of-work problem*, and the reward is given to the first miner who solves the problem. Then the verified transactions are stored in the public ledger.

This PoW is not without its own disadvantages; this type of algorithm can create all sorts of problems in today's world. For instance, if one mining pool controls more than 51 percent of the total mining power, the entire blockchain security is at risk as you have one central collective not much different than having one computer. A DDOS attack against the network can put the entire trustworthiness of the network at risk.

This actually happened and is not just a theory. At the time of writing, bitcoin gold, a forked version of bitcoin, has suffered a DDOS attack.

A distributed denial-of-service (DDoS) attack happens when multiple systems are attacking a target's system resource/bandwidth.

On PoW, as the difficulty goes up, that means less profit. Less profit results in less incentive to mine coins. Ethereum cryptocurrency is facing a problem of reduced miners in the network, and in 2018 Ethereum had to plan a "difficulty bomb," which reduced the difficulty (raising profit for miners), as well as switch from PoW to PoS to increase scalability.

How is an attack is achieved? A pool that accounts for 51 percent of the network's hashing power is able to create its own block and post it faster than the main blockchain updates. The block holds 51 percent of the network and is able to double spend coins by removing transactions after spending so that the coins are not taken from the originating wallet. This threat is real. At the time of writing, Bitmain, a mining company, controls more than 40 percent of the total bitcoin's hash rate.

Many view PoW as unsustainable and insufficient because of the amount of electricity a miner uses and the slow transaction speed compared to other algorithms. To put things in perspective, bitcoin's current estimated annual electricity consumption is about 60 to 73 terawatt hour (TWh) per year. That's a similar amount of electricity that it takes to power Switzerland in a year; imagine multiple coins becoming as popular as bitcoin utilizing PoW.

Read more about PoW in the bitcoin white paper at `https://bitcoin.org/bitcoin.pdf` written by Satoshi Nakamoto.

Proof of Stake

PoS was created by Sunny King and Scott Nadal in 2012 as an alternative to solve the PoW cons mentioned earlier.

PoS relies on how many coins a peer holds. The peer needs to stake the number of coins it wants to mine.

Instead of hashing power, we have stake power, and there is no dependency on energy consumption because there is no puzzle to solve. PoS provides a similar hashing block scheme to bitcoin's PoW, but it limits the number of peers. This provides the needed security yet lowers the cost and power consumption. A network fee is provided to peers instead of giving a reward for solving a mathematical puzzle as in PoW.

PoS determines what peer does the work by the size of the stake the peer holds. This achieves a distributed consensus at less energy and less cost. DDOS attacks and frauds are still possible. However, attackers cannot transact more digital currency than they are staking. Otherwise, they would lose their deposits, so the chances are lower for an attack. Keep in mind that attackers can stake other people coins and won't care to lose these coins as they are not theirs, so there are still ways for a DDOS attack.

Any peer can participate in the mining process by staking coins in order to validate a new transaction. To become a miner, there are two options; you can stake your coins to be used by a trustworthy node (but you can lose your coin via a fraud of the PoS network by the node), or you can submit a full node to be selected as a miner. Decentralization is limited as only a few miners can hold most of the coins and have majority control. For the work, each miner gets selected randomly; it's not based on solving a puzzle. Take a look at Table 1-1, which compares PoW and PoS.

Table 1-1. *PoW vs. PoS*

Category	PoW	PoS
Generating new blocks	First miner to solve problem selected based on hashing power	Random selection based on stake power (how many coins a peer holds)
Reward	Block reward	Network fees
Energy and resource consumption	ASIC miner and large footprint	Little resource and low energy consumption

You can set a staking wallet that holds the coins you need for the PoS. Your coins can earn a return annually in some blockchain networks.

Here is a list of some popular cryptocurrency coins that use PoS:

- **Dash**: You need 1,000 units to be a master node. It gives an annual return of approximately 7.5 percent per year.

- **NEO**: Staking wallets return approximately 5.5 percent per year. There's no need to mine; you get gas coins just by holding coins.

- **Others**: LSK, PIVX, NAV, RDD, BEAN, Linda, DCR, NEBL, OK, STRAT.

Although some coins provide annual returns, keep in mind that in case the coin market cap stays stable, a single coin will be worth less over time, as new coins are generated. By staking a wallet, the hold (HODL) wallet's value is less affected as you get more coins to maintain your wallet value. Similar to how a bank gives you an X% interest rate and the inflation is X%, your balance shows more funds, but realistically you own the same amount of money.

Note   HODL is a slang term coined in association with cryptocurrency to describe holding cryptocurrency disregarding price fluctuation.

Let's examine NEO as an example. You won't need to mine NEO to get a reward. You will get gas coin just for holding coins as a reward for help with staking transactions. You can calculate how much gas coin you will receive by using this URL: `https://neotogas.com/`. At the time of writing, if you purchase five NEO coins and hold them for a year, you will get 0.4799 gas coins (currently at a price of $7.73) by placing them in staking wallets. See Figure 1-4.

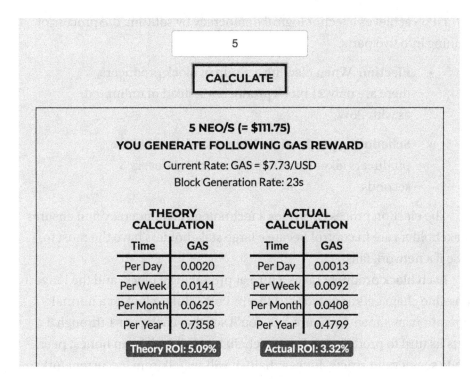

Figure 1-4. *Neotogas.com gas staking calculation*

I encourage you to read the white paper about PoS here: https://peercoin.net/assets/paper/peercoin-paper.pdf.

Delegated Proof of Stake

Delegated proof of stake is a census algorithm method invented by Dan Larimer discussed in the white paper at https://github.com/EOSIO/ Documentation/blob/master/TechnicalWhitePaper.md. DPoS is aimed at improving PoS cons by providing a democracy instead of the random process of selecting a miner.

Note   In DPoS, the miners are called *block producers*.

DPoS achieves a technological democracy by splitting the process of mining into two parts.

- **Election**: When electing a group of block producers, there are only 21 block producers instead of unlimited as with PoW.

- **Scheduling production**: Each one of the 21 block producers takes turns to produce a block every 3 seconds.

The election process provides a technological democracy and ensures stakeholders are in control because large stakeholders have the most to lose if a network fails.

Each block producer takes a turn at producing a block, and the longest possible chain gets adopted (just like in PoW). Take a look at a normal operation, as shown in Figure 1-5. You'll see that each peer 1 through 3 gets its turn to produce the longest chain block. Anytime an honest peer node sees a valid strictly longer chain, it will switch from its current fork to the longer one.

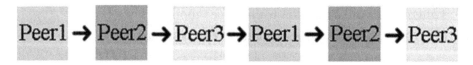

Figure 1-5. *DPoS normal operation*

DPoS is able to continue and function even when most of the producers fail. Figure 1-6 shows a minority fork, where peer 2 only gets to post the longest chain once during a cycle. During a fail process, the community can vote and replace a failed peer producer, in this case peer 1, or peer producers until the network resumes to normal operation.

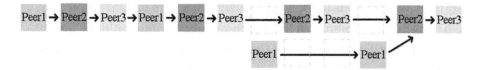

Figure 1-6. *DPoS minority fork*

This white paper describes in detail this process and how blocks are being produced and the rules to handle fail chains: `https://steemit.com/ dpos/@dantheman/dpos-consensus-algorithm-this-missing-white-paper`.

Setting a community of block producers and staked users who agree to these sets of rules gives the efficiency of PoS with the decentralized way that PoW operates. DPoS uses the power of stakeholders to approve voting of the consensus algorithm rules such as incentive fees, block intervals, forks, and transaction sizes.

These rules can be fine-tuned by the elected delegates. This type of consensus can decrease the transaction time significantly (1 second versus 10 minutes for PoW). Further, the consensus protocol is designed to protect all the participants against unwanted interference of a group of nodes as possible in POW. Examples of popular DPOS blockchains are Bitshares, Steem, and EOS.

Mining Layer

What the miners are doing behind the scenes on networks could be described as competition to do the blockchain's work, which is really doing the network bookkeeping. For bitcoin and most coins out there that utilize PoW, each peer needs to hold the entire public ledger, which holds a record of all the transactions that were ever conducted. PoW miners are based on computing power and pools, while other networks take into account other considerations.

For bitcoin, transactions must be validated by the miners who check the ledger, ensure the sender is not transferring funds it doesn't have, and only then add the transaction to the ledger. Finally, to ensure protection from hackers, the miners seal these transactions behind multiple layers of computational work, requiring too much work for a hacker to possibly achieve. This service is rewarded by providing bitcoins as a fee to the miner.

For bitcoin, the size of each batch of coins drops by half about every four years; around 2140 (unless a faster calculation than SHA2 is discovered), it will be cut to zero, and the total number of bitcoins in circulation will be 21 million.

Propagation Layer

The propagation layer is responsible for deciding how the shared ledger and the blocks are transmitted on the P2P network. This layer is described in detail in the blockchain white papers.

Each of the peers can transmit a new transaction to other nodes on the network. This architecture allows nodes to communicate indirectly. For instance, you can send a transaction affecting two wallets without each wallet being connected directly to each other.

Any node that receives a valid transaction it has not seen before will immediately forward it to all other nodes to which it is connected. This is a propagation technique known as *flooding*. Thus, the transaction rapidly propagates out across the P2P network, reaching a large percentage of the nodes within seconds.

Semantic Layer

The semantic layer takes care of how new blocks relate to previous blocks and provides the protocol for verifying the consensus rules.

As you have seen, there are different types of consensus mechanisms based on how many trusted machines are connected, staking, speed, hashing power, and more, but they do work similarly to how new blocks are related with previous blocks to ensure security. Every blockchain has specifications. In this layer, transactions happen where coins/tokens are transferred between accounts. I discussed the best block chain and how each block contains data, and a chain of blocks has each block referencing the block preceding it. The consensus in the blockchain holds the same blocks in their validated best block chain and follows the same rules (consensus rules). That's how a blockchain ensures security.

Application Layer

This layer takes care of deploying applications on top of the blockchain.

For instance, dapps, smart contracts, exchanges, and sites that provide information about a blockchain are applications built on top of blockchains.

For the application layer, the blockchain needs to expose APIs. Different blockchains are similar as they all provide a way for a client to communicate with the network.

Bitcoin offers a full node, which is currently about 27 GB and includes a fully enforced node and all the rules of the blockchain. That is needed for mining as well as ensuring the peer you run that gets connected to the application layer is synced with the latest blocks.

These full nodes contribute to the functionality of the P2P network and help support the network and its security.

It's common for a blockchain to also offer a "light" node version. In fact, the bitcoin light client is referencing a trusted full node's copy of the blockchain. The light client allows users to interact with the bitcoin's blockchain and makes and confirms transactions without committing the large 27 GB disk space, which helps less capable devices such as mobile.

It's important to understand that a light client is trustworthy and does not include all the consensus rules. A full node is trustless and will reject blocks that violate consensus rules, even if all the other nodes on the network recognize the transaction as valid.

I used NEO as an example of a popular PoS blockchain. NEO also provides NEO-CLI, which includes an API that supports a consensus function that can be used for the application layer.

Similarly, EOS delegated proof of stake provides a full-node and light-node option. You will start noticing that although there are many blockchain options out there, there are many similarities in the way the blockchain is implemented.

Summary

In this chapter, I laid the foundations and explained basic concepts regarding blockchain; I explained concepts such as encryption and decryption, cryptography, digital assets, cryptography, and cryptocurrency.

I covered the pieces that make up a blockchain, including blocks, double spending, cryptocurrency, cryptomining, cryptominers, and cryptocurrency wallets. I covered different types of cryptocurrencies: bitcoin, tokens, and altcoins.

Lastly, I covered the blockchain P2P network and the different layers that make up the network: consensus layer, miner layer, propagation layer, semantic layer, and application layer. You also learned about the peer-to-peer network core logic and proof of work (PoW), proof of stake (PoS), and delegated proof of stake blockchain (DPOS).

In this chapter, I introduced many terms that will be useful throughout this book such as digital asset, public and private keys, decentralized, double spending, smart contracts, and HODL.

In the next chapter, you will install and learn about the bitcoin core API as well as learn how to create a full peer in different blockchains. This will enable you to access the blockchain P2P network and even be able to understand and create peers that can act as miners.

CHAPTER 2

Blockchain Nodes

In the previous chapter, I covered basic concepts related to blockchain and the pieces that make up an individual blockchain. I covered how blockchain technology solved the double spending problem by utilizing a P2P network, which led to the creation of a global distributed shared ledger and digital cash. The blockchain P2P network is stitched together by connecting multiple nodes, and in this chapter, you will be taking a closer look at the nodes that make up the network.

The nodes or peers are machines that maintain the transactions and records on the blockchain network. Each cryptocurrency has its own blockchain and nodes; however, I will cover how to install three different blockchains that utilize different consensus mechanisms.

In addition, I will cover how to interact with a node. I will be using the bitcoin core API as an example so you will have a better understanding of the ledger, blocks, transactions, and wallets. These concepts will continue to lay out the foundations and basic concepts that are needed in the next chapters.

Running a Blockchain Node

As we mentioned, the blockchain P2P network consists of peers that store a full copy of all the blocks in the network, which is the shared ledger. Each blockchain validates blocks via a specific consensus mechanism and is able to reject blocks that do not conform with the set of rules agreed on by

© Elad Elrom 2019
E. Elrom, *The Blockchain Developer*, https://doi.org/10.1007/978-1-4842-4847-8_2

the network. To be able to connect to blocks and execute commands, you need to have a peer connected to the blockchain. In this chapter, you will be setting up a full node and will learn how to get rewarded for helping the network; therefore, you will fully understand how the nodes on different networks operate. You will be creating nodes for the following: bitcoin, NEO, and EOS. Because blockchain technologies operate on different consensus mechanisms, they also have different names for the node capable of managing the blockchain.

- For bitcoin, a node that can create blocks is called a *miner*.

- For NEO, a node that has management rights is called a *book-keeping node*.

- For EOS, a node running the underlying network layer and able to process all transactions is called a *block producer*.

The reason I selected these blockchains is so you can examine how different peers working on different networks with different consensus mechanism operate. Once you are able to work with different blockchains, you will start noticing a pattern and be well rounded in blockchain technology.

Create a Bitcoin Miner

In this section, you will turn your own computer into a bitcoin cryptominer and start cryptomining. Before doing that, you need to understand that the hashing power of your computer is not going to generate enough hash power for the mining of bitcoin to be profitable. Nevertheless, it will allow you to fully understand the full cycle, and you may be able to find other coins where mining using your CPU/GPU is profitable such as ETN, BCN, XMR, and ETH. The process is similar in all PoW-based networks.

Today, for a miner to be profitable, it's a matter of hash rate and power consumption, price of electricity, bitcoin puzzle difficulty rate, and maintenance costs as well as other factors.

Note   *Hash rate* is the number of calculations in a second that your computer can perform trying to solve the mathematical puzzle.

In the early days of bitcoin, your desktop could use your central processing unit (CPU) or graphics processing unit (GPU) for processing bitcoin, and it would have been enough for bitcoin mining to be profitable. Your computer would have been able to support the bitcoin network; however, the competition has increased, and you now need a field programmable gate array (FPGA) or application-specific integrated circuit (ASIC) miner to be profitable.

What are ASIC and FPGA miners? An FPGA is an integrated circuit that is able to be configured after being built. The miners have better performance than CPUs and GPUs mining; they can hash 750 megahashes per second.

ASICs are computers that have an integrated circuit dedicated to performing the single task of mining instead of operating as a regular computer. There is nothing more on that computer; everything else was stripped out.

This makes the computer much faster and more efficient in processing transactions, and it is able to hash more. At the time of writing, there are ASICs that can hash over 56 TH/sec, and they use less power than older generation ASCIs.

This type of mining equipment is not only unique to bitcoin; at the time of writing, there are ASIC miners for other cryptocurrency such as litecoin, zCash, ethereum, and others.

To get started, you first need mining software. There is a lot of mining software to choose from. For instance macOS users can, this one is free, open source, and easy to use: http://downloads.fabulouspanda.co.uk/macminer/.

Once you have downloaded the software, install it. Next, you need to join a mining pool. Here I'll show how to connect to Antpool, the largest bitcoin pool; however, any pool would work. Sign up on Antpool here: https://www.antpool.com.

Antpool calls a miner a *worker*. You can create a worker by clicking the Dashboard tab, then clicking the Worker link, and finally clicking Create Worker, as shown in Figure 2-1.

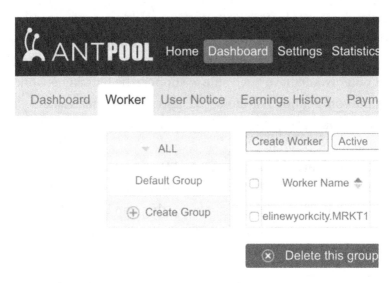

Figure 2-1. *Antpool dashboard page for creating a mining worker*

Now that you have your worker ready, you will set up your miner as a CPU miner utilizing your CPU, and for your GPU, you could set your miner to utilize your graphics card.

Open the MacMiner software you downloaded and click File and then Preference option from the File drop menu. In the Preferences section, set the miner as a CPU and/or GPU miner, as shown in Figure 2-2.

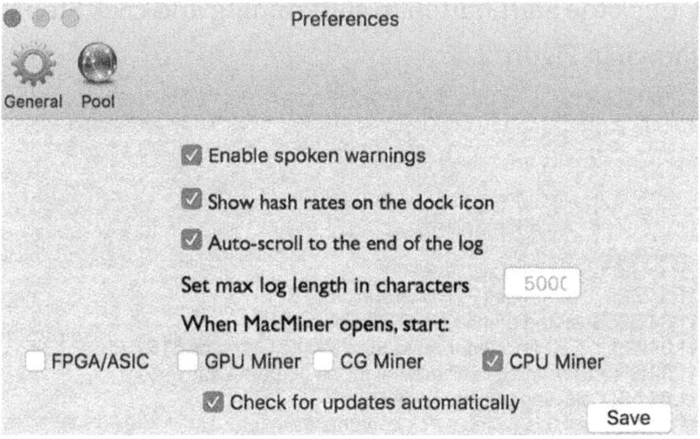

Figure 2-2. *MacMiner preferences*

In the next step of the preferences, you set the pool URL and your username. Antpool is set up without a password, so it's not needed, and the pool URL is listed on the Antpool site:

```
startum+tcp://startum.antpool.com:3333
```

See Figure 2-3.

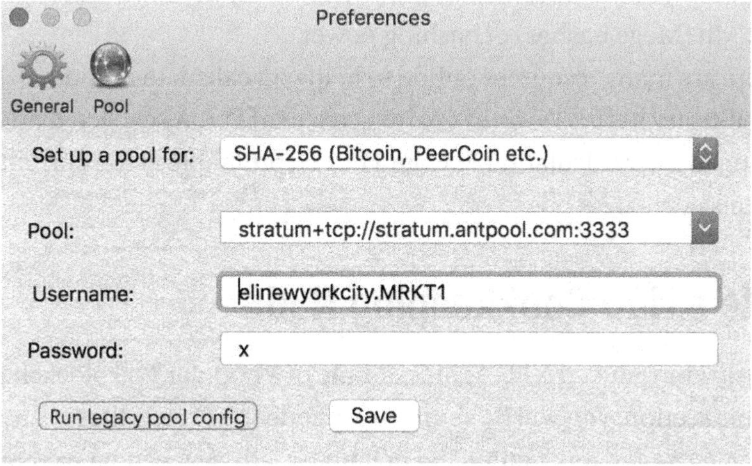

Figure 2-3. *MacMiner Preferences window for setting up a miner pool*

That's it. Click the Start button to start mining and click Stop to stop mining, as shown in Figure 2-4.

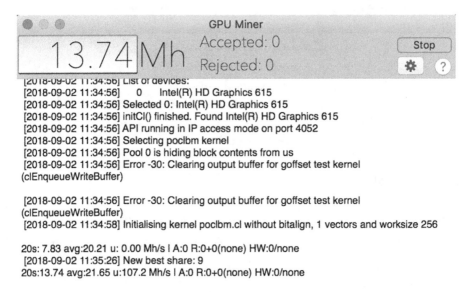

Figure 2-4. *MacMiner starting a miner*

Six years ago, you would have been able to mine more than 100 BTC on your GPU. As you can see, my mining power on my 2018 MacBook resulted in 13.74 Mh (Mega hashes) of hashing power.

There are many resources online to help you calculate mining profitability; try `http://www.bitcoinx.com/profit/`. As expected and according to their calculation, it would not be profitable at the current conditions.

Create a NEO Bookkeeping Node

Previously I introduced NEO as an example of a popular PoS blockchain.

In this section, you will be setting up a node (NEO calls these *bookkeeping nodes*) and getting the machine ready so it can be selected to help manage the network and receive a transaction reward.

Note   NEO does not call its managing node a miner. A miner can be an analogy for the hard work that nodes do to maintain a PoW-based blockchain. As NEO uses the PoS census algorithm and uses a technological democracy to selecting the managing nodes, there is no hashing power and no hard labor when using the PoW census algorithm. To better understand how Neo node works, it is recommended to read the NEO white paper at `https://github.com/neo-project/docs/blob/master/en-us/whitepaper.md`.

The node validates the blockchain blocks and pays in a cryptocurrency coin called *gas*. To be selected, you need to set a full node on a capable machine. The minimum required machine is listed on the NEO project wiki at `https://github.com/neo-project/neo/wiki/Bookkeeping-Node-Deployment`.

Next, you need to obtain a consensus authority certificate and get staking gas to be nominated as a bookkeeping node.

Note   You may need to be a Chinese citizen and set up a Chinese business to receive an identification certificate; see the NEO docs at `http://docs.neo.org/en-us/index.html`. You also need 1,000 staking gas to be nominated as a bookkeeping node.

To receive a fee from supporting the NEO network, you will need to create a full node by following these steps:

1. Set up a full NEO node.

2. Request a consensus authority certificate.

3. Stake 1,000 gas.

4. Be elected by NEO holders.

To set up a full NEO node, you also need to meet the system minimum requirement listed here: https://github.com/neo-project/neo/wiki/Bookkeeping-Node-Deployment.

Setting Up a NEO Node on AWS Ubuntu

As my computer does not meet the minimum requirement list, I will be utilizing AWS to set up a full node. However, if you have a machine that meets these requirements, feel free to skip using Amazon AWS or select another service provider to set your Node.

For AWS, go to the following URL: https://aws.amazon.com/free/. Select "Create free account" and sign up.

Once you complete the sign-up process, select the free Basic Plan. Then sign into the console at https://us-east-2.console.aws.amazon. com/console/home and select "Launch a virtual machine."

In the first step, you can select the machine type. Select Ubuntu. "On the Step 1, wizard page: Choose an Amazon Machine Image (AMI)" ➤ Next, select: Ubuntu Server 16.04 LTS (HVM), SSD Volume Type ➤ Click the "select" button. See Figure 2-5.

Figure 2-5. *AWS, selecting Ubuntu Server 16.04 LTS*

On the next screen, select General purpose - t2.micro - free tier eligible check-box. See Figure 2-6.

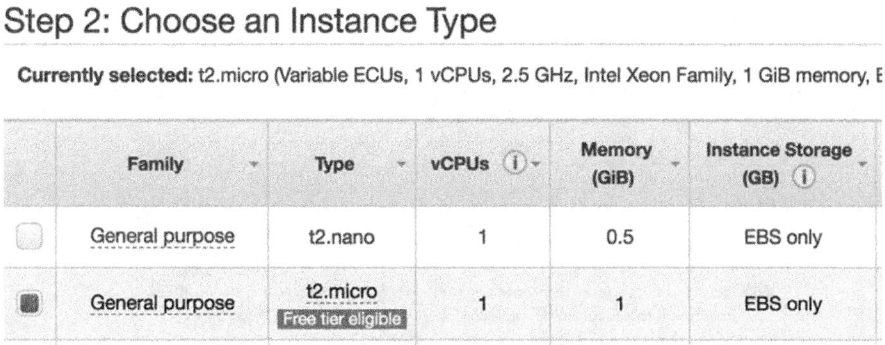

Step 2: Choose an Instance Type

Currently selected: t2.micro (Variable ECUs, 1 vCPUs, 2.5 GHz, Intel Xeon Family, 1 GiB memory, E

	Family	Type	vCPUs ⓘ	Memory (GiB)	Instance Storage (GB) ⓘ
☐	General purpose	t2.nano	1	0.5	EBS only
■	General purpose	t2.micro Free tier eligible	1	1	EBS only

Figure 2-6. *AWS, selecting t2.micro machine*

On the next screen, you will be prompted to create key pairs: Select "create a new key pair" ➤ next, select "key pair name" ➤ call the key "neo" ➤ then download the key: "download key pair" ➤ Lastly, select "Launch Instances." See Figure 2-7. Make sure you download the key, as you won't be able to connect via SSH to the box without the key.

Note   Secure Shell (SSH) uses port 22 to connect your computer to another computer on the Internet.

Figure 2-7. *AWS key pairs*

Next, you will get a message, with a link: your instances are now launching. The following instance launches have been initiated: [instance id].

Click the link and you will be able to view the instance, as shown in Figure 2-8.

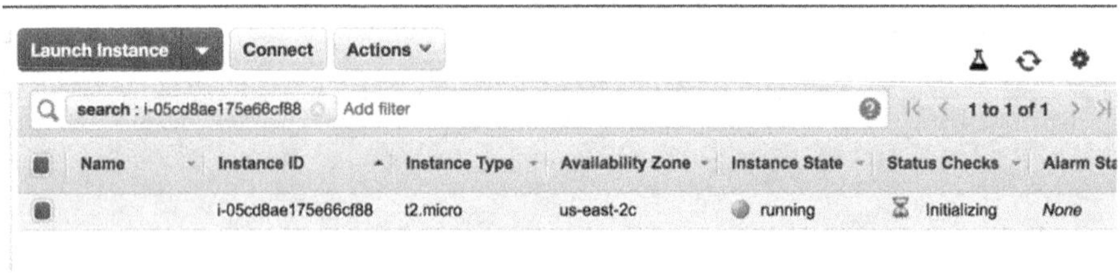

Figure 2-8. *AWS, launching an instance*

In the instance, you will find a link to the security settings. Scroll to the right of the screen, or go to the top-left navigation bar, and select Network & Security ➤ Security Groups. You will be able to change the security settings.

For HTTP and SSH, you want to open the port to the world (0.0.0.0/0), but SSH limits you to your own computer, called My IP. See Figure 2-9.

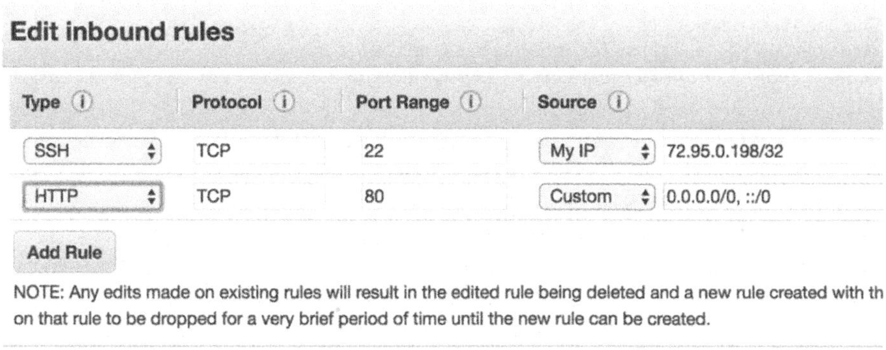

Edit inbound rules

Type ⓘ	Protocol ⓘ	Port Range ⓘ	Source ⓘ	
SSH ⬍	TCP	22	My IP ⬍	72.95.0.198/32
HTTP ⬍	TCP	80	Custom ⬍	0.0.0.0/0, ::/0

Add Rule

NOTE: Any edits made on existing rules will result in the edited rule being deleted and a new rule created with th
on that rule to be dropped for a very brief period of time until the new rule can be created.

Figure 2-9. *AWS inbound security rules*

Next, you can create an SSH shortcut to access the server via one command, as shown here:

```
> mkdir ~/.ssh
> vim ~/.ssh/config
```

Paste the following into the config file:

```
Host NEO
HostName [ip address]
User ubuntu
IdentityFile /[location of key]/neo.pem
```

Configure these settings with the IP address of the machine and with the location of your key. Next set the permissions for the key.

```
> chmod 400 /[location of key]/neo.pem
```

Now, you can access your machine with one command, as shown in Figure 2-10.

```
> ssh NEO
```

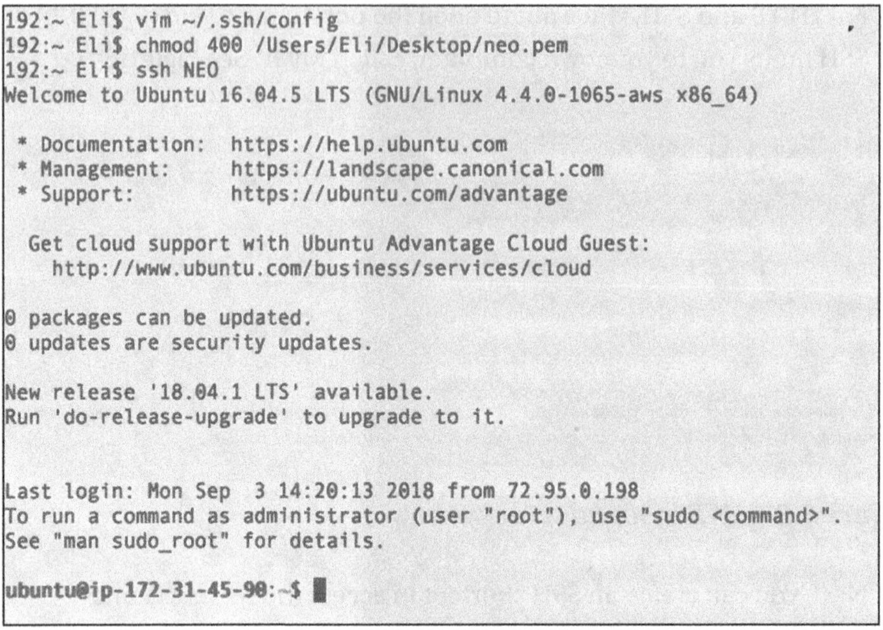

```
192:~ Eli$ vim ~/.ssh/config
192:~ Eli$ chmod 400 /Users/Eli/Desktop/neo.pem
192:~ Eli$ ssh NEO
Welcome to Ubuntu 16.04.5 LTS (GNU/Linux 4.4.0-1065-aws x86_64)

 * Documentation:  https://help.ubuntu.com
 * Management:     https://landscape.canonical.com
 * Support:        https://ubuntu.com/advantage

  Get cloud support with Ubuntu Advantage Cloud Guest:
    http://www.ubuntu.com/business/services/cloud

0 packages can be updated.
0 updates are security updates.

New release '18.04.1 LTS' available.
Run 'do-release-upgrade' to upgrade to it.


Last login: Mon Sep  3 14:20:13 2018 from 72.95.0.198
To run a command as administrator (user "root"), use "sudo <command>".
See "man sudo_root" for details.

ubuntu@ip-172-31-45-90:~$ 
```

Figure 2-10. *Connecting to an AWS machine via SSH*

If you run into any problems connecting to the machine, use the AWS Troubleshooting page, which you can find at https://docs.aws.amazon. com/AWSEC2/latest/UserGuide/TroubleshootingInstancesConnecting. html#TroubleshootingInstancesConnectingMindTerm.

Installing Bookkeeping-Node-Deployment on Ubuntu 16.04

Now that you have a machine to fit the minimum needs of a full node, you can install the software needed. Start by installing dependencies, as shown here:

> sudo sh -c 'echo "deb [arch=amd64] https://apt-mo. trafficmanager.net/repos/dotnet-release/ trusty main" > /etc/ apt/sources.list.d/dotnetdev.list'

```
> sudo apt-key adv --keyserver apt-mo.trafficmanager.net
  --recv-keys 417A0893
> sudo apt-get update
> sudo apt-get install dotnet-dev-1.0.4
```

It appears that the current installation instructions in the NEO docs produce errors during installation, as shown here:

```
Depends:
dotnet-sharedframework-microsoft.netcore.app-1.0.4,
dotnet-sharedframework-microsoft.netcore.app-1.1.1
```

The workaround is to install a different dotnet core environment sources list and update; then you will be able to install the dotnet-dev-1.0.4 core environment.

```
> sudo sh -c 'echo "deb [arch=amd64] https://apt-mo.
  trafficmanager.net/repos/dotnet-release/ xenial main" >
  /etc/apt/sources.list.d/dotnetdev.list'
> sudo apt-key adv --keyserver hkp://keyserver.ubuntu.com:80
  --recv-keys 417A0893
> sudo apt-get update
```

Remember to change the sources list back to the following:

```
> sudo sh -c 'echo "deb [arch=amd64] https://apt-mo.
  trafficmanager.net/repos/dotnet-release/ trusty main" >
  /etc/apt/sources.list.d/dotnetdev.list'
```

Now that the dotnet core environment is installed, check whether the dotnet core environment is successfully installed with the following command:

```
> mkdir hwapp
> cd hwapp
> dotnet new xunit --framework netcoreapp1.1
```

```
> dotnet restore hwapp.csproj
> dotnet run
> cd ..
> rm -rf hwapp/
```

Bookkeeping Node Deployment

Now that you have the dotnet core environment installed, you can install additional dependencies and check out the NEO project.

```
> sudo apt-get install libleveldb-dev sqlite3 libsqlite3-dev
  libunwind8-dev
> git clone https://github.com/neo-project/neo-cli
> git branch -a
> git checkout v3.0
> git checkout head
```

To run the NEO node, you will need version 1.1.2 of .NET Core. Download the SDK binary; for Ubuntu 16.4, the commands are listed here: https://www.microsoft.com/net/download/linux-package-manager/ubuntu16-04/sdk-2.1.300.

Next, run the dpkg package manager to install the package:

```
> wget -q https://packages.microsoft.com/config/ubuntu/16.04/
  packages-microsoft-prod.deb
> sudo dpkg -i packages-microsoft-prod.deb
```

Now you can restore the NEO build and compile, as shown here:

```
> dotnet restore
> dotnet publish -c Release
```

Once you compile the code, you get the location of the DLLs.

```
neo-cli -> /home/ubuntu/neo-cli/neo-cli/bin/Release/
netcoreapp2.0/neo-cli.dll .
```

```
neo-cli -> /home/ubuntu/neo-cli/neo-cli/bin/Release/
netcoreapp2.0/publish/
```

Run the full node:

```
> dotnet /home/ubuntu/neo-cli/neo-cli/bin/Release/
  netcoreapp2.0/neo-cli.dll .
```

This command opens a terminal command call "neo" with the version.

```
NEO-CLI Version: 3.0.0.0
```

In the neo terminal, you can query the version to ensure it's working correctly.

```
neo> show state
```

You can also create a wallet.

```
neo> create wallet wallet.db3
```

This command will request a password.

```
password: [select a password]
password: [select a passwrod]
```

Then it generates a public key and address for your wallet.

```
address: AXZmWZckF55xb1p566No2qh19uj8vt5d2R
 pubkey: 03b80edc66c9324077c8c1c4bbad1e1ace7e1b7e8ac63945a3
         b5bb9f642f4520f1
```

You now have a NEO node on an AWS machine, and you are able to interact with the NEO command-line interface (CLI). In the next chapters, you will be interacting with the CLI. Feel free to get a head start and review the documentation for smart contracts and dapp development at the NEO site here: http://docs.neo.org/en-us/node/cli.html.

Request Consensus Authority Certificate

Now that you have a working node on a qualified Ubuntu server, you can obtain a consensus authority certificate. The NEO white paper discusses the need to have an actual real identity:

> *"DBFT combines digital identity technology, meaning the bookkeepers can be a real name of the individual or institution. Thus, it is possible to freeze, revoke, inherit, retrieve, and affect judicial decisions on them. This facilitates the registration of compliant financial assets in the NEO network. The NEO network plans to support such operations when necessary."*

You can obtain CA certificates from OnChain/Neo directly. Additionally, you can find more information on the NEO forums: `https://www.reddit.com/r/NEO/`. This process is beyond the scope of this book, but it's needed in order to be selected as a node.

Getting Gas

To be selected as a node, you also need 1,000 gas to stake in order to become a bookkeeper. The easiest way to purchase gas is on exchanges. The other option is to hold NEO, and you will get 0.33 gas per 1,000. See Figure 2-11 shows a button to claim gas coins once you hold NEO coins.

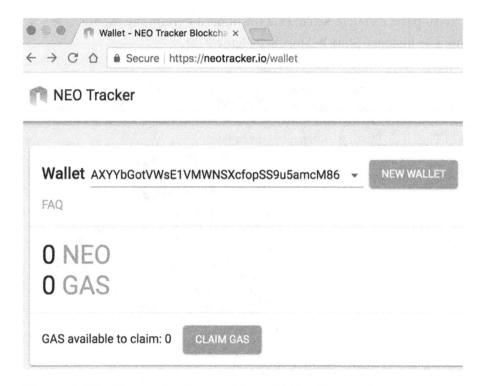

Figure 2-11. *Neotracker.io provides a Claim Gas option*

A simple calculation of prices of NEO and gas at the time of writing shows it's a large investment.

Elected as a Bookkeeper

NEO is an electronic democracy, and NEO holders can vote on who should be a bookkeeper. At the time of writing, the NEO team has not implemented the voting features; however, they are likely to be implemented in the near future as the GitHub wiki shows a payment structure with fees, including 10 gas for voting a bookkeeper: `https://github.com/neo-project/neo/wiki/Network-Protocol`.

For now, stop the EC2 node so you won't be charged.

To stop the instance, select EC2 Dashboard ➤ Running instances ➤ Actions ➤ Instance State ➤ Stop. See Figure 2-12.

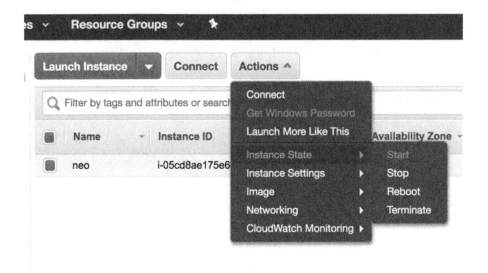

Figure 2-12. *AWS, stop instance action*

Tip   Amazon can charge storage fees for the EBS volumes attached to a stopped instance. The cost is five cents per gigabyte. Amazon provides one year for free. To completely avoid being charged, you need to "terminate" the instance instead of just stopping it.

You can make sure you are not charged at this URL: `https://console.aws.amazon.com/billing/home`.

Create an EOS Block Producer

You will now learn how to run a full EOS node on a dedicated server; you just need to make sure you meet the minimum hardware requirement. The requirements are listed here: `https://developers.eos.io/ eosio-nodeos/docs/install-nodeos`.

At the time of writing, the system requirements on all platforms are as follows:

- 7 GB RAM free required

- 20 GB of available storage

You will learn how to set up an Ubuntu server. I will be using AWS. In AWS, select Ubuntu Server 16.04 LTS (HVM), SSD Volume Type ➤ Choose an Instance Type ➤ General purpose ➤ t2.large. This type of machine has 8 GB RAM free.

An EOS node needs at least 20 GB of a storage space, so you'll set this machine to 25 GB to be safe. To do that, select Configure Instance Detail. Next select: add storage. In the next window select: Size (GiB) 25 GB. The next wizard window you will be able to: Review and Launch. Launch the instance.

For security, set the same settings as you did for the NEO full-node server: select an existing security group. Next, select: launch-wizard-1 that includes port 22 for SSH and public HTTP/HTTPS. Now we can: Review and Launch in the next window and lastly, Launch.

In the key pairs, use the same key you created for NEO or create a new key. To select the same key, select Choose an existing key pair. We will call the key: EOS.

That's it. You can now update the SSH config file with the new server to be able to connect quickly.

```
> vim ~/.ssh/config
```

And paste the following:

```
Host EOS
HostName [ip address]
User ubuntu
IdentityFile /[location of key]/EOS.pem
```

Now you can connect to the EOS server.

```
> ssh EOS
```

Installing an EOS Full Node

Now that you have the Ubuntu server configured with 8 GB of memory and a 25 GB hard drive, you can clone the project and build.

```
> git clone https://github.com/EOSIO/eos --recursive
> cd eos
> ./eosio_build.sh #takes about 30 mins to an hour.
```

Once the build is completed, you will see the screen shown in Figure 2-13.

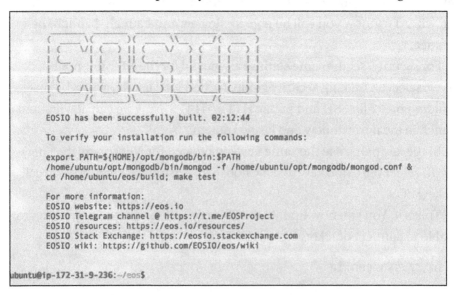

Figure 2-13. *EOS full-node build, complete output*

Ensure that the daemon is working correctly by running the -h flag to get a list of commands.

```
> cd build/programs/nodeos
> ./nodeos -h #list of commands
```

Now you can run the EOS node daemon; Figure 2-14 shows the output.

```
> ./nodeos -e -p eosio --plugin eosio::chain_api_plugin
  --plugin eosio::history_api_plugin
```

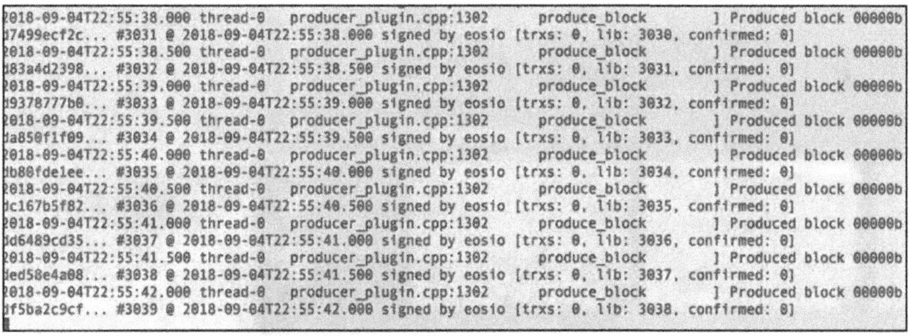

Figure 2-14. *EOS full node running*

EOS provides a portal at https://developers.eos.io/ to get started with nodes, dapps, smart contract, tokens, and much more. In the next chapters, you will be interacting more with the EOS platform.

Marketing and Listing

Now that you have an EOS node running, you need to create a marketing campaign to be elected. You can set the submission profile to be similar to this URL: https://github.com/consenlabs/eos-bp-profile.

Next, you are ready to receive votes. You can get voting through the imToken 2.0 app (iPhone or Android). It offers block producers voting; follow this guide for instructions: https://medium.com/imtoken/guide-imtoken-2-0-block-producers-voting-141983f9a76e.

Terminating an EOS Node

You want to ensure that you terminate the node so you won't get charged, as this machine configuration is not part of the free tier server on Amazon. Just you did before, select EC2 Dashboard ➤ Running instances ➤ Actions ➤ Instance State ➤ Terminate.

You'll also want to terminate the 25 GB volume you created. Select Volume from the left navigation menu and then select Actions ➤ Detach Volume. Then select Delete Volume. See Figure 2-15.

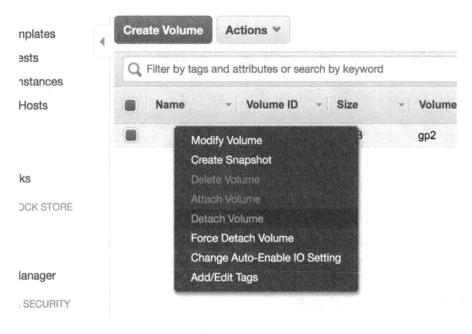

Figure 2-15. *Detaching a volume and deleting a volume*

Bitcoin Core API

As a developer, you want to have deep understanding of how a technology works, so to better understand blockchain in general and the bitcoin blockchain specifically, you will be downloading and installing the bitcoin core code. The full node and the bitcoin miner you set up previously on bitcoin core can be compiled from source code, or you can use a precompiled executable.

Previously you set up a bitcoin node capable of doing mining on your computer. To interact with the bitcoin core API, you need a full node. What is the difference between a full node and a miner then?

A full node is a complete copy of the blockchain that is able to verify all the transactions that ever occurred on the blockchain since the first block was created. This requires 180 GB at the time of writing. However, as you will see, you can set the full node not to download the entire ledger. A full node does not need to solve any mathematical problem, and hashing is not an issue.

A miner is a node in the network; however, as you have seen, its job is to generate blocks by working on transactions and coming up with the best block (or hash) to store the information. Miners compete and spend about 10 minutes coming up with a solution to the problem. Full nodes keep blocks forever in the database and are verified by other nodes. Miners, on the other hand, don't need to know about previous blocks, just the block before, and they focus on hashing. However, a bitcoin miner does download the entire 180 GB blockchain ledger.

In the following exercise, you will be installing and configuring a full node to be able to connect and interact with the bitcoin core API.

INSTALLING AND CONFIGURATING A FULL BITCOIN NODE

Setting Up Your System

In this exercise, you will set up your environment and then download, configure, and start a full working node of bitcoin. This will come in handy as you continue to examine how bitcoin and blockchain work. You will be using the bitcoin core source code. Bitcoin core code includes docs that give complete instructions for installing the code on different OSs. In this book, I am focusing on macOS, so I am providing instructions to expedite the installation process for your convenience; however, you can install bitcoin core on other platforms. Here is the link for the complete instructions for Mac and PC:

- macOS install instructions: `https://github.com/bitcoin/bitcoin/blob/master/doc/build-osx.md`

- Windows: `https://github.com/bitcoin/bitcoin/blob/master/doc/build-windows.md`

To get started, you need Xcode and the Xcode tools installed, so this would be a good time to install these tools if you don't have them already. To check whether Xcode is installed on your computer, open a command-line terminal by clicking the Spotlight Search and type **Terminal**.

At the command line, type the following command to check whether you have Xcode installed:

```
> xcode-select –v
```

It should return `xcode-select` and the version number, as shown in Figure 2-16.

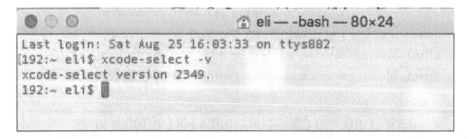

Figure 2-16. *Terminal xcode-select version*

If you don't have Xcode installed, you can download it from `https://developer.apple.com/xcode/`.

Note   This installation can take hours, depending on your Internet connection.

Now that you have Xcode downloaded, execute the command-line tools for Xcode.

```
> xcode-select -install
```

With command-line tools installed, you can install Homebrew and the wget tools by using these commands:

```
> /usr/bin/ruby -e "$(curl -fsSL https://raw.githubusercontent.
  com/Homebrew/install/master/install)"
> brew install wget
```

After Homebrew and wget are installed, you are able to install the rest of the needed dependencies for bitcoin core, as shown here:

```
> brew install automake berkeley-db4 libtool boost miniupnpc
  openssl pkg-config protobuf python qt libevent qrencode librsvg
```

Installing Bitcoin Core

At this point you have the needed tools and dependencies installed, and you can clone the bitcoin code project, compile, and run it.

```
> git clone https://github.com/bitcoin/bitcoin.git
> cd bitcoin/
```

Now, you can build the Berkeley DB version 4, used by the bitcoin core node:

```
> ./contrib/install_db4.sh .
Continue the installation;
> ./autogen.sh
> ./configure
> make
> make check && sudo make install
```

Bitcoin core code includes two tools: bitcoind and bitcoin-CLI.

- *bitcoind (the bitcoin daemon)*: This implements the bitcoin protocol for remote procedure call (RPC) use. Once it's installed, you can make API calls. There is a list of all the API calls here: `https://en.bitcoin.it/wiki/Original_Bitcoin_client/API_Calls_list`.

- *bitcoin-CLI (the bitcoin command-line interface)*: This enables you to interact with the bitcoin core daemon. To ensure the installation went well, you can check that the bitcoin daemon and bitcoin-CLI are configured and working as expected.

To ensure these tools were installed correctly, you can execute the `which` command on these tools to get the location of them.

```
> which bitcoind
> which bitcoin-cli
```

The output returns the location of the bitcoind and bitcoin-cli:

```
/usr/local/bin/bitcoind
/usr/local/bin/bitcoin-cli
```

Configuring and Compiling Bitcoin Core

Next, you want to configure a node. Each bitcoin core node does not do mining but contributes to the bitcoin network and consists of clients, miners, wallets, and so on. To configure the node, you can find the configuration files' location by typing the following command in Terminal:

```
> bitcoind -printtoconsole
```

After a few seconds, stop this service (Control+C). The command shows the `bitcoin.conf` configuration file location. See Figure 2-17 for the output.

```
"> Using config file /[path]/.bitcoin/bitcoin.conf"
```

Figure 2-17. *bitcoin.conf file location*

At the time of writing, a full-index bitcoin core node requires 2 GB RAM and at least 180 GB of disk space (`https://blockchain.info/charts/blocks-size`). Additionally, as the bitcoin nodes send and receive transactions and blocks constantly, you will need a fast internet connection.

The full node is advisable for a working project running a miner as you can run a dedicated server and interact with the bitcoind via Bitcoin-CLI; however, for the purpose of this book, most of the time you won't need a full node. I recommend that you constrain bitcoin node resources usage on your computer so it won't hog your computer's resources and Internet bandwidth.

To limit your node from downloading the entire shared ledger, use vim or your favorite editor to edit the `bitcoin.conf` file.

```
> vim /[path]/.bitcoin/bitcoin.conf
```

After vim opens up `bitcoin.conf`, paste the following configurations:

```
alertnotify=myemailscript.sh "Alert: %s"
prune=3000
maxconnections=10
dbcache=150
maxmempool=100
maxsendbuffer=500
maxreceivebuffer=2000
txindex=0
```

Make sure you don't erase the following lines already there:

```
rpcuser=bitcoinrpcrpc
password=[password]
```

For your knowledge, the configuration file holds the following params:

- **prune**: Utilizing `prune`, you can limit the disk usage. Set this to 3000.

- **Maxconnections**: By setting a limited `maxconnections` value, you are limiting the maximum nodes number to ten connections

- **dbcache**: In `dbcache`, you reduce the size of the UTXO cache from 300 MiB to 100 MiB.

- **Maxsendbuffer and maxreceivebuffer**: You can limit the memory buffer per connection to the number you set; for instance, set `maxreceivebuffer` to 2000 MB.

- **Txindex**: Set this to 1 to get transaction data for any transaction on the blockchain; however, this will use up more disk space.

Running Bitcoin Core Daemon

Now that you have configured your node, you can start the bitcoin core daemon. To run the bitcoind, execute the following command in Terminal:

```
> bitcoind -printtoconsole
```

The first time running the daemon, it will download the blockchain. This can take several hours (depending on your Internet connection). Because you set the parameter to print to the console (-printtoconsole), you will be able to watch the process as it downloads the entire blockchain. See Figure 2-18.

```
te='2013-08-05T19:46:26Z' progress=0.064338 cache=28.8MiB(132970txo)
2018-08-19T20:22:20Z UpdateTip: new best=000000000000000003c7a2705aeabe9cae96d93e391fa1fff07534c244a88636fe9 height=250405
e='2013-08-05T19:49:21Z' progress=0.064338 cache=28.8MiB(133384txo)
2018-08-19T20:22:20Z UpdateTip: new best=000000000000000387c486e6e53a58d4d63fa5272234c15ffad1e1d9bb49526ea height=250406
te='2013-08-05T20:07:06Z' progress=0.064339 cache=28.9MiB(133724txo)
2018-08-19T20:22:20Z UpdateTip: new best=0000000000000004979d0e32a48a8309df1dfc7f18e9a46449eff3c1afa7fa071 height=250407
te='2013-08-05T20:07:12Z' progress=0.064340 cache=28.9MiB(133927txo)
2018-08-19T20:22:20Z UpdateTip: new best=00000000000000071514801e13fcb088fa4fc2cfea987683797fd2db9f4799e37 height=250408
te='2013-08-05T20:08:33Z' progress=0.064340 cache=28.9MiB(134120txo)
2018-08-19T20:22:20Z UpdateTip: new best=00000000000000025784711e9dfa95d14d7ce8dfd976a348f361b8644d027ab9c height=250409
te='2013-08-05T20:24:20Z' progress=0.064342 cache=29.0MiB(134547txo)
2018-08-19T20:22:20Z UpdateTip: new best=000000000000002b89a1686f1c9f36af7ee1b7663a8e828654eb246a15335f78 height=250410
te='2013-08-05T20:51:21Z' progress=0.064343 cache=29.0MiB(134961txo)
2018-08-19T20:22:20Z UpdateTip: new best=0000000000000000280b700b5df666212e7144ad1d5c8fbf8a18e84db11b101aa6 height=250411
te='2013-08-05T20:52:10Z' progress=0.064343 cache=29.1MiB(135042txo)
2018-08-19T20:22:20Z UpdateTip: new best=000000000000002b993875ecd9b83a9dfe710154d1d7efbd71a6f11720121429 height=250412
te='2013-08-05T21:06:18Z' progress=0.064345 cache=29.1MiB(135313txo)
2018-08-19T20:22:20Z UpdateTip: new best=0000000000000015e1d460c3733e2432bf21f1d75f908ed29b85892963e5d1d7 height=250413
te='2013-08-05T21:06:56Z' progress=0.064345 cache=29.1MiB(135674txo)
2018-08-19T20:22:20Z UpdateTip: new best=000000000000000666c575f54b147865670fdf7639904bbf4ee3887b5d1fc85cd height=250414
te='2013-08-05T21:39:18Z' progress=0.064347 cache=29.2MiB(136160txo)
```

Figure 2-18. *Bitcoin core daemon (bitcoind)*

While the process is running, open a second Terminal window to query the bitcoind interact with the APIs via the bitcoin-cli. Note: you can call the help feature and get help about the available APIs. For instance, to get a list of all available APIs, use this:

> bitcoin-cli --help # outputs list of command-line options.

> bitcoin-cli help # outputs list of RPC commands when the daemon is running.

> bitcoin-cli help getblockhash # get help on specific API, for instance "getblockhash";

To be able to retrieve the complete information, you would need to run a full node. To run a full node in the config file, change txindex=1 in the bitcoin.conf file and remove prune=3000. Open bitcoin.conf using your favorite editor.

> vim /[path]/.bitcoin/bitcoin.conf

Change the params as follows:

txindex=1 # prune=3000 - comment out this line

This change will allow you to run a full node and provide the index information so you can review transaction data for any transaction on the blockchain. Now you can start the bitcoin core daemon again and tell the daemon to re-index all the data.

```
> bitcoind -reindex -printtoconsole
```

Once again, this process can take hours; however, as it is downloading the blocks, you will be able to interact with the downloaded blocks.

To get the blockchain information, you can query the daemon to show the progress of your node. See the expected output in Figure 2-19.

```
> bitcoin-cli getblockchaininfo
```

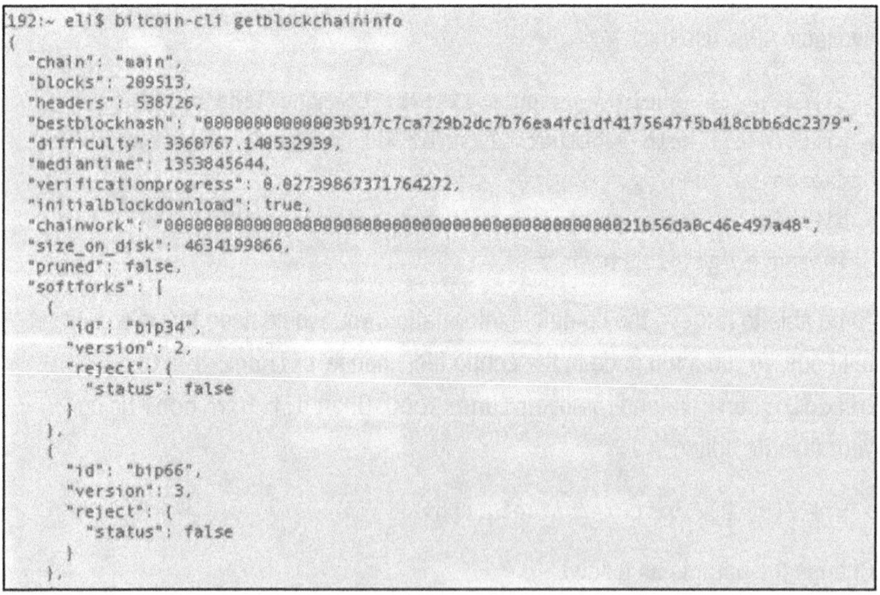

```
192:~ eli$ bitcoin-cli getblockchaininfo
{
  "chain": "main",
  "blocks": 209513,
  "headers": 538726,
  "bestblockhash": "00000000000003b917c7ca729b2dc7b76ea4fc1df4175647f5b418cbb6dc2379",
  "difficulty": 3368767.140532939,
  "mediantime": 1353845644,
  "verificationprogress": 0.02739867371764272,
  "initialblockdownload": true,
  "chainwork": "000000000000000000000000000000000000000000000000021b56da8c46e497a48",
  "size_on_disk": 4634199866,
  "pruned": false,
  "softforks": [
    {
      "id": "bip34",
      "version": 2,
      "reject": {
        "status": false
      }
    },
    {
      "id": "bip66",
      "version": 3,
      "reject": {
        "status": false
      }
    },
```

Figure 2-19. *Getting blockchain information*

This did not complete the full download of the bitcoin node; however, you already have 209,513 blocks and 538,726 block headers. The node first downloads the block headers of the best chain blocks and then downloads the full blocks.

In this exercise, you set your environment and downloaded blocks, configured them, and started a bitcoin node.

Serialized Blocks

Each full node holds the same validated blocks and follows the same rules (consensus rules). Each bitcoin block in the chain contains a 1 MB serialized code according to the current bitcoin consensus rules.

The block header holds encoded information that includes the following:

- Version
- Previous block header
- Merkle root hash
- Time
- nBits
- nounce
- txn_count (holds the total number of transactions)
- txns (raw transaction)

This data is being hashed and is part of the proof-of-work algorithm and the consensus rules. The Satoshi Nakamoto white paper explains the consensus rules.

"They vote with their CPU power, expressing their acceptance of valid blocks by working on extending them and rejecting invalid blocks by refusing to work on them. Any needed rules and incentives can be enforced with this consensus mechanism."

—*Bitcoin: A Peer-to-Peer Electronic Cash System.*

The proof of work (PoW) in bitcoin is based on Adam Back's Hashcash. Each miner is racing to solve the problem; once the problem is solved, the process restarts. The problem is a mathematical puzzle known as a *proof-of-work problem,* and the reward is given to the first miner who solves the problem. Then the verified transactions are stored in the public ledger. You'll learn more about this in the next section. It takes 9.9 minutes to generate about 25 bitcoins. Per the Satoshi white paper:

"A block header with no transactions would be about 80 bytes. If we suppose blocks are generated every 10 minutes, 80 bytes ∗ 6 ∗ 24 ∗ 365 = 4.2MB per year"

—*Bitcoin: A Peer-to-Peer Electronic Cash System.*

At the time of writing, bitcoin processes three transactions per seconds, and if the bitcoin transactions increase to four transactions per second, then bitcoin will be operating at peak capacity. Ethereum, on the other hand, is running five transactions per seconds, and if it goes to eight, that would be peak capacity. This design creates a scalability flaw as large corporations need to process hundreds of thousands of transactions per seconds not just four to eight per second.

Block Header

As mentioned, a block is shared between nodes on the bitcoin network. Each block header is a serialized 80-byte format. The following information is encoded in each block header:

- **Version**: At the time of writing, there are four block versions. Version 1 is the genesis block (2009), and version 2 was a soft fork in bitcoin core 0.7.0 (2012). Version 3 blocks were a soft fork in bitcoin core 0.10.0 (2015). Version 4 blocks are BIP65 in bitcoin core 0.11.2 (2015).

Note   What is BIP? BIP is a *bitcoin improvement proposal* (BIP). It is a document for introducing features or information to bitcoin. BIP is the standard for communicating ideas as bitcoin is open source and has no formal structure.

- **Previous block header hash**: This is an SHA256(SHA256()) hash of the previous block's header. This ensures integrity because changing one previous block will require changing each previous block.

- **Merkle root hash**: A Merkle tree is a binary tree that holds all the hashed pairs of the tree.

- **Time**: This is a Unix epoch time when the miner started hashing the header.

- **nBits**: nBits is the target section of the block header.

- **nonce**: This is an arbitrary number that miners change to modify the header hash in order to produce a hash that is less than or equal to the target threshold.

You already downloaded a portion of the blockchain, and you are able to query the block height already downloaded.

> bitcoin-cli getblockhash 375617

The daemon returned a string with the block hash of the best block chain at index 375617. You can then request to get the actual block.

> bitcoin-cli getblock 00000000000000000f270563d7f2187beec75 cdc04f98823572e5a31baf0a261

Figure 2-20 shows the results. As you can see, the block information includes the previousblockhash key and the nextblockhas key. These keys are SHA256(SHA256()) hash-encrypted keys. The rules ensure blocks cannot be changed. These rules are part of the consensus rules that are set to maintain the blockchain security by untrusted nodes.

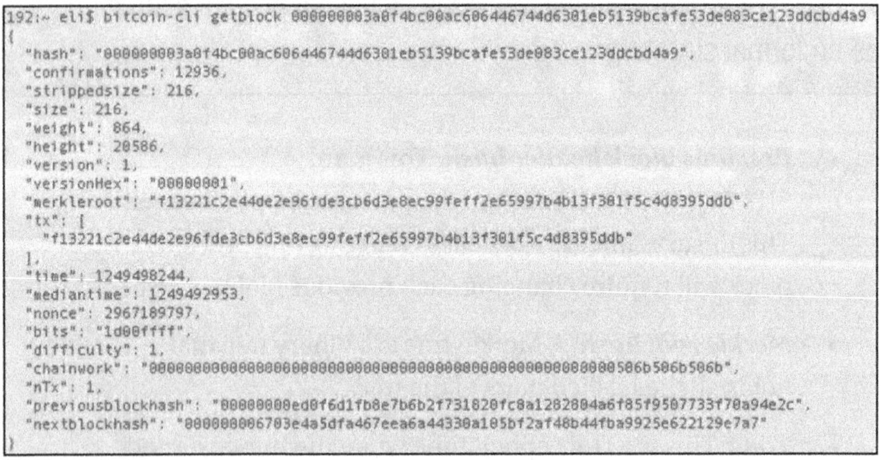

```
192:~ eli$ bitcoin-cli getblock 000000003a0f4bc00ac606446744d6301eb5139bcafe53de083ce123ddcbd4a9
{
  "hash": "000000003a0f4bc00ac606446744d6301eb5139bcafe53de083ce123ddcbd4a9",
  "confirmations": 12936,
  "strippedsize": 216,
  "size": 216,
  "weight": 864,
  "height": 20586,
  "version": 1,
  "versionHex": "00000001",
  "merkleroot": "f13221c2e44de2e96fde3cb6d3e8ec99feff2e65997b4b13f301f5c4d8395ddb",
  "tx": [
    "f13221c2e44de2e96fde3cb6d3e8ec99feff2e65997b4b13f301f5c4d8395ddb"
  ],
  "time": 1249498244,
  "mediantime": 1249492953,
  "nonce": 2967189797,
  "bits": "1d00ffff",
  "difficulty": 1,
  "chainwork": "0000000000000000000000000000000000000000000000000000000586b506b506b",
  "nTx": 1,
  "previousblockhash": "00000000ed0f6d1fb8e7b6b2f731820fc8a1282804a6f85f9507733f70a94e2c",
  "nextblockhash": "000000006703e4a5dfa467eea6a44330a105bf2af48b44fba9925e622129e7a7"
}
```

Figure 2-20. *Getting block information*

Block Version

The block version is part of the block header. You can see the block versions used in the block. In Figure 2-20 you can see that only version 1 is used for block 00000000000000000f270563d7f2187beec75cdc04f9882 3572e5a31baf0a261.

The consensus mechanism can only be changed by the bitcoin open source development team, which published instructions on how to handle upgrades suggestions. The BIP that introduced the upgrade method to handle the path for versioned transactions and blocks was used in versions 2, 3, and 4.

The function added to bitcoin core manages the soft forking. You can learn more about this BIP feature here: https://github.com/bitcoin/ bips/blob/master/bip-0034.mediawiki.

Merkle Trees

You called to retrieve the block information and received a Merkle root hash key. A Merkle tree is a binary tree. The root node of the Merkle tree holds all the hashed pairs of the tree. To help visualize this process, look at the following simple ASCII example of a binary list of a hashed tree:

```
Transactions list: H(A)->H(B)->H(C)->H(D)
          Hash(A|B|C|D)
       /                 \
  Hash(A|B)           Hash(C|D)
    / \                 /      \
Hash(A)  Hash(B)   Hash(C)    Hash(D)
```

The block headers included in this Merkle root are a representation of the descendants of all the transactions in that block. HASH(A|B|C|D) is the Merkle root. Each element A, B, C, and D would be a hash of all the transactions in that block. In our example we have only one transaction in each block.

```
Merkle Root: H(A)
        /
    Hash(A)
```

Target nBits

The block header includes nBits. nBits is the target section of the block header. nBits is a 32-bit compact encoding of the 256-bit target threshold. It works like scientific notation but uses base-256 instead of base-10. Every 2,016-block bitcoin core re-target point and adjusts nBits according to bitcoin difficulty rules. Bitcoin difficulty increases or decreases depending on whether it took less time or more time than two weeks to find 2,016 blocks. In other words, the difficulty will increase if the hash rate increases or decrease if the network hash rate decreases.

For instance, to convert an nBits 0x181b8330 into the target threshold, you would calculate it using the same shorthand you use with regular scientific notation; see Figure 2-21.

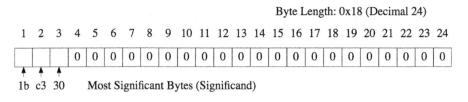

Quickly Converting nBits 0x181bc330 Into The Target
Threshold 0x1bc330000000000000000000000000000000000000000000000

Figure 2-21. *Calculating nBits. Photo credit. stackexchange.com.*

Convert 0x1bc330000000000000000000000000000000000000000000000 to nBits of 0x181b8330. That will be our target threshold.

txn_count

The txn_count parameter represents the total number of transactions in a given block including the coinbase transaction.

Coinbase is a special field used as an input for coinbase transactions. The coinbase allows you to claim the block reward and provides up to 100 bytes for arbitrary data.

Each block contains transactions, and the first transaction in a block is created by a miner; it includes a single coinbase.

Block Reward

Bitcoin miners claim the reward for creating a block. The reward is the sum of block subsidies plus the transaction fees paid by transactions included in the block.

A block subsidy is the newly available satoshis reward. It started at 50 bitcoins and is being halved every 210,000 blocks, approximately once every four years. At the time of writing, it's about 12.5 bitcoins. Eighty percent of the block subsidy has already been paid, and only 4.2 million bitcoins are left to mine until the 21 million supply cap is reached. At that point, the miners will receive a reward of only transaction fees.

As mentioned, each block contains transactions, and the first transaction in a block is created by a miner; it includes a single coinbase, the reward.

txns: Decode a Transaction

txns is the raw transaction in the block. To better understand this process, let's work with an actual transaction. Bitcoin transactions that are stored in the blockchain ledger are broadcast between different peers in serialized byte format (raw format or raw transaction). To decode the SHA256 raw transaction, you can call the bitcoin client and utilize the different APIs.

To start, you can retrieve a block you would like to work with. The daemon you are running lists the blocks as the new best, as shown in Figure 2-22.

```
2018-08-27T21:24:24Z UpdateTip: new best=000000000000015e8254b57a63a832a7915ffb85481a59da386c78b6f746a7913 height=116529 version=0x00000001
b67912 date='2011-04-03T18:48:07Z' progress=0.001150 cache=30.7MiB(198732txo)
2018-08-27T21:24:24Z UpdateTip: new best=000000000000ea2ca199cafd1362ece59d7c6f3867b5e0d6f20c12af6752fb48 height=116530 version=0x00000001
b07923 date='2011-04-03T18:49:00Z' progress=0.001150 cache=30.7MiB(198742txo)
2018-08-27T21:24:24Z UpdateTip: new best=0000000000000035223cb13dc1807cbe7e6c029ecce26f065244510013e7451df height=116531 version=0x00000001
b07935 date='2011-04-03T18:53:13Z' progress=0.001150 cache=30.7MiB(198754txo)
```

Figure 2-22. *Bitcoin daemon printing to console result*

As you can see, you are able to find the new best block by looking at the output of the bitcoin daemon. In this case, you choose the hash 000000000000ea2ca199cafd1362ece59d7c6f3867b5e0d6f20c12af6752fb48.

The best block chain is the block selected that is the hardest chain to re-create. Remember, in a chain of blocks, each block refers to the block that came before it; that's how you have a blockchain that creates the security and prevents the double spending.

Now that you have the new best block, you can retrieve the hash data of that block.

```
> bitcoin-cli getblock 000000000000ea2ca199cafd1362ece59d7
  c6f3867b5e0d6f20c12af6752fb48
```

The getblock command returns to a coded SHA256 hash data about the block you requested (Figure 2-23).

```
[192:~ eli$ bitcoin-cli getblock 000000000000ea2ca199cafd1362ece59d7c6f3867b5e0d6f20c12af6752fb48
{
  "hash": "000000000000ea2ca199cafd1362ece59d7c6f3867b5e0d6f20c12af6752fb48",
  "confirmations": 2937,
  "strippedsize": 2975,
  "size": 2975,
  "weight": 11900,
  "height": 116530,
  "version": 1,
  "versionHex": "00000001",
  "merkleroot": "9bf29601a9b7fb950748eac3ab492a39beea6bce80ac6532d6d4c1688462b758",
  "tx": [
    "a73226fc261f95db14eba45cd734aeb0b8784911aeb24f301f94858a09184036",
    "62d6634772d3686a55ccc84ad7f5ac2c0b03a299e0f2891abf427d0841309bab",
    "fb089405d99ab60a57bd345300e3eb1e9834bb9543adda3e183f482e9407ac62",
    "b10e64a838b39528e1937df490e9b555bf63dfe2cd1a63ddd0798fd8d37e0dfc",
    "98aea178e034319543755f34a696dc33fb963d4156d100fdd7bddde85210056b",
    "625f713effd396f7c7779f8655e062ee1258c64961719311f1547c5a5ec4a21e0",
    "7d194190448a00f8ef3518c4237560ce75739d12d0dd2d8681f3c446f8daf86d",
    "d673cbc0d561603c0f093969d00360cfb9a57559aa662977744deac7b12c20f7",
    "7253c524624ac9e16677e6e7a7f9a741cd00645f0f1bb4df43e35b0ee6039144",
    "ad986e692ac7adb1944563029631c6490241d91ea9a8f6c3e5aaecce96e949b5",
    "089903d7c985da07a8d44d434e456a4cc0741cef40d9003da9047f9d3a97db06"
  ],
  "time": 1301856540,
  "mediantime": 1301854026,
  "nonce": 821049821,
  "bits": "1b00f339",
  "difficulty": 68977.78463020959,
  "chainwork": "000000000000000000000000000000000000000000000000002bc6aa2bd7fdcaa3",
  "nTx": 11,
  "previousblockhash": "0000000000000815e8254b57a63a032a7915ffb05481a59da386c78b6f746a7913",
  "nextblockhash": "00000000000000035223cb13dc1007cbe7e6c829ecce28f865244518013e7451df"
}
```

Figure 2-23. *getblock retrieving block information*

Let's examine the result of the getblock call. You got a Merkle root as a hash as well as hash tx of all the transactions in that block.

```
"tx": [
  "a73226fc261f95db14eba45cd734aeb0b8784911aeb24f301f94858
  a09184036",
  Transaction hash 02,
  Transaction hash 03,
  and so on...
]
```

As you can see, there are multiple tx (transactions) in the array of this block. You can now request to retrieve the raw transaction data of each transaction (tx).

The getrawtransaction command will return the raw data.

```
> bitcoin-cli getrawtransaction a73226fc261f95db14eba45cd734
  aeb0b8784911aeb24f301f94858a09184036
```

Here is the raw transaction SHA256 data:

010000000010000000000000000000000000000000000000000000000000000000
000000000000ffffffff070439f3001b0141ffffffff0100f2052a01000000
434104b5a750a0ca4bb5a47b6f169b8a8f42b39e2dbb7967d046f1bf018d
927d102c280f1123ebfd973f6e651f2e5ff4486e18a90cc67d6d17ccdb95cd6
bf028d791cfac00000000

You can now decode the SHA256 raw transaction data with the
decoderawtransaction command.

```
> bitcoin-cli decoderawtransaction 010000000010000000000000000000
  00000000000000000000000000000000000000000ffffffff070439
  f3001b0141ffffffff0100f2052a01000000434104b5a750a0ca4bb5a47
  b6f169b8a8f42b39e2dbb7967d046f1bf018d927d102c280f1123ebfd973
  f6e651f2e5ff4486e18a90cc67d6d17ccdb95cd6bf028d791cfac00000000
```

The command returns the transaction result in a readable format, as
shown in Figure 2-24.

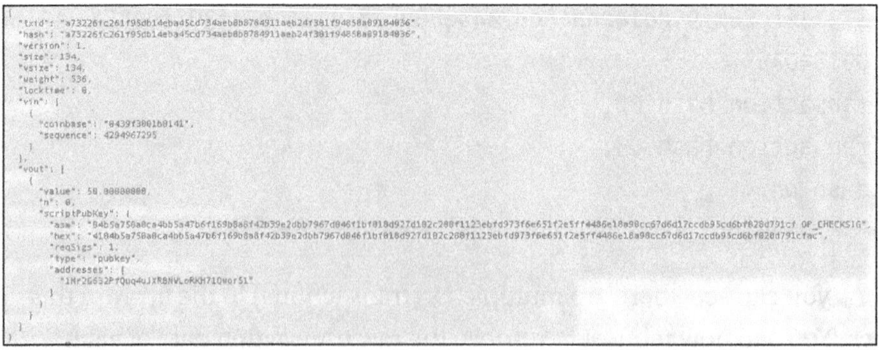

Figure 2-24. *Decode transaction utilizing the decoderawtransaction*
command

Bitcoin Wallet

As you saw in Figure 2-24, the wallet address is 1Mr2G632PfQuq4uJXRBN WLoRKH71Qwor51, and the value is 50 coins.

You can also confirm the transactions of this wallet online by visiting services that contain a full node and checking the wallet's balance. Figure 2-25 shows a screenshot from `https://bitref.com/1Mr2G632PfQuq 4uJXRBNWLoRKH71Qwor51`.

Figure 2-25. *1Mr2G632PfQuq4uJXRBNWLoRKH71Qwor51 wallet balance*

Similarly, you can query your wallet's available funds via the CLI:

```
> bitcoin-cli getbalance 1Mr2G632PfQuq4uJXRBNWLoRKH71Qwor51
```

In the next chapters, I will be covering wallets, so I will explain in more detail the wallet's operations, but for now, you can see that the user purchased 50 coins in 2003 and sold them in 2012. Notice that although you do not know the identity of the person who owns the wallet, you are able to view the wallet's current balance as this is public information.

Summary

In this chapter, you learned how to run a blockchain node that can help manage a blockchain. For bitcoin, you created a node called a *miner*. For NEO, you created a node that has management rights called a b*ookkeeping node*, and for EOS you created a *block producer*. You also explored what you need to do to have your node elected or running so it is profitable.

Next, you installed a full bitcoin node that is capable of running the bitcoin core API. You installed and configured your node and learned how to run the bitcoin core demon. You then interacted with the bitcoin core API and were able to learn how to serialize blocks and understand better the data inside each block.

I covered block rewards, transactions, and the bitcoin wallet. In the next chapter, you will be building your very own blockchain P2P network to get a much deeper understanding of how a blockchain works.

CHAPTER 3

Creating Your Own Blockchain

In this chapter, I will cover how to build your very own blockchain P2P network. This is a seven-step process, so in each section I'll start with a brief introduction followed by an exercise. You can download the code for each of the following exercises from GitHub and follow along:

- Creating a basic P2P network

- Sending and receiving blocks

- Registering miners and creating new blocks

- Setting up a name-value database, LevelDB

- Creating a private-public wallet

- Using API services

- Creating a command-line interface

This chapter will drill down into the code, and the examples in this chapter are simple in nature and intended for learning purposes. They will give you a better understanding of blockchain and the elements that are needed to achieve a fully working prototype of a blockchain.

© Elad Elrom 2019
E. Elrom, *The Blockchain Developer*, https://doi.org/10.1007/978-1-4842-4847-8_3

Note   It's not feasible to create a full production-grade blockchain in this short instructional chapter; however, I will give you the fundamentals for creating a basic working one.

Creating a Basic P2P Network

The first step in creating your blockchain is to create a P2P network. As you saw in previous chapters, the P2P network was the key to making blockchain work. In cryptocurrency the P2P network can help prevents the double spending issue for PoW and is also the core architecture behind PoS. In a blockchain, it allows you to sync any data needed on a network.

Note   Peer-to-peer (P2P) is a type of computer network that uses a distributed architecture. Each peer or node shares the workload and is equal to the other peers, meaning there should not be any privileged peer.

"We have proposed a system for electronic transactions without relying on trust. We started with the usual framework of coins made from digital signatures, which provides strong control of ownership, but is incomplete without a way to prevent double-spending. To solve this, we proposed a peer-to-peer network using proof-of-work to record a public history of transactions that quickly becomes computationally impractical for an attacker to change if honest nodes control a majority of CPU proof-of-worker."

—*Bitcoin: A Peer-to-Peer Electronic Cash System*

In this chapter, I will show you how to create your blockchain with Node.js, but you can do this with any other programming language because the principles are the same. You will be setting up your machine with the WebStorm integrated development environment (IDE) that will be used throughout this book. To download WebStorm, go to `https://www.jetbrains.com/webstorm/`. WebStorm offers a 30-day trial; however, it's not necessary, and you can choose any IDE of your liking and achieve the same results. At the time of writing, the WebStorm version is 2018.2.

STEP 1: BASIC P2P NETWORK EXERCISE

Setting Up Your Project

In this exercise, you will set up your project and create a basic P2P network to send and receive messages. After you are able to send and receive messages, you will be able to create a block class and a chained library and tie several blocks together to create a blockchain. You will need Node.js installed on your machine; there are many ways to install it. One easy way is through the prebuilt installer manager; find one that fits your platform here: `https://nodejs.org/en/download/`.

After you have downloaded WebStorm, you can create a new project. Select File ➤ Create New Project ➤ Node.js Express App ➤ CREATE. In Location, call the project **Blockchain**, and click Create (see Figure 3-1).

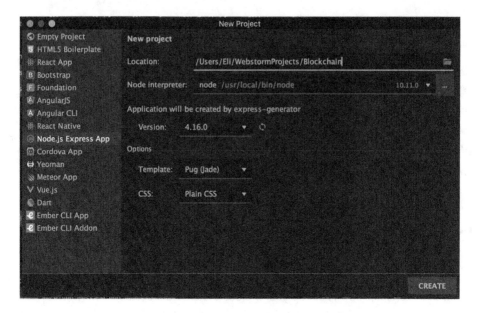

Figure 3-1. *WebStorm, creating a new project wizard*

Creating a P2P Network

Create a folder and name it **Blockchain**. Then create a file and name it p2p.js and write the following code. Alternatively, you could just clone the code from GitHub.

```
https://github.com/Apress/the-blockchain-developer/blob/master/
chapter2/step1/p2p.js
> git clone https://github.com/Apress/the-blockchain-developer
```

Tip   You can clone the entire code listings in this book from GitHub. Use the following Terminal command: > git clone
https://github.com/Apress/the-blockchain-developer/
chapter3/step1/

Listing 3-1. Shows Node.js P2P Network initial code to send and receive messages

```
const crypto = require('crypto'),
    Swarm = require('discovery-swarm'),
    defaults = require('dat-swarm-defaults'),
    getPort = require('get-port');

const peers = {};
let connSeq = 0;
let channel = 'myBlockchain';

const myPeerId = crypto.randomBytes(32);
console.log('myPeerId: ' + myPeerId.toString('hex'));

const config = defaults({
    id: myPeerId,
});

const swarm = Swarm(config);

(async () => {
    const port = await getPort();

    swarm.listen(port);
    console.log('Listening port: ' + port);

    swarm.join(channel);
    swarm.on('connection', (conn, info) => {
        const seq = connSeq;
        const peerId = info.id.toString('hex');
        console.log(`Connected #${seq} to peer: ${peerId}`);
        if (info.initiator) {
            try {
                conn.setKeepAlive(true, 600);
```

```javascript
            } catch (exception) {
                console.log('exception', exception);
            }
        }

        conn.on('data', data => {
            let message = JSON.parse(data);
            console.log('----------- Received Message start ----
            ---------');
            console.log(
                'from: ' + peerId.toString('hex'),
                'to: ' + peerId.toString(message.to),
                'my: ' + myPeerId.toString('hex'),
                'type: ' + JSON.stringify(message.type)
            );
            console.log('----------- Received Message end -----
            --------');

        });

        conn.on('close', () => {
            console.log(`Connection ${seq} closed, peerId:
            ${peerId}`);
            if (peers[peerId].seq === seq) {
                delete peers[peerId]
            }
        });

        if (!peers[peerId]) {
            peers[peerId] = {}
        }
        peers[peerId].conn = conn;
        peers[peerId].seq = seq;
        connSeq++
    })
})();
```

```
setTimeout(function(){
    writeMessageToPeers('hello', null);
}, 10000);

writeMessageToPeers = (type, data) => {
    for (let id in peers) {
        console.log('-------- writeMessageToPeers start -------- ');
        console.log('type: ' + type + ', to: ' + id);
        console.log('-------- writeMessageToPeers end ----------- ');
        sendMessage(id, type, data);
    }
};

writeMessageToPeerToId = (toId, type, data) => {
    for (let id in peers) {
        if (id === toId) {
            console.log('-------- writeMessageToPeerToId start
            -------- ');
            console.log('type: ' + type + ', to: ' + toId);
            console.log('-------- writeMessageToPeerToId end ---
            -------- ');
            sendMessage(id, type, data);
        }
    }
};

sendMessage = (id, type, data) => {
    peers[id].conn.write(JSON.stringify(
        {
            to: id,
            from: myPeerId,
            type: type,
```

```
            data: data
      }
   ));
};
```

To get this example to work, you need to run two instances of this code. You can run it from two separate machines as would be done in real life, or you could run two instances from the same machine via Terminal.

Your code needs to find and connect peers, deploy servers that are used to discover other peers, and get an available TCP port. That is done by utilizing these three libraries:

- **discovery-swarm**: Used to create a network swarm that uses `discovery-channel` to find and connect peers

- **dat-swarm-defaults**: Deploys servers that are used to discover other peers

- **get-port**: Gets available TCP ports

To install these libraries, run this command:

```
> npm install crypto discovery-swarm dat-swarm-defaults get-port
--save
```

Now that are libraries are installed, open two Terminal instances and navigate to the location of the library. Run the following command:

```
> node p2p.js
```

To run the code from the clone library on GitHub, navigate to the code, follow these Terminal commands to install the libraries, and run a node.js instance attaching our p2p.js code:

```
> cd [location]/chapter2/step2
> npm install
> node p2p.js
```

Figure 3-2 shows the output of running the Node.js code.

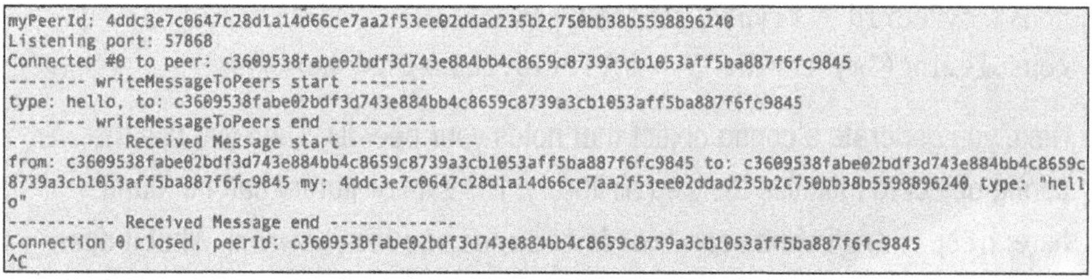

```
myPeerId: 4ddc3e7c0647c28d1a14d66ce7aa2f53ee02ddad235b2c750bb38b5598896240
Listening port: 57868
Connected #0 to peer: c3609538fabe02bdf3d743e884bb4c8659c8739a3cb1053aff5ba887f6fc9845
-------- writeMessageToPeers start --------
type: hello, to: c3609538fabe02bdf3d743e884bb4c8659c8739a3cb1053aff5ba887f6fc9845
-------- writeMessageToPeers end -----------
----------- Received Message start -------------
from: c3609538fabe02bdf3d743e884bb4c8659c8739a3cb1053aff5ba887f6fc9845 to: c3609538fabe02bdf3d743e884bb4c8659c
8739a3cb1053aff5ba887f6fc9845 my: 4ddc3e7c0647c28d1a14d66ce7aa2f53ee02ddad235b2c750bb38b5598896240 type: "hell
o"
----------- Received Message end -------------
Connection 0 closed, peerId: c3609538fabe02bdf3d743e884bb4c8659c8739a3cb1053aff5ba887f6fc9845
^C
```

Figure 3-2. *P2P running two peers in Terminal*

As you can see in Figure 3-2, the network generated a random peer ID for your machine and picked a random port utilizing the discovery libraries you installed. Then the code was able to discover other peers on the network and send and receive messages to and from these peers. You are now connected on a P2P network with other users.

Let's walk through the code to better understand how it all works. The first lines of code are an import statement for the open source libraries that you are using in your code.

```
const crypto = require('crypto'),
    Swarm = require('discovery-swarm'),
    defaults = require('dat-swarm-defaults'),
    getPort = require('get-port');
```

Notice that you use const to set your variable instead of let. You want to ensure there is no rebinding, and you always refer to the same object, so selecting const is advised according to best practices.

Next, you set your variables to hold an object with the peers and connection sequence, and you choose a channel name that all your nodes will be connecting to. You also set a randomly generated peer ID for your peer utilizing the crypto library.

```
const peers = {};
let connSeq = 0;
let channel = 'myBlockchain';
```

```
const myPeerId = crypto.randomBytes(32);
console.log('myPeerId: ' + myPeerId.toString('hex'));
```

Next, you generate a config object that holds your peer ID. Then you use the config object to initialize the swarm library. The swarm library can be found here: https://github.com/mafintosh/discovery-swarm. What it does is create a network swarm that uses the discovery-channel library to find and connect peers on a UCP/TCP network.

```
const config = defaults({
    id: myPeerId,
});

const swarm = Swarm(config);
```

Now that everything is set up and ready, you will be creating a Node.js async function to continuously monitor swarm.on event messages.

```
(async () => {
```

You listen on the random port selected, and once a connection is made to the peer, you use setKeepAlive to ensure the network connection stays with other peers.

```
    const port = await getPort();

    swarm.listen(port);
    console.log('Listening port: ' + port);

    swarm.join(channel);
    swarm.on('connection', (conn, info) => {
        const seq = connSeq;
        const peerId = info.id.toString('hex');
        console.log(`Connected #${seq} to peer: ${peerId}`);
        if (info.initiator) {
            try {
                conn.setKeepAlive(true, 600);
```

```
    } catch (exception) {
        console.log('exception', exception);
    }
  }
```

Once you receive a `data` message on the P2P network, you parse the data using `JSON.parse`, which is a Node.js native command, so you do not need to include any `import` statement. This command decodes your message back into an object, and the `toString` command converts bytes into a readable string data type.

```
conn.on('data', data => {
    let message = JSON.parse(data);
    console.log('----------- Received Message start ----
    ---------');
    console.log(
        'from: ' + peerId.toString('hex'),
        'to: ' + peerId.toString(message.to),
        'my: ' + myPeerId.toString('hex'),
        'type: ' + JSON.stringify(message.type)
    );
    console.log('----------- Received Message end -----
    --------');
});
```

You also listen to a `close` event, which will indicate that you lost a connection with peers, so you can take action, such as delete the peers from your `peers` list object.

```
conn.on('close', () => {
    console.log(`Connection ${seq} closed, peerId: ${peerId}`);
    if (peers[peerId].seq === seq) {
        delete peers[peerId]
    }
});
```

```
        if (!peers[peerId]) {
            peers[peerId] = {}
        }
        peers[peerId].conn = conn;
        peers[peerId].seq = seq;
        connSeq++
    })
})();
```

Here, you will be using a setTimeout Node.js native function to send a message after ten seconds to any available peers. The first message you will be sending is just an "hello" message. You create methods called writeMessageToPeers and writeMessageToPeerToId to handle your object, so it's formatted with the data you want to transmit and who you want to send it to.

```
setTimeout(function(){
    writeMessageToPeers('hello', null);
}, 10000);
```

The writeMessageToPeers method will be sending messages to all the connected peers.

```
writeMessageToPeers = (type, data) => {
    for (let id in peers) {
        console.log('-------- writeMessageToPeers start ------
        -- ');
        console.log('type: ' + type + ', to: ' + id);
        console.log('-------- writeMessageToPeers end ---------
        -- ');
        sendMessage(id, type, data);
    }
};
```

Additionally, you will be creating another method,
writeMessageToPeerToId, that will be sending the message to a specific
peer ID, in case you want to communicate with just one specific peer.

```
writeMessageToPeerToId = (toId, type, data) => {
    for (let id in peers) {
        if (id === toId) {
            console.log('-------- writeMessageToPeerToId start
            -------- ');
            console.log('type: ' + type + ', to: ' + toId);
            console.log('-------- writeMessageToPeerToId end ---
            -------- ');
            sendMessage(id, type, data);
        }
    }
};
```

Lastly, sendMessage is a generic method that you will be using to send a
message formatted with the params you would like to pass and includes the
following:

- **to/from**: The peer ID you are sending the message from and to

- **type**: The message type

- **data**: Any data you would like to share on the P2P network

These params will be useful once you share your blockchain block. Notice
that the message you pass needs to be a string and cannot be an object, so
you are using a JSON.stringify native function to encode your messages
before sharing them over the P2P network.

```
sendMessage = (id, type, data) => {
    peers[id].conn.write(JSON.stringify(
        {
            to: id,
            from: myPeerId,
```

```
                type: type,
                data: data
        }
    ));
};
```

In this exercise, you downloaded and installed the WebStorm IDE and created your project, which includes a basic P2P network. You were able to keep a connection to a TCP network random port and send and receive messages including encoding and decoding these messages. You are ready to move to the next exercise and send an actual block between each node on your network.

Creating Genesis Block and Sharing Blocks

In the next exercise, you will be creating block objects that you can share between your nodes. But before you do that, let's take a closer look at the Block object. The Block object is not the same for every blockchain. Different blockchains utilize different types of Block objects; you will be using a Block object similar to bitcoin; I covered in details during Chapter 2. To better understand the architecture, take a look at a Unified Modeling Language (UML) diagram of the Block and the BlockHeader objects you will be using in the next exercise, as shown in Figure 3-3.

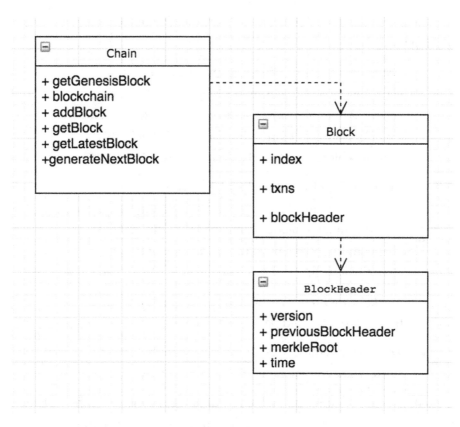

Figure 3-3. *Block and BlockHeader UML diagram*

As a reminder, from Chapter 2, the Block object contains the following properties:

- *index*: GenesisBlock is our first block, we assign the block index with the value of 0.

- *txns*: This is the raw transaction in the block. I don't want to focus on just cryptocurrencies in this chapter, so think of this as any type of data you want to store.

Included in the `Block` object is the `BlockHeader` object, which contains the following properties:

- **Version**: At the time of writing, there are four block versions. Version 1 is the genesis block (2009), and version 2 is a soft fork of bitcoin core 0.7.0 (2012). Version 3 blocks were a soft fork of bitcoin core 0.10.0 (2015). Version 4 blocks are BIP65 in bitcoin core 0.11.2 (2015).

- **Previous block header hash**: This is an SHA-256 (Secure Hash Algorithm) hash function of the previous block's header. It ensures that the previous block cannot be changed as this block needs to be changed as well.

- **Merkle root hash**: A Merkle tree is a binary tree that holds all the hashed pairs of the tree.

- **Time**: This is the Unix epoch time when the miner started hashing the header.

As you recall, bitcoin also includes a difficulty property for the miners that gets recalculated every 2,016 blocks. Here you won't use the nBits and nounce params, as you are not doing PoW.

- **nounce**: The nonce in a bitcoin block is a 32-bit (4-byte) field whose value is adjusted by miners so that the hash of the block will be less than or equal to the current target of the network.

- **nBits**: This refers to the target. The target is a 256-bit number and inversely proportional to the difficulty. It is recalculated every 2,016 blocks.

In terms of P2P communication, the flow of blocks between each peer on the P2P network consists of requesting the latest block from a peer on the network and then receiving a block request. Figure 3-4 shows the flow diagram.

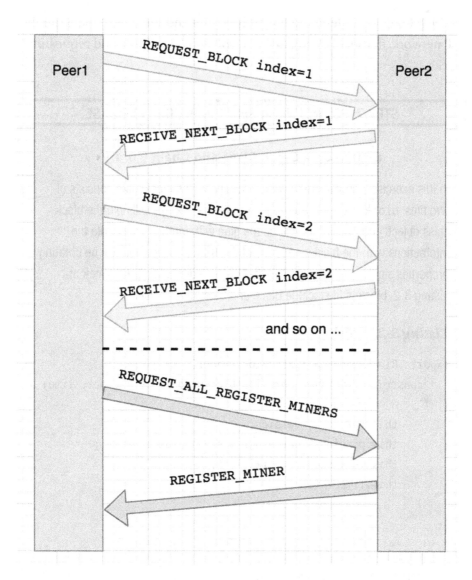

Figure 3-4. *Flow diagram of P2P communications requesting latest block and receiving latest block*

Now that you understand the architecture and the flow of blocks in the P2P network, in the following exercise you will be sending and requesting blocks.

STEP 2: P2P NETWORK SENDING BLOCKS EXERCISE

Setting Up a Block Class and Chain Library

In this exercise, you will create your blockchain. The blockchain consists of two files: block.js and chain.js. The file Block.js will hold the block class object, and chain.js will be the glue with methods to handle the interactions with the blocks. In terms of the Block object, you will be creating properties similar to the properties that bitcoin core holds. Take a look at Listing 3-2, block.js file include Block and BlockHeader objects.

Listing 3-2. block.js

```
exports.BlockHeader = class BlockHeader {
    constructor(version, previousBlockHeader, merkleRoot, time)
{
        this.version = version;
        this.previousBlockHeader = previousBlockHeader;
        this.merkleRoot = merkleRoot;
        this.time = time;
    }
};

exports.Block = class Block {
    constructor(blockHeader, index, txns) {
        this.blockHeader = blockHeader;
        this.index = index;
        this.txns = txns;
    }
}
```

As you can see, chain.js contains the first block, which is called the *genesis* block, as well as a method to receive the entire blockchain object, add a block, and retrieve a block. Note that you will be adding a library called moment to save the time in a Unix time format in your chain.js library. To do so, install moment with npm.

```
> npm install moment --save
```

Now that you have the block.js file created, you can create the chain.js class; see Listing 3-3.

Listing 3-3. chain.js

```
let Block =  require("./block.js").Block,
    BlockHeader =  require("./block.js").BlockHeader,
    moment = require("moment");

let getGenesisBlock = () => {
    let blockHeader = new BlockHeader(1, null, "0x1bc33000000000
    00000000000000000000000000000000000000", moment().unix());
    return new Block(blockHeader, 0, null);
};

let getLatestBlock = () => blockchain[blockchain.length-1];

let addBlock = (newBlock) => {
    let prevBlock = getLatestBlock();
    if (prevBlock.index < newBlock.index && newBlock.
    blockHeader.previousBlockHeader === prevBlock.blockHeader.
    merkleRoot) {
        blockchain.push(newBlock);
    }
}

let getBlock = (index) => {
    if (blockchain.length-1 >= index)
```

```
        return blockchain[index];
    else
        return null;
}

const blockchain = [getGenesisBlock()];

if (typeof exports != 'undefined' ) {
    exports.addBlock = addBlock;
    exports.getBlock = getBlock;
    exports.blockchain = blockchain;
    exports.getLatestBlock = getLatestBlock;
}
```

You now have a block object that is included in chain.js. Your library can create your genesis block and add a block to your blockchain object. You also will be able to send and request blocks.

Next, in your P2P network class, you can use the chain.js file you created. First you need to import the class chain.js.

```
const chain =  require("./chain");
```

Then you can define a message type to request and receive the latest block. When you send messages in your P2P network, you need to be able to figure out the purpose of messages. By using a MessageType property, you can define a switch mechanism so different messages types will be used for different functions.

```
let MessageType = {
    REQUEST_LATEST_BLOCK: 'requestLatestBlock',
    LATEST_BLOCK: 'latestBlock'
};
```

Once a connection data event message is received, you can create your switch code to handle the different types of requests, as shown in Listing 3-4.

Listing 3-4. Message Switch and Handlers

```
switch (message.type) {
    case MessageType.REQUEST_BLOCK:
        console.log('-----------REQUEST_BLOCK-------------');
        let requestedIndex = (JSON.parse(JSON.stringify(message.
        data))).index;
        let requestedBlock = chain.getBlock(requestedIndex);
        if (requestedBlock)
        writeMessageToPeerToId(peerId.toString('hex'),
        MessageType.RECEIVE_NEXT_BLOCK, requestedBlock);
        else
            console.log('No block found @ index: ' + requestedIndex);
        console.log('-----------REQUEST_BLOCK-------------');
        break;
    case MessageType.RECEIVE_NEXT_BLOCK:
        console.log('-----------RECEIVE_NEXT_BLOCK-------------');
        chain.addBlock(JSON.parse(JSON.stringify(message.data)));
        console.log(JSON.stringify(chain.blockchain));
        let nextBlockIndex = chain.getLatestBlock().index+1;
        console.log('-- request next block @ index: ' +
        nextBlockIndex);
        writeMessageToPeers(MessageType.REQUEST_BLOCK, {index:
        nextBlockIndex});
        console.log('-----------RECEIVE_NEXT_BLOCK-------------');
        break;
}
```

Lastly, you will set a timeout request that will send a request to retrieve the
latest block every 5,000 milliseconds (5 seconds).

```
setTimeout(function(){
writeMessageToPeers(MessageType.REQUEST_BLOCK, {index: chain.
getLatestBlock().index+1});
}, 5000);
```

You can download the complete exercise from here: `https://github.com/Apress/the-blockchain-developer/tree/master/chapter3/step2/`.

In this exercise, you were able to generate your genesis block and create a mechanism to request and receive blocks by sending messages requests. The ability to request and receive blocks allows you to sync new peers that enter the P2P network. You also need a sync for any additional blocks you generate after the genesis block creation.

Registering Miners and Creating New Blocks

At this point, you have a basic P2P network, and you are able to connect peers in the network, create a genesis block, and send and receive blocks. The next step is being able to generate new blocks. As you saw in Chapter 2, proof of work is based on creating a mathematical problem and rewarding miners that find the solution for the problem first. However, in this example, you will take an approach of proof of stake (PoS) where you trust each miner to generate your blocks. Each peer will register as a miner and will take a turn to mine a block. You can see an overview of each miner generating a block in Figure 3-5.

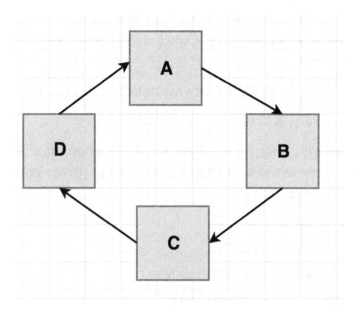

Figure 3-5. *Your blockchain handles mining using a simple PoS mechanism*

Lastly, before you start your next exercise, revisit Figure 3-4 to better understand your flow. The flow shows how your P2P network handles peer communications requesting the latest block and receiving the latest block. In the next exercise, you will register your peers as miners and create new blocks.

STEP 3: REGISTER MINERS AND CREATING NEW BLOCKS EXERCISE

Register Miners

In this exercise, you will register miners and create new blocks. You can download the complete exercise from here: https://github.com/Apress/the-blockchain-developer/tree/master/chapter3/step3.

To automate the process of generating a block every x number of minutes, you can use a Node.js library called `cron`, which is similar to the Linux library that automates tasks.

To install the `cron` open source library, run the following command:

```
> npm install cron --save
```

Next, in your `p2p.js` file, you will create two variables to keep track of the registered miners as well as who mined the last block so you can assign the next block to the next miner.

```
let registeredMiners = [];
let lastBlockMinedBy = null;
```

You are also going to add two messages types.

- REQUEST_ALL_REGISTER_MINERS

- REGISTER_MINER

```
let MessageType = {
    REQUEST_BLOCK: 'requestBlock',
    RECEIVE_NEXT_BLOCK: 'receiveNextBlock',
    RECEIVE_NEW_BLOCK: 'receiveNewBlock',
    REQUEST_ALL_REGISTER_MINERS: 'requestAllRegisterMiners',
    REGISTER_MINER: 'registerMiner'
};
```

Before you register your peers as miners, you will request to receive all the existing registered miners in the network, and then you will add your peer as a miner in a `registeredMiners` object. You do that by running a timer to update your miners every five seconds.

```
setTimeout(function(){
writeMessageToPeers(MessageType.REQUEST_ALL_REGISTER_MINERS,
null);
}, 5000);
```

Now, that have an automated timeout command that can point to a handler
to update the list of registered miners you can also automate a command to
register your peer as a miner;

```
setTimeout(function(){
    registeredMiners.push(myPeerId.toString('hex'));
    console.log('----------Register my miner --------------');
    console.log(registeredMiners);
    writeMessageToPeers(MessageType.REGISTER_MINER,
    registeredMiners);
    console.log('---------- Register my miner --------------');
}, 7000);
```

In your switch command, you want to modify the code to be able to set
handlers for incoming messages regarding the registrations of miners. You
want to keep track of the registered miners as well as handle a message once
a new block is mined. See Listing 3-5 for the miner's handlers.

Listing 3-5. Miner's Handlers

```
case MessageType.REQUEST_ALL_REGISTER_MINERS:
        console.log('-----------REQUEST_ALL_REGISTER_
        MINERS------------- ' + message.to);
        writeMessageToPeers(MessageType.REGISTER_MINER,
        registeredMiners);
        registeredMiners = JSON.parse(JSON.stringify(message.
        data));
        console.log('-----------REQUEST_ALL_REGISTER_
        MINERS------------- ' + message.to);
        break;
    case MessageType.REGISTER_MINER:
        console.log('-----------REGISTER_MINER------------- ' +
        message.to);
        let miners = JSON.stringify(message.data);
        registeredMiners = JSON.parse(miners);
```

```
console.log(registeredMiners);
console.log('-----------REGISTER_MINER------------ ' +
message.to);
break;
```

Unregister Miners

You also need to unregister a miner once a connection with the miner is closed or lost.

```
console.log(`Connection ${seq} closed, peerId: ${peerId}`);
if (peers[peerId].seq === seq) {
    delete peers[peerId];
    console.log('--- registeredMiners before: ' + JSON.
    stringify(registeredMiners));
    let index = registeredMiners.indexOf(peerId);
    if (index > -1)
        registeredMiners.splice(index, 1);
    console.log('--- registeredMiners end: ' + JSON.
    stringify(registeredMiners));
}
});
```

Mine a New Block

As opposed to bitcoin, which generates a block every 10 minutes, your blockchain will be improved and will generate a block every 30 seconds. To achieve that, you already installed the open source cron library for Node.js. The cron library works the same as the Linux cron. You can utilized the cron library to set how often to call the same code again, which will be used to call your miners every 30 seconds.

To do so, first include the library in your code's import statement on top of the p2p.js file.

```
let CronJob = require('cron').CronJob;
```

Next, you can set your `cronjob` to run every 30 seconds, and `job.start();`
will start the job, as shown in Listing 3-6.

Listing 3-6. crobjob to Mine a New Block

```
const job = new CronJob('30 * * * * *', function() {
    let index = 0; // first block
    if (lastBlockMinedBy) {
        let newIndex = registeredMiners.indexOf(lastBlockMinedBy);
        index = ( newIndex+1 > registeredMiners.length-1) ? 0 :
        newIndex + 1;
    }
    lastBlockMinedBy = registeredMiners[index];
    console.log('-- REQUESTING NEW BLOCK FROM: ' +
    registeredMiners[index] + ', index: ' + index);
    console.log(JSON.stringify(registeredMiners));
    if (registeredMiners[index] === myPeerId.toString('hex')) {
        console.log('-----------create next block -------------
        ----');
        let newBlock = chain.generateNextBlock(null);
        chain.addBlock(newBlock);
        console.log(JSON.stringify(newBlock));
        writeMessageToPeers(MessageType.RECEIVE_NEW_BLOCK,
        newBlock);
        console.log(JSON.stringify(chain.blockchain));
        console.log('-----------create next block -------------
        ----');
    }
});
job.start();
```

Reviewing the code, notice that the first block's index is 0, so after the first block is mined, `lastBlockMinedBy` will be set, and you will be requesting the next block from your next miner.

```
let newIndex = registeredMiners.indexOf(lastBlockMinedBy);
index = ( newIndex+1 > registeredMiners.length-1) ? 0 : newIndex
+ 1;
```

To generate and add a new block, you will be calling `chain generateNextBlock` and `addBlock`. Lastly, you will broadcast the new block to all the connected peers.

```
let newBlock = chain.generateNextBlock(null);
chain.addBlock(newBlock);
writeMessageToPeers(MessageType.RECEIVE_NEW_BLOCK, newBlock);
```

In your code, your switch will handle the new incoming blocks.

```
case MessageType.RECEIVE_NEW_BLOCK:
    if ( message.to === myPeerId.toString('hex') && message.from
    !== myPeerId.toString('hex')) {
        console.log('-----------RECEIVE_NEW_BLOCK------------- '
        + message.to);
        chain.addBlock(JSON.parse(JSON.stringify(message.data)));
        console.log(JSON.stringify(chain.blockchain));
        console.log('-----------RECEIVE_NEW_BLOCK------------- '
        + message.to);
    }
    break;
```

To see this code in action, run three instances of your code.

```
> node p2p.js
```

You can see the messages of registering each peer as a miner, as well as your code starting to mine blocks every 30 seconds in order, as shown in Figure 3-6.

```
----------REGISTER_MINER------------- ede97c6d7d1c7ebff06f9a20610d2e6730d9aa438a8d16a9e1e6c162f10551c0
[ 'ede97c6d7d1c7ebff06f9a20610d2e6730d9aa438a8d16a9e1e6c162f10551c0',
  '6e0ee3456858dc3e275503b7afe5d14444bfa656e324e76f6d34f9e1f049a3a1',
  '782ac554fda194991843f4a33a6b6926b6cf6774922fe3fc3b74e41f1a2ad4e8' ]
----------REGISTER_MINER------------- ede97c6d7d1c7ebff06f9a20610d2e6730d9aa438a8d16a9e1e6c162f10551c0
-- REQUESTING NEW BLOCK FROM: ede97c6d7d1c7ebff06f9a20610d2e6730d9aa438a8d16a9e1e6c162f10551c0, index: 0
["ede97c6d7d1c7ebff06f9a20610d2e6730d9aa438a8d16a9e1e6c162f10551c0","6e0ee3456858dc3e275503b7afe5d14444bfa656e324e76f6d34f9e1f049a3a1","
782ac554fda194991843f4a33a6b6926b6cf6774922fe3fc3b74e41f1a2ad4e8"]
-----------create next block -----------------
{"blockHeader":{"version":1,"previousBlockHeader":"0x1bc330000000000000000000000000000000000000000000000000","merkleRoot":"4ea5c508a6566e7624
0543f8feb06fd457777be39549c4016436afda65d2330e","time":1540148550},"index":1,"txns":null}
-------- writeMessageToPeers start --------
type: receiveNewBlock, to: 6e0ee3456858dc3e275503b7afe5d14444bfa656e324e76f6d34f9e1f049a3a1
-------- writeMessageToPeers end -----------
-------- writeMessageToPeers start --------
type: receiveNewBlock, to: 782ac554fda194991843f4a33a6b6926b6cf6774922fe3fc3b74e41f1a2ad4e8
-------- writeMessageToPeers end -----------
[{"blockHeader":{"version":1,"previousBlockHeader":null,"merkleRoot":"0x1bc330000000000000000000000000000000000000000000000000","time":154014
8483},"index":0,"txns":null},{"blockHeader":{"version":1,"previousBlockHeader":"0x1bc330000000000000000000000000000000000000000000000000","me
rkleRoot":"4ea5c508a6566e76240543f8feb06fd457777be39549c4016436afda65d2330e","time":1540148550},"index":1,"txns":null}]
-----------create next block -----------------
```

Figure 3-6. *Code registering miners and generating new blocks*

In this exercise, you were able to register your peers as a miners, generate new blocks, and share blocks with other peers; you used a simple PoS for the consensus mechanism and were able to test the functionality by creating three peers. The consensus mechanism is simple and does not take into account every use case that can happen or security. In the next step, you will save your blocks in a LevelDB database.

Storing Blocks in LevelDB

If you run your blockchain for a few hours, you will notice that the number of blocks created grows, which can become a problem as currently these blocks are stored in your computer's memory cache. As you add more and more blocks, the memory usage will grow, and eventually your code will crash. Further, without storing your blocks in a database, you will not be able to start and stop your P2P network, as the blocks are not saved.

To accommodate these use cases and others, you will be using a LevelDB database.

Note   A LevelDB database stores name-value pairs in what is called a *level-up* and *level-down* fashion. It is an ideal option for blockchain networks. In fact, bitcoin uses LevelDB to store not only block information but also transaction information. See `https://github.com/bitcoin-core/leveldb`.

STEP 4: LEVELDB TO STORE BLOCKS EXERCISE

LevelDB

In this exercise, you will implement a database to store your blocks. You can download the complete exercise from here: `https://github.com/Apress/the-blockchain-developer/tree/master/chapter3/step4/blockchain`. Remember to run the `install` command to retrieve all the npm modules.

```
> npm install
```

To get started on your own from the previous step, you will be using a Node.js LevelDB wrapper so you can communicate with LevelDB through your code. Install the library via npm.

```
>   npm install level -save
```

Next, make a directory where you will be saving the database.

```
> mkdir db
```

You can now implement the database. In your `chain.js` library, you will add some code to save your block in the LevelDB database, as shown in Listing 3-7.

Listing 3-7. Storing Blocks in LevelDB

```
let level = require('level'),
    fs = require('fs');

let db;

let createDb = (peerId) => {
    let dir = __dirname + '/db/' + peerId;
    if (!fs.existsSync(dir)){
        fs.mkdirSync(dir);
        db = level(dir);
        storeBlock(getGenesisBlock());
    }
}
```

As you can see, you use the __dirname Node.js native class to give you the directory path location because you need the full path to save your database.

Because you are running multiple instances of your P2P network on the same machine, you cannot use the same path for each peer because the database needs to be separate. What you can do is set each database's location in a separate path location using the folder name as the name of your peer ID; then each database can be stored in the db folder. Also notice that you save the first block, getGenesisBlock().

Next, you create a storeBlock method to store the new block.

```
let storeBlock = (newBlock) => {
    db.put(newBlock.index, JSON.stringify(newBlock), function (err) {
        if (err) return console.log('Ooops!', err) // some kind
        of I/O error
        console.log('--- Inserting block index: ' + newBlock.
        index);
    })
}
```

When you generate a new block using the generateNextBlock method, you can now store the block in the LevelDB database.

```
storeBlock(newBlock);
```

You are also going to add a method to be able to retrieve a block from the LevelDB database.

```
let getDbBlock = (index, res) => {
    db.get(index, function (err, value) {
        if (err) return res.send(JSON.stringify(err));
        return(res.send(value));
    });
}
```

Make sure you expose the createDb and getDbBlock methods.

```
if (typeof exports != 'undefined' ) {
    exports.createDb = createDb;
    exports.getDbBlock = getDbBlock;}
```

Lastly, in your P2P network code, all you need to do is create a database once you start the code.

```
chain.createDb(myPeerId.toString('hex'));
```

To see the code in action, run an instance of the P2P network.

```
> node p2p.js
```

You can monitor the database's data in the db folder using the tail command with the -f flag. Terminal will stay open and can show you new blocks as they are being generated (see the output in Figure 3-7).

```
> cd step4/db/[our peer Id]
> tail -f 000003.log
```

```
Eli@Elis-MacBook-Pro ~/Desktop/step4/db/b34d183470ad2a96a12fadf9a08bcaa85e60a6c2d037e9a374f3b3dc7a7a62b7 $
 tail -F 000003.log
"'<c?0?{"blockHeader":{"version":1,"previousBlockHeader":null,"merkleRoot":"0x1bc330000000000000000000000
00000000000000000000000","time":1555830838},"index":0,"txns":null}q???1?{"blockHeader":{"version":1,"previo
usBlockHeader":"0x1bc3300000000000000000000000000000000000000000000000000","merkleRoot":"4ea5c508a6566e76240543f
8feb06fd457777be39549c4016436afda65d2330e","time":1555830870},"index":1,"txns":null}d[??2?{"blockHeader":{
"version":1,"previousBlockHeader":"4ea5c508a6566e76240543f8feb06fd457777be39549c4016436afda65d2330e","merk
leRoot":"4ea5c508a6566e76240543f8feb06fd457777be39549c4016436afda65d2330e","time":1555830930},"index":2,"t
xns":null}m    %?3?{"blockHeader":{"version":1,"previousBlockHeader":"4ea5c508a6566e76240543f8feb06fd4577
77be39549c4016436afda65d2330e","merkleRoot":"4ea5c508a6566e76240543f8feb06fd457777be39549c4016436afda65d23
30e","time":1555830990},"index":3,"txns":null}???e?4?{"blockHeader":{"version":1,"previousBlockHeader":"4e
a5c508a6566e76240543f8feb06fd457777be39549c4016436afda65d2330e","merkleRoot":"4ea5c508a6566e76240543f8feb0
6fd457777be39549c4016436afda65d2330e","time":1555831050},"index":4,"txns":null}▮
```

Figure 3-7. tail command with the LevelDB database showing new blocks being generated

In this exercise, you created a LevelDB database. You are storing your blocks so you will be able to retrieve them instead of relying on your cache memory. I am keeping things simple; if this were a real working blockchain, you would implement the following steps:

1. Mitigate all the possible security risks.

2. Store and retrieve your blocks from the LevelDB database.

3. Create a method to restore LevelDB's entries.

4. Clean old databases because new ones are created on every init.

Creating a Blockchain Wallet

In cryptocurrency, a wallet is necessary in order to reward miners for generating blocks as well as to be able to create transactions and send transactions. In this section, you will create a wallet. You need to create a combination of public and private keys not just to authenticate a user but so you can store and retrieve data that the user owns. You will create a wallet with public and private keys.

In bitcoin, the wallet's original software is the bitcoin core protocol you downloaded in Chapter 2; it needs the entire ledger of all transactions since 2009, which is more than 150 GB at the time of writing. For that reason, most wallets in use are "light" wallets or what's called *simplified payment verification* (SPV) wallets that sync to bitcoin core. In blockchain, there are many different wallets available, from online all the way to a paper wallet where you write your private key on a piece of paper.

Before proceeding, let's take a quick look at how you can communicate with a bitcoin wallet. As you recall, in Chapter 2 you were able to get the balance of a certain bitcoin wallet. To better understand wallets, you can create a bitcoin wallet using the bitcoin core.

First, you need to run the bitcoin daemon.

```
> bitcoind -printtoconsole
```

Next, you can request an address.

```
> bitcoin-cli help getnewaddress
```

Then, you are able to dump your private keys into a text file.

```
> bitcoin-cli dumpwallet ~/mywallet.txt
```

You can get the location of your private key and view the key.

```
> vim /Users/[location]/mywallet.txt
```

For reference, check the C++ bitcoin core wallet code here:

```
> vim /[Bitcoin Core Location]/bitcoin/src/wallet/init.cpp
```

STEP 5: WALLET EXERCISE

Create a Blockchain Wallet

In this exercise, you will generate public-private keys to be used for your wallet. You can download the complete exercise from https://github. com/Apress/the-blockchain-developer/tree/master/chapter3/ step5/blockchain and run the npm install command. Additionally, create a folder named wallet.

```
> npm install
> mkdir wallet
```

You will be using the `elliptic-curve` cryptography library implementation to generate private-public key combos. Note that the `elliptic-curve` library uses `secp256k1` as the ECDSA curve algorithm.

Note   *Elliptical curve cryptography* (ECC) is the public key encryption technique used by bitcoin. It's based on elliptic curve theory to generate the cryptographic keys. Secp256k1 is the graph elliptic curve ECDSA algorithm.

To install the library, run the following command:

```
> npm install elliptic --save
```

Next, add a file and name it `wallet.js`. Take a look at the complete code in Listing 3-8.

Listing 3-8. wallet.js

```
let EC = require('elliptic').ec,
    fs = require('fs');

const ec = new EC('secp256k1'),
    privateKeyLocation = __dirname + '/wallet/private_key';

exports.initWallet = () => {
    let privateKey;
    if (fs.existsSync(privateKeyLocation)) {
        const buffer = fs.readFileSync(privateKeyLocation, 'utf8');
        privateKey = buffer.toString();
    } else {
        privateKey = generatePrivateKey();
        fs.writeFileSync(privateKeyLocation, privateKey);
    }
```

```
    const key = ec.keyFromPrivate(privateKey, 'hex');
    const publicKey = key.getPublic().encode('hex');
    return({'privateKeyLocation': privateKeyLocation,
    'publicKey': publicKey});
};

const generatePrivateKey = () => {
    const keyPair = ec.genKeyPair();
    const privateKey = keyPair.getPrivate();
    return privateKey.toString(16);
};
```

In the wallet file, you create and initialize the EC context.

```
const ec = new EC('secp256k1'),
```

You then store the location of your wallet's private key,
privateKeyLocation.

```
privateKeyLocation = __dirname + '/wallet/private_key';
```

Next, you are able to create a method exports.initWallet to generate the
actual public-private key, generatePrivateKey.

```
    const keyPair = ec.genKeyPair();
    const privateKey = keyPair.getPrivate();
```

Notice that you will be generating a new wallet only if one doesn't exist.

```
if (fs.existsSync(privateKeyLocation))
```

In this exercise, you create a wallet.js file utilizing the Elliptic Curve
Cryptography library to generate your private-public key combo.

To see the code working, add the following code temporarily at the end of the wallet.js file. The script will create the public and private keys.

```
let wallet = this;
let retVal = wallet.initWallet();
console.log(JSON.stringify(retVal));
```

Next, create a wallet directory to store the private key and run the script. The code will initialize the script and create your public key.

```
> mkdir wallet
> node wallet.js
> cat wallet/private_key
```

When you run the node wallet.js command, you can see the public key. See Figure 3-8 for the output.

```
Eli@Elis-MacBook-Pro ~/Desktop/step5 $ mkdir wallet
Eli@Elis-MacBook-Pro ~/Desktop/step5 $ node wallet.js
{"privateKeyLocation":"/Users/Eli/Desktop/step5/wallet/private_key","publicKey":"04d0ada455947912bbb02812d37a395f
44aa007896546dc88a2ed12e74356f348049c2be4e4c0ebb6e2f843b8a82f5adbc11149f1281aedb210d1e9db2d25e8d0e"}
Eli@Elis-MacBook-Pro ~/Desktop/step5 $ cat wallet/private_key
d5209dda97530efd382007ae4b2438c7e5c02b56ae5697a2045031c7e25ffd9fEli@Elis-MacBook-Pro ~/Desktop/step5 $
```

Figure 3-8. *Generating a wallet's private-public key*

Remember to comment out these lines because in the next exercise, you will create an API to be able to create your keys via the browser.

Creating an API

The next step is creating an application program interface (API) to be able to access the code you write. This is an important part of a blockchain, as you want to access your blocks and wallet or any other P2P network operation using an HTTP service. In this section, you will be using the express library, as it's easy to run, and you will be able to create your API easily.

STEP 6: API P2P BLOCKCHAIN EXERCISE

Creating API

In this exercise, you will create an API to interact with your P2P blockchain network. You can download the complete exercise from here: `https://github.com/Apress/the-blockchain-developer/tree/master/chapter3/step6/blockchain`.

You will be creating the following services:

- **blocks**: Retrieves all the blocks in the blockchain

- **getBlock**: Retrieves a specific block by index

- **getDBBlock**: Retrieves a block from the database

- **getWallet**: Creates a new wallet by generating a public-private key

You will install `express` and `body-parser`. These libraries will allow you to create a server and display pages in the browser.

```
> npm install express body-parser --save
```

You also need to import the `wallet.js` file you created.

```
let express = require("express"),
    bodyParser = require('body-parser'),
    wallet = require('./wallet');
```

Next, you create a method called `initHttpServer` that will initiate the server and create the services. As you utilize different instances of the P2P network and run instances on the same computer, you want to utilize different port numbers. It's common to use port 80 or 8081 for HTTP services but not required. What you will do is pass the random port number you are using and utilize the slice method to get the last two digits of the port number.

```
let initHttpServer = (port) => {
    let http_port = '80' + port.toString().slice(-2);
    let app = express();
    app.use(bodyParser.json());
```

The Blocks service will be retrieving all of your blocks.

```
app.get('/blocks', (req, res) => res.send(JSON.stringify(
chain.blockchain )));
```

The getBlock service will be retrieving one block based on an index.

```
app.get('/getBlock', (req, res) => {
    let blockIndex = req.query.index;
    res.send(chain.blockchain[blockIndex]);
});
```

The getDBBlock service will be retrieving a LevelDB database entry based on an index.

```
app.get('/getDBBlock', (req, res) => {
    let blockIndex = req.query.index;
    chain.getDbBlock(blockIndex, res);
});
```

The getWallet service will be utilizing the wallet.js file you created in the previous step and generate your public-private key pair.

```
app.get('/getWallet', (req, res) => {
    res.send(wallet.initWallet());
});
```

Lastly, you will utilize the Express listen method.

```
app.listen(http_port, () => console.log('Listening http on
port: ' + http_port));
};
```

You will call the `initHttpServer` method you created after you start the P2P network and a random port was selected.

```
(async () => {
    const port = await getPort();
    initHttpServer(port);
}
```

To call your services, run the P2P network, and then you can open a browser and call the API.

```
http://localhost:80[port]/getWallet
http://localhost:80[port]/blocks
http://localhost:80[port]/getBlock?index=0
http://localhost:80[port]/ getDBBlock?index=0
```

See Figure 3-9, for instance, as you retrieve all the blocks in your blockchain.

Figure 3-9. *Retrieving all the blocks in your blockchain*

In this exercise, you created API services, and you can now interact with your P2P network. You created your services so you will be able to create multiple instances of the P2P networks on the same machine; however, in reality, every machine will be holding only one peer. In the next exercise, you will create a command-line interface (CLI) to easily call these services.

Creating a Command-Line Interface

For the last step in this chapter, you will be creating a command-line interface (CLI). The CLI is needed to be able to easily access the services you created. I won't get into the entire internal process of the CLI script, as it's beyond the scope of this chapter; however, you can download the whole example and review it.

STEP 7: CLI EXERCISE

Block Command

In this exercise, you will create a CLI to interact with and access your P2P blockchain network. You can download the complete exercise from here: https://github.com/Apress/the-blockchain-developer/tree/master/chapter3/step7/blockchain.

Next, install the libraries you will be utilizing to run promises, run the async function, add colors to the console, and store cookies.

```
> npm babel-polyfill async update-notifier handlebars colors
  nopt --save
```

In the block.js command, you will be setting two commands: get and all. Take a look at the entire code in Listing 3-9.

Listing 3-9. Block Command Code

```
let logger = require('../logger');

function Block(options) {
    this.options = options;
}
```

```
Block.DETAILS = {
    alias: 'b',
    description: 'block',
    commands: ['get', 'all'],
    options: {
        create: Boolean
    },
    shorthands: {
        s: ['--get'],
        a: ['--all']
    },
    payload: function(payload, options) {
        options.start = true;
    },
};

Block.prototype.run = function() {
    let instance = this,
        options = instance.options;

    if (options.get) {
        instance.runCmd('curl http://localhost:' + options.argv.
        original[2] + '/getBlock?index=' + options.argv.original[3]);
    }

    if (options.all) {
        instance.runCmd('curl http://localhost:' + options.argv.
        original[2] + '/blocks');
    }
};

Block.prototype.runCmd = function(cmd) {
    const { exec } = require('child_process');
    logger.log(cmd);
    exec(cmd, (err, stdout, stderr) => {
```

```
        if (err) {
            logger.log(`err: ${err}`);
            return;
        }
        logger.log(`stdout: ${stdout}`);
    });
};

exports.Impl = Block;
```

As you can see, the `wallet.js` command will include the `get` and `all` methods to point to a `curl` command to run the HTTP service call.

Wallet Command

Similarly, the `block.js` command will include a `create` method and a `curl` command to run the HTTP service call. See Listing 3-10.

Listing 3-10. Wallet Command Code

```
let logger = require('../logger');

function Wallet(options) {
    this.options = options;
}

Wallet.DETAILS = {
    alias: 'w',
    description: 'wallet',
    commands: ['create'],
    options: {
        create: Boolean
    },
    shorthands: {
        c: ['--create']
    },
```

```
    payload: function(payload, options) {
        options.start = true;
    },
};

Wallet.prototype.run = function() {
    let instance = this,
        options = instance.options;

    if (options.create) {
        instance.runCmd('curl http://localhost:' + options.argv.
        original[2] + '/getWallet');
    }
};

Wallet.prototype.runCmd = function(cmd) {
    const { exec } = require('child_process');
    logger.log(cmd);
    exec(cmd, (err, stdout, stderr) => {
        if (err) {
            logger.log(`err: ${err}`);
            return;
        }
        logger.log(`stdout: ${stdout}`);
    });
};

exports.Impl = Wallet;
```

Now that you have your commands set up, you can add your CLI to the bash_
profile as an alias to be able to run the CLI from any path location.

```
> vim ~/.bash_profile
alias cli='node /[project location]/step7/bin/bin/cli.js
```

Save and run `bash_profile` to apply these changes.

```
> . ~/.bash_profile
```

You can call the CLI once you run the P2P and know the ports you are using.

```
> cli block --get [port] 1 #port #index
> cli block -all [port] #port
> cli wallet --create [port]
```

For instance, run an instance of the P2P network in Terminal.

```
> node p2p.js
```

Next, open a new window terminal and run the CLI command to retrieve the first generated block.

```
> cli block --get [port] 1
```

You can see the output in Figures 3-10 and 3-11.

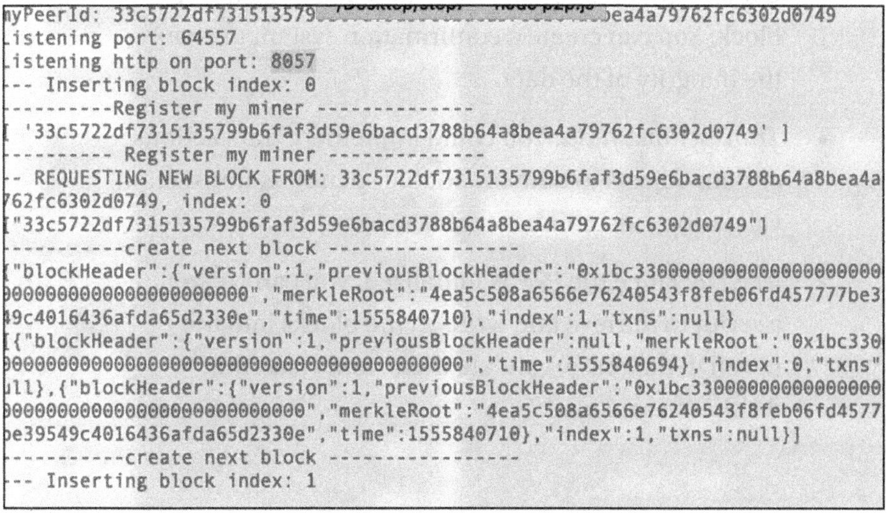

```
myPeerId: 33c5722df731513579                                ea4a79762fc6302d0749
Listening port: 64557
Listening http on port: 8057
--- Inserting block index: 0
---------Register my miner ------------
[ '33c5722df7315135799b6faf3d59e6bacd3788b64a8bea4a79762fc6302d0749' ]
--------- Register my miner --------------
-- REQUESTING NEW BLOCK FROM: 33c5722df7315135799b6faf3d59e6bacd3788b64a8bea4a
762fc6302d0749, index: 0
["33c5722df7315135799b6faf3d59e6bacd3788b64a8bea4a79762fc6302d0749"]
----------create next block ----------------
{"blockHeader":{"version":1,"previousBlockHeader":"0x1bc3300000000000000000000
00000000000000000000000000","merkleRoot":"4ea5c508a6566e76240543f8feb06fd457777be3
49c4016436afda65d2330e","time":1555840710},"index":1,"txns":null}
[{"blockHeader":{"version":1,"previousBlockHeader":null,"merkleRoot":"0x1bc330
00000000000000000000000000000000000000","time":1555840694},"index":0,"txns"
ull},{"blockHeader":{"version":1,"previousBlockHeader":"0x1bc33000000000000000
00000000000000000000000000000","merkleRoot":"4ea5c508a6566e76240543f8feb06fd4577
be39549c4016436afda65d2330e","time":1555840710},"index":1,"txns":null}]
----------create next block ----------------
--- Inserting block index: 1
```

Figure 3-10. *Running the P2P blockchain network on port 8057*

```
Eli@Elis-MacBook-Pro ~/Desktop/step7 $ cli block --get 8057 1
curl http://localhost:8057/getBlock?index=1
stdout: {"blockHeader":{"version":1,"previousBlockHeader":"0x1bc3300000000000000
0000000000000000000000000000000","merkleRoot":"4ea5c508a6566e76240543f8feb06fd457
777be39549c4016436afda65d2330e","time":1555840710},"index":1,"txns":null}
Eli@Elis-MacBook-Pro ~/Desktop/step7 $
```

Figure 3-11. *Retrieving blocks on port 8057*

In this exercise, you created two commands for getting blocks and creating your wallet. This is a starting point for your CLI, and you will be able to continue to add commands as needed.

Where to Go from Here

I already mentioned that the code in this chapter does not take into account many use cases and has no security to keep it simple. There are many things you can do to improve the code.

- *Confirmations*: Each miner sends a message with a block. You can create a confirmation system to ensure the integrity of the data.

- *Transactions/data*: You could implement transactions or data objects to address double spending, transaction validation, and coinbase transactions.

- *levelDB*: Once the P2P is initialized, you can create a script to retrieve and write all the blocks into the LevelDB database, validate them, and clean the database as needed.

Summary

This chapter covered how to create your very own basic P2P blockchain network; you were able to send and receive messages and include blocks in these messages. You were able to register and unregister miners and implement a simple PoS consensus mechanism. You created new blocks and sent them between the peers. You also set up a name-value LevelDB database to store blocks. You continued and created a wallet that consists of private-public key pairs. Lastly, you created ways to communicate with your P2P network via API services and the CLI. In the next chapter, you will be diving deep into understanding bitcoin wallets and transactions by interacting with the bitcoin core API.

CHAPTER 4

Bitcoin Wallets and Transactions

In this chapter, you will be diving deep into bitcoin's core RPC and learn about wallets and transactions. You will learn how to utilize legacy and SegWit's bitcoin wallets. You will extract a wallet's public and private keys.

The majority of this chapter will deal with transactions, from sending funds in a simple way utilizing bitcoin's testing blockchain to more complex transactions. Additionally, you will learn how to send coins via bitcoin's core wallet GUI, and you will learn how to view transactions in the Block Explorer and understand confirmations. You will look into raw transactions and learn how to create a raw transaction with one output as well as how to create transactions with multiple users signing them. Additionally, you will replace your transaction and set a lock time. You will also learn the difference between pay options and fees.

Lastly, I will cover how to pass data in a raw transaction. By the end of this chapter, you will have a much better understanding of transactions, wallets, fees, payment options, and bitcoin's core RPC.

Bitcoin Core RPC Resources

You learned how to interact with bitcoin core utilizing the bitcoin daemon and bitcoin core function as an HTTP JSON-RPC server, and you are now

© Elad Elrom 2019

E. Elrom, *The Blockchain Developer*, https://doi.org/10.1007/978-1-4842-4847-8_4

able to make calls and receive JSON responses. In this section, you will build on these skills to understand wallets and transactions.

The first step is to initialize and run the bitcoin daemon.

```
> bitcoind -printtoconsole
```

Then in a different Terminal window, you can view the available RPC commands by running the help command.

```
> bitcoin-cli help
```

You can also request help on any command you run by adding help before the command. For instance, add help before the getnewaddress command like this:

```
> bitcoin-cli help getnewaddress
```

At the time of writing, the latest RPC version is bitcoin core version v0.18.99.0-56376f336 (release build); as new versions of bitcoin core are released, the commands in this chapter may change, so it's useful to check https://bitcoincore.org/en/doc/ for the latest RPC commands.

Note that documentation for v0.18 is not live at the time of writing; v0.17 is the latest doc (https://bitcoincore.org/en/doc/0.17.0/). In the menu on the right, select RAWTRANSACTIONS and WALLET for a list of RPC commands relevant to this chapter.

Note   In addition to bitcoin core documentation, there are two free web resources that can help you better understand the bitcoin RPC command line beyond what is covered in this chapter. They are https://github.com/ChristopherA/Learning-bitcoin-from-the-Command-Line and http://learnmeabitcoin. com/guide/transactions.

Bitcoin Wallet

In Chapter 2, you queried a wallet's available funds via the `getbalance` command, and you created a new bitcoin wallet utilizing the `getnewaddress` command.

In Chapter 3, you created your very own blockchain wallet for your blockchain; you did so by creating a `wallet.js` file utilizing the Elliptic Curve Cryptography Node.js library and generating a private-public key combo that you then were able to expose using a CLI. In this section, I will expand on this knowledge by looking at bitcoin's core and how wallets and transactions are generated.

Bitcoin allows users to send and receive coins. A user can generate a wallet, which holds a public key, and the sender will send the coins to the receiver's wallet's public key address.

Sending coins follows the same process but in reverse. The receiver provides the sender with a wallet's public key address where they expect to be paid, and the sender sends coins to that public key address. The wallet address is the public key that was generated by the public/private key hashing algorithm. The receiver can generate a new public key every time the user expects payment. Users who don't need to be anonymous can use just one public key for multiple transactions; however, bitcoin's original vision encourages users to give a different public key for each transaction, as well as set many private keys that correspond with many public keys. The private keys are stored in a wallet, and each public key represents a wallet address.

Create a Legacy Wallet Address and Retrieve Private Keys

The most common bitcoin address and the type you generated in Chapter 2 is called a Pay to PubKey Hash (P2PKH) address. P2PKH is the public key, and the public key address gets hashed by an algorithm.

Bitcoin also supports the P2SH-SEGWIT protocol, which I will discuss later in this chapter.

Note   Segregated Witness (SegWit) was an addition to bitcoin core code via a soft fork that increased bitcoin's block size limit by removing the signature data that unlocks the transaction. When the unlocking code is removed, the additional space is used to include more transactions in the chain.

To generate an address with P2SH-SEGWIT and P2PKH support, just run the following:

```
> bitcoin-cli getnewaddress
2N96AMUEX4VMNTApPAbUaA6wzP4V9QrbveK
```

To generate the P2PKH address, you will be using the legacy flag.

```
> bitcoin-cli getnewaddress "" legacy
13oWKiVQ7C5Ewwjv6KRpP3Xm5YstzqFixT
```

As you can see, the commands return the public keys. The wallet's private keys can be viewed via dumping the keys into a file, as you did previously, or just by using the dumpprivkey command.

```
> bitcoin-cli dumpprivkey "13oWKiVQ7C5Ewwjv6KRpP3Xm5YstzqFixT"
L5gDpFvfEkUSFeMSQb92kueD1BuX4JeZLAhQkXoEtjcZMog3uXB4
```

Private keys should not be shared with anyone, as they unlock the funds associated with the public address. With that said, I am sharing this one with you here as a learning example.

Note   Protect your private keys. If your private keys are lost, you lose your coins/funds.

As you know, you are able to dump the private keys into a text file.

```
> bitcoin-cli dumpwallet ~/mywallet.txt
{
  "filename": "/Users/Eli/mywallet.txt"
}
```

Then, you can get the location of the wallet and can view your keys.

```
> vim /Users/[location]/mywallet.txt
```

The data file you saved contains not only the public and private keys but also transactions related to your wallet.

Another useful RPC feature, as you might recall, is that you can query the bitcoin daemon for a specific wallet's funds.

```
> bitcoin-cli getbalance 1Mr2G632PfQuq4uJXRBNWLoRKH71Qwor51
```

To get the available funds in your wallet, you just run the getbalance command, which returns a 0 balance because you have not deposited any funds yet.

```
> bitcoin-cli getbalance
0.00000000
```

Pay to Witness a Public Key Hash (P2WPKH): SegWit Soft Fork

Bitcoin (BTC) and bitcoin cash (BCH) have hard-forked mainly over a disagreement of the block size, meaning how much data can be included in each block. In 2017, bitcoin core code was hard-forked into bitcoin cash and allowed to increase the block's size limit. In 2019, bitcoin cash forked once again because of a dispute over several new features for each fork.

The block size limitation in bitcoin means transactions sometimes have to wait to be included in a block; however, because of the 1 MB limitation, they might not be included in the next block, causing slow transaction times when there too many transactions in the network, resulting in an increase of miner fees. To correct this, bitcoin open source developers created a soft fork and included Segregated Witness (SegWit). SegWit increased bitcoin's block size limit by removing the signature data that unlocks the transaction. When the unlocking code is removed, the additional space can be used to include more transactions in the chain. This method increases the block size to 4 MB.

Note   SegWit is a process where the block size limit on a blockchain is increased by removing the signature data from bitcoin transactions. This process frees up space and allows you to add more transactions. SegWit uses a Bech32 address defined in BIP173. It is 90 characters and consists of a human-readable part, separator, and data.

The unlocking validation code is the *witness* data. You can say that the new code "segregated the witness." That's where the name came from.

In the build we are using, v17.0, there is a Witness Public Key Hash option in a wallet and transaction to replace the scriptSig parameters and check the transaction validity. The old legacy code still works, as this is a soft fork.

You have seen this in the getaddressinfo command, which includes both scriptPubKey to support the legacy addresses as well as iswitness. You can run the getaddressinfo command and see these parameters.

```
> bitcoin-cli getaddressinfo $address1
```

Prior to bitcoin core v0.16, you would have had to use the addwitnessaddress command to turn a legacy address into a P2WPKH. Since bitcoin core v0.16.0, an address accommodates both P2SH and P2WPKH. Thus, the wallet is a P2SH-P2WPKH. If you are using v0.18, you can see that getaddressinfo addresses have both parameters for legacy scriptSig and for SegWit.

Elliptic Curve Digital Signature Algorithm

Bitcoin core allows you to create a signature by utilizing the Elliptic Curve Digital Signature Algorithm (ECDSA). This can be achieved by utilizing the signmessage command. Adding a signature allows you to prove that you own the private keys of the wallet and thus adds another security layer for the sender to ensure they are sending the funds to the correct address.

```
> bitcoin-cli signmessage "13oWKiVQ7C5Ewwjv6KRpP3Xm5YstzqFixT"
  "John Doe"
```

This command outputs a hash:

```
HzicuTXMl1COVh7Xw9ky9A/cl7ZjMSWNH1oY/invAgHWa74gS8EOvio3FJkofpH
OnunIA7pJoGwWLRaoUdD7dc8=
```

The sender can verify the wallet prior to sending the funds.

```
> bitcoin-cli verifymessage "13oWKiVQ7C5Ewwjv6KRpP3Xm5YstzqFixT"
  "HzicuTXMl1COVh7Xw9ky9A/cl7ZjMSWNH1oY/invAgHWa74gS8EOvio3FJk
  ofpHOnunIA7pJoGwWLRaoUdD7dc8=" "John Doe"
```

The verify command will output a true or false response. In this case, it will respond with this:

```
true
```

This allows users to confirm they actually own a wallet. This is useful, for instance, on the code level, because the P2PKH address will be utilizing the private key to generate a signature. A P2PKH address is a hash of the public key corresponding to the private key that made the signature.

Note   ECDSA is the cryptographic algorithm utilized by bitcoin to ensure ownership of funds. It is used to generate the public/private keys and can also include the signature in the algorithm.

The ECDSA signature can be checked against up to four possible ECDSA public keys. These public keys will be reconstructed from the signature hash; each key is hashed and compared against the P2PKH wallet address provided for a match. The result is either true or false. As you saw earlier, the example received a true once you ran the verifymessage command.

Note   QR code is an image representation of a string. QR readers are used for things such as reading URLs or encoding a wallet's public key address.

You can generate QR code via the Chart Google API: https://chart.googleapis.com. For instance to generate a QR code for address: 13oWKiVQ7C5Ewwjv6KRpP3Xm5YstzqFixT in the amount of 0.00016 BTC you would generate the following URL:

https://chart.googleapis.com/chart?chs=250x250&cht=qr&chl=bitcoin:13oWKiVQ7C5Ewwjv6KRpP3Xm5YstzqFixT?&amount=0.00016. See Figure 4-1.

Figure 4-1. *Bitcoin QR code via Chart.googleapi.com*

Transactions

In this section, I will cover transactions. You will learn how to send coins with bitcoin's daemon on a testnet utilizing both the command line and the bitcoin core wallet GUI. You will learn how to use the bitcoin explorer to view your transactions. Then I will cover more advanced creation of transactions by showing how to create a raw transaction with one output as well as more complex transactions with utilizing Multisignature (multisig), which is requesting more than a single key to authorize a transaction. Additionally, I will cover how to change other options such as replacing a transaction for a change of fee as well as setting a locktime. You will learn the difference between P2PKH and P2SH-SEGWIT. Lastly, you will learn how to attach other data than just coins with bitcoin using OP_RETURN params. Let's get started.

Simple Command

The first transaction in a block is called the *coinbase* transaction; this transaction consists of the transaction fees paid by transactions included in the block. To send a transaction, you need to pay a transaction fee to the miners. If there is a low fee or no fee is paid, the transaction may get stuck for a long period of time or even forever in the P2P network until the fee is changed.

To set the transaction fee, you can add a parameter to the `bitcoin.conf` file with a default fee. First, you need to find the file location. To do so, right after you run the daemon, you can track down the location of the file.

```
> bitcoind -printtoconsole
```

After a few seconds, stop this service by pressing Control+C. The command shows the `bitcoin.conf` file location. It returns the location of the configuration file. Then you can open the file and modify it by adding the default fee. In this case, it was nested inside the Application Support folder.

```
/Users/[my user]/Library/Application Support/Bitcoin/bitcoin.conf
```

When you open the file, you can see that the default transaction fee is set to 0.00000020 (`mintxfee=0.00000020`).

Note   There are other fees and settings in bitcoind. You can modify transactions you send (`paytxfee`), maximum total fees (`maxtxfee`), fallback fees, and so on. Visit this bitcoin page for all the available options: `https://en.bitcoin.it/wiki/Running_Bitcoin`.

Monitor and updating the bitcoin transaction fee can ensure the funds being sent get changed by market forces. There are web sites, apps, and forms that can try to predict the fee that needs to be paid. There are many

sites that help calculate transaction fee prediction, such as this API, that
you can call from your code:

```
https://bitcoinfees.earn.com/api/v1/fees/recommended
```

The API returned at the time of writing a fee of 20 satoshis.

```
{"fastestFee":20,"halfHourFee":20,"hourFee":18}
```

Another example is `https://bitcoinfees.net/`. This site shows a
majority of transactions are at five to six satoshis at less than six hours, or
49 to 50 satoshis for less than 20 minutes at the time of writing.

Note   A satoshi is a hundredth of a millionth BTC and is named after
Satoshi Nakamoto. It's the smallest fraction of a bitcoin that can be
sent: 0.00000001 BTC. A faster fee would be 50 satoshi at the time
of writing.

Now that you know the fee, you can modify the config file with the
minimum fee to a higher fee such as 50 satoshis.

```
> vim '/[location]/bitcoin/bitcoin.conf'
mintxfee=0.00000050
txconfirmtarget=3
```

The `mintxfee` value sets a minimum transaction fee of 50 satoshis, or
0.00000050 ฿. That will set a 20 satoshis/byte of data in your transaction.
This means the floating fee needs to figure out a good amount to get the
transaction into the next three blocks. As you recall, each block takes about
10 minutes to hash, so it will aim at 30 minutes to include your transaction.

Once you have modified the config file, remember to restart bitcoind.

```
> bitcoind -printtoconsole
```

Testnet

In this section, you will learn more about transactions, and to understand transactions better, you will need to send and receive bitcoins. To get bitcoins on mainnet (the actual production chain), you would need to either mine coins or trade them. However, you don't want to handle actual coins as you learn, because you would have to pay fees as well as risk losing coins if you make mistakes. Also, the price of the bitcoin may go down.

Luckily, bitcoin offers an alternative blockchain that is used for testing; it's called *testnet*. This alternative blockchain enables you to experiment without using real bitcoins or abusing the bitcoin chain. You can start a bitcoin core instance with the -testnet flag. On testnet, this is done through *faucets*, the pretend coins. You connect to the testnet blockchain instead of the main blockchain by stopping the bitcoin core demon and restarting it with the testnet flag.

```
> bitcoind -testnet
```

Keep in mind that just as with bitcoin's mainnet chain, the syncing and indexing portions may take hours, depending on your Internet connection. Run the command and take a long coffee break if you want to start working with blocks.

The BTC testnet offers you free faucet bitcoins that you can use for testing. Testnet requests that you return these coins once you complete testing as this service is free, and returning these coins will benefit the next developer who needs them.

You can read more about testnet here: https://en.bitcoin.it/wiki/Testnet. At the time of writing, testnet3 is the latest blockchain used for testing.

You will be using coinfaucet.eu, which can be found at https://coinfaucet.eu/en/btc-testnet/. However, there are other faucets in case this one ceases to exist. The first step is to send coins to your wallet. First generate a new P2PKH wallet address using the following command:

```
> bitcoin-cli getnewaddress "" legacy
mnMs77edsGV8VKwtB3d7fsnvrNuZ8ECKfh
```

As you can see, the output you receive is the public key that you can use to receive funds. Next, paste that address into `https://coinfaucet.eu`, choose "Bitcoin testnet," verify you are not a robot, and click the "Get bitcoins!" button, as shown in Figure 4-2.

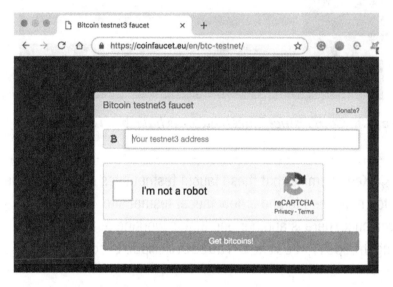

Figure 4-2. *Coin testnet faucet, requesting funds for testing*

Once the coins have been sent to your wallet, you receive a confirmation with the `tx` number, as shown in Figure 4-3.

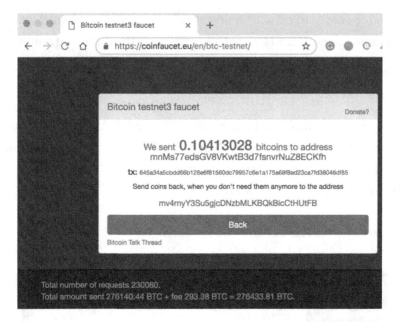

Figure 4-3. *Coin testnet faucet, bitcoins have been sent*

Note   Keep in mind that these faucet testnet sites often go offline, and you may need to find a new faucet testnet site. For your convenience, here is another one that is working at the time of writing: `https://testnet-faucet.mempool.co/`.

Viewing Transactions on Block Explorer

On the testnet faucet, you can monitor the bitcoins that have been sent just as can be done on the maintest production bitcoin's blockchain. This is done in the testnet Blockchain Explorer; see the "tx" link, as shown in Figure 4-3. As you recall, "tx ID" stands for the transaction ID. Alternatively, you can paste that transaction ID directly into the Block Explorer at `https://live.blockcypher.com/btc-testnet/`. See Figure 4-4.

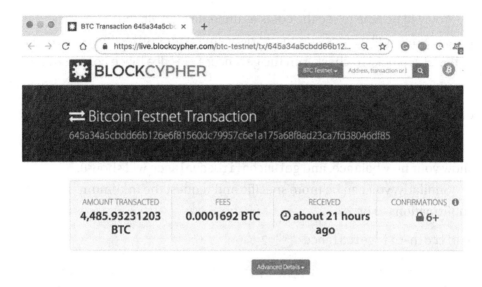

Figure 4-4. *Viewing transaction information on live.*
blockcypher.com

In fact, every transaction that ever occurs on the blockchain is publicly available to view by anyone in the Blockchain Explorer; that includes all the transaction data except for the users' private keys. Although the transaction data is publicly available, the identifying information about the owner is not public information and is not needed to perform transactions. What connects the user to the coins you send is the private key associated with the public key.

Similarly, you can do the same check of information via the RPC command line. You already know how to check your wallet's balance, as shown here:

```
> bitcoin-cli getbalance
0.0000000
```

When coins have been received, they will not be available to spend until the transaction has been confirmed by the mined blocks' confirmations. That's why if you check your balance right away, it will still show 0.

You will be able to see the coins as unconfirmed via the getunconfirmedbalance command right after your transaction is included in the next block. To check, run the getunconfirmedbalance command.

```
> bitcoin-cli getunconfirmedbalance
0.10413028
```

Once you have enough confirmations, the getbalance command will show your new balance, and getunconfirmedbalance will show 0.

Similarly, you can be more specific and request the minimum confirmations to be 2.

```
> bitcoin-cli getbalance "*" 2
```

Note   A transaction stays "unconfirmed" until the next new block is created. Once the new block is created, the new transaction is verified and included in that block. Now, the transaction will have one confirmation. About ten minutes pass, and a new block is created, and the transaction is confirmed again. Each confirmation increases the safety of the transaction, and the chances of the transaction being reversed decrease. The norm on exchanges is that four to six confirmations are required to allow you to use the coins; it may be wise to wait for even sixty confirmations for large amounts of coins, which takes about ten hours.

Another useful command is the listtransactions command; it provides the full list of transaction data related to your wallet.

```
> bitcoin-cli listtransactions
[
  {
    "address": "mnMs77edsGV8VKwtB3d7fsnvrNuZ8ECKfh",
    "category": "receive",
```

```
"amount": 0.10413028,
"label": "",
"vout": 0,
"confirmations": 420,
"blockhash": "0000000000125d2714882704562c8442a6700c58a41ca
              d0b4108305474be3bb1",
"blockindex": 4,
"blocktime": 1541783585,
"txid": "645a34a5cbdd66b126e6f81560dc79957c6e1a175a68f8ad23
         ca7fd38046df85",
"walletconflicts": [
],
"time": 1541783585,
"timereceived": 1541890511,
"bip125-replaceable": "no"
    }
]
```

Sending Testnet Coins via the Bitcoin Core Wallet GUI

You initialized a bitcoin core instance with the testnet flag; however, there is another even easier way to send and receive coins. Bitcoin core includes a GUI wallet you can use. You will be utilizing the GUI software that comes out of the box with bitcoin core. To get started, terminate the bitcoind daemon in Terminal by pressing Control+C and then run `bitcoin-qt` in a command-line terminal with the `testnet` flag so you connect to testnet and not mainnet.

```
> bitcoin-qt -testnet
```

This command opens a new window and then syncs with the testnet blockchain. Just as before, if you did not complete a testnet sync, it may take hours, depending on your Internet connection, as shown in Figure 4-5. However, at the wallet GUI, you will see an estimated time for how long the sync will take.

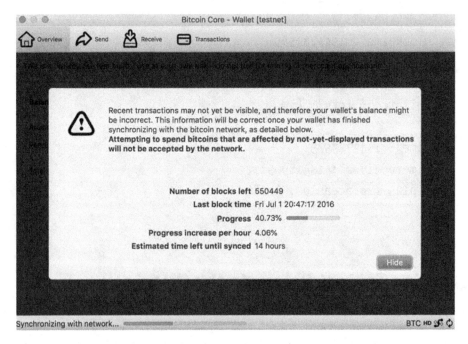

Figure 4-5. *Bitcoin wallet testnet GUI sync with testnet network*

As before, you need to wait for the sync to complete; only then can you retrieve your wallet's public key address and spend your coins. In the Overview menu you will see the balances, including the confirmed (Available) funds and the unconfirmed (Pending) funds. You can also get a list of transactions by clicking the Transactions button at the top. See Figure 4-6.

Figure 4-6. *Bitcoin core wallet overview screen*

To create a new wallet's public key address, click Receive at the top and then click the Request Payment button. This will generate an address for your wallet, as shown in Figure 4-7.

Figure 4-7. *Bitcoin core wallet, receive coins screen*

As you can see, the GUI created a QR code for your convenience. You can scan it when you send coins, where this feature is supported. Now, let's go ahead and send some more coins to your wallet via the testnet faucet at `https://live.blockcypher.com/btc-testnet/`.

As you can see, you can then receive coins just as you did via the command line. Next, you will send some coins.

You will be sending 0.01 BTC back to the testnet faucet for other developers to use. To do so, click the Send button at the top of the GUI and paste in the testnet faucet wallet address that was provided to you when you sent coins to your wallet.

Notice that there is a Choose button next to Transaction Fee in the bitcoin core wallet GUI. This allows you to select the fee, as well as the number of confirmations. It also includes a way to enable a "replace by" fee. This feature allows you to change the fee in case the fee is too low and the transaction is not getting included in the block. See Figure 4-8.

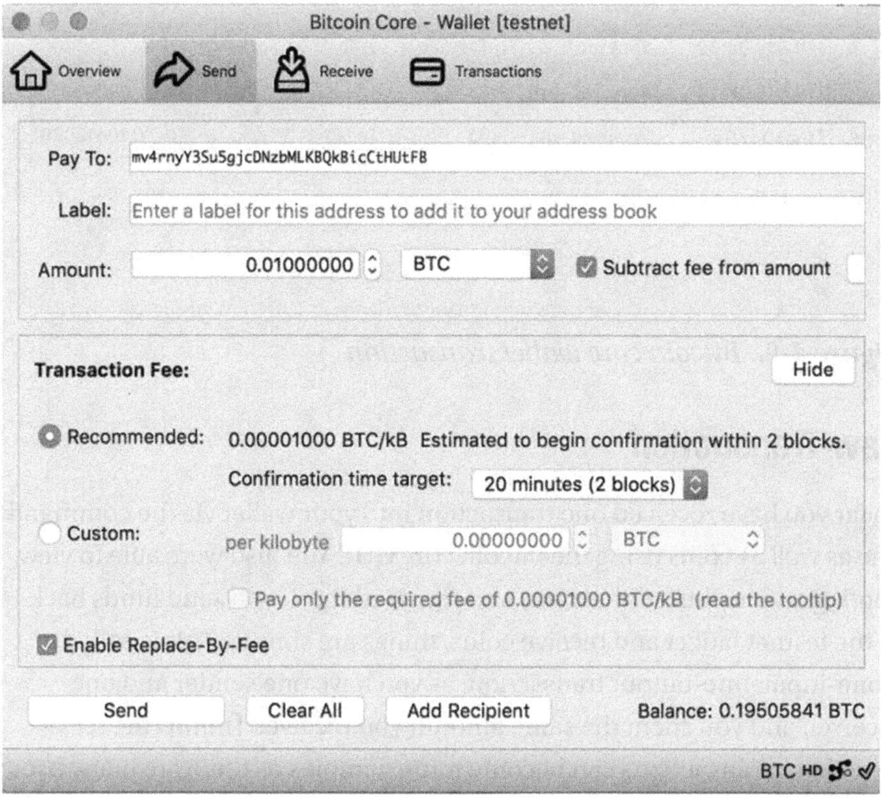

Figure 4-8. *Bitcoin core wallet send screen*

The testnet faucet sends coins to the wallet address you provided. When you send and receive coins, you get a notification pop-up from the GUI and an updated balance on the overview screen. Click the Transactions button to see the transaction's information. You can also click each transaction to see the actual transaction data. This is similar to what you saw with the listtransactions command. See Figure 4-9.

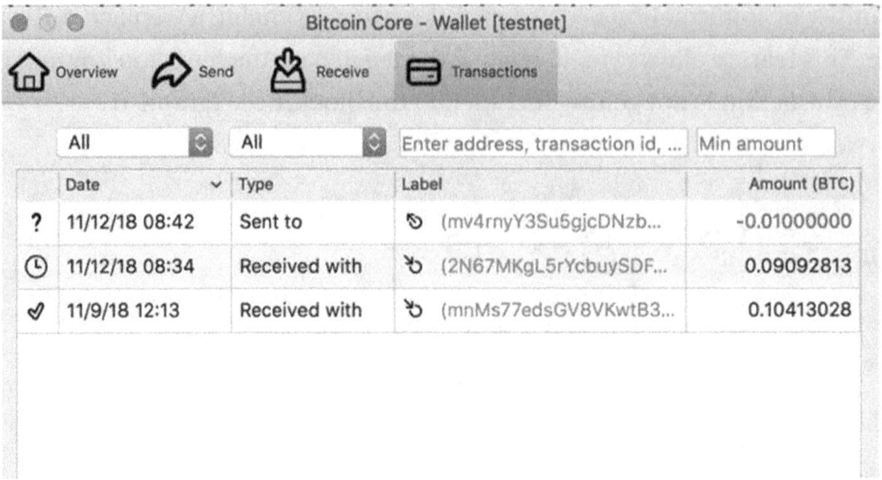

Figure 4-9. *Bitcoin core wallet transaction*

Raw Transaction

So far you have received one transaction into your wallet via the command line as well as coins using the bitcoin core GUI. You also were able to view confirmations, the fees balance, and transactions. If you send funds back to the testnet faucet and receive coins, things are simple. This is called a one-input, one-output transaction, as you have one sender and one receiver, and you spent the same amount you received (minus the fees). In real life, transactions can become more complex as there are many use cases where there are one input and multiple outputs or multiple inputs and multiple outputs. Bitcoin core provides you with sets of commands to access a raw transaction (`RawTransaction`) so you can have more granular control over your transaction.

You will start with the simple one-input, one-output transaction via the RPC command line.

Note   Creating and understanding `RawTransaction` is useful for building software, as you have full granular control over your transaction. However, making mistakes can result in a catastrophic outcome and loss of coins, so use caution and double-check everything before sending any funds.

When you receive a transaction, the transaction stays in a state called *unspent transaction output* (UTXO) in your wallet. To send a one-input, one-output transaction, you need your amount to be equal to the funds you want to send. You can then generate a new UTXO for the receiver you are sending the coins to. The receiver can use these UTXOs to send transactions to a new receiver or receivers, and this process can continue endlessly.

Note   A UTXO is an individual incoming coin transaction in your wallet. When you receive multiple transactions to one or multiple wallets' addresses, each stays as a UTXO, so you will have multiple UTXOs. To create a new outgoing transaction, you collect one or more UTXOs as needed depending on how much you are trying to send.

Now, what if your UTXO includes a larger amount than you would like to spend? Then you would need to send the remaining of the coins back to your wallet. To get a list of unspent coins, you can use the `listunspent` command.

Close the bitcoin core GUI wallet via Control+C and start the daemon again with the testnet flag.

```
> bitcoind -testnet
```

When you run the getbalance command, you get your wallet's balance, which includes the two transactions you received from https://live.blockcypher.com/btc-testnet/ less the transaction you sent back to the testnet faucet.

```
> bitcoin-cli getbalance
0.18505841
```

I would like to point out that at any time you can use the -named flag instead of using order arguments. The named argument is useful to ensure you are not making mistakes when working with mainnet. For instance, a getbalance command with the named argument would look as follows:

```
> bitcoin-cli -named getbalance minconf=2
0.18505841
```

Next, let's take a look at the listunspent command. As the name suggests, it returns JSON with transactions for coins you did not spend, in other words, your UTXOs. The listunspent command also returns JSON with a variable called vout, which represents the index number of the output in a transaction.

Note   The vout value represents the index number of the output of a transaction. You will be using a txid and a vout to select the existing output as the input of a new transaction.

```
> bitcoin-cli listunspent
[
  {
    "txid": "50e91c9b73a90bd883f4a9a8a51be729770df20fae0445a
             9090b80a8621f4538",
    "vout": 0,
```

```
    "address": "2N67MKgL5rYcbuySDFUdypU5DvKjmwZoYEb",
    "label": "",
    "redeemScript": "0014c27b4e6bd8eb821ee80a239e0edd59070f
                    57233d",
    "scriptPubKey": "a9148d1c6e108c60cfdfa61565ac328be66245
                    91404b87",
    "amount": 0.09092813,
    "confirmations": 17,
    "spendable": true,
    "solvable": true,
    "safe": true
},
{
    "txid": "be05d068d1245f1c60ea4229c00eb5e96f2a5c5527f1deb7c6
            de5e1e20a4b4db",
    "vout": 1,
    "address": "2MveVhMe6PTzuhsJHx5zXAjDBwQvzdyqGjM",
   "redeemScript": "00142e29123ba343c577ab9517ede9b74f047d2c2ea3",
    "scriptPubKey": "a914254f0e95fb26c0f29975f866e69543519bf5
                    65e787",
    "amount": 0.09413028,
    "confirmations": 16,
    "spendable": true,
    "solvable": true,
    "safe": true
}
]
```

These UTXOs show you a property called txid, which is included in bitcoin's blocks. The txid property allows you to track transactions, as you saw via the Blockchain Explorer.

Notice that the index starts at 0, and because you have two transactions, it is now 0 and then 1. If you had more transactions, this index would continue. Figure 4-10 illustrates the `listunspent` result if you have two UTXOs.

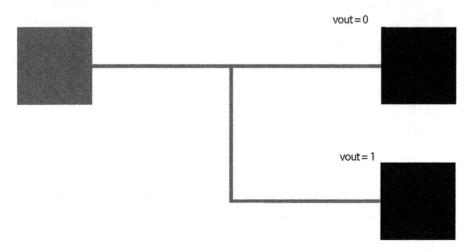

Figure 4-10. *vout index illustration*

You can get all the data regarding the transaction via the `getrawtransaction` command. Here I picked the first `tx` property from the UTXO you received, and then I added the 1 flag to decode the hex-encoded transaction data; take a look at the command and entire output, shown here:

```
> bitcoin-cli getrawtransaction
  50e91c9b73a90bd883f4a9a8a51be729770df20fae0445a9090b80a862
  1f4538 1

{
    "txid": "50e91c9b73a90bd883f4a9a8a51be729770df20fae0445a9090b
            80a8621f4538",
    "hash": "e420b350f5b95e29f51b722a5bd44ea2e9d27a7239d2
            e17da02f28e04c757b14",
```

```
"version": 2,
"size": 248,
"vsize": 166,
"weight": 662,
"locktime": 1443113,
"vin": [
  {
    "txid": "2645c128d68194640a7207eeae6ea42e8e528bcba2369
            eec0ba572566228b507",
    "vout": 0,
    "scriptSig": {
      "asm": "00143bfa0326c076fa6cab0d23aea170bac38ac9a164",
      "hex": "1600143bfa0326c076fa6cab0d23aea170bac38ac9a164"
    },
    "txinwitness": [
      "3045022100fb7f0fc2cf99c8174eb3d14169e1c206157d434d
      8290b2efbefa5a37d0773923022065f0b671c0596816c062b9bdc7
      b30931edfd99a846a0f1633d301bfb7c03db3c01",
      "02d208ff6da0583b99392d30e33c5a12da61b9d9de4c35bb0
      d20c33ba3bfc49302"
    ],
    "sequence": 4294967294
  }
],
"vout": [
  {
    "value": 0.09092813,
    "n": 0,
    "scriptPubKey": {
      "asm": "OP_HASH160 8d1c6e108c60cfdfa61565ac328be66
            24591404b OP_EQUAL",
```

```
      "hex": "a9148d1c6e108c60cfdfa61565ac328be6624591404b87",
       "reqSigs": 1,
       "type": "scripthash",
       "addresses": [
         "2N67MKgL5rYcbuySDFUdypU5DvKjmwZoYEb"
       ]
    }
  },
  {
    "value": 1453.63689543,
    "n": 1,
    "scriptPubKey": {
      "asm": "OP_HASH160 f4eb3fe1578076853a774d36f193684f86f
             71d5f OP_EQUAL",
     "hex": "a914f4eb3fe1578076853a774d36f193684f86f71d5f87",
      "reqSigs": 1,
      "type": "scripthash",
      "addresses": [
        "2NFaEgWoTNL5akkTuGtYQhzTvWhUaCbxBtL"
      ]
    }
  }
],
"hex": "0200000000010107b528625672a50bec9e36a2cb8b528e2ea46
       eaeee07720a649481d628c1452600000000171600143bfa0326c
       076fa6cab0d23aea170bac38ac9a164feffffff02cdbe8a00000
       0000017a9148d1c6e108c60cfdfa61565ac328be6624591404b8
       747e059d82100000017a914f4eb3fe1578076853a774d36f1936
       84f86f71d5f8702483045022100fb7f0fc2cf99c8174eb3d1416
       9e1c206157d434d8290b2efbefa5a37d0773923022065f0b671c
       0596816c062b9bdc7b30931edfd99a846a0f1633d301bfb7c03d
```

```
        b3c012102d208ff6da0583b99392d30e33c5a12da61b9d9de4c3
        5bb0d20c33ba3bfc4930229051600",
  "blockhash": "00000000000000321b56aece3932b187927ac3e7d
                c4532f8811aa612bcfa639a",
  "confirmations": 17,
  "time": 1542029870,
  "blocktime": 1542029870
}
```

Notice that you have information about the block, confirmation, in, out, and much more.

Generating Raw Transactions with One Output

Transactions can get complicated easily because there is often a need for more than one input or more than one output. For instance, if you want to send the unspent coins back to your wallet, as well as send coins to multiple addresses, it starts to get complicated. Using RawTransaction, you get full access to where the coins go and are able to achieve complex transactions.

You will start by creating a simple RawTransaction by sending one UTXO from one wallet to another. Previously, you sent coins back to the testnet faucet via the bitcoin core wallet GUI. Let's do the same thing but with the RawTransaction command.

To get started, let's confirm your wallet's balance prior to sending coins.

```
> bitcoin-cli getbalance
0.18505841
```

Next, let's pick the UTXO you will be using to fund the transaction. As you recall, you can get a list of UTXOs, via the listunspent command, and then look at the JSON response and pick the transaction txid. Pick

a transaction that has enough funds to feed your new transaction and a
transaction that has been confirmed.

```
> utxo_txid="50e91c9b73a90bd883f4a9a8a51be729770df20fae0445a909
  0b80a8621f4538"
```

As you probably recall, vout is the index number for an output in a
transaction. In this example, I will be pointing to a vout and generating a
new transaction. The new transaction can include multiple other vouts, as
illustrated in Figure 4-11.

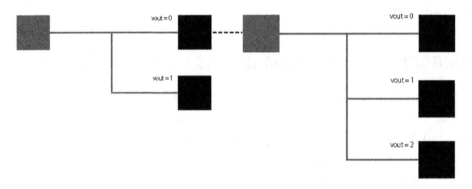

Figure 4-11. *vout new transaction illustration*

In this example, you will set the first index for vout.

```
> utxo_vout="0"
```

The last but most important variable you need to set is the recipient
address. Here, you will be using the same wallet address as you used
previously to send your coins.

```
> recipient="mv4rnyY3Su5gjcDNzbMLKBQkBicCtHUtFB"
```

Lastly, you can use the echo command to verify and double-check that you set your variables correctly.

```
> echo $utxo_txid
> echo $utxo_vout
> echo $recipient
```

Now that you have your variables set, you can generate a RawTransaction object via the createrawtransaction command. You do that by including all the variables you set and declaring the amount you would like to spend. You are using 0.xxx, but you need to use the UTXO less the fee you would like to pay to send the entire coins you have in the UTXO.

```
> rawtxhex=$(bitcoin-cli createrawtransaction "'[ { "txid":
  "'$utxo_txid'", "vout": '$utxo_vout' } ]"'
  "'{ "'$recipient'": 0.xxx }"')
```

Next, you can extract the rawtxhex value.

```
> echo $rawtxhex
020000000138451f62a8800b09a94504ae0ff2
0d7729e71ba5a8a9f483d80ba9739b1ce9500000000000ffff
ffff0140420f00000000001976a9149f9a7abd600c0caa03983
a77c8c3df8e062cb2fa88ac00000000
```

The rawtxhex value includes your new transaction information as a hex-encoded data. The following decoderawtransaction command will return some JSON output with decoded data for your transaction:

```
> bitcoin-cli decoderawtransaction $rawtxhex
{
  "txid": "91d4e108f8957251d2997e1f8dcdd0eec97192e8accf85a9e81
          f772f586118af",
```

```
"hash": "91d4e108f8957251d2997e1f8dcdd0eec97192e8accf85a9e81
        f772f586118af",
"version": 2,
"size": 85,
"vsize": 85,
"weight": 340,
"locktime": 0,
"vin": [
  {
    "txid": "50e91c9b73a90bd883f4a9a8a51be729770df20fae0445a9
            090b80a8621f4538",
    "vout": 0,
    "scriptSig": {
      "asm": "",
      "hex": ""
    },
    "sequence": 4294967295
  }
],
"vout": [
  {
    "value": 0.01000000,
    "n": 0,
    "scriptPubKey": {
      "asm": "OP_DUP OP_HASH160 9f9a7abd600c0caa03983a77c
              8c3df8e062cb2fa OP_EQUALVERIFY OP_CHECKSIG",
      "hex": "76a9149f9a7abd600c0caa03983a77c8c3df8e062cb2fa
              88ac",
      "reqSigs": 1,
      "type": "pubkeyhash",
      "addresses": [
```

```
        "mv4rnyY3Su5gjcDNzbMLKBQkBicCtHUtFB"
      ]
    }
  }
 ]
}
```

As you have seen, to create a transaction, you generate a signature from the wallet's public hash and the private key hash. The transaction output script takes the public key and the signature and checks to see whether you have a match to the public key hash. If results are true, you are able to spend the coins; otherwise, you can't.

Note   A public key visible in the transaction is a type of transaction called Pay to Pubkey (P2PK). A hidden public key as you have been using is a type of transaction called Pay to PubKey Hash (P2PKH).

You will sign your transaction via P2PKH to match your wallet's type. There are two ways to sign the transaction; you can use `signrawtransactionwithkey` or `signrawtransactionwithwallet`.

These two signed methods are available in 0.18.0 RPC, including inputs for raw transactions in a serialized hex-encoded format.

The `signrawtransactionwithwallet` command format is as follows:

```
signrawtransactionwithwallet "hexstring" ( [{"txid":"id","vout":
n,"scriptPubKey":"hex","redeemScript":"hex"},...] sighashtype )
```

Notice that the `signrawtransactionwithwallet` command allows you to include a second argument called "prevtxs". "prevtxs" is formatted as an array that includes the previous transaction outputs. If you decide to utilize and insert value for "prevtxs" the transaction will depends on the previous transaction that may not even be in the blockchain yet. In case you don't need this feature just set "prevtxs" to null.

The signrawtransactionwithkey command format is as follows:

signrawtransactionwithkey "hexstring" ["privatekey1",...]

Notice that the second argument is a base58-encoded array of private keys that will be the only keys used to sign the transaction. The third optional argument is an array of previous transaction outputs that this transaction depends on but may not yet be in the blockchain.

In our case, you will not include the second argument because your transaction does not need to depend on other conditions.

```
> bitcoin-cli signrawtransactionwithwallet $rawtxhex
{
  "hex": "0200000000010138451f62a8800b09a94504ae0ff20d7729e71ba
          5a8a9f483d80ba9739b1ce950000000000017160014c27b4e6bd8eb
          821ee80a239e0edd59070f57233dffffffff0140420f0000000000
          1976a9149f9a7abd600c0caa03983a77c8c3df8e062cb2fa88
          ac0247304402205cc4b04859e34aa6b1e924745f33a7643fbe45
          fcd6e900fdaa29281feae3f8f6022059d4083a3cf81c3bb8226
          7931660afb8ffc4bae87ede8dfa11efcb6af6a14ac90121028
          926735fcd5bf6580e6f669c240da8975dddf23a6d4015e
          4e0bc1ca3f1d2b7f100000000",
  "complete": true
}
```

The previous command returned signed, hex-encoded data in the JSON response. Use that data to set the hex for the signedtx variable.

```
> signedtx="0200000000010138451f62a8800b09a94504ae0ff20d7729e71
  ba5a8a9f483d80ba9739b1ce950000000000017160014c27b4e6bd8eb821ee8
  0a239e0edd59070f57233dffffffff0140420f00000000001976a9149f9a7
  abd600c0caa03983a77c8c3df8e062cb2fa88ac0247304402205cc4b04859
  e34aa6b1e924745f33a7643fbe45fcd6e900fdaa29281feae3f8f6022059d
  4083a3cf81c3bb82267931660afb8ffc4bae87ede8dfa11efcb6af6a14ac9
```

0121028926735fcd5bf6580e6f669c240da8975dddf23a6d4015e4e0bc
1ca3f1d2b7f100000000"

That's it; you can now send your transaction via the
sendrawtransaction command.

```
> bitcoin-cli sendrawtransaction $signedtx
ff75dbb08da6f4dc6463dd32d8f9b1a4781e1eeee338e93e8282
0d0fdfbd43ff
```

The output gets you a txid response that you can check in the
Blockchain Explorer as you did before. You can also verify that the funds
were removed from your account via the getbalance command.

```
> bitcoin-cli getbalance
0.09413028
```

As well as listunspent command.

```
> bitcoin-cli listunspent
[
  {
    "txid": "be05d068d1245f1c60ea4229c00eb5e96f2a5c5527f1de
            b7c6de5e1e20a4b4db",
    "vout": 1,
    "address": "2MveVhMe6PTzuhsJHx5zXAjDBwQvzdyqGjM",
    "redeemScript": "00142e29123ba343c577ab9517ede9b74f047d
                    2c2ea3",
    "scriptPubKey": "a914254f0e95fb26c0f29975f866e69543519b
                    f565e787",
    "amount": 0.09413028,
    "confirmations": 86,
    "spendable": true,
    "solvable": true,
```

```
    "safe": true
  }
]
```

Additionally, you can view the transaction via the `listtransactions`
command.

```
> bitcoin-cli listtransactions
[
...
  {
    "address": "mv4rnyY3Su5gjcDNzbMLKBQkBicCtHUtFB",
    "category": "send",
    "amount": -0.01000000,
    "label": "",
    "vout": 0,
    "fee": -0.08092813,
    "confirmations": 1,
    "blockhash": "0000000000000016ba1c314375d9bb17b6a857e091fd
                  4924bda5c9d7d9a2fd15",
    "blockindex": 1,
    "blocktime": 1542070705,
    "txid": "ff75dbb08da6f4dc6463dd32d8f9b1a4781e1eeee338e93e82
            820d0fdfbd43ff",
    "walletconflicts": [
    ],
    "time": 1542070656,
    "timereceived": 1542070656,
    "bip125-replaceable": "no",
    "abandoned": false
  }
]
```

Transactions that Require Multisignature

So far you have been doing standard "single-signature transactions," as you needed only one signee with one signature to sign a transaction and perform the transfer. However, the bitcoin network supports a more complicated transaction. These transactions can be set to require a signature of multiple signees. For instance, institutions, partners, spouses, or programmed scripts may want to have all parties sign instead of just one. These cases would need all the users' private keys before funds could be sent.

To do a multiple-signees transaction, you will create two separate wallets for testing. You can run bitcoin core on two separate machines and use the RPC calls to generate a new public address for each wallet, or you can download the Electrum wallet at https://electrum.org/#download and run it in testnet mode to generate your second wallet.

As a first example, you will run Electrum because you can use its built-in multisignature wallet to understand this process. Once you complete downloading Electrum, run Electrum as testnet via the command line.

```
> open -n /Applications/Electrum.app --args –testnet
```

Setting Electrum with a Multisignature Wallet

After Electrum starts, select "Multi-signature wallet" for the create wallet option and then click Next. See Figure 4-12.

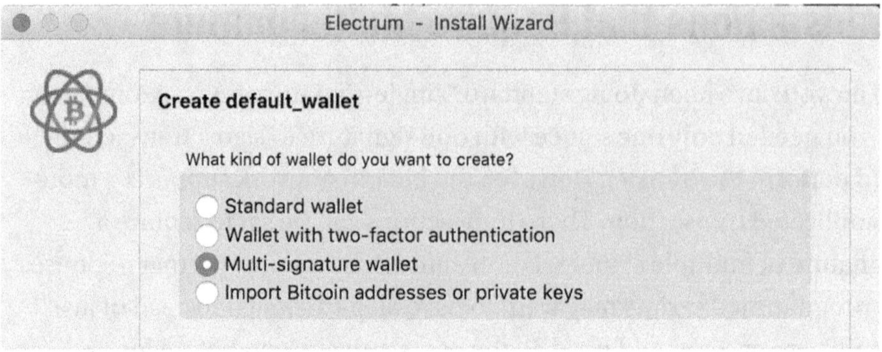

Figure 4-12. Electrum multisignature wallet

On the next screen, you can select how many cosigners are required and how many signatures are needed. These transactions are often referred to as *M-of-N transactions*, for instance, a 2-of-3 scenario. A 2-of-3 would mean you need at least two private keys (signatures) from three cosigners to authorize the transaction. You can move the sliders to better understand this feature, as shown in Figure 4-13.

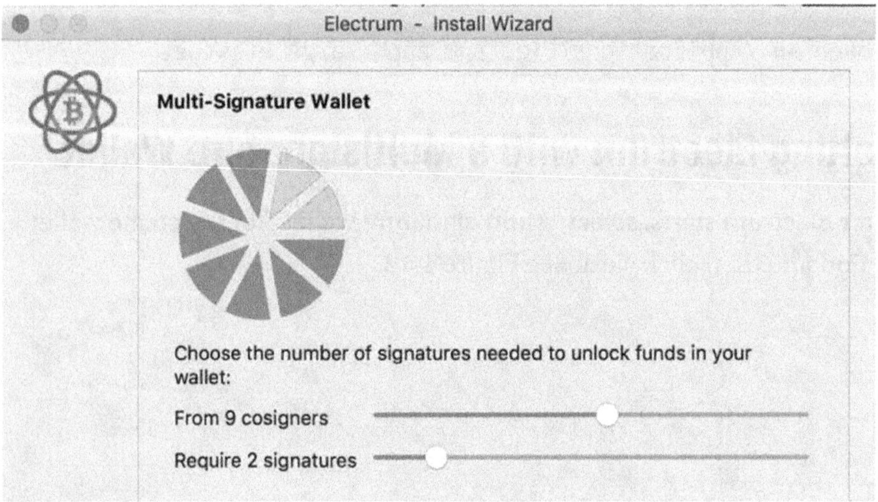

Figure 4-13. Electrum multisignature wallet cosigners and signatures

Here, select a 2-of-2 multisignature wallet, which means two cosigners and two signatures. Then click the Next button. On the following screen, click "Create a new seed" and click the Next button.

On the following screen, you can choose the seed type. Standard means P2PKH or SegWit, which means a P2SH-SEGWIT, so select Standard and click Next.

For the next step, you are given a seed that represents your private key. Store your seed and be careful not to share it with anyone. You are then provided with what Electrum calls your *master* public key, and you are asked to share it with your cosigners, as shown in Figure 4-14.

Figure 4-14. Electrum install wizard master public key

Note   The Electrum public master key is part of the Electrum Hierarchical Deterministic (HD) wallet that generates an address for you based on a master seed that can be used to back up all your funds. The seed consists of words used to retrieve your wallet's private keys; losing your seeds would mean losing your private keys.

Click Next, and you can enter a cosigner's public key or private key. See Figure 4-15.

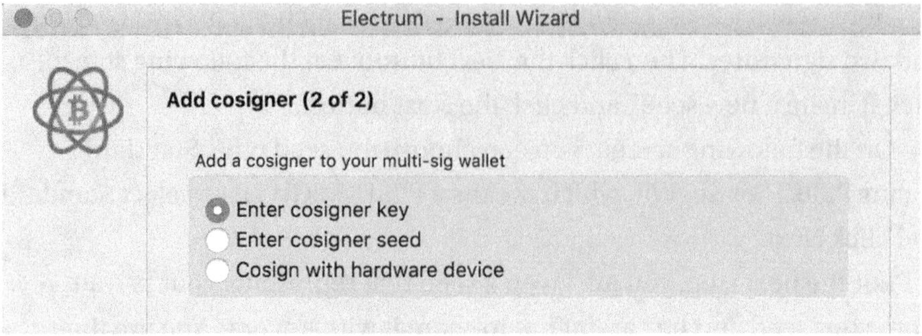

Figure 4-15. *Electrum install wizard cosigner key*

On the next screen of the wizard, you will be using the master private key of your bitcoin core's wallet to allow Electrum to sign the second wallet on your behalf. You can retrieve the private key from inside your private key backup file. It shows under extended private masterkey.

```
> vim /Users/[location]/mywallet.txt
# extended private masterkey: [key]
```

The Electrum wizard sets your cosigners for you, and the next step of the install wizard asks you to set up your password, if you like, for extra security.

That's it. Now that the wizard has completed setting up your account, you can send and receive funds from and to your cosigner wallet. Click Receive at the top to get your wallet address, as shown in Figure 4-16.

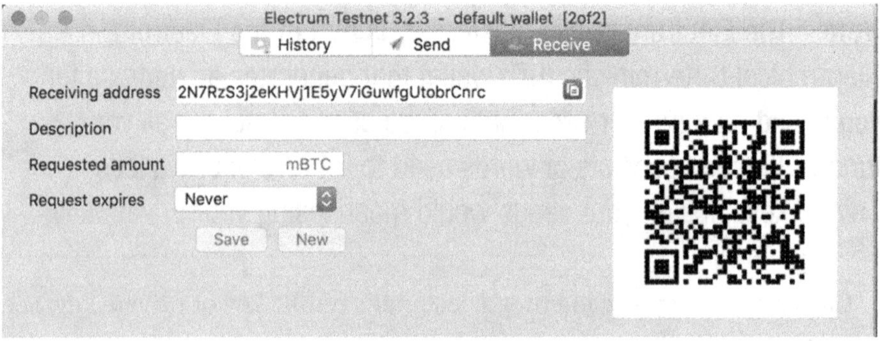

Figure 4-16. *Electrum wallet receive address and QR code*

You will be using Coinfaucet.eu again to fund your new wallet:
`https://coinfaucet.eu/en/btc-testnet/`.

Then you can send these coins back to the Coinfaucet.eu wallet's
address after the coins have been confirmed; here is Coinfaucet.eu wallet's
address:

`2N7RzS3j2eKHVj1E5yV7iGuwfgUtobrCnrc`

Since you have been providing both of the cosigner's private keys, this
transaction will be happening using the send command. However, in case
you set two accounts and provide only one public key, the second cosigner
would need to approve this transaction on his account before the send
command will actually send the coins.

Similarly, you can do this transaction via the RPC command line.

To get started, click File ➤ Delete at the top of Electrum to create a
standard wallet instead of a cosigner wallet.

Once this wallet is removed, you can start over and create a new
Standard (P2PKH) wallet that you will be using as the second cosigner. To
retrieve your wallet's address, click the View link at the top and then click
Addresses.

Next, right-click an address for which you'd like to see its public key.
This will show the address public key. See Figure 4-17.

- Here is the example's wallet address:
  `mxaFFFW5CFfJi6fbhn1qFDi8gv6eFsSBKQ`

- Here is the example's public key:
  `038e6fb8b842c750eb68bfccfd0fa1aa1c`
  `e8e455d58137e260a067e6d2fb853ea6`

Figure 4-17. *Electrum Standard wallet address and public key*

Next, you will create a new address for your cosigner via command-line RPC.

```
> bitcoin-cli getnewaddress
2Msggcttx7wDDbcib6yD8ng2oKRdq8Bz4wV
```

Next, you can set the two cosigners' addresses.

```
> address1=2Msggcttx7wDDbcib6yD8ng2oKRdq8Bz4wV
> address2=mxaFFFW5CFfJi6fbhn1qFDi8gv6eFsSBKQ
```

Ensure the address is correct via the `validateaddress` command.

```
> bitcoin-cli validateaddress $address2
```

You need both cosigners' public keys to create your cosigner wallet. You already have the Electrum wallet's public key; now you need bitcoin core's RPC public key. To get this, you use the `getaddressinfo` command to take a look at the RPC JSON response and `pubkey` variable.

```
> bitcoin-cli getaddressinfo $address1
{
    "address": "2Msggcttx7wDDbcib6yD8ng2oKRdq8Bz4wV",
    "scriptPubKey": "a91404d0a132b5796d4462f39865d56af4ff7255d1b
                287",
    "ismine": true,
    "iswatchonly": false,
    "isscript": true,
    "iswitness": false,
    "script": "witness_v0_keyhash",
    "hex": "001440bbb1a949badb3a12a941a44bc994f7127c595c",
    "pubkey": "034ffed96ffc416b90daa97df5c09b618d7fbf99076ed8100
            900cfa0890e763ac0",
    "embedded": {
      "isscript": false,
      "iswitness": true,
      "witness_version": 0,
      "witness_program": "40bbb1a949badb3a12a941a44bc994f7127c595c",
      "pubkey": "034ffed96ffc416b90daa97df5c09b618d7fbf99076ed81
              00900cfa0890e763ac0",
      "address": "tb1qgzamr22fhtdn5y4fgxjyhjv57uf8ck2u4glnj9",
      "scriptPubKey": "001440bbb1a949badb3a12a941a44bc994f7127c5
                  95c"
    },
    "label": "",
    "timestamp": 1541782726,
    "hdkeypath": "m/0'/0'/9'",
    "hdseedid": "572deaa922cbf31076701942878c3e5fc2e23b60",
    "hdmasterkeyid": "572deaa922cbf31076701942878c3e5fc2e23b60",
    "labels": [
      {
```

```
      "name": "",
      "purpose": "receive"
    }
  ]
}
```

Now, you are ready to create your cosigners' multisigned address via the createmultisig command because you have both cosigners' public keys.

```
> bitcoin-cli -named createmultisig nrequired=2 keys="'["034ffe
  d96ffc416b90daa97df5c09b618d7fbf99076ed8100900cfa0890e763ac0",
  "038e6fb8b842c750eb68bfccfd0fa1aa1ce8e455d58137e260a067e6d2
  fb853ea6"]"'
{
  "address": "2MtBkhgVLJ6VA1nFbjam36iUY1dCiWFf4ix",
  "redeemScript": "5221034ffed96ffc416b90daa97df5c09b618d7fbf99
                   076ed8100900cfa0890e763ac021038e6fb8b842c
                   750eb68bfccfd0fa1aa1ce8e455d58137e260a0
                   67e6d2fb853ea652ae"
}
```

Next, you need to pick a UTXO txid and vout to sign your transaction, just as you did in previous raw transactions.

```
> bitcoin-cli listunspent
[
  {
    "txid": "ea3fb46ab103d15120e02ed6b60e3d83b265fed26794e3ed
            739496b62445410b",
    "vout": 0,
    ...
]
```

Then you set the utxo_txid property.

```
> utxo_txid=ea3fb46ab103d15120e02ed6b60e3d83b265fed26794e3ed73
  9496b62445410b
> utxo_vout=0
> recipient="mv4rnyY3Su5gjcDNzbMLKBQkBicCtHUtFB"
> rawtxhex=$(bitcoin-cli -named createrawtransaction
  inputs="'[ { "txid": "'$utxo_txid'", "vout": '$utxo_vout' } ]"'
  outputs="'{ "'$recipient'": 0.001}"')
```

Now decode and set the hexstring property.

```
> bitcoin-cli -named decoderawtransaction hexstring=$rawtxhex
> bitcoin-cli signrawtransactionwithwallet $rawtxhex
{
  "hex": "020000000001010b414524b6969473ede39467d2fe65b2833d0eb
          6d62ee02051d103b16ab43fea0000000017160014040c578cf60bf
          00980bfde1920f54459eaab3a09ffffffff01a086010000000000
          1976a9149f9a7abd600c0caa03983a77c8c3df8e062cb2fa88ac0
          24730440220603883ace41bdf5cf85c87e80f7362b45e35949114
          f46ac5e5b89f5e13d8d95002205c5eb45ca7de8b2da88c41c4311
          711beb14e8e0d679e40d1fbc2cb8e81e053fb01210205e848e0f2
          2dfe0c428d02c356d0c9a8d064a789a6bbcaa43a245d701948aba
          200000000",
  "complete": true
}
```

Lastly, sign your transaction via the signedtx command.

```
> signedtx="020000000001010b414524b6969473ede39467d2fe65b283
  3d0eb6d62ee02051d103b16ab43fea0000000017160014040c578cf
  60bf00980bfde1920f54459eaab3a09ffffffff01a0860100000000
  001976a9149f9a7abd600c0caa03983a77c8c3df8e062cb2fa88ac
  024730440220603883ace41bdf5cf85c87e80f7362b45e35949114
  f46ac5e5b89f5e13d8d95002205c5eb45ca7de8b2da88c41c43117
```

11beb14e8e0d679e40d1fbc2cb8e81e053fb01210205e848e0f22dfe0
c428d02c356d0c9a8d064a789a6bbcaa43a245d701948aba200000000"

You are ready to send your transaction using sendrawtransaction value.

```
> bitcoin-cli sendrawtransaction $signedtx
```

Replaceable Transactions and Locktime

When creating a RawTransaction with the createrawtransaction command you can includes two more variables you can utilize: locktime and replaceable.

```
createrawtransaction [{"txid":"id","vout":n},...] [{"address":a
mount},{"data":"hex"},...] ( locktime ) ( replaceable )
```

You can learn more about these arguments here:
https://bitcoincore.org/en/doc/0.17.0/rpc/rawtransactions/createrawtransaction/

As the name suggests, replaceable allows a raw transaction to be replaced by a new transaction with higher fees. This happens when the fee you set is too low, causing the transaction not to go through. For instance, if the fee you are trying to pay is too high, you can get the following error message:

```
absurdly-high-fee, 11563419 > 10000000 (code 256)
```

Bitcoin core supports the locktime argument in the raw transaction; this argument allows you to send transactions at some time in the future, and until they're sent, the sender can cancel the transaction.

There are two options. Block height is used for small numbers, and UNIX timestamps are used for big numbers. These arguments mean that the transaction is not inserted into the block until the conditions are met.

> **Note**   Block height is the number of blocks in the chain between any specific block and the first chain block on the chain.

Bitcoin Colored Coins

Bitcoin transactions hold a property called OP_RETURN. This property can be used to hold up to 80 bytes of data, which can be used for passing data. This may not seem much, but it's enough for proof of ownership or passing small pieces of data to authenticate. Utilizing the OP_RETURN property is done by setting data code word in the vout property of the transaction. To pass the data we want to include in your transaction, you still need to send funds for the transaction to be included in the blockchain, but you can set the recipient to be your own wallet in case you don't want to pay someone. That way you get to store data in the Bitcoin persistence Blockchain and you only need to pay the transaction fee as you don't pay anyone.

> **Note**   OP_RETURN is the opcode script that defines the transaction as valid or invalid; it can be used to insert data into the transaction that will result in storing that data in the bitcoin blockchain. Keep in mind that there are different opinions about whether it's okay to utilize this property. Some believe that storing noncurrency data in the blockchain is a bad idea; because there are less costly and more efficient ways to store data, it really depends on usage.

Sending a Transaction with OP_RETURN

Before you set your transaction, you will want to introduce a small lightweight utility program called jq to streamline creating a RawTranaction object. This is a command-line JSON processor that you can use to process your RPC JSON in the terminal. You can download it from https://stedolan.github.io/jq/download.

Install it with Brew.

```
> brew install jq
```

The jq utility allows you to retrieve pieces of the returned JSON so you will be able to stream your transaction quicker and with fewer mistakes.

Next, you can set some data to send via the OP_RETURN param. This example will create an MD5 for a file. In real life, this can be a version of a contract between parties or any piece of code you need.

Note   The Message-Digest 5 (MD5) algorithm is a function that generates a 128-bit hash value. It's common to create a file that holds checksum files and that ensures the integrity of data because each file change would result in a new MD5 result.

You can pick one of bitcoin's core files such as config.log to generate an MD5 hash and set the op_return_data variable.

```
> md5 config.log
MD5 (config.log) = 634ef85e038cea45bd20900fc97e09dc
> op_return_data="634ef85e038cea45bd20900fc97e09dc"
```

As you saw previously in this chapter, you can use the listunspent command to select your UTXO that you want to spend.

```
> bitcoin-cli listunspent
```

Now using the jq utility, you can stream the process, so you don't need to do a copy and paste and can avoid errors.

```
> utxo_txid=$(bitcoin-cli listunspent | jq -r '.[0] | .txid')
> utxo_vout=$(bitcoin-cli listunspent | jq -r '.[0] | .vout')
> recipient=$(bitcoin-cli getrawchangeaddress)
```

Notice a few things here. You set the first JSON item [0] here, but you can set any item you want, such as [1] or [2]. Also, notice that you need to run the `listunspent` command to find out the "amount" the UTXO has. For this example, the amount is 0.1166341, and since you want to pay 0.00000200 for fees (200 satoshis), you will be sending 0.1166321 in total.

If you don't set the fee correctly, you may end up spending too much on fees or getting an error message such as the following:

- `min relay fee not met, 29 < 161 (code 66)`
- `absurdly-high-fee, 24432219 > 10000000 (code 256)`

You can use the `echo` command to ensure your variable is set correctly. Then you can continue and set your transaction's data.

```
> rawtxhex=$(bitcoin-cli -named createrawtransaction
  inputs="'[ { "txid": "'$utxo_txid'", "vout": '$utxo_vout' } ]'"
  outputs="'{ "data": "'$op_return_data'", "'$recipient'":
  0.1166321}'")
```

Next, you need to sign and send the transaction.

```
> signedtx=$(bitcoin-cli signrawtransactionwithwallet
  $rawtxhex | jq -r '.hex')
> bitcoin-cli sendrawtransaction $signedtx
43a14c3b1ac446e4774c5338e5ae4e23839ab65a38c45da8b790f44
49b090ae5
```

Now, you can track the `RawTransaction` object on the testnet Blockchain Explorer ledger, as shown in Figure 4-18. Here's the URL:

https://live.blockcypher.com/btc-testnet/tx/43a14c3b1ac44
6e4774c5338e5ae4e23839ab65a38c45da8b790f4449b090ae5/

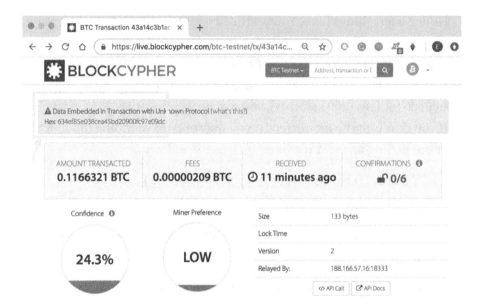

Figure 4-18. *Block Explorer testnet, transaction with data*

As you can see in Figure 4-18, you are getting the message "Data Embedded in Transaction with Unknown Protocol." If you were to design some software that uses this method on a regular basis, you would want to include a keyword to identify your data.

Bitcoin's Colored Coins

The colored coins name stuck from bitcoin core's older implementations of the EPOBC protocol where an asset is associated with satoshis (thus "coloring"). Now you are able to achieve coloring with the OP_RETURN param.

OP_RETURN colored your coins and provided a new capability for bitcoin's blockchain, as you were able to embed data that provided proof of ownership. You can also set other conditions to happen at a specific time or pass data related to the transaction you inserted into the blockchain. OP_RETURN is powerful, and later in this book you will see how OP_RETURN is utilized in production-grade projects to solve all sorts of issues.

Summary

In this chapter, you dove deep into the bitcoin core RPC. You generated a legacy and SegWit bitcoin wallets, and you were able to retrieve the wallet's private keys and better understand the Elliptic Curve Digital Signature Algorithm (ECDSA) and how the public and private keys are created.

You spent the majority of this chapter looking into transactions; you sent coins with bitcoin's daemon on testnet as well as utilizing bitcoin's core wallet GUI to send coins. After coins were sent, you learned how to view your transactions in bitcoin's Block Explorer. You continued by looking into RawTransaction and learned how to generate transactions with one output as well as more complex transactions with multiple signers via Electrum as well as the command line.

Additionally, you learned other options such as replacing your transaction for a change of fee as well as setting the locktime variable. You learned the difference between P2PKH and P2SH-SEGWIT. Lastly, I covered how to pass data using the OP_RETURN params, which can be used for bitcoin colored coins or just to pass additional data utilizing bitcoin's blockchain for more than spending coins. In the next chapter, you will take a closer look at Ethereum and how to write smart contracts.

CHAPTER 5

Ethereum Wallets and Smart Contracts

In Chapter 1, I introduced Ethereum when I covered bitcoin, altcoins, and different consensus mechanisms. Specifically, I covered Ethereum's PoW consensus and how utilizing Ethereum enables developers to create their own smart contracts and tokens. I mentioned that the Ethereum tokens can be generated as Ethereum requests for comment (ERCs) such as ERC-20, ERC-223, or ERC-777. In Chapter 3, you created your own blockchain, and I covered bitcoin wallets and transactions.

In this chapter, I will be expanding on Ethereum in more detail. Ethereum allows you to create code (*smart contracts*) to handle funds utilizing blockchain technology to overcome downtime and third-party interference. The Ethereum platform is mostly credited to Vitalik Buterin and Gavin Wood. According to the Ethereum web site, the definition of Ethereum is as follows:

> *"Ethereum is a decentralized platform that runs smart contracts: applications that run exactly as programmed without any possibility of downtime, censorship, fraud or third-party interference."*

> —Ethereum.org

© Elad Elrom 2019
E. Elrom, *The Blockchain Developer*, https://doi.org/10.1007/978-1-4842-4847-8_5

In previous chapters, you were able to pass and store data such as the bitcoin colored coins use case with the OP_RETURN param. This is useful because you're able to generate an MD5 hash of a file and store it on bitcoin's network. The MD5 you stored could be of a document, a contract, or anything you want. However, as you saw, bitcoin is limited to only storing the information, and you were unable to interact with the data. Specifically, you are able to pass and store data on the network, but you are unable to run code against your file such as to perform operations against your data. Ethereum solves this lack of functionality by allowing you to create a smart contract utilizing the power of blockchain.

Note   Smart contracts are programmable code used to handle funds. The code runs on its own, absent of the need of third parties. Solidity is a popular Ethereum contact-oriented programming language and can be used to write smart contracts and deploy the code on multiple blockchains.

At the heart of Ethereum is the Ethereum Virtual Machine (EVM). The EVM is where the smart contracts run in Ethereum. A good way to help you understand the EVM is to think about the EVM as a distributed global computer where the smart contracts can be executed.

Note   The EVM is a distributed global computer to run arbitrary, algorithmic, complex code. More simply, the EVM consists of all the nodes in the Ethereum network connected as a singular consensus and able to take a smart contract's code, process it, and execute it. The EVM uses 256 bits as the fundamental consensus mechanism; it can handle a 1 TB block, and the standard block time is 15 seconds.

Decentralized application developers write smart contracts and then run the code on the EVM with the help of front-end code. See Figure 5-1. The EVM executes the code in parallel connections on all the connected Ethereum nodes. This ensures the consensus of the nodes. The size of the Ethereum blockchain can be as big as 1 TB at the time of writing versus bitcoin's block height, which is limited to 4 MB per block. Additionally, bitcoin takes about 10 minutes to create a new block versus 15 seconds on the EVM.

Although it is advantageous for the decentralized code to run as a singular consensus, there are also drawbacks. For instance, the smart contract's code is slower and more expensive than a traditional computer as it runs on all nodes.

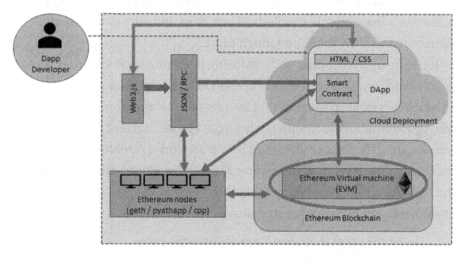

Figure 5-1. *Ethereum 10,000-foot perspective. Photo credit: xbt.net.*

To run an Ethereum miner, you need to run a full-node EVM. The miners are running a PoW consensus mechanism to verify transactions just like bitcoin. During the mining process, five coins are mined on every block. Just as you saw with NEO in Chapter 1, the Ethereum miners get paid for running smart contracts with Ethereum coins, which get changed into what is called *gas*.

Note   Ethereum gas is a fraction of an Ethereum token. Ethereum gas is changed and used by the contract to pay the miner for their efforts. Think of a car. It needs gas to operate, and so does Ethereum. Absent Ethereum gas, you cannot execute the smart contract.

Because Ethereum offers the ability to build interesting applications, the platform has been acknowledged for its potential and is utilized in one way or another by Microsoft, Intel, Amazon, J.P. Morgan, and even governments. This has turned Ethereum into an extensive ecosystem with many options to choose from to help you create your smart contracts easily. You can choose from a large number of development tools, apps communicating with other tools, best practices, infrastructure, testing, security, monitoring tools, and much more.

It can be overwhelming and confusing to choose tools to use, especially when many of the tools are still in alpha, beta, or not fully tested. However, keep in mind that by now you are already equipped with a good fundamental understanding of blockchain technologies, including transactions, wallets, and how it all works. Additionally, the blockchain you developed in Chapter 3 was in JavaScript utilizing Node.js, which is fundamental for many Ethereum tools. There are two lists that I recommend you bookmark, listed here:

- `https://github.com/ConsenSys/ethereum-developer-tools-list`

- `https://github.com/ConsenSys/ethereum-developer-tools-list/blob/master/EcosystemResources.md`

These resources provide an extensive list of all the development tools and resources related to Ethereum. It's beyond the scope of this book to cover all these different tools, but I recommend you review these tools at some point if you focus on Ethereum development so you can make your own determination about which tool fits your project best.

In this chapter, I will be focusing on Ethereum smart contracts and running them on a testnet, just as you have done in the previous chapters for bitcoin. I will show how to set up your development tools and IDE and give you basic information for dapp mainnet deployment, which I will expand upon in later chapters in this book.

Ganache Simulated Full-Node Client

Ganache (previously known as ethereumjs-testrpc) allows you to run a simulated full-node client of Ethereum on your machine and to interact with your contract via a CLI. This tool is useful because you will be setting up a development network and a private testnet network to test your smart contract code.

Just as you saw in the previous chapter, setting up a testnet network allows you to test your code with pretend money before committing your code to mainnet. I decided to use Ganache in this chapter as it is part of the Truffle development suite and integrates well with Truffle.

Install Ganache

To get started, you can install Ganache globally with npm and confirm it's working correctly by calling the help command.

```
> npm install -g ganache-cli
> ganache-cli help
```

If you have installation issues or want to get more information regarding the tool, visit the Ganache GitHub page: https://github.com/trufflesuite/ganache-cli. You can also check the version of CLI by running this command:

```
> ganache-cli -v
```

This command outputs the version. At the time of writing, the Ganache CLI is version v6.4.3 (ganache-core: 2.5.5).

Ganache CLI: Listen to Port

You can run Ganache on your machine while you develop and debug your contracts. To do this, you set up the Ganache CLI in Terminal to listen to the port you will be setting in `truffle.js` later in this chapter.

```
> ganache-cli -p 8584
```

Notice that at this point there is nothing running on port 8584, so let's assume you will be setting up port 8584. The command should output the following:

```
Listening on 127.0.0.1:8584
```

IntelliJ IDEA Plugin for Solidity

In Chapter 3, you downloaded and used WebStorm as your IDE to develop your blockchain. WebStorm is a subset of IntelliJ IDEA and has a plugin for the Solidity language, which provides an easy way to write your contracts. Also, it provides highlights and code completion to make development easier. You can use the WebStorm version you previously installed and just add the Solidity plugin. To do so, first download the plugin here: `https://plugins.jetbrains.com/plugin/9475-intellij-solidity`.

To get the plugin installed, follow these steps:

1. Select WebStorm ➤ Preferences (or press command + ,).

2. Select Plugins.

3. Search in "Plugins" for "*Solidity*". It will say "No Plugins founds." With a link to "Search in repositories". Click the "Search in repositories" link. "Intellij-Solidity" plugin will show. See Figure 5-2.

4. Install both "Intellij-Solidity" plugins: LANGUAGES
    and INSPECTION. See Figure 5-2.

5. Click IntelliJ-Solidity ➤ install. See Figure 5-2.

Figure 5-2. *Installing IntelliJ-Solidity and Solidity Solhint in WebStorm*

6. Under Plugins search for Solidity Solhint. It will say "No
    Plugins founds." With a link to "Search in repositories".
    Click the "Search in repositories" link. Click Solidity
    Solhint INSPECTION ➤ and then click Install.

7. Restart WebStorm.

Note that if you are a Visual Studio fan, there is also a Solidity extension
for Visual Studio; see `https://marketplace.visualstudio.com/`
`items?itemName=ConsenSys.Solidity`. At the time of writing, the plugin
works only for Visual Studio 2015 or earlier.

Keep in mind that, as always, you can use your favorite IDE, text editor,
or even vim to write your code; there's no need to buy an IDE.

Truffle Suite

You will be using Truffle as it's one of the most popular tools and has
integrated libraries that help expedite the development cycle. Truffle Suite
includes Truffle, Ganache, and Drizzle; see Figure 5-3.

"Truffle is a development environment, testing framework and asset pipeline for Ethereum, aiming to make life as an Ethereum developer easier."

—*https://github.com/trufflesuite/truffle*

The Truffle documentation includes installation instructions, which can be found at `https://truffleframework.com/docs`.

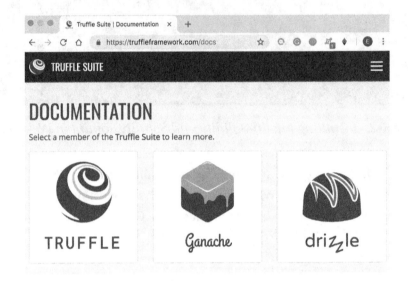

Figure 5-3. *Truffle Suite documentation*

To get started, open a new Terminal window and install Truffle globally on your machine (at the time of writing, the current Truffle version is 5.0.14). Then ensure it's installed correctly by running the `help` command to view a list of all available commands.

```
> npm install -g truffle
+ truffle@5.0.14
> truffle help
Truffle v5.0.14 - a development framework for Ethereum
Usage: truffle <command> [options]
```

Create Your Smart Contracts

To get started, let's create your folder and initialize the Truffle wizard to generate all the code needed to get started. In Terminal, type the following:

```
> mkdir MySmartContract && cd $_
> truffle init
```

These commands create a folder named MySmartContract and change the directory location to the new project; then the truffle init command initializes the project. You can see the output in Figure 5-4.

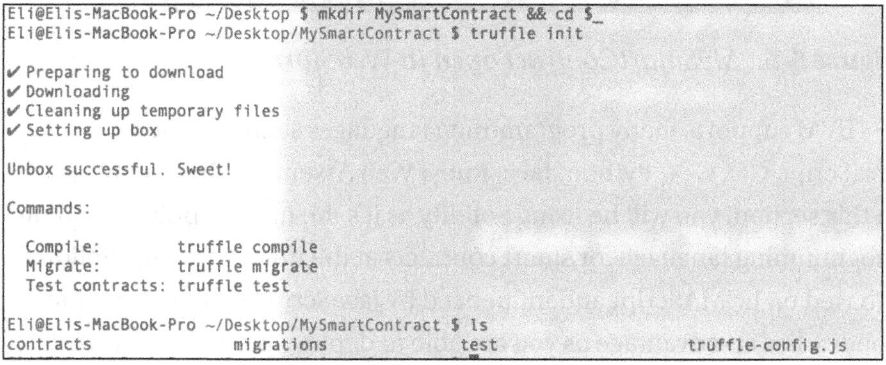

```
Eli@Elis-MacBook-Pro ~/Desktop $ mkdir MySmartContract && cd $_
Eli@Elis-MacBook-Pro ~/Desktop/MySmartContract $ truffle init

✔ Preparing to download
✔ Downloading
✔ Cleaning up temporary files
✔ Setting up box

Unbox successful. Sweet!

Commands:

  Compile:          truffle compile
  Migrate:          truffle migrate
  Test contracts:   truffle test

Eli@Elis-MacBook-Pro ~/Desktop/MySmartContract $ ls
contracts              migrations          test              truffle-config.js
```

Figure 5-4. *Creating the MySmartContract project and initializing with the truffle init command*

Next, open WebStorm and open the project you created by selecting File ➤ Open. Navigate to the MySmartContract project directory and click Open. WebStorm will open the project, as shown in Figure 5-5.

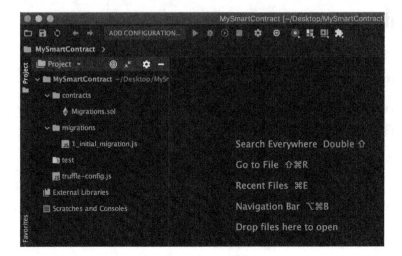

Figure 5-5. *MySmartContract open in WebStorm*

EVM supports many programming languages such as Solidity, JavaScript, GO, C++, Python, Java, Ruby, Web Assembly, Rust, and Haskell. In this section, you will be using Solidity as it's the most popular Ethereum programming language for smart contracts at the time of writing. Solidity is based on ECMAScript and influenced by JavaScript, C++, and Python. Solidity has an advantage as you are able to deploy your smart contract transactions on other various blockchain platforms beside Ethereum, such as Ethereum Classic, Tendermint, ErisDB, and Counterparty.

Solidity uses the `.sol` file extension; in fact, if you check in the `contracts` folder of your project, you will find a file called `Migrations.sol`, as shown in Figure 5-5. This file was generated automatically for you when you initialized the Truffle wizard. The migration files help you deploy contracts to the Ethereum network. As your project progresses, you will create new migration files.

Connect Truffle to the Ganache Network

Next, you will customize your environment by calling your network development and setting the URL and port. As you recall, you are already running Ganache and have programmed your network to listen on 127.0.0.1, port 8584. You'll use these settings for deploying your contracts on your Ethereum blockchain network.

To get started, open MySmartContract/truffle-config.js and inside the network object add a development object with these configuration settings:

```
module.exports = {
    networks: {
        development: {
            host: "127.0.0.1",
            port: 8584,
            network_id: "*",
            gas: 4712388,
            gasPrice: 100000000000
        }
    }
}
```

You set the host, port, and network ID, as well as the gas and gasPrice parameters. The following is according to Truffle docs (https://truffleframework.com/docs/truffle/reference/configuration#networks):

- gas: This is the gas limit used for deploys. The default is 4712388.

- gasPrice: This is the gas price used for deploys. The default is 100000000000 (100 Shannon).

You are setting the default values, which you can achieve also by omitting the gas and gasPrice tags; however, for the live mainnet network, at the time of writing, I recommend setting a 21,000 gas price that is a reasonable value. Check the ETH Gas Station (`https://ethgasstation.info/`) to figure out how much the `gasPrice` value should be, as shown in Figure 5-6.

Figure 5-6. *Ethgasstation.info calculates a recommended gas price*

As you can see, at the time of writing, paying a fiat of $0.014 provides a standard 5.6 transaction time.

You have set up a development environment only; however, as you move your code from development to a public testnet network and then production, you can add more environments to the `truffle-config.js` file.

"Hello, World" Smart Contract

As mentioned, smart contracts are account objects on the Ethereum blockchain; you can write functions to interact with other contracts, send coins, make decisions, and store data. Generally speaking, the contracts are built to be decentralized; however, keep in mind they can be programmed with a regulated option, making them centralized. For instance, the Ethereum Gemini dollar has the option to freeze transactions or even reverse them, and other coins can be built with a self-destruct function by the owner.

You'll start by creating a simple "Hello, World" contract. This is the minimum code, and the intention here is not to create anything useful but to help you understand how to create a smart contract.

In Terminal, at the project location, create a new contract and call it HelloWorldContract using the command truffle.

```
> truffle create contract HelloWorldContract
```

If the CLI worked correctly and without errors, it doesn't output anything.

Next, open the contract you created; it will show up under contracts/HelloWorldContract.sol. As you can see, the Truffle wizard created your contract for you.

This first smart contract is a minimal working example; it just holds a message and allows you to retrieve the message by calling your main function. Replace the existing code in contracts/HelloWorldContract.sol with the following below;

```
pragma solidity ^0.5.0;
contract HelloWorldContract {
  string greeting;
  constructor() public {
    greeting = 'Hello World';
  }
  function greet() public view returns (string memory) {
    return greeting;
  }
}
```

As you can see, Solidity scripting is similar to JavaScript or C++, and it's easy to read. The first line of code is the Solidity compiler version; you will be using 0.5.0. In the HelloWorldContract constructor, you are setting the greeting variable to 'Hello World'. The main function is greet(). Once you call the main function, you can retrieve the value of the greeting variable.

"MD5SmartContract" Smart Contract

Now you will create a second contract that is more practical. This contact will allow you to store the MD5 hash you stored in the previous chapter, but this time you will be able to interact with it instead of just storing the MD5 data on the blockchain.

In Terminal, at the project level, create a new contract called MD5SmartContract using the command truffle.

```
> truffle create contract MD5SmartContract
```

Next, open the contract you created called contracts/RegisterContract.sol. You will be running the following contact:

```
pragma solidity ^0.5.0;
contract MD5SmartContract {
  bytes32 public signature;
  event signEvent(bytes32 signature);
  constructor() public {
  }
  function sign(string memory document) public {
    signature = sha256(bytes(document));
    emit signEvent(signature);
  }
}
```

The code creates a variable call signature. Then your main function signs your document. You pass the document MD5, and using SHA256, you sign the document. You create an event to get dispatched once you sign your document.

Note   Secure Hash Algorithm (SHA) is one of a number of cryptographic hash functions. A cryptographic hash function acts as a signature for text or data; it is one-way and cannot be decrypted. The generated SHA256 hash is a fixed-size, 256 bits (32 bytes), and almost unique.

Create Truffle Migration Files for Your Smart Contract Deployment

As mentioned, Truffle migration files help you deploy your contracts on the Ethereum network. You will create a migration file for your deployment. To do so, create a new deployment file; call it 2_deploy_contracts.js, and place the file here: migrations/2_deploy_contracts.js. You can point to the smart contract code you created as follows:

```
const HelloWorldContract = artifacts.
require("HelloWorldContract.sol");
module.exports = function(deployer) {
    deployer.deploy(HelloWorldContract);
};
```

Create another deployment file, called 3_deploy_contracts.js, and place the file here: migrations/3_deploy_contracts.js.

```
const MD5SmartContract = artifacts.require("MD5SmartContract.sol");
module.exports = function(deployer) {
    deployer.deploy(MD5SmartContract);
};
```

At this point, your project includes two smart contracts and migration files. You can compare your project directory and files with mine; see Figure 5-7.

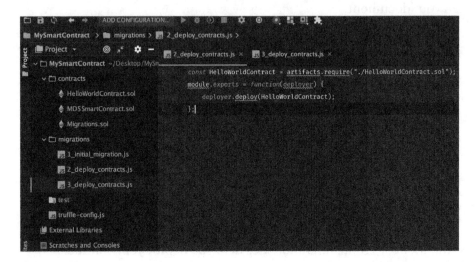

Figure 5-7. *MySmartContract including two smart contracts and migration files*

Another technique for lazier developers is to use the Truffle create wizard to generate the migration file.

```
> truffle create migration deploy_my_contract
```

This command generates the migration file automatically for you.

Compile Your Smart Contract with Truffle

In a separate Terminal window, you will run Truffle to compile your smart contract. The compile command turns your Solidity code to bytecode, which can be interpreted by the EVM. For now, Ganache simulates the EVM.

```
> truffle compile
```

You can see your contract's bytecode in the JSON file found here: build/contracts/HelloWorldContract.json and build/contracts/ MD5SmartContract.json. Look for the bytecode tag shown here:

"bytecode": "0x608060405234801561001057600080fd5b5061031...",

---

Note   Keep in mind that ideally you should delete the contract's contracts/*.json file manually before compiling again. This will ensure the latest code gets compiled because the CLI does not always recognize changes right away.

Deploy the Smart Contract to Your Development Network

Now that you have bytecode compiled from your smart contract, you can migrate the bytecode into your development environment so you can run the migration command to switch to the network you set in the truffle.js file.

```
> truffle migrate --network development
```

Running this command will return the response shown in Figure 5-8. This shows you that three migration files have been deployed successfully on the network. You have a successful deployment for each contract.

```
Running migration: 1_initial_migration.js
  Deploying Migrations...
  ... 0x13d3029f9bb6ec1eeedc67e5ae54130c95aaf6a95ce028954e470eb2b206830c
  Migrations: 0x1c6782a6f3c88a8482aab388baae9bc86a3e46c3
Saving successful migration to network...
  ... 0xeb11bc26a67a9430a6a371f0678399b3b5bb273c004c192b18d4ffee66631a79
Saving artifacts...
Running migration: 2_deploy_contracts.js
  Deploying HelloWorldContract...
  ... 0x959b3db385e172189292098b5079d73fa43c20873ee5b956e4a00468dd58e9fe
  HelloWorldContract: 0x5961b3a58759fb00cbfc1b2ababd2adcc28e9257
Saving successful migration to network...
  ... 0x3939e3e237cafbc40042cfec8258703b4882387611109e86205be30629c71f0d
Saving artifacts...
Running migration: 3_deploy_contracts.js
  Deploying MD5SmartContract...
  ... 0xb39a645bd3a53982050c927d5a8121ca3750280fcc54e00da59c2c4c67e0498e
  MD5SmartContract: 0xd223c4c19a2f7ecb48a0daf34ba5ec9a5d46428a
Saving successful migration to network...
  ... 0x5abb2fd7fdf2d2aaa18ddceab4c2bd4ea74d54327f4322b81c1bbd1f0089b3c9
Saving artifacts...
```

Figure 5-8. *Truffle migrate command response*

Keep in mind that the --reset flag is useful when you change your code, as you need to recompile, and re-deploy.

```
> truffle migrate --reset
```

Truffle Console

Now that your contract has been deployed to your development network you can communicate with your smart contract via the Truffle CLI. To do so, you can open a console and connect it to your development network.

```
> truffle console --network development
```

Once you run the console command, your Terminal shows you are in Truffle CLI development mode.

```
truffle(development)>
```

To get out of CLI mode, click Control+C twice or type .exit in the console.

Interact with Your Smart Contract via the Truffle CLI

You set two variables, hello and sign, for your smart contracts so that you can interact with them.

```
truffle(development)> HelloWorldContract.deployed().then(_app
=> { hello = _app })

undefined

truffle(development)> MD5SmartContract.deployed().then(_app =>
{ doc = _app })
undefined
```

To interact with your HelloWorldContract contract, you can call the main public function you created because you exposed the function greet.

```
truffle(development)> hello.greet()
'Hello World'
```

Similarly, you can interact with the MD5SmartContract.sol contract. You will pass the same MD5 hash you generated in Chapter 3 (634ef85e038cea45bd20900fc97e09dc) and call your main function called sign. That function will generate an SHA256 hash, as shown in Figure 5-9.

```
truffle(development)> doc.sign('634ef85e038cea45bd20900fc97e09dc')
```

```
truffle(development)> doc.sign('634ef85e038cea45bd20900fc97e09dc');
{ tx:
   '0xc284194c7b5d0a8bbfbbee1ecd1c0c0dfac9ca9540a8b928adaae56d10f03c79',
  receipt:
   { transactionHash:
      '0xc284194c7b5d0a8bbfbbee1ecd1c0c0dfac9ca9540a8b928adaae56d10f03c79',
     transactionIndex: 0,
     blockHash:
      '0x95c1cc58adf6e2f976d74ddc29a3103374ab2d0a8a46b320c9ea2a35c49a3aec',
     blockNumber: 7,
     from: '0x2ad080abff43e735970d883e885523dbe6a0b8f2',
     to: '0xd223c4c19a2f7ecb48a0daf34ba5ec9a5d46428a',
     gasUsed: 46744,
     cumulativeGasUsed: 46744,
     contractAddress: null,
     logs: [ [Object] ],
     status: '0x1',
     logsBloom:
      '0x000008000000000000000000000000000000010000000000000002000000000000000000
00000000000000000000080000000000000000000000000000000000000000000000000000000000
000000000200000000000000000000000000000000000800000000000000000000000000000000000
000000000000000000000000000000000000000000000000000000000000000000000000000000000
000000000000000000000000000000000000000', 
     v: '0x1b',
     r:
```

Figure 5-9. *Creating a doc.sign transaction*

Now you can confirm that you have an SHA256 hash by calling the
signature function; see the output in Figure 5-10.

```
truffle(development)> doc.signature()
'0x7869cd540ff8c3b2635ec87251f361e21ad3c72fbc2f79897b9816
bec54b0a48'
```

```
logs:
  [ { logIndex: 0,
      transactionIndex: 0,
      transactionHash: '0xff480d15dca9e8a3715ff0dc6e1911276fa49ea91fc48765a0c7434a54a46e12',
      blockHash: '0x1c2429d9f7b6ff7ab2790bb2c5d6080c5e3fb47dd9b0dbb3ca5884dbc7837d38',
      blockNumber: 132,
      address: '0x3A1C6c201f36f0968f736251Dad9447fb34b3F0E',
      type: 'mined',
      id: 'log_f9330bba',
      event: 'signEvent',
      args: [Object] } ] }
truffle(development)> doc.signature()
'0x7869cd540ff8c3b2635ec87251f361e21ad3c72fbc2f79897b9816bec54b0a48'
```

Figure 5-10. *Interacting with the MD5SmartContract smart contract to produce a signature*

You can download the entire smart contract project from here:
https://github.com/Apress/the-blockchain-developer/chapter5/step1/.

Compile with Remix

So far you used the Truffle tools, Ganache network, and WebStorm IDE to create, compile, deploy, and interact with your contract; however, there is another even easier way. Remix offers an online IDE that can do the same as WebStorm and Truffle.

To see this work, go to the Remix site: https://remix.ethereum.org.

Paste in the "Hello, World" smart contract code from your example. Ensure that the right-side panel is set to the correct compiler; you will be using "Current version:0.4.22." Then click "Start to compile (Ctrl-S)." See Figure 5-11.

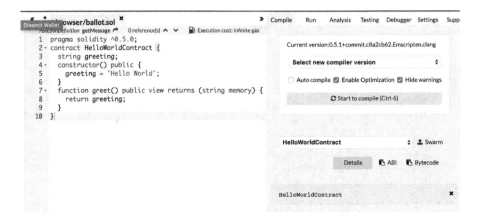

Figure 5-11. *"Hello, World" smart contract*

Create a new folder in your project and name it remix; then create a file and name it HelloWorldContract.js. Click the Details button in Remix Online IDE and copy and paste the WEB3DEPLOY content into the HelloWorldRemix.js file you created, as shown in Figure 5-12.

```
WEB3DEPLOY

var helloworldcontractContract = web3.eth.contract([{"const
var helloworldcontract = helloworldcontractContract.new(
    {
        from: web3.eth.accounts[0],
        data: '0x6080604052348015610010576000080fd5b50604080518
        gas: '4700000'
    }, function (e, contract){
    console.log(e, contract);
    if (typeof contract.address !== 'undefined') {
        console.log('Contract mined! address: ' + contract
    }
})
```

Figure 5-12. *"Hello, World" smart contract WEB3DEPLOY code*

Note   web3.js is Ethereum JavaScript API; its libraries allow you to interact with an Ethereum node via an HTTP or IPC connection. The WEB3DEPLOY code can be deployed on a local or remote node.

Private Ethereum Blockchain with Geth

You have interacted with your smart contract on your local machine. Next, it's advisable to run a full node and test your smart contract on a testnet blockchain; this tests it in a more realistic environment. Geth offers a full Ethereum node implemented in Go that you can run locally. This private testnet will allow you to develop and test your current smart contract in isolation from the real Ethereum blockchain.

To get started, first install Geth using Brew.

```
> brew tap ethereum/ethereum
> brew install ethereum
```

To ensure installation went well, run the `--version` command for the current Geth version (I am using 1.8.27 at the time of writing).

```
> geth version
Version: 1.8.27-stable
```

Initialized Geth Private Blockchain

Now that you have Geth installed, you will create your first block, or block 0, which is called the *genesis* block. Create a file called genesis_block.json and place it in the project root. For now just paste the provided JSON, but note that you can generate a custom genesis block with the Python script found here: https://blog.ethereum.org/2015/07/27/final-steps/.

For the scope of this book, you will use this script and set a low difficulty of 1000 and gas limit of 1000000 for easy mining and low gas fees; however, feel free to adjust as needed in your own experiments. See genesis_block.json.

```
{
  "config": {
  "chainId": 1,
  "homesteadBlock": 0,
  "eip155Block": 0,
  "eip158Block": 0
},
  "difficulty": "0x1000",
  "gasLimit": "0x1000000",
    "alloc": {
      "0x44dc998cbc1c7504bec0a96af4a9aef6606a768a":
      {"balance": "0x1337000000000000000000"}
    }
}
```

Next you will create your private testnet. In Terminal, run this command:

```
> geth --identity "MyTestNet" --nodiscover --networkid 1999
  --datadir testnet-blockchain init genesis_block.json
```

You will need an account for your testnet-blockchain; use the account command. Select a simple password as you are running a local test network, but on mainnet you need to be mindful of security; here I'm choosing password 123.

```
> geth account new --datadir testnet-blockchain
Passphrase: 123
Repeat passphrase: 123
Address: { a8eceb3e2dd7af9c6fdb12edd8a7e84290932c2d}
```

As you can see, you received a wallet address after picking a password. You can compare your output with mine, as shown in Figure 5-13.

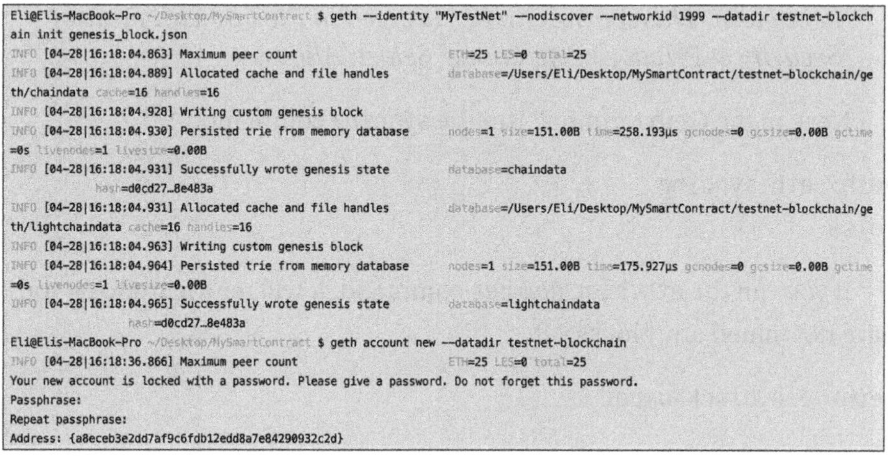

```
Eli@Elis-MacBook-Pro ~/Desktop/MySmartContract $ geth --identity "MyTestNet" --nodiscover --networkid 1999 --datadir testnet-blockch
ain init genesis_block.json
INFO [04-28|16:18:04.863] Maximum peer count                       ETH=25 LES=0 total=25
INFO [04-28|16:18:04.889] Allocated cache and file handles         database=/Users/Eli/Desktop/MySmartContract/testnet-blockchain/ge
th/chaindata cache=16 handles=16
INFO [04-28|16:18:04.928] Writing custom genesis block
INFO [04-28|16:18:04.930] Persisted trie from memory database      nodes=1 size=151.00B time=258.193µs gcnodes=0 gcsize=0.00B gctime
=0s livenodes=1 livesize=0.00B
INFO [04-28|16:18:04.931] Successfully wrote genesis state         database=chaindata
              hash=d0cd27_8e483a
INFO [04-28|16:18:04.931] Allocated cache and file handles         database=/Users/Eli/Desktop/MySmartContract/testnet-blockchain/ge
th/lightchaindata cache=16 handles=16
INFO [04-28|16:18:04.963] Writing custom genesis block
INFO [04-28|16:18:04.964] Persisted trie from memory database      nodes=1 size=151.00B time=175.927µs gcnodes=0 gcsize=0.00B gctime
=0s livenodes=1 livesize=0.00B
INFO [04-28|16:18:04.965] Successfully wrote genesis state         database=lightchaindata
              hash=d0cd27_8e483a
Eli@Elis-MacBook-Pro ~/Desktop/MySmartContract $ geth account new --datadir testnet-blockchain
INFO [04-28|16:18:36.866] Maximum peer count                       ETH=25 LES=0 total=25
Your new account is locked with a password. Please give a password. Do not forget this password.
Passphrase:
Repeat passphrase:
Address: {a8eceb3e2dd7af9c6fdb12edd8a7e84290932c2d}
```

Figure 5-13. *Creating a private testnet and wallet with Geth*

Geth Console

Now that you have your account set and `testnet-blockchain` chain, you can open a Geth console to interact with the chain.

```
> geth --identity "MyTestNet" --datadir testnet-blockchain
  --nodiscover --networkid 1999 console 2>> geth.log
```

Notice that I used the `2>> geth.log` param to output the logs into a custom file location. Once the Geth console starts, you can run the `eth.syncing` command to check the current block being synced. In this case, it will return `false` because there is nothing to sync; you are starting from block 0 on a local network.

You will receive a pop-up alert asking you the following:

"Do you want the application "geth" to accept incoming network connections? Clicking Deny may limit the application's behaviour. This setting can be changed in the Firewall pane of Security & Privacy preferences." Select "Allow".

Next, in the Geth terminal, run the syncing command.

```
geth> eth.syncing
false
```

If you run the eth.blockNumber command, it will return a zero as you have not mined any blocks yet.

```
geth> eth.blockNumber
0
```

Mine Ethereum for Your Private Testnet

You can then confirm you have a balance in your account with the getBalance command.

```
geth> eth.getBalance(eth.accounts[0])
0
```

With the eth.accounts command, you will get the new account you created.

```
geth> eth.accounts
["0xa2a6d8fe7e39645613e74fe19c79071ee52009ba"]
```

You can either generate or mine ether coins on the private Ethereum chain you created. Regardless, you need to know how to mine coins, because you will need transactions to be included in mined blocks as you test your code. To start mining, just run the miner.start command.

```
geth> miner.start()
null
```

Similarly, to stop mining, simply run the miner.stop command.

```
> miner.stop()
null
```

If you let the mining run, you will mine some blocks, so when you check the block number, you will now see results as well as funds.

```
geth> eth.blockNumber
1672
geth> eth.getBalance(eth.accounts[0])
8.36e+21
```

Deploy Remix to Geth

Now that your node is synced and you know how to mine, you can deploy your contracts to the testnet. First, you need to unlock your main Geth account to be able to use it. Ensure your account holds a balance; otherwise, you won't be able to deploy your contract on the network. On Geth, unlock your account with your password so Geth can use it.

```
geth> personal.unlockAccount(eth.accounts[0], "123", 24*3600)
true
```

I used the password 123, but you need to change it to your password if you used a different password. Next, load the web3.js script you generated on Remix.

```
> loadScript("remix/HelloWorldContract.js")
null [object Object]
true
```

It takes a few seconds to mine the next block and include this contract; once it's mined, you will receive the following message:

```
Contract mined! address: 0x9905f1663f1b808d52dca42ce26e0d264
8f8be07 transactionHash: 0x66b80787eb3eae16c9535a1bd86ff1a
623c1914ac9ffc2addde74655aed09157
```

If you are not seeing this message, make sure you are mining.

```
geth> miner.start()
```

Once the contact is mined, you will get the following message in Terminal, which includes the address and transaction hash:

```
Contract mined! address: 0xe49da16551c5c5735de46e07e8ab9e
713310a13b transactionHash: 0x36d3ec593f63280ca6aae1b079bfb6
f00eea719468e04960643c23f39cbef5b3
```

Deploy Truffle to Geth

Similarly, to deploy the web3.js contract's script via Truffle, you run the migrate --reset command. The --reset flag tells Truffle to run all the migrations from the beginning. Ensure you use .exit to exit the Truffle console prior to running the migrate command. Truffle will compile your contract automatically.

```
truffle(development)> .exit
> truffle migrate --reset
Using network 'development'.
Network up to date.
```

Now you can open a development console again.

```
> truffle console --network development
truffle(development)> HelloWorldContract.deployed().then(_app
=> { hello = _app })
undefined
truffle(development)> hello.greet() 'Hello World'
```

The contract is redeployed, and you can interact with your contract again. You can download this step from here: https://github.com/Apress/the-blockchain-developer/chapter5/step2/.

Useful Commands in Geth

You can stop the Geth process by pressing Command+C and then exit, or you can stop the process via aux to check whether there are any processes open. Or you can use the killall command to stop the process.

```
> ps aux | grep geth
> killall -HUP geth
```

At any time, you can run the help flag to get a list of commands.

```
> geth -help
```

To get a list of the pending transactions, run the following:

```
> geth --identity "MyTestNet" --datadir testnet-blockchain
  --nodiscover --networkid 1999 console 2>> geth.log
geth> eth.pendingTransactions
```

To remove your locally synced blockchain data from the public testnet, use this:

```
geth> geth removedb
```

To remove your private blockchain testnet data, use this:

```
geth> geth removedb --datadir test-net-blockchain
```

To synchronize the blockchain more quickly, use the --fast flag to perform a fast Ethereum sync. Note that you will not retain the past transaction data with this command. The cache flag sets the cache limit.

```
geth> geth --fast --cache=1024
```

Connect the Mist Ethereum Wallet to Your Private Network

It would be useful to have a wallet to connect to your private network. That's where Mist is helpful. You can connect your private blockchain to Mist and perform transactions, conducting realistic transactions as if people were using your contracts.

To get started, download Mist from here: `https://github.com/ethereum/mist/releases`.

For Mac, the file to download is called `Mist-macosx-0-11-1.dmg` at the time of writing. Note that you can also achieve the same results with an Ethereum wallet, which you can download from the same URL.

Next, you will be starting Mist and connecting it to your testnet blockchain. At the command line, point to Mist's location and the `geth.ipc` database.

```
> /Applications/Mist.app/Contents/MacOS/Mist --rpc /[project
  location]/MySmartContract/testnet-blockchain/geth.ipc
```

Mist opens and shows your active account and balance, as shown in Figure 5-14.

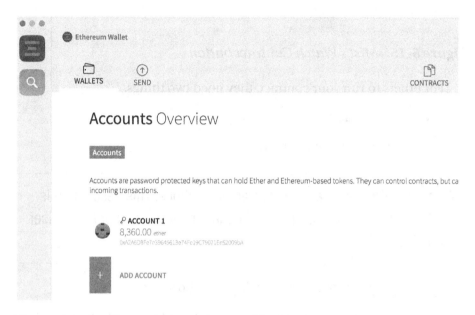

Figure 5-14. *Mist active account and balance*

Others to Interact with Your Smart Contract

Once the contract is published, anyone can use the address and application binary interface (ABI) to connect and interact with the contract. You can start and interact with your contract as if an actual person is using your contract prior to publishing it to mainnet.

Mist is a desktop app that can be used for testing. To watch a contract, in Mist, click the Contracts link at the top right and then click Watch Contract, as shown in Figure 5-15.

Figure 5-15. *Mist's Watch Contract button*

For others to run your contract, they need two things.

- Contract address

- Application binary interface

Note   An ABI describes the contract's functions. This description is needed in order to know how to call the function. Think of it as a user manual.

You can retrieve the contract address, as shown here:

```
truffle(development)>var hello = HelloWorldContract.deployed().
then(_app => { hello = _app })
truffle(development)>hello.address
'0x0b4f69f88390bc8cec93e730128a5e5c5dffd56c'
```

Similarly, you can retrieve the contract's ABI with this command:

```
truffle(development)>JSON.stringify(hello.abi)
'[{"inputs":[],"payable":false,"stateMutability":"nonpayable","
type":"constructor","signature" '[{"inputs":[],"payable":false,
"stateMutability":"nonpayable","type":
"constructor","signature":"constructor"},{"constant":true,
"inputs":[],"name":"greet","outputs":[{"name":"","type":"string"}],
"payable":false,"stateMutability":"view","type":"function",
"signature":"0xcfae3217"}]'
```

Then pass the contract address and ABI in Mist, as shown in Figure 5-16.

Figure 5-16. *Passing info in Mist*

Notice that you omit the single quote from the ABI and address before pasting it into Mist.

Now click OK, and you can see your contract in the watched contracts list. See Figure 5-17.

Figure 5-17. *Mist's watched contracts*

You have your contract in Mist, and you can interact with it, send funds, listen to events, and interact with functions, just as users will interact with your contract on mainnet.

MetaMask

Similar to Mist, another way to interact with your contracts, without even downloading a desktop app, is in your Chrome or Firefox browser with a plugin called MetaMask. Just as with Mist, you can utilize MetaMask to connect your contract to mainnet, a public testnet, and a local blockchain (such as the one you created with Ganache), or you can even connect to Truffle Develop. To get started, download the MetaMask plugin for Chrome or Firefox.

- *Chrome Web Store*: `https://chrome.google.com/webstore/detail/metamask/nkbihfbeogaeaoehlefnkodbefgpgknn`. Click the Add to Chrome button. See Figure 5-18.

- *Firefox Add-ons page*: `https://addons.mozilla.org/en-US/firefox/addon/ether-metamask`. Click the Add to Firefox button.

Figure 5-18. *MetaMask beta Chrome add-on*

Click the MetaMask icon and then the Continue button. Next, select a password, accept the terms, save your secret backup phrase, and create your account.

Now that the account is created, you have an option in the top drop-down of which network to connect to, as shown in Figure 5-19.

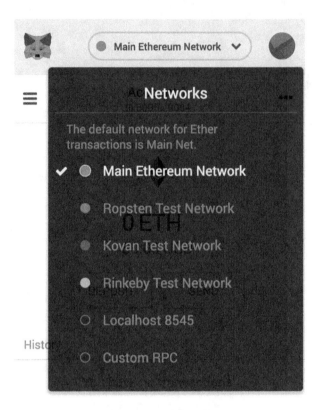

Figure 5-19. *MetaMask beta Chrome network drop-down*

As you might recall, you programmed the `truffle.js` values to set a network on localhost port 8584, which matches the default network; however, you can set a custom RPC or connect to testnet or mainnet.

For more information regarding connecting Truffle with Metamask, visit the Truffle framework docs;

`https://truffleframework.com/docs/truffle/getting-started/truffle-with-metamask`

Public Testnet

Now that you are able to run your smart contract on a development network, you can take an additional step prior to going to mainnet. You can run your contract on a public testnet network.

Syncing Blocks

There are three well-known testnets: Ropsten, Kovan, and Rinkeby. You can program Geth to connect to a testnet with the --testnet flag, which will connect to the public testnet network (Ropsten).

```
> geth --testnet --syncmode "fast" --cache=512 console
```

As before, the rpc flag is needed to accept the Geth RPC connections and for Truffle to be able to connect to Geth. You are also setting it to fast sync and limiting the cache size to 512. This command includes starting the Geth console.

To check the status of the syncing command, use this:

```
geth> eth.syncing
{
  currentBlock: 1011878,
  highestBlock: 3569550,
  knownStates: 2058862,
  pulledStates: 2056745,
  startingBlock: 968873
}
```

Once complete, the syncing command will return false. Keep in mind that there are millions of state entries and 3,569,550 blocks at the time of writing, which could take hours depending on your connection speed. The currentBlock value is the current block being retrieved out of a total number of blocks (the highest block). This can give you an idea of how long the download will take.

As you recall, you can check current block number being sync by running the eth.blockNumber command in a Geth console, as well as check your balance in your account to see whether it has been updated yet.

```
> eth.blockNumber
> eth.getBalance(eth.accounts[0])
```

Public Testnet Faucet

In addition to the testnet coins, you can get additional testnet coins via a faucet, just as you did with bitcoin. Go to https://faucet.ropsten.be/, as shown in Figure 5-20, and request coins to your wallet address set in Mist.

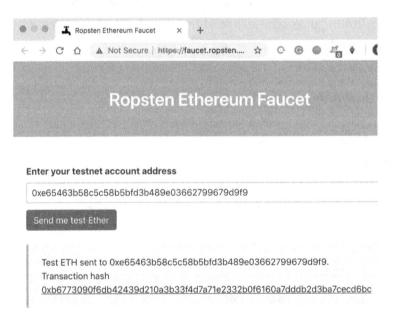

Figure 5-20. *Ropsten Ethereum faucet*

Ethereum Mainnet

From the Ganache console, you were able to publish to a public testnet network (Ropsten). The next step is to publish to the Ethereum mainnet. To do so, you will restart Geth and connect this time to the mainnet.

```
> geth --fast --cache=512
```

Just as with the public testnet, you will have to wait for Geth to sync. Once syncing is complete, you can call the Truffle `migrate` command to deploy, and as before, you need your account to have ether coins.

```
> truffle migrate --reset
```

Recommended Tools for Smart Contracts

In this chapter, I covered Ganache, Solidity, IntelliJ, Truffle, Geth, Remix, and MetaMask; however, there are other tools worth mentioning.

- *Solium*: Solidity code cleaning solution

- *conteract.io*: Interacting with smart contracts

- *Populus*: Development framework for Ethereum smart contracts

- *Parity*: Light-weight Ethereum node

- *Drizzle*: Front-end dapp solution

Summary

In this chapter, I covered how to utilize Ganache to simulate a full-node Ethereum client. You installed Ganache, and once you were able to connect to the Ganache CLI, you were able to create a network and listen to a port. You learned how to use the IntelliJ IDEA plugin for Solidity to

211

easily develop smart contracts with autocomplete and highlights. You also learned about the Truffle Suite and how to create your own smart contracts using the command-line wizard. You connected Truffle to the Ganache network and then created a "Hello, World" smart contract as well as "MD5SmartContract" smart contract.

Once you created your contracts, you were able to migrate your smart contract utilizing the Truffle deployment process. You compiled and deployed your smart contract code with Truffle to your development network. Then, you used the Truffle console to interact with your smart contract via the Truffle CLI. Next, you created a private Ethereum blockchain with Geth and initialized the blockchain. You utilize the Geth console and mined pretend Ethereum on your Geth private testnet.

Next, you deployed your Remix web3.js to the Geth private testnet you created, as well as deployed your Truffle contracts. In addition, you looked at some useful Geth commands that will help you while developing smart contracts. You connected your Mist Ethereum wallet to the private Geth network you created and were able to interact with your smart contract. You were able to use MetaMask in your browser as a replacement for a desktop client.

Once you were able to see your contract working, you set a public testnet and synced blocks as well as got coins via a faucet. Lastly, you learned how to migrate your code to the Ethereum mainnet.

In next chapters, you will learn how to build front-end code for smart contracts and publish a complete dapp.

CHAPTER 6

EOS.IO Wallets and Smart Contracts

In Chapter 2, I introduced EOS.IO when I covered bitcoin, altcoins, and different consensus mechanisms. Specifically, I covered how EOS.IO is an example of altcoins that turn into tokens; you created an EOS block producer and were able to create a full node capable of mining EOS tokens. Ethereum was the beginning of your blockchain smart contract development, and you learned to use the Solidity language to write smart contracts and dapps. EOS.IO has created a more robust architecture than Ethereum for smart contract and dapp development.

In this chapter, I will expand on the EOS.IO blockchain and show how to build a EOS.IO smart contract that can be used in decentralized applications (dapps). You will set up a local testnet environment and learn how to configure the EOS.IO tools and libraries. You will learn about EOS.IO wallets and how to create, delete, and back up wallets as well as perform operations such as opening, locking, and unlocking a wallet. I will cover the wallet's key pairs and how to spin up and re-spin up a local testnet block producer. You will learn about permissions and single-signature and multisignature options.

To better understand EOS.IO smart contracts, you will create a "HelloWorld" smart contract and smart contract token. You will create accounts, write smart contract C++ code, compile code, and generate WebAssembly and ABI files as well as Ricardian contracts. You then will learn how to deploy your smart contracts and interact with them, as well as issue tokens and transfer tokens to another user.

© Elad Elrom 2019
E. Elrom, *The Blockchain Developer*, https://doi.org/10.1007/978-1-4842-4847-8_6

Lastly, you will connect to a public testnet block producer for testing in a more realistic environment as well as connecting and publishing on a mainnet block producer.

Note   EOS is the native cryptocurrency (token) that powers the EOS.IO software. EOS.IO is an industrial-scale, fully customized blockchain architecture protocol that enables decentralized applications by providing access to the parts that make up the blockchain. Think of EOS.IO as a blockchain OS as it emulates a real computer and enables access to resources such as the CPU, GPU, RAM, and hard disk. EOS.IS does not charge transaction fees while performing millions of transactions per second. An EOS token is a utility token, and owning the token (staking) provides bandwidth and storage on the EOS.IO blockchain. You receive resources in proportion to the total stake you own to the total stake (owning 1 percent of EOS tokens gives usage up to 1 percent of total EOS.IO bandwidth).

"EOS.IO software introduces a new blockchain architecture designed to enable vertical and horizontal scaling of decentralized applications. This is achieved by creating an operating system-like construct upon which applications can be built. The software provides accounts, authentication, databases, asynchronous communication, and the scheduling of applications across many of CPU cores or clusters. The resulting technology is a blockchain architecture that may ultimately scale to millions of transactions per second, eliminates user fees, and allows for quick and easy deployment and maintenance of decentralized applications, in the context of a governed blockchain."

—EOS.IO block.one white paper

As mentioned in Chapter 2, EOS.IO is built on the delegated proof of stake (DPoS) consensus. EOS.IO is able to handle low latency and tens of millions of active users daily (bypassing Ethereum). This is achieved by the DPoS consensus as well as EOS.IO running as multithreaded (running on multiple computer cores) and acting as an OS.

This type of scalability can enable adoption of blockchain technology by large businesses. EOS.IO offers many additional features such as the following:

- Free rate-limited transactions

- Low-latency transactions (such as 0.25 seconds broadcast time or 0.5 block time)

- Recovery of stolen keys

- Parallel execution of applications

- Atomic transactions with multiple accounts

I encourage you to read the EOS.IO white paper and visit the GitHub page for a full list of features.

- `https://github.com/EOSIO/eos`

- `https://github.com/EOSIO/Documentation/blob/master/TechnicalWhitePaper.md`

Financially speaking, EOS was developed by a private company called block.one and was able to raise an astonishing $4 billion in initial coin offering (ICO) via an ERC-20 tokens sale. At the time of writing, EOS's price is selling around $2 to $8, and it has a total market capitalization of around $2 billion, which makes EOS the seventh largest cryptocurrency by market cap.

EOS offers a few repositories to help with the development of EOS.IO contracts; they are listed at `https://github.com/EOSIO` and include the following: eos, eosio.cdt, eosjs, demux-js, and eosio.contracts. You will be installing the EOS and EOSIO.CDT libraries in this chapter. The EOS library is an open source smart contract platform, and the EOSIO.CDT library is a suite of tools for building EOS.IO contracts.

At the time of writing, the EOS.IO platform has a steep learning curve. The code keeps changing, and the documentation and examples of EOS.IO are not being updated in timely manner, so it may feel like chasing a moving target at times. This results in code sometimes not compiling, commands not working, and documentation and examples containing code and commands that have been deprecated. It's easy to find yourself stumped a few times while developing a contract; however, once you understand EOS.IO, it's easy to overcome these obstacles.

Setting Up a Testnet Environment

Before jumping into coding, let's start by installing EOS.IO and EOSIO. CDT. You will build your EOS.IO version and set up a local testnet block producer. Then you will learn about the EOS.IO tools called `cleos`, `keosd`, and `nodeos` and how to configure them and create and manage a wallet with `cleos`. These tools and libraries are necessary for development.

Install EOS.IO

The easiest way to install EOS.IO on macOS is with Brew.

```
> brew tap eosio/eosio
> brew install eosio
```

The current EOS.IO is version 1.7.3. I recommend checking the repo and issues section on GitHub (`https://github.com/eosio/eos`) or doing a Google search in case you encounter errors when installing or building EOS.IO. Also see `https://github.com/EOSIO/eos/issues`.

Once the installation is complete, you will see the message in Figure 6-1 in Terminal.

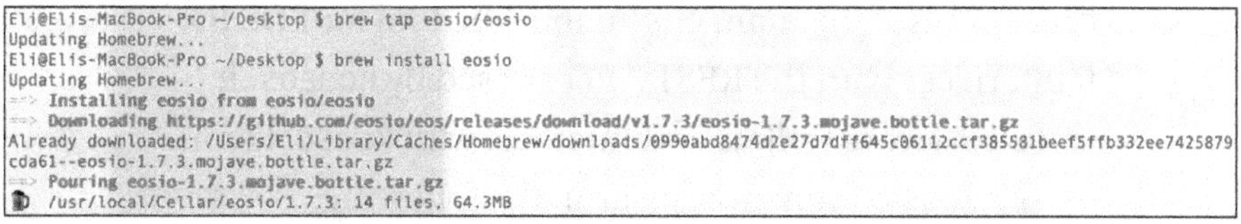

```
Eli@Elis-MacBook-Pro ~/Desktop $ brew tap eosio/eosio
Updating Homebrew...
Eli@Elis-MacBook-Pro ~/Desktop $ brew install eosio
Updating Homebrew...
==> Installing eosio from eosio/eosio
==> Downloading https://github.com/eosio/eos/releases/download/v1.7.3/eosio-1.7.3.mojave.bottle.tar.gz
Already downloaded: /Users/Eli/Library/Caches/Homebrew/downloads/0990abd8474d2e27d7dff645c86112ccf385581beef5ffb332ee7425879
cda61--eosio-1.7.3.mojave.bottle.tar.gz
==> Pouring eosio-1.7.3.mojave.bottle.tar.gz
🍺  /usr/local/Cellar/eosio/1.7.3: 14 files, 64.3MB
```

Figure 6-1. *EOS.IO successfully built*

Next, add the EOS.IO binaries location to your environment, so you can run nodeos from anywhere.

> export PATH=$PATH:/usr/local/eosio/bin

This will set the path variable on this Terminal session, but you want to set the path environment variable permanently, so add it to your bash_profile file by opening the file with vim or your favorite text editor.

> vim ~/.bash_profile

Next, insert the following lines:

# Setting PATH for EOSIO
PATH="/usr/local/eosio/bin:${PATH}"

Lastly, run bash_profile to commit the changes.

> . ~/.bash_profile

EOS.IO comes out of the box with built-in tools and programs; they are here: /usr/local/eosio/. Figure 6-2 shows an architecture diagram of these tools.

- nodeos: This is the core EOS.IO daemon that enables you to run a blockchain node component. nodeos can be configured with plugins. Additionally, nodeos can be configured to run a block producer in a local development environment or on dedicated endpoints. It interacts with a blockchain by creating blocks.

- cleos: This is the main command-line tool for EOS.IO.
  It interfaces with the REST API exposed by nodeos. It
  can also access wallets as it interacts with keosd. For a
  list of cleos commands, just run the following:

  ```
  > cleos
  ```

- keosd: This is the wallet daemon to load and manage
  the wallet's keys. It does this by loading wallet-related
  plugins, such as the HTTP interface and the RPC API.

- eosio-launcher: This tool will help you deploy a
  multinode blockchain network.

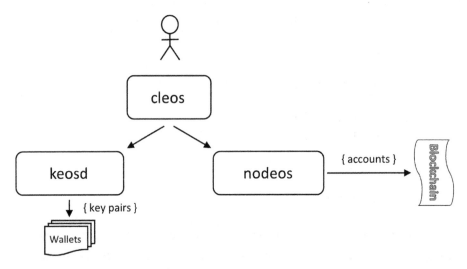

Figure 6-2. *Basic architecture of EOS. Photo credit: developers.eos.io.*

Install EOSIO.CDT

You installed EOS.IO. The other important library you need is EOSIO.CDT
(CDT stands for "contract development toolkit"). EOSIO.CDT is the suite
of tools used to build EOS.IO contracts. To get the library installed, you will
be using Brew.

```
> brew tap eosio/eosio.cdt
> brew install eosio.cdt
```

The latest EOSIO.CDT at the time of writing is version 1.6.1. Run brew update if you have an older version.

```
> brew upgrade eosio.cdt
```

To ensure installation went well, run the eosio-cpp command with the help argument.

```
> eosio-cpp --help
```

As you recall, you used Truffle and Remix to generate the Ethereum's application binary interface (ABI) files. For EOS.IO smart contracts, you use eosio-cpp, which is a compiler that generates a WebAssembly (.wasm) file, which is the ABI that is needed to be uploaded to the blockchain for the smart contract. eosio-cpp also generates helper functions that serialize/deserialize the types defined in the ABI code for the smart contract development.

You can find more information about EOSIO.CDT on the GitHub page: https://github.com/EOSIO/eosio.cdt.

In the future, if you need to remove EOSIO and EOSIO.CDT, run the following commands:

```
> brew remove eosio
> brew remove eosio.cdt
```

Note   eosio-cpp is the replacement for eosiocpp, which has been deprecated. Originally eosiocpp was part of the EOS.IO installation, but now it's part of CDT.

Build EOS.IO

A good way to visually understand EOS.IO and the tools associated with
EOS.IO is to look at Figure 6-2.

keosd and nodeos Configuration Files

The default ports for keosd and nodeos utilize the same port: 8888.

To configure nodeos, see this config file:

```
> vim "/Users/[user]/Library/Application Support/eosio/nodeos/
  config/config.ini"
```

Inside the config.ini file, a notable variable to change is the plugins
list that you load. You won't make changes, but as you advance in your
development, you may need to make changes.

Like with nodeos, you can configure keosd by editing this config file:

```
> vim ~/eosio-wallet/config.ini
```

Once you open the file, note that there is a variable named http-
server-address that can be used to change from port 8888 in case you
need that port for other software. Here let's set it to any port you like.

The variable is commented out. To set it to port 9000, change it
from this:

```
# http-server-address =
```

to the following:

```
http-server-address = http://127.0.0.1:9000
```

You could use the default port; however, it's good to know how to
configure EOS.IO.

Create and Manage a Wallet with cleos

In the previous section, I introduced some EOS.IO built-in programs and tools.

As mentioned, `cleos` provides a REST API interface that is exposed by nodeos. The `cleos` reference guide can be found here: `https://developers.eos.io/eosio-cleos/reference`.

To find the `cleos --version` number, run the `--version` client command. At the time of writing, you get to build d4ffb4eb.

```
> cleos version client
d4ffb4eb
```

As mentioned, to get a list of commands, just type `cleos`. or `cleos --help;`.

```
> cleos --help
```

If you don't remember a specific subcommand, type the command and get the subcommands list in the output; for instance, the `get` command outputs the subcommands list such as `info` for your block producer's info.

```
> cleos get
> cleos get info
Failed to connect to nodeos at http://127.0.0.1:8888/; is
nodeos running?
```

Notice that as you don't have a node running, you get no results and an error message; however, later in this chapter, when you spin up nodeos, you will get information about your block producer.

EOS.IO Wallets

The EOS.IO wallets use keys and offer a locked (encrypted) state and an unlocked (decrypted) state to protect the keys. The lock and unlock commands need the high entropy password that is provided to you once you create a wallet. The wallet's keys can be associated with an account to provide permission to the account's tokens, but it's not necessary for the creation of a wallet.

The wallet's software uses `cleos` as the intermediary layer between `keosd` key retrieval operations and the `nodeos` blockchain actions. For instance, you can use `cleos` to access an account as it requires signatures to be generated from the keys. To create the default wallet, just run the `create wallet` command. Use the `--to-console` flag to get the master key (password).

```
> cleos wallet create --to-console
Creating wallet: default
Save password to use in the future to unlock this wallet.
Without password imported keys will not be retrievable.
"[ DEFAULT_MASTER_KEY]"
```

Make sure you store the password. Now you can check that the wallet was created and run the `wallet list` command, and you will be able to see an array that lists the wallets and includes the default wallet you created.

```
> cleos wallet list
Wallets:
[
  "default *"
]
```

Notice that once you create your default wallet, there is an asterisk next to the wallet's name. The asterisk means that it's unlocked. You'll learn more about the lock and unlock states in the next section.

Delete and Back Up Wallets

To remove the wallet you created, you need to remove the actual wallet's file; it's located here: ~/eosio-wallet.

```
> rm -rf ~/eosio-wallet
```

Run the wallet list command, and you can see that the wallet array is empty.

```
> cleos wallet list
"/usr/local/eosio/bin/keosd" launched
Wallets:
[]
```

To back up the wallet, copy the wallet's files and store them in a safe location.

EOS.IO Wallet with Custom Name

So far, you created the default wallet. Now let's say you want to create another wallet and name it mywallet. All you have to do is utilize the -n or --name flag. Choose a name and be careful about the strict name restrictions (a–z and 1–5 are allowed only, with a length of 12). I am choosing mywallet.

```
> cleos wallet create -n mywallet --to-console
Creating wallet: mywallet
Save password to use in the future to unlock this wallet.
Without password imported keys will not be retrievable.
"[DEFAULT_MASTER_KEY]"
```

EOS.IO: Open, Lock, and Unlock a Wallet

When you created your wallet, you got a high entropy master key, which is your password. This password is used to encrypt (lock) and decrypt (unlock) your wallet file. To lock and unlock your wallet, use the following commands:

```
> cleos wallet lock -n mywallet
> cleos wallet unlock -n mywallet
password: [DEFAULT_MASTER_KEY]
password: Unlocked: mywallet
```

The lock and unlock commands enable your wallet to set a state of encryption and decryption that is protected by your password. What you are protecting are the wallet's keys.

To unlock the default wallet, just run the following:

```
> cleos wallet unlock
```

Also, to perform operations on your wallets, you need to first open the wallet. When keosd gets restarted, the wallet will be closed. Run the open command to open the wallet as needed.

```
> cleos wallet open
Opened: default
```

Generating EOS.IO Keys

Just as in other blockchains, EOS.IO stores keys in a wallet. You generate these keys and assign them to an EOS.IO account. There are multiple ways to create keys. You will be using cleos here. First let's re-create the default wallet, in case you deleted it previously.

```
> cleos wallet create --to-console
Creating wallet: default
```

Save password to use in the future to unlock this wallet.
Without password imported keys will not be retrievable.

```
"[DEFAULT_MASTER_KEY]"
```

Running wallet list should show you two wallets.

```
> cleos wallet list
Wallets:
[
  "default",
  "mywallet *"
]
```

Next, to create two public/private key pairs, run the create key command.

```
> cleos create key --to-console
Private key: [PRIVATE_KEY_1]
Public key: [PUBLIC_KEY_1]
> cleos create key --to-console
Private key: [PRIVATE_KEY_2]
Public key: [PUBLIC_KEY_2]
```

As you noticed, you ran the create key command twice. This is not a typo; you need to have two keys: one for the active user and one for the owner. You'll learn more about this concept once you create an account.

The command you ran output key pairs of public and private keys. Notice that the public key starts with the EOS keyword. These arbitrary key pairs are meaningless by themselves because they have no authority (they do not belong to any wallet or account). To assign these key pairs to a wallet, you can import these keys into your wallet.

```
> cleos wallet import --private-key [PRIVATE_KEY_1]
imported private key for:
[PRIVATE_KEY_1]
```

```
imported private key for: [key]
> cleos wallet import --private-key [PRIVATE_KEY_2]
imported private key for: [PRIVATE_KEY_2]
```

In the output of your command, you received a confirmation message from the command line that the key pairs were added. However, you can also confirm that the key pairs were added by calling the wallet keys command.

```
> cleos wallet keys
[PUBLIC_KEY_1, PUBLIC_KEY_2]
```

Additionally, you can request to view the key pairs.

```
> cleos wallet private_keys --password [DEFAULT_MASTER_KEY]
[[PUBLIC_KEY_1, PRIVATE_KEY_2],[ PUBLIC_KEY_1, PUBLIC_KEY_2]]
```

In the previous command, you passed the --password argument instead of waiting for the command line to ask that you enter your master password.

Lastly, you need to import a special EOS.IO parent account. This special parent account is used to bootstrap the EOS.IO nodes. Without this private key, you won't be able to create your account. EOS.IO accounts need a parent account to create another account; that's how EOS.IO allocates resources and protects against spam and hackers.

```
> cleos wallet import --private-key
  5KQwrPbwdL6PhXujxW37FSSQZ1JiwsST4cqQzDeyXtP79zkvFD3
imported private key for:
EOS6MRyAjQq8ud7hVNYcfnVPJqcVpscN5So8BhtHuGYqET5GDW5CV
```

Note   At the time of writing, the parent wallet works; however, this can change, and you may need to find a parent wallet that can be used to bootstrap the EOS.IO wallet.

Take a look at your output in case you would like to compare yours with mine; see Figure 6-3.

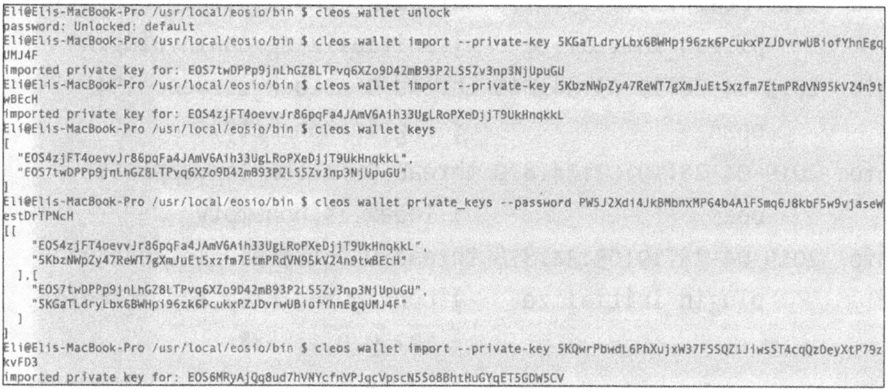

```
Eli@Elis-MacBook-Pro /usr/local/eosio/bin $ cleos wallet unlock
password: Unlocked: default
Eli@Elis-MacBook-Pro /usr/local/eosio/bin $ cleos wallet import --private-key 5KGaTLdryLbx6BWHpi96zk6PcukxPZJDvrwUBiofYhnEgq
UMJ4F
imported private key for: EOS7twDPPp9jnLhGZ8LTPvq6XZo9D42mB93P2LS5Zv3np3NjUpuGU
Eli@Elis-MacBook-Pro /usr/local/eosio/bin $ cleos wallet import --private-key 5KbzNWpZy47ReWT7gXmJuEt5xzfm7EtmPRdVN95kV24n9t
wBEcH
imported private key for: EOS4zjFT4oevvJr86pqFa4JAmV6Aih33UgLRoPXeDjjT9UkHnqkkL
Eli@Elis-MacBook-Pro /usr/local/eosio/bin $ cleos wallet keys
[
  "EOS4zjFT4oevvJr86pqFa4JAmV6Aih33UgLRoPXeDjjT9UkHnqkkL",
  "EOS7twDPPp9jnLhGZ8LTPvq6XZo9D42mB93P2LS5Zv3np3NjUpuGU"
]
Eli@Elis-MacBook-Pro /usr/local/eosio/bin $ cleos wallet private_keys --password PW5J2Xd14JkBMbnxMP64b4A1FSmq6J8kbF5w9vjaseW
estDrTPNcH
[[
    "EOS4zjFT4oevvJr86pqFa4JAmV6Aih33UgLRoPXeDjjT9UkHnqkkL",
    "5KbzNWpZy47ReWT7gXmJuEt5xzfm7EtmPRdVN95kV24n9twBEcH"
  ],[
    "EOS7twDPPp9jnLhGZ8LTPvq6XZo9D42mB93P2LS5Zv3np3NjUpuGU",
    "5KGaTLdryLbx6BWHpi96zk6PcukxPZJDvrwUBiofYhnEgqUMJ4F"
  ]
]
Eli@Elis-MacBook-Pro /usr/local/eosio/bin $ cleos wallet import --private-key 5KQwrPbWdL6PhXujxW37FSSQZ1JiwsST4cqQzDeyXtP79z
kvFD3
imported private key for: EOS6MRyAjQq8ud7hVNYcfnVPJqcVpscN5So8BhtHuGYqET5GDW5CV
```

Figure 6-3. *Setting up EOS.IO wallet keys with a special parent account*

Spin Up a node with nodeos

Transactions are attached to a block, and you need a block producer to be able to pass these transactions to the network.

You can skip creating an EOS node (nodeos) if you connect directly to a public testnet or the mainnet; however, it's better to first run your smart contracts on a local testnet network before committing your code to a public testnet or mainnet.

At this point, you should be used to this process as you did the same thing when you developed a smart contract for Ethereum. Feel free to revisit Figure 6-2, where you can see the diagram of nodeos and the EOS. IO blockchain relationship.

To start your own single-node local blockchain block producer, in a separate terminal, run nodeos.

```
> nodeos -e -p eosio --plugin eosio::chain_api_plugin --plugin
  eosio::history_api_plugin --contracts-console
```

This command starts the block producer and should display the process on the console.

```
info   2019-04-28T19:03:34.776 thread-0  chain_plugin.cpp:333
         plugin_initialize    ] initializing chain plugin
info   2019-04-28T19:03:34.811 thread-0  block_log.cpp:134
         open                 ] Log is nonempty
info   2019-04-28T19:03:34.820 thread-0  block_log.cpp:161
         open                 ] Index is nonempty
info   2019-04-28T19:03:34.878 thread-0  http_plugin.cpp:422
         plugin_initialize    ] configured http to listen on
                               127.0.0.1:8888
. . .
. . .
. . .
```

As you can see, the console shows that your local network starts producing blocks. Notice the command you used sets the plugins, and also you set the --contracts-console flag.

This flag is necessary to be able to see messages you print to the console while in development mode.

Note   You can also set the --contracts-console flag inside the config.ini file instead of passing this argument with nodeos every time.

As you recall, you previously were running the cleos get info command and getting no results, as you did not have a block producer running; now if you run the same command in a new Terminal, you can observe information about your blocks.

```
> cleos get info
{
  "server_version": "d4ffb4eb",
  "chain_id": "cf057bbfb72640471fd910bcb67639c22df9f92470936cd
             dc1ade0e2f2e7dc4f",
  "head_block_num": 73699,
  "last_irreversible_block_num": 73698,
  "last_irreversible_block_id": "00011fe2a80bf11315396c85e70860
122dddc24ac083911fba31f7ee2d64eb3e",
  "head_block_id": "00011fe36fab1fc2d4885067e1391c72782895d43f14
                 cf7970ac282ddef17d67",
  "head_block_time": "2019-04-28T19:04:06.500",
  "head_block_producer": "eosio",
  "virtual_block_cpu_limit": 200000000,
  "virtual_block_net_limit": 1048576000,
  "block_cpu_limit": 199900,
  "block_net_limit": 1048576,
  "server_version_string": "v1.5.1-dirty"
}
```

Re-spin Up a Testnet Local node (nodeos)

If you want to clear the block producer's history, delete all the blocks, and re-spin up your local testnet, you will use what is called a *hard replay* by using the following flags:

```
--delete-all-blocks --delete-state-history --hard-replay
```

These arguments will clear the accounts on the local testnet as well as the blocks. The complete command will look as follows:

```
> nodeos -e -p eosio --plugin eosio::chain_api_plugin --plugin
  eosio::history_api_plugin --delete-all-blocks --delete-state-
  history --hard-replay --contracts-console
```

EOS.IO Accounts

EOS.IO accounts hold a human-readable name that is stored on the EOS. IO blockchain.

To create an account on the mainnet, someone with an EOS.IO account needs to create it for you. The reasons behind this regulated process are spam and hacker prevention and resource allocation. By default, the account holds two native names/permissions.

- Owner: This is used to recover other permissions, which is useful in the event that the permission has been compromised.

- Active: This is used for high-level account changes such as transferring funds or voting for block producers.

When you created your testnet account, you imported a special EOS.IO parent account key to bootstrap. Each permission name needs a "parent." The parent authority is to be able to make changes to any of the permission settings for all of its children. EOS.IO provides a special account's parent key for the local testnet that you imported in order to create your account. See Figure 6-4.

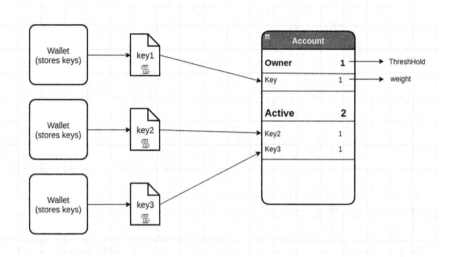

Figure 6-4. *Account high-level architecture and permission structure.*
Photo credit: hackernoon.com.

For a transaction to be valid and signed, each named permission needs
conditions to be met such as a client with an unlocked wallet, and the
wallet has to grant authority permission for the account. If you don't meet
these conditions, the transaction will fail.

Now that you understand accounts, you are ready to create your own
account. You already created a wallet and imported the parent key. To
create an account, you run the following command's syntax:

```
> cleos create account eosio [ACCOUNT_NAME] [OWNER_PUBLIC_KEY]
  [ACTIVE_PUBLIC_KEY]
```

The OWNER_KEY value is the public key of the account owner authority,
and the ACTIVE_KEY value is the public key of the account's active
authority.

In this example, let's call the account myaccount and use the two keys you created. The command will look like so (see Figure 6-5 for the expected output):

```
> cleos create account eosio myaccount [PUBLIC_KEY_1]
  [PUBLIC_KEY_2]
```

Figure 6-5. *Creating your first EOS.IO account called myaccount*

You generated two keys, so it doesn't matter which key you decide to use as your active and which one as an owner; just remember which key you used for which.

To see the list of the account, use this:

```
> cleos get accounts [PUBLIC_KEY_1]
{
  "account_names": [
    "myaccount"
  ]
}
```

Note   You may get an error message while trying to create the account if you missed any of the steps provided in this chapter. The error is "Error 3090003: provided keys, permissions, and delays do not satisfy declared authorizations."

Wallets, Keys, and Accounts: Complete Commands

To ensure you fully understand the process, here is a summary of how to create an account:

1. Ensure nodeos is running in a separate Terminal window.

   ```
   > nodeos -e -p eosio --plugin eosio::chain_api_plugin
   --plugin eosio::history_api_plugin --delete-all-blocks
   --delete-state-history --hard-replay --contracts-
   console
   ```

2. Ensure your wallet is unlocked. Run > cleos wallet list (check that there is an asterisk next to the wallet's name).

3. The EOS.IO special account's parent key (5KQwrPbwd L6PhXujxW37FSSQZ1JiwsST4cqQzDeyXtP79zkvFD3) was imported to bootstrap the EOS.IO.

   ```
   cleos wallet import --private-key 5KQwrPbwdL
   6PhXujxW37FSSQZ1JiwsST4cqQzDeyXtP79zkvFD3
   ```

4. Check the key's list using > cleos wallet keys. It should output an array with the keys you imported.

To summarize what you have done so far or to redo the entire process of creating an account, here are the complete steps:

```
> rm -rf ~/eosio-wallet
> cleos wallet create --to-console
> cleos wallet open
> cleos wallet unlock --password [DEFAULT_MASTER_KEY]
> cleos create key --to-console
> cleos create key --to-console
> cleos wallet import --private-key [PRIVATE_KEY_1]
```

```
> cleos wallet import --private-key [PRIVATE_KEY_2]
> cleos wallet import --private-key
  5KQwrPbwdL6PhXujxW37FSSQZ1JiwsST4cqQzDeyXtP79zkvFD3
> cleos wallet keys
> cleos create account eosio myaccount [EOS* OWNER_KEY] [EOS*
  ACTIVE_KEY]
```

Custom, Single Signature (Single-Sig), and Multisignature (Multisig)

By default, you configured your account with a single signature (aka single-sig) because it's authorized for actions with the default (active and owner) permissions. However, it's possible to configure your accounts with a multisignature (aka multisig) or with custom permissions. For instance, you can configure your account with multiple keys to authorize specific owner actions and active actions. You could use this feature, for instance, to create a permission called "publish" and give this permission to an account to allow only published smart contracts without the ability to withdraw tokens.

"HelloWorld" Smart Contract

You will be writing a smart contract with the minimal code. You will call your smart contract "HelloWorld."

"HelloWorld" Smart Contract Accounts

To get started, you will create two accounts for your smart contract, one to publish your smart contract and one for interacting with a user. See the output in Figure 6-6.

```
> cleos create account eosio helloworld [PUBLIC_KEY]
> cleos create account eosio john [PUBLIC_KEY]
```

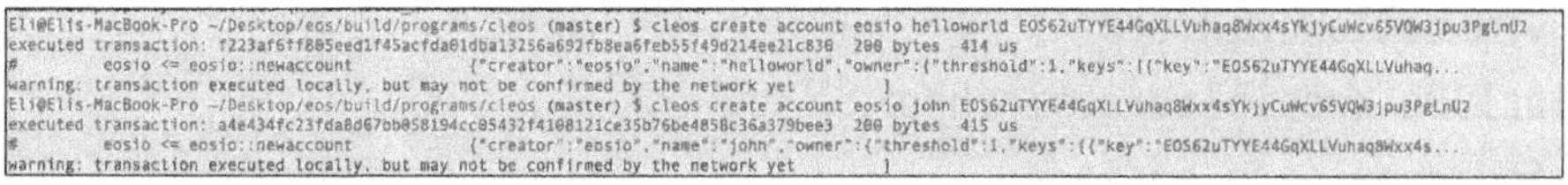

```
Eli@Elis-MacBook-Pro ~/Desktop/eos/build/programs/cleos (master) $ cleos create account eosio helloworld EOS62uTYYE44GqXLLVuhaq8Wxx4sYkjyCuWcv65VOW3jpu3PgLnU2
executed transaction: f223af6tf885eed1f45acfda81dba13256a692fb8ea6feb55f49d214ee21c838  200 bytes  414 us
#     eosio <= eosio::newaccount        {"creator":"eosio","name":"helloworld","owner":{"threshold":1,"keys":[{"key":"EOS62uTYYE44GqXLLVuhaq...
warning: transaction executed locally, but may not be confirmed by the network yet        ]
Eli@Elis-MacBook-Pro ~/Desktop/eos/build/programs/cleos (master) $ cleos create account eosio john EOS62uTYYE44GqXLLVuhaq8Wxx4sYkjyCuWcv65VQW3jpu3PgLnU2
executed transaction: a4e434fc23fda8d67bb058194cc85432f4108121ce35b76be4858c36a379bee3  200 bytes  415 us
#     eosio <= eosio::newaccount        {"creator":"eosio","name":"john","owner":{"threshold":1,"keys":[{"key":"EOS62uTYYE44GqXLLVuhaq8Wxx4s...
warning: transaction executed locally, but may not be confirmed by the network yet        ]
```

Figure 6-6. *Creating your accounts for the "HelloWorld" smart contract*

"HelloWorld" C++ Code

EOS selected C++, which resulted in mixed reviews from the blockchain development community. C++ is a low-level language, and it allows better management of resources such as memory pointers and operator overloading. This can result in better performance; however, it comes with a cost of increased code effort, especially if you are not familiar with C++.

The EOS.IO infrastructure is written in C++, so it should not be a surprise that C++ was selected by EOS.IO's team. EOS.IO smart contracts are written in C++ saved as the CPP file format; then you compile the C++ code to WebAssembly that is then used for deployment.

Note   EOS.IO smart contract source files can be broken into three: CPP, HPP, and Ricardian. The HPP file defines the smart contract class, actions, and tables. The CPP file is the C++ code, which implements the action logic. The Ricardian file is the digital document (more about this in the next section).

Start by creating the helloworld contract directory by navigating into the directory.

```
> mkdir ~/Desktop/helloworld && cd $_
```

Notice that you used your desktop but can use any directory you like. Next, paste the helloworld.cpp code with vim or your favorite text editor.

```
> vim helloworld.cpp
#include <eosiolib/eosio.hpp>
using namespace eosio;
class helloworld : public contract {
  public:
      using contract::contract;
      [[eosio::action]]
      void hello( name user ) {
         print( "World: User: ", user);
      }
};
EOSIO_DISPATCH(helloworld, (hello))
```

The code imports EOS.IO libraries. The class HelloWorld is of type contract, and you create a method called hello. The method is your action; you pass the user and print the word *world* and the username. Once a user interacts with your contract and calls the hello action, they will get world with the user's name.

Notice that in this example you included the eosio.hpp file. To debug the EOS.IO smart contract, you need to use old-fashioned caveman debugging.

Note   Caveman debugging, aka printf() debugging, is nothing more than adding print statements around your code. The EOS.IO Print API supports the char array, 64-bit and 128-bit unsigned integer, and others. The print is done by wrapping the C++ code printi, prints_l, printi128, and others in print.hpp, which includes the import eosio.hpp library statement.

Smart Contract IDE

Using Terminal is perfectly acceptable, but as the code becomes more complex, using a professional IDE can be helpful for code completion, highlights, and readability. You can use the IDE of your liking. As you already used WebStorm, you can continue and import the project to WebStorm. WebStorm already includes a C++ plugin, so there's no need to install any special plugin. Figure 6-7 shows HelloWorld project open in WebStorm.

To import your project, select File ➤ Open and navigate to the project's location: ~/Desktop/helloworld.

Figure 6-7. *HelloWorld project imported into WebStorm version 2018.2.4*

Compile a Contract and Generate an ABI

As mentioned, the eosio-cpp tool takes C++ code and outputs WebAssembly and ABI. This is done by running the following command:

```
> eosio-cpp -o helloworld.wasm helloworld.cpp --abigen
```

Notice that in the command you specify the output file's name, which is helloworld.wasm. After running this command, the compiler generates the following files: helloworld.wasm and helloworld.abi.

To ensure the compiler worked as expected, you should be able to see these two files; see Figure 6-7.

Ricardian Contracts

Once you generate your WASM and ABI files, notice that you are getting more than 20 warnings. Among these warnings, you should find the following warnings in the output:

```
Warning, empty ricardian clause file
Warning, empty ricardian clause file
Warning, action <hello> does not have a ricardian contract
```

Note   Ricardian contracts were invented by Ian Grigg in 1996 to help bridge the gap between software application and court of law. The Ricardian contracts file in EOS is a digital document in Markdown Language format (.md, .markdown) and defines the terms and conditions of the interaction between the parties. It is set as parameters but written as readable text. EOS uses cryptographically to sign and verify the Ricardian contracts.

To help generate the Ricardian contracts, you can copy a Python script and template from a contributor that generates the files automatically: https://github.com/EOS-Mainnet/governance.

As it's just three files, instead of using clone, you can use wget to download these files.

Check that you have wget installed on your machine.

```
> wget --help
```

In case it's not installed, install wget on macOS via Ruby and Brew.

```
> ruby -e "$(curl -fsSL https://raw.githubusercontent.com/
  Homebrew/install/master/install)" < /dev/null 2> /dev/null
> brew install wget
> brew upgrade wget
```

Next, inside your helloworld project, create the directory and download the files you need.

```
> cd ~/desktop/helloworld
> mkdir rc && cd $_
> wget https://raw.githubusercontent.com/EOS-Mainnet/
  governance/master/scripts/abi_to_rc/abi_to_rc.py
> wget https://raw.githubusercontent.com/EOS-Mainnet/
  governance/master/scripts/abi_to_rc/rc-action-template.md
> wget https://raw.githubusercontent.com/EOS-Mainnet/
  governance/master/scripts/abi_to_rc/rc-overview-template.md
```

Next, run the Python script.

```
> cd ../
> python rc/abi_to_rc.py helloworld.abi
```

The script generates for you automatically `helloworld-rc.md` and `helloworld-hello-rc.md` already formatted in the Markdown language. If you view these files, you will notice that the Python script used the templates you downloaded to generate your files, and you can fill in the terms and conditions about your smart contract.

You can lay out the guidelines of what exactly your users are purchasing/exchanging and allow better trust between parties; it can include terms and conditions such as intent, warranty, remedies, force majeure, dispute resolution, governing law, and many others. Pay close attention to the terms you set as these can be enforced in a court of law. These terms allow skipping middlemen such as attorneys to have the smart contract set the terms and conditions that both parties agree to.

Deploy a Contract

To deploy your smart contract to your local testnet network, the `set contract` command is used to upload the contract. See Figure 6-8 for the expected output.

```
> cleos set contract helloworld ~/Desktop/helloworld -p
  helloworld@active
```

Figure 6-8. *Terminal output of deploying your smart contract*

Interact with a Smart Contract Action

Now that you have your smart contract deployed on your local blockchain, you can interact with the hello action you created. You will call the hello action and pass your username to the user's active key. See the output in Figure 6-9.

```
> cleos push action helloworld hello '["john"]' -p john@active
```

```
Eli@Elis-MacBook-Pro ~/Desktop/eos/build/programs/cleos (master) $ cleos push action helloworld hello '["john"]' -p john@active
executed transaction: 1fdae85b5ac6e9d840dd51f239d540f32442b82b04442fc9c6fefd1bc24667e9  104 bytes  1037 us
#    helloworld <= helloworld::hello          {"user":"john"}
>> World: User: john
```

Figure 6-9. *Terminal output of push action on a smart contract*

You can download the entire smart contract project from here: https://github.com/Apress/the-blockchain-developer/chapter6/helloworld/.

Smart Contact Tokens

The EOS.IO GitHub project has a library of smart contracts as examples that can be used. One of these libraries is a smart contract called eosio.token. This contract enables developers to create other tokens as well as transfer a token. You will be using these libraries to create your own tokens. To get started, you will create a new smart contract project and call it eosio.token.

```
> mkdir ~/Desktop/eosio.token && cd $_
```

Create Accounts

Token gets issued by an "issuer" account. You will start off by creating the "issuer" account and an account called jane that you can use to transfer some tokens.

```
> cleos create account eosio eosio.token [public key]
> cleos create account eosio jane [public key]
```

Compile wasm with the Latest eosio.token Code

To issue eosio.token, you will be using the eosio.token.hpp file that defines the contract's class, actions, and tables, as well as eosio.token. cpp that holds the logic and coding. You can find these files and the entire SmartContract project here: https://github.com/Apress/the-blockchain-developer/chapter6/eosio.token/.

Next, ensure you change the include statement in the CPP code to point to the HPP file you downloaded from GitHub using vim or your favorite text editor.

```
> vim eosio.token.cpp
```

Change the eosio.token.cpp file on line 6 to point to the location of eosio.token.hpp file; in this case, it's here:

```
include "~/Desktop/eosio.token/eosio.token.hpp"
```

Deploy eosio.token

Equipped with eosio.token.hpp and eosio.token.cpp, you have all the files needed. You can compile the latest HPP and CPP files to generate the .wasm code with the eosio-cpp command, just as you did in the HelloWorld smart contract example.

```
> eosio-cpp -o eosio.token.wasm eosio.token.cpp --abigen
```

Next, deploy the eosio.token contract using the set contract command.

```
> cleos wallet unlock --password [DEFAULT_MASTER_KEY]
> cleos set contract eosio.token ~/Desktop/eosio.token --abi
  eosio.token.abi -p eosio.token@active
```

Create the EOS.IO Token

To create your new token, you utilize the create action. You will be passing the symbol_name type, which includes two parameters.

- *Maximum supply float*: In this example, you'll set this to 20 million as your max tokens: 20000000.0000.

- *Symbol*: For symbol_name, you need to pick a name. The name must be capital alpha characters only; in this example, select the name TOKEN.

The "issuer" account has the authority to make a call issue action or any other actions such as recalling, freezing, and whitelisting owners.

To create a new token action, run the following command. See Figure 6-10 for the expected output.

```
> cleos wallet unlock --password [DEFAULT_MASTER_KEY]
> cleos push action eosio.token create '[ "eosio",
  "20000000.0000 TOKEN"]' -p eosio.token@active
```

```
Eli@Elis-MacBook-Pro ~/Desktop/eos/build/programs/cleos (master) $ cleos wallet unlock --password PW5JRVgAgM6pTWcWMwpKu5yvQ5
AHmnWaQ36WPg6DUEstfbTRSf7bA
Unlocked: default
Eli@Elis-MacBook-Pro ~/Desktop/eos/build/programs/cleos (master) $ cleos push action eosio.token create '[ "eosio", "2000000
0.0000 TOKEN"]' -p eosio.token@active
executed transaction: 2eeeb4935a40753d9cf1d121bb74b8e5da82006f8d8bd04a199e955b95b5d747   120 bytes   515 us
#   eosio.token <= eosio.token::create          {"issuer":"eosio","maximum_supply":"20000000.0000 TOKEN"}
warning: transaction executed locally, but may not be confirmed by the network yet          ]
```

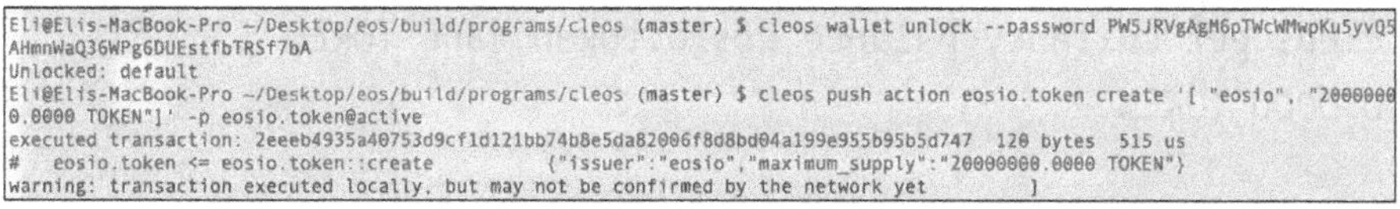

Figure 6-10. *Expected output for creating an eosio.token action*

You can confirm the tokens were issued by calling the currency stats command.

```
> cleos get currency stats eosio.token TOKEN
{
  "TOKEN": {
    "supply": "0.0000 TOKEN",
```

```
    "max_supply": "20000000.0000 TOKEN",
    "issuer": "eosio"
  }
}
```

Issue Tokens

Let's create another account that you can use to send some of the tokens you issued. We'll call this account jane.

```
> cleos create account eosio jane [public key]
```

Next, call the "issue" action to issue tokens. In this example, you will issue jane 500 tokens.

```
> cleos push action eosio.token issue '[ "jane", "500.0000
  TOKEN", "move tokens to Jane" ]' -p eosio@active
```

To see the TOKEN balance in the jane account, you can use the get currency command.

```
> cleos get currency balance eosio.token jane TOKEN
500.0000 TOKEN
```

Transfer Tokens

To transfer tokens, you run the transfer action. As an example, let's transfer tokens from Jane's account to John's account.

```
> cleos push action eosio.token transfer '[ "jane", "john",
  "100.0000 TOKEN", "transfer tokens" ]' -p jane@active
```

You can confirm John's account received the tokens by running the currency balance command on both accounts to ensure the math adds up.

```
> cleos get currency balance eosio.token jane TOKEN
  400.0000 TOKEN
> cleos get currency balance eosio.token john TOKEN
  100.0000 TOKEN
```

Figure 6-11 shows the expected output.

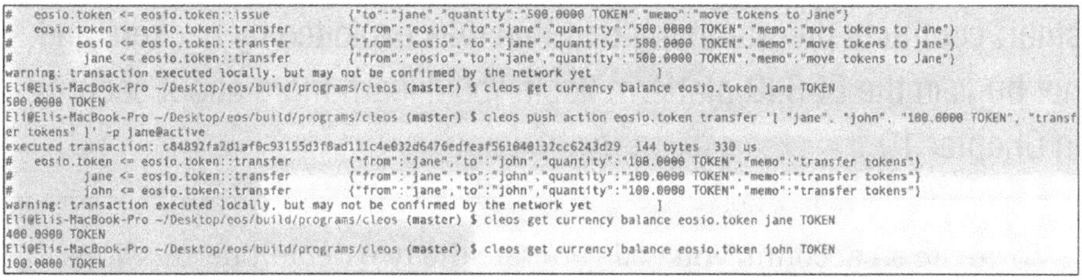

Figure 6-11. *Expected output for creating, transferring, and balancing eosio.token actions*

Connecting to a Public Testnet Block Producer

At the time of writing, EOS.IO provides two public testnets so you can test in a more realistic environment before committing your code to mainnet.

- *Jungle2.0*: https://jungletestnet.io/

- *Kylin*: https://www.cryptokylin.io/

I chose Jungle2.0 for the public testnet in this example, but feel free to test both; it's the same process just with different endpoints.

To get started, visit the Jungle project's GitHub page here: https://github.com/CryptoLions/EOS-Jungle-Testnet.

The EOS Jungle testnet is almost identical to your local testnet. You just need to set up the Jungle API endpoint and generate EOS faucet tokens to pay for the account's creation and RAM usage.

The testnet API endpoint is `https://jungle.eosio.cr:443`; just add the endpoint so your previous commands will work.

Note   Always test on testnet before publishing your code to mainnet. In September 2018 alone, $240,000 worth of EOS tokens were stolen from EOSBet's smart contract accounts, and it was because of a smart contracts programming bug that was exploited by hackers and not bugs in the EOS.IO platform itself. You'll learn more about security in Chapter 10.

To create an account, you will generate the two default permissions: owner and active. You can do this at `https://nadejde.github.io/eos-token-sale/` or by running the same command line you used before twice.

```
> cleos create key --to-console
Private key: [key]
Public key: [key]
```

Next, you need to create an account. You can create an account by visiting the Jungle page and using the public keys you generated: `https://monitor.jungletestnet.io/#account`.

I picked a random name of `liontestaa11`, but feel free to use any name you want. Just be careful of the strict name restrictions (a–z and 1–5 are allowed only, with a length of 12). If you don't comply with this strict name restriction, your account won't get created. See Figure 6-12.

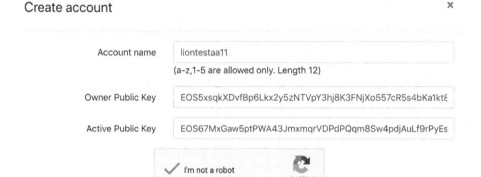

Figure 6-12. *Jungle2.0's liontestaa11 account was created*

Notice that you get the same warning as you got on your local testnet regarding the transaction being executed, but it's not confirmed.

To get information about the testnet, you can run the same get info command you ran for your local testnet. Just add the Jungle endpoint URL argument.

```
> cleos --url https://jungle.eosio.cr:443 get info
```

All the cleos commands need the URL endpoint argument; you can edit your bash file to point cleos to the URL you want. Edit the bash profile and point to the public testnet for the block producer, while still pointing to your local machine for the wallet.

```
> vim ~/.bash_profile
```

Add the following line:

```
alias cleos-testnet='cleos --url https://jungle.eosio.cr:443
--wallet-url http://localhost:8888'
```

You did not set the `config.ini` file here with a custom port, but you are changing the port to 8888. Remember, to run the bash profile to commit the changes, run this:

```
> . ~/.bash_profile
```

Now you can run the all the commands with `cleos-testnet`.

```
> cleos-testnet get info
```

Buy Resource Allocation on the Public Testnet Block Producer

Now you will be publishing your "HelloWorld" smart contract you created in the previous section.

If you were publishing your contract on mainnet, you would need to buy RAM and pay to create your account so you could publish your smart contract. EOS tokens are used to purchase resources. In the public testnet, you don't need to spend actual money for your resources. You get fake faucet tokens that can be used for the Jungle block producer to purchase your resources.

To get these tokens, all you need is your account name. Type your account name to get tokens from the Jungle faucet: `http://monitor.jungletestnet.io/#faucet`. See Figure 6-13.

I'll explain resource allocation in more detail in the next section when you ready to publish to mainnet.

Jungle Faucet   ✕

Account name   liontestaa11

✓ I'm not a robot

reCAPTCHA
Privacy · Terms

Send Coins

executed transaction: ccb5768eead43c0e4ebe8077834e6b6e1065b7b29a1de164b221b253284b11ad
144 bytes 519 us warn 2018-12-27T10:42:26.380 thread-0 main.cpp:482 print_result] warning:
transaction executed locally, but may not be confirmed by the network yet executed transaction:
f30ef94477531e3ecf95c949a3a2f1b304a22174884bae4d441cb5da12e1da21 144 bytes 514 us warn
2018-12-27T10:42:26.920 thread-0 main.cpp:482 print_result] warning: transaction executed locally, but
may not be confirmed by the network yet

eosio.token <= eosio.token::transfer {"from":"junglefaucet","to":"liontestaa11","quantity":"100.0000
EOS","memo":"Jungle Faucet"} # junglefaucet <= eosio.token::transfer
{"from":"junglefaucet","to":"liontestaa11","quantity":"100.0000 EOS","memo":"Jungle Faucet"} #
liontestaa11 <= eosio.token::transfer {"from":"junglefaucet","to":"liontestaa11","quantity":"100.0000

Figure 6-13. *Jungle2.0 gets tokens through the Jungle faucet*

You can check the account balance with the get account command;
see the output in Figure 6-14.

```
> cleos --url https://jungle.eosio.cr:443 get account liontestaa11
```

```
Eli@Elis-MacBook-Pro ~/Desktop/eosio.token $ cleos --url https://jungle.eosio.cr:443 get account liontestaa11
created: 2018-12-27T10:25:10.500
permissions:
     owner     1:    1 EOS5xsqkXDvf8p6Lkx2y5zNTVpY3hj8K3FNjXo557cR5s4bKalkt8
        active 1:    1 EOS67MxGaw5ptPWA43JmxmqrVDPdPQqm8Sw4pdjAuLf9rPyEsUH3U
memory:
     quota:    558.7 KiB    used:      25.62 KiB

net bandwidth:
     staked:           1.0000 EOS         (total stake delegated from account to self)
     delegated:        0.0000 EOS         (total staked delegated to account from others)
     used:             1.547 KiB
     available:        131.3 KiB
     limit:            132.9 KiB

cpu bandwidth:
     staked:           1.0000 EOS         (total stake delegated from account to self)
     delegated:        0.0000 EOS         (total staked delegated to account from others)
     used:             3.055 ms
     available:        45.26 ms
     limit:            48.32 ms

EOS balances:
     liquid:           90.0000 EOS
     staked:            2.0000 EOS
     unstaking:         0.0000 EOS
     total:            92.0000 EOS

producers:     <not voted>
```

Figure 6-14. *Jungle faucet account balance*

Now that you have EOS tokens, you can run the cleos system buyram command to purchase RAM so you can publish your smart contract.

```
> cleos --url https://jungle.eosio.cr:443 system buyram
  liontestaa11 liontestaa11 "10 EOS"
```

Publish Your HelloWorld Contract on the Public Testnet

Now that you have tokens, you can publish your HelloWorld smart contract on the public testnet. Run the set contract command.

```
> cleos --url https://jungle.eosio.cr:443 set contract
  liontestaa11 ~/Desktop/helloworld
```

You can confirm the code was published using the get code command. You can see the entire expected output in Figure 6-15.

```
> cleos --url https://jungle.eosio.cr:443 get code liontestaa11
```

```
Eli@Elis-MacBook-Pro ~/Desktop/eos/contracts/eosio.token (master) $ cleos --url https://jungle.eosio.cr:443 system buyra
m liontestaa11 liontestaa11 "10 EOS"
executed transaction: 32163b0ffa717c657790a0b224fa17ca4e082b569d24f06ec096dddc2e3de3b3  128 bytes  1454 us
#         eosio <= eosio::buyram                    {"payer":"liontestaa11","receiver":"liontestaa11","quant":"10.0000 EOS"}
#   eosio.token <= eosio.token::transfer           {"from":"liontestaa11","to":"eosio.ram","quantity":"9.9500 EOS","memo":"
buy ram"}
#   liontestaa11 <= eosio.token::transfer          {"from":"liontestaa11","to":"eosio.ram","quantity":"9.9500 EOS","memo":"
buy ram"}
#     eosio.ram <= eosio.token::transfer           {"from":"liontestaa11","to":"eosio.ram","quantity":"9.9500 EOS","memo":"
buy ram"}
#   eosio.token <= eosio.token::transfer           {"from":"liontestaa11","to":"eosio.ramfee","quantity":"0.0500 EOS","memo
":"ram fee"}
#   liontestaa11 <= eosio.token::transfer          {"from":"liontestaa11","to":"eosio.ramfee","quantity":"0.0500 EOS","memo
":"ram fee"}
#   eosio.ramfee <= eosio.token::transfer          {"from":"liontestaa11","to":"eosio.ramfee","quantity":"0.0500 EOS","memo
":"ram fee"}
#   eosio.token <= eosio.token::transfer           {"from":"eosio.ramfee","to":"eosio.rex","quantity":"0.0500 EOS","memo":"
transfer from eosio.ramfee t...
#   eosio.ramfee <= eosio.token::transfer          {"from":"eosio.ramfee","to":"eosio.rex","quantity":"0.0500 EOS","memo":"
transfer from eosio.ramfee t...
#     eosio.rex <= eosio.token::transfer           {"from":"eosio.ramfee","to":"eosio.rex","quantity":"0.0500 EOS","memo":"
transfer from eosio.ramfee t...
warning: transaction executed locally, but may not be confirmed by the network yet              ]
Eli@Elis-MacBook-Pro ~/Desktop/eos/contracts/eosio.token (master) $ cleos --url https://jungle.eosio.cr:443 set contract
 liontestaa11 ~/Desktop/eos/contracts/helloworld
Reading WASM from /Users/Eli/Desktop/eos/contracts/helloworld/helloworld.wasm...
Publishing contract...
executed transaction: 3cc5da4295624d95abac48812a95eceb8b1fd71a1550c508352c200af6082497  1456 bytes  745 us
#         eosio <= eosio::setcode                  {"account":"liontestaa11","vmtype":0,"vmversion":0,"code":"0061736d01000
00001390b60027f7e086000017f6...
#         eosio <= eosio::setabi                   {"account":"liontestaa11","abi":"0e656f73696f3a3a6162692f312e31000105686
56c6c6f00010475735736572046e616...
warning: transaction executed locally, but may not be confirmed by the network yet              ]
Eli@Elis-MacBook-Pro ~/Desktop/eos/contracts/eosio.token (master) $ cleos --url https://jungle.eosio.cr:443 get code lio
ntestaa11
code hash: 6d12cb789ab1c916f1809e731b10a4c49c25064b764c9bd89c339af973339c04
```

Figure 6-15. *Expected output when publishing contract on public testnet*

Connecting to Mainnet

The EOS.IO mainnet is almost the same as the testnet; you just need to use a different API endpoint and actually pay for the accounts and RAM with real EOS tokens.

There are three main ways to get EOS tokens:

- *Mine*: This creates a block producer and mines EOS.

- *Purchase EOS tokens*: They can be purchased on crypto exchanges.

- *Gift*: This gets an EOS as a gift from someone.

As you saw in previous chapters, creating a block producer and getting selected by the EOS.IO network is not an easy process or guaranteed, and as you just need coins to buy RAM for opening an account and getting resources, you don't need too many coins. At this point, it's easy to just purchase these tokens.

You would need to first purchase bitcoin, Ethereum, or other coins on a fiat exchange such as Coinbase, CEX.io, or Coinmama. Then use exchanges such as Binance or Changelly to change your coins to EOS tokens. The reason is that there is no known exchange available at the time of writing that can directly change your fiat to EOS.

Next, you need an endpoint. The 21 selected block producers are able to provide you with an endpoint. You can find all the available block producers and other data regarding the blocks being mined here:

- `http://eosnetworkmonitor.io/`

- `https://eostracker.io/producers`

Once you find a block producer you would like to use, you append `/bp.json` to the end of the URL to find the endpoint. Here's an example: `https://api.eosnewyork.io/bp.json`.

The JASON output gives you the block producer's information and ensures it's ready for usage. To set the URL, just adjust the `--url` flag to the block producer you would like to connect to; the rest of the commands are all the same as the public testnet.

```
> cleos --url https://api.eosnewyork.io:443 get info
```

As before, you can edit the bash profile file as you did with the public testnet.

```
alias cleos-mainnet='cleos --url https://api.eosnewyork.io:443
--wallet-url http://localhost:8888'
```

Your bash profile should look like this:

```
PATH="/usr/local/eosio/bin:${PATH}"
alias cleos-testnet='cleos --url https://jungle.eosio.cr:443
--wallet-url http://localhost:8888'
alias cleos-mainnet='cleos --url https://api.eosnewyork.io:443
--wallet-url http://localhost:8888'
```

Confirm it works by running the get info command.

```
> cleos-mainnet get info
```

I'll spare you from repeating the same steps as in the public testnet section and spending actual tokens on the "HelloWorld" sample smart contract. However, I will cover resource allocation, as you need a good understanding of it to publish smart contracts on mainnet.

Resource Allocation Explained

I spoke a bit about resource allocation when I covered testnets, as you needed to get EOS tokens to publish your smart contract on a public testnet.

For mainnet, you need actual EOS tokens to buy RAM and create your account. There are three types of resources consumed by EOS.IO accounts.

- *Disk*: Bandwidth and log storage (disk)

- *CPU*: Staking computation and computational backlog (CPU)

- *Ram*: Staking state storage

Buy RAM on Mainnet

To free up RAM, you need to delete data from the account state mechanism, and then the RAM can be sold on the RAM marketplace at the current RAM price. The RAM marketplace price can be found here: https://www.feexplorer.io/EOS_RAM_price.

Create an EOS.IO Account on Mainnet

EOS.IO accounts are necessary, as they are needed to interact with the EOS.IO network and create an account. As I explained previously, someone who already has an account needs to vouch for creating new accounts. If you don't have someone with an EOS account who can create your account, you can get an account created with third-party providers. The third-party providers normally charge you a fee. For instance, you can download EOS Lynx on your phone and pay $2 to create an EOS.IO account.

Change Your Account's Public and Private Keys

Once you get a mainnet account, you are not done. You need to make sure you change your private key before funding your account, as the service that creates your account could just store your private keys and take your funds. You are already familiar with all these steps; the only new command here is remove_key, which removes the old key from your wallet. You create a new key, unlock your wallet, reset the permissions with the new key, and remove the old public key as well as import the new private key. Follow these steps:

```
> cleos create key
> cleos wallet unlock
> cleos set account permission [ACCOUNT NAME] active [PUBLIC
  KEY] owner -p [ACCOUNT NAME]@owner
> cleos set account permission MYACCOUNT owner [PUBLIC KEY] -p
  [ACCOUNT NAME]@owner
> cleos wallet remove_key [OLD PUBLIC KEY]
> cleos wallet import [PRIVATE KEY]
```

CPU and Bandwidth Allocations

To get bandwidth and CPU, you need to allocate EOS tokens, and the resource will be available automatically for you proportional to the amount held in the staking contract period.

For instance, during the staking window, say you would like to consume 1 CPU unit. To do so, you would need to compete with other accounts so you have 0.1 percent of all CPU-staked tokens under your account or have someone else delegate these tokens to your account.

After the staking period, the consumed resources free up, and you can reuse the same staked tokens, so there's no need to keep purchasing more EOS tokens each time. The EOS tokens can be undelegated after you are done.

Where to Go from Here

EOS.IO offers an online resource with links; see `https://developers.eos.io`. The developer resource provides valuable documentation as well as information about other tools I did not cover such as these:

- *State handler*: `demux-js`

- *JavaScript library:* `eosjs`

I also recommend exploring the EOS GitHub smart contracts examples, which can help you learn about all the functionally and what's possible with EOS.IO.

Summary

In this chapter, I covered the EOS.IO blockchain in more detail. You set up a local testnet environment by installing the EOS.IO and EOSIO.CDT libraries and learned how to configure `keosd` and `nodeos`. You learned about EOS.IO wallets, including how to create, delete, and back up wallets as well as how to create a wallet with custom names and perform operations such as opening, locking, and unlocking a wallet.

Next, I covered a wallet's key pairs and how to spin and re-spin up a local node (nodeos) to run a local block producer. You learned about active and owner permissions as well as single-signature (single-sig) and multisignature (multisig) are accounts.

To understand EOS.IO smart contracts, you created a "HelloWorld" smart contract and tokens by first creating accounts and then writing C++ code. You then compiled and generated WebAssembly and ABI files as well as Ricardian contracts. You then learned how to deploy the contracts you created and interact with them. Once your tokens were generated, you were able to issue and transfer tokens between accounts.

You continued by connecting to a public testnet block producer to test your smart contracts in a more realistic environment, and lastly you learned how to connect and publish on mainnet and learned about resource allocations on an EOS.IO network.

In the next chapter, I will cover NEO blockchain wallets and NEO smart contracts.

CHAPTER 7

NEO Blockchain and Smart Contracts

In Chapter 1, I covered the NEO proof of stake (PoS) blockchain consensus mechanism. In Chapter 2, you created a NEO bookkeeping node on AWS Ubuntu and learned how to request a consensus authority certificate and get elected as a bookkeeper.

In this chapter, I will expand on the NEO blockchain, and you will learn how to set up a local environment, do operations in NEO wallets, create smart contracts (NeoContracts), and publish. In this chapter, I will cover NEO's blockchain high-level architecture and how to set up your local environment, create a local testnet chain, create "Hello, World" projects in both C# and Python, publish these smart contracts, and learn the criteria to compare Ethereum versus EOS versus NEO.

As you can see, understanding smart contracts, blockchain, and the process of publishing is similar between projects, and covering three projects is sufficient to gain an understanding of how to work with the rest of the 40 (at the time of writing) projects available for writing smart contracts that are out there.

© Elad Elrom 2019
E. Elrom, *The Blockchain Developer*, https://doi.org/10.1007/978-1-4842-4847-8_7

257

NEO's High-Level Blockchain Architecture

NEO was founded in 2014 with the name of AntShares by Da Hongfei and Erik Zhang and then was open sourced on GitHub in June 2015 with the name of NEO. The NEO consensus mechanism is called Byzantine Fault Tolerant (dBFT), which is a modified PoS. This type of mechanism makes NEO a scalable blockchain. Bookkeeping nodes are randomly selected to validate transactions and can support up to 10,000 transactions per second.

> *"NEO is a non-profit community-driven blockchain project. It utilizes blockchain technology and digital identity to digitize assets and automate the management of digital assets using smart contracts. Using a distributed network, it aims to create a 'Smart Economy.'"*
>
> —Neo.org

NEO transactions are charges with NEO gas tokens. The NEO genesis block includes 100 million NEO. Half were sold to early investors, and half were locked in NEO smart contract tokens. Each year 15 million NEO tokens are unlocked to be used for the NEO development team to fund development goals. NEO charges fees for transactions as well as a smart contract's related transactions. The NEO fee structure related to smart contracts is listed in the NEO white paper: `http://docs.neo.org/en-us/sc/systemfees.html`.

In term of programming languages, NEO smart contracts support the NeoVM (NEO's Universal Lightweight Virtual Machine) compiler, Microsoft.net, Java, Kotlin, Go, and Python.

Here are some notable NEO development features:

- NEO can create smart contract tokens built with the Communications Standard (NEP5). These tokens are able to communicate with other NEO tokens.

- Smart contracts can communicate with other blockchains (this feature is called NeoX).

- NEO can pass information via a file sharing protocol (called NeoFS).

- It uses a lattice-based cryptographic mechanism called quantum-safe (NeoQS).

NEO's "smart economy" infrastructure (I will explain this concept in the next section) enables smart contracts to support front-end applications and integrate with other smart contracts and other blockchains through an open API.

NEO's open API allows you to integrate data from external sources. Figure 7-1 shows a high-level architecture diagram of the NeoVM. The NeoVM core is the deployment box (the dashed box). As you can see, the external data with the execution engine (green box) enables smart contracts to interact and perform operations. Then data can be stored on the NEO distributed ledger.

> *"We hope the platform can be used for different front end scenarios, such as the Digital asset wallet, Forum, Voting, Profile management and Mobile applications. The platform also features an open API that can be used for integration with other systems."*

> —Da Hongfei, Zhao Chen founder of NEO

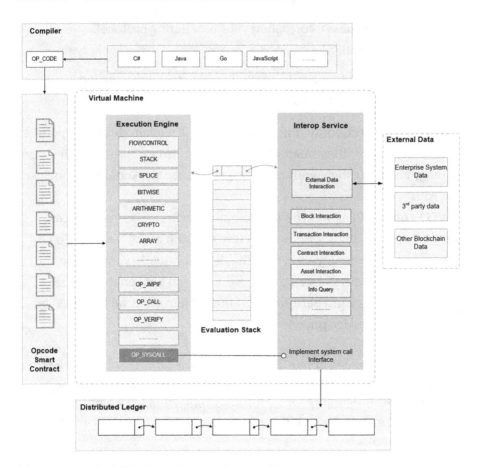

Figure 7-1. *NEO's virtual machine architecture diagram. Image credit: docs.neo.org.*

What Is NEO's Smart Economy?

NEO coined the term *smart economy*, which explains NEO's vision. This vision consists of changing your existing market from a traditional economy to the smart economy with the power of a decentralized blockchain. To achieve this goal, NEO integrates digital assets, digital identities, and smart contracts into its platform.

Note   NEO's smart economy vision is aimed to change the way existing markets work, from a traditional economy to a "smart economy," with the power of a decentralized blockchain. This is achieved by integrating digital assets, digital identities, and smart contracts.

NEO's smart economy concept consists of integrating the following three components:

- *NEO digital assets*: These assets contain electronic data and can be programmed. Placing the digital assets on a blockchain provides the benefit of PoS blockchains, such as decentralization, trust, traceability, and transparency. The NEO blockchain enables users to register, trade, and transfer different types of assets. Physical assets get digitization through digital identity; then these digital assets can be protected by law through validation. For an ICO, it costs 5,000 gas to register a digital asset. Then there is a renewal fee of 5,000 gas per year.

- *NEO digital identity*: This is the digitization of the identity of individuals, organizations, or any other entities. A NEO digital identity is based on the public key infrastructure (PKI) X.509 standard implementation that also supports web of trust point-to-point certificates.

- *NEO smart contract*: Smart contracts on NEO are called NeoContracts, and they support the C#, VB.NET, F#, Java, Kotlin, and Python languages. Supporting these languages gives the benefits of having sophisticated development, debugging, and compilation in the Visual Studio, Eclipse, and WebStorm IDEs. NeoVM is built for scalability.

261

Setting Up Your Local Environment

As mentioned, NEO supports enterprise-level programming languages such as C#, VB.NET, F# Java, Kotlin, and Python. This selection of programming languages gives NEO an advantage in building NeoContracts because you can utilize the Visual Studio 2017 IDE, which offers enterprise tools for development. In this chapter, I will be using the following .NET tools:

- *Visual Studio 2017 IDE*: To follow along, install the Visual Studio (VS) Community Edition for Mac.

- *.NET Core*: To follow along, install .NET Core to be able to publish DLL library files.

In addition to .NET, you need the following tools:

- *Xcode 10.1*: You need Xcode 10.2 for the tools and libraries you will be installing.

- *Docker*: Docker is a popular tool for creating containers and integrating software. You will be using Docker for your private net to run a whole NEO blockchain to simulate four consensus nodes in a single, lightweight Docker container.

- *neo-compiler*: The NEO compiler is needed to turn your code to an `.avm` file that can be deployed on the NEO blockchain.

- *neo-cli*: You will install and use the NEO command-line tools for wallets, operations, and RPC calls to the NEO API.

Now that you know what needed, let's get started.

Xcode 10.2

At the time of writing, you need Xcode with at least version 10.1 for the tools and libraries needed for NEO. The latest Xcode at the time of writing is Xcode 10.2.1.

You can check whether you already have Xcode installed via the command line.

```
> xcodebuild --version
Xcode 10.1
Build version 10B61
```

This command will output the version if Xcode is installed. If you need to upgrade or install, visit the Apple developer portal: https://developer. apple.com/download/.

Install Visual Studio 2017 IDE

Next, download and install the latest version of Visual Studio (VS) Community Edition for Mac. The community edition is free and can be downloaded from the following URL: https://visualstudio.microsoft. com/vs/community/.

For future reference, to uninstall a portion or all of VS, follow the instructions here: https://docs.microsoft.com/en-us/visualstudio/ mac/uninstall#net-core-script.

The complete VS 2017 consumes a lot of disk space; however, you don't need all the packages downloaded. You need only Xamarin Workbooks in order to develop NeoContracts, so only download what's needed.

During the installation process, the wizard gives you an option of what platforms and tools to install. Select Xamarin Workbooks by clicking the checkbox and click the Install button. See Figure 7-2.

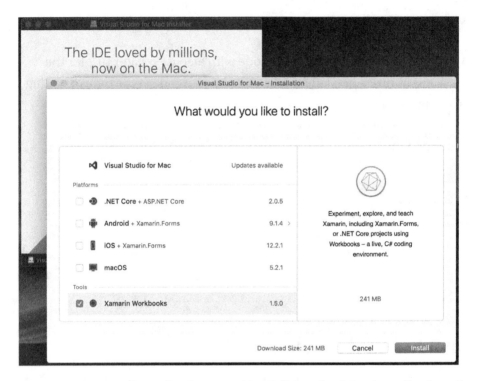

Figure 7-2. *Visual Studio Community Edition for Mac install wizard*

Install .NET Core

You will be installing .NET Core so you will be able to publish DLL libraries files via the command line. This will be done via the `dotnet publish` command. To download it, go to the dotnet Microsoft site; see Figure 7-3.

```
https://dotnet.microsoft.com/download
```

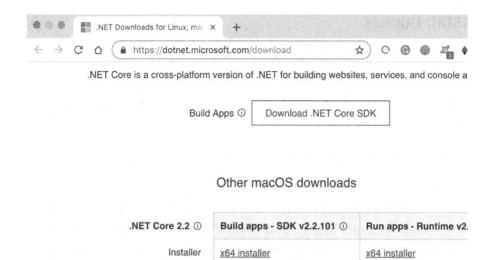

Figure 7-3. *Downloading Microsoft dotnet core*

You will be downloading both: Build apps - SDK v2.2.101 and Run apps - Runtime v2.2.0.

To confirm the installation went well, run the dotnet --version command.

```
> dotnet --version
2.2.101
```

This command will output the dotnet version, which at the time of writing is 2.2.101.

If the SDK is not installed, you will get the following error message:

```
Did you mean to run dotnet SDK commands? Please install dotnet
SDK from: http://go.microsoft.com/fwlink/?LinkID=798306&clcid=
0x409
```

You can also output your machine info via the info command.

```
> dotnet --info
```

Install Docker

Next, you will install Docker. Docker is needed to create a container that you will be using to create your local blockchain.

- *Download Docker from here*: https://download.docker.com/mac/ beta/Docker.dmg

- *Installation instructions*: https://runnable.com/docker/ install-docker-on-macos

Once Docker is downloaded and installed, double-click Docker from the Applications menu to get Docker running. You will see the Docker icon in the top menu on your computer. You can verify it's installed correctly by typing docker at the command line; it lists the Docker commands.

```
> docker
```

Run docker ps to view containers running to ensure you do not get any error messages.

```
> docker ps
```

If Docker is not running, you will get the following message:

```
Cannot connect to the Docker daemon at unix:///var/run/docker.
sock. Is the docker daemon running?
```

Just open Docker in case you get this message. Additionally, if your container is not running but it was already created, you can use the -a (all) flag and find the container ID.

```
> docker ps -a
List containers
```

Then when you have the container ID, you can start that container.

```
> docker start [CONTAINER ID]
```

For now, you won't see any list of containers as you have not created your containers yet.

Download NeoCompiler and Generate neon.dll

To create your NeoContract, you need to generate an .avm file. To do so, you need to create a neon.dll file to be able to generate the smart contract. To get started, you will clone the neo-compiler to your desktop and then generate the neon.dll file.

```
> cd ~/Desktop
> git clone https://github.com/neo-project/neo-compiler
> cd ~/Desktop/neo-compiler/neon/
```

To publish your self-contained .avm file, you need to set a runtime identifier. You can set the neon.csproj runtime identifier to the correct OS. As I am using a Mac and not a PC here, I need to change the neon.csproj file. To follow along, first make a copy of the original.

```
> cp neon.csproj neon.csproj.backup
```

I am using vim, but feel free to use your favorite editor.

```
> vim neon.csproj
```

Once the file is open, replace the following configuration, which sets a target framework.

Note   You can compare your output and settings with my project here: chapter7/NEO/neo-compiler/neon/. Also, you can find neon.csproj there.

```xml
<Project Sdk="Microsoft.NET.Sdk">

  <PropertyGroup>
    <Copyright>2016-2017 The Neo Project</Copyright>
    <AssemblyTitle>Neo.Compiler.MSIL</AssemblyTitle>
    <Version>2.3.1.1</Version>
    <Authors>The Neo Project</Authors>
    <TargetFramework>netcoreapp2.0</TargetFramework>
    <PlatformTarget>anycpu</PlatformTarget>
    <AssemblyName>neon</AssemblyName>
    <OutputType>Exe</OutputType>
    <PackageId>Neo.Compiler.MSIL</PackageId>
    <RuntimeIdentifiers>osx.10.12-x64</RuntimeIdentifiers>
    <RootNamespace>Neo.Compiler</RootNamespace>
    <Company>The Neo Project</Company>
    <Product>Neo.Compiler.MSIL</Product>
    <Description>Neo.Compiler.MSIL</Description>
  </PropertyGroup>

  <PropertyGroup Condition="'$(Configuration)|$(Platform)'==
  'Release|AnyCPU'">
    <DefineConstants>RELEASE;NETCOREAPP1_0</DefineConstants>
    <DebugType>none</DebugType>
    <DebugSymbols>False</DebugSymbols>
    <AllowUnsafeBlocks>true</AllowUnsafeBlocks>
  </PropertyGroup>

  <PropertyGroup Condition="'$(Configuration)|$(Platform)'==
  'Debug|AnyCPU'">
    <AllowUnsafeBlocks>true</AllowUnsafeBlocks>
  </PropertyGroup>
```

```
<ItemGroup>
  <PackageReference Include="Mono.Cecil" Version="0.10.0" />
  <PackageReference Include="Neo.VM" Version="2.3.0" />
</ItemGroup>
```

```
</Project>
```

Now `publish` pointing to the runtime identifier `osx.10.11-x64` by passing the `RuntimeIdentifier` setting param.

```
> dotnet publish -r osx.10.11-x64
```

The compiler created your `neon.dll` file here:

```
bin/Debug/netcoreapp2.0/osx.10.11-x64/publish/neon.dll
```

See Figure 7-4 for the output.

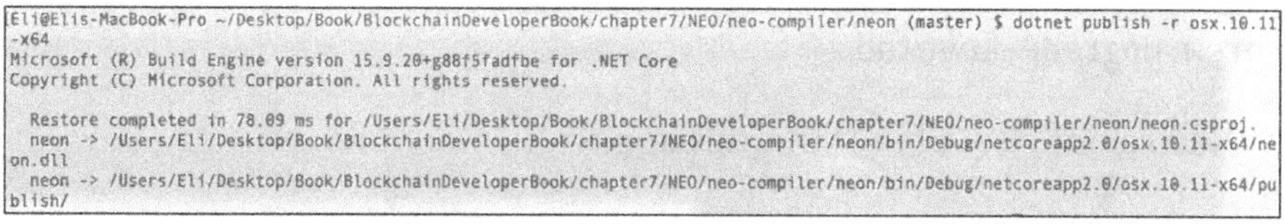

Figure 7-4. *Compiling neon.dll for the target osx.10.11-x64*

neo-cli to Generate a NEO Node

Next, you want to create a fill NEO node. To generate a full NEO node, there are two full-node options.

- *neo-gui*: This can be used by both developers and NEO users. It can be used to do basic user-client operations such as managing wallets but also publishing smart contracts. It has a visual user interface. However, it works only on Windows at the time of writing.

– *neo-cli*: This provides an external API for basic wallet operations. It also helps other nodes keep a consensus with the network and generate new blocks.

In this case, I am installing on a Mac, so you will be using `neo-cli` to manage your wallet via the command line. However, it's good for you to know that you can install `neo-gui` and create a virtual PC that way.

neo-cli

For `neo-cli`, you need to install the LevelDB package as it's a dependency. As you recall, you already installed LevelDB in Chapter 3 via Homebrew. If you did not install LevelDB previously, here is the command again:

```
> brew install leveldb
```

Alternatively, you can check if you have it and upgrade.

```
> brew upgrade leveldb
```

Next, clone `neo-cli` to your desktop.

```
> cd ~/Desktop
> git clone https://github.com/neo-project/neo-cli
```

Now, you can use dotnet to publish `neo-cli` from the source code you downloaded.

```
> cd neo-cli
> dotnet restore
> dotnet publish -c Release
```

The `.dll` file should be created in the `Release` folder; see Figure 7-5 for the output.

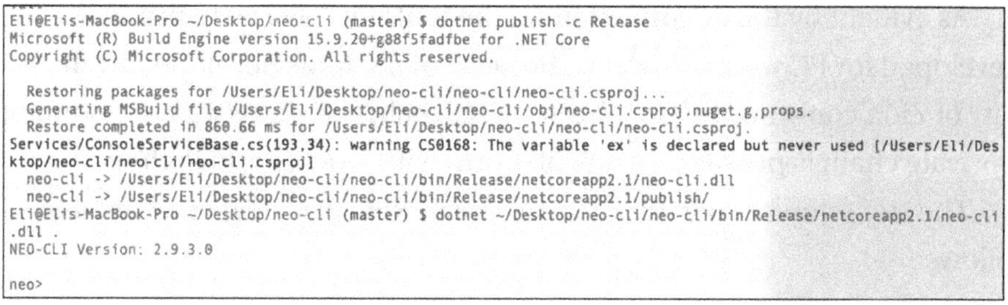

```
Eli@Elis-MacBook-Pro ~/Desktop/neo-cli (master) $ dotnet publish -c Release
Microsoft (R) Build Engine version 15.9.20+g88f5fadfbe for .NET Core
Copyright (C) Microsoft Corporation. All rights reserved.

  Restoring packages for /Users/Eli/Desktop/neo-cli/neo-cli/neo-cli.csproj...
  Generating MSBuild file /Users/Eli/Desktop/neo-cli/neo-cli/obj/neo-cli.csproj.nuget.g.props.
  Restore completed in 860.66 ms for /Users/Eli/Desktop/neo-cli/neo-cli/neo-cli.csproj.
Services/ConsoleServiceBase.cs(193,34): warning CS0168: The variable 'ex' is declared but never used [/Users/Eli/Des
ktop/neo-cli/neo-cli.csproj]
  neo-cli -> /Users/Eli/Desktop/neo-cli/neo-cli/bin/Release/netcoreapp2.1/neo-cli.dll
  neo-cli -> /Users/Eli/Desktop/neo-cli/neo-cli/bin/Release/netcoreapp2.1/publish/
Eli@Elis-MacBook-Pro ~/Desktop/neo-cli (master) $ dotnet ~/Desktop/neo-cli/neo-cli/bin/Release/netcoreapp2.1/neo-cli
.dll .
NEO-CLI Version: 2.9.3.0

neo>
```

Figure 7-5. *Building the neo-cli DLL*

Note   You can compare your output and settings with my project here: `chapter7/NEO/neo-cli`.

To run the `.dll` file, you use `dotnet` and the location of the DLL file, which starts a NEO command-line terminal.

> `cd bin/Release/netcoreapp2.1/`
> `dotnet neo-cli.dll.`

`neo-cli` also supports plugins. For instance, you can enable logs in `neo-cli` with application logs, or you can improve security in RPC nodes via RPC Security. A list of plugins can be found here: `https://github.com/neo-project/neo-plugins`.

Create a Local NEO Private Testnet

You can run your NeoContracts on public testnets just as you have done with other blockchains; however, it's much better to run your own private testnet so you have full control of it. A private testnet can be on the cloud, but you will have to pay for the service provider, so it's better if you set up your testnet on your local box.

As evident by the documentation, the tools for NEO were primarily developed for PC users. However, because of the tools developed by the City of Zion community (CoZ, https://github.com/CityOfZion), running a private chain is possible on any platform with Docker and Python.

The steps you need to take to run a local NEO private testnet are as follows:

1. *Install neo-python*: This allows you to run a full NEO node and to interact with the blockchain.

2. *Create neo-privatenet-docker*: This allows you to run a whole NEO blockchain with four consensus nodes in a single, lightweight Docker container.

3. *Create a NEO wallet*: This connects to the private net and creates a wallet.

4. *Claim*: This is initially 100,000,000 NEO.

5. *Bootstrap the testnet*: This synchronizes the network.

Python 3.6

neo-python needs Python 3.6 or later. Mac comes out of the box with Python, and you can verify you have python3 installed via the --version command.

```
> python3 --version
Python 3.6.x
```

If you are running a previous version of Python and need to install/re-install Python, follow these steps:

```
> brew unlink python
```

Next, install Python with Brew.

```
> brew install --ignore-dependencies
  https://raw.githubusercontent.com/Homebrew/homebrew-core/
  f2a764ef944b1080be64bd88dca9a1d80130c558/Formula/python.rb
```

Now switch the Python versions.

```
> brew switch python 3.7.0
> brew switch python 3.6.5_1
```

In case you don't have pip installed, run this:

```
> curl -O https://bootstrap.pypa.io/get-pip.py
> sudo python get-pip.py
> pip
```

Install neo-python

Next, clone neo-python from the City of Zion and check out the development branch.

```
> cd ~/Desktop
> git clone https://github.com/CityOfZion/neo-python.git
> cd neo-python
> git checkout development
```

You can create a virtual environment using Python 3.6 and then run the activate script.

```
> python3.6 -m venv venv
> source venv/bin/activate
```

Ensure you have the latest pip version by running this command:

```
(venv)> pip install --upgrade pip
```

Now you can install the package in an editable form.

```
(venv)> pip install -e.
```

You can compare your output with mine; for the steps you took so far, see Figure 7-6.

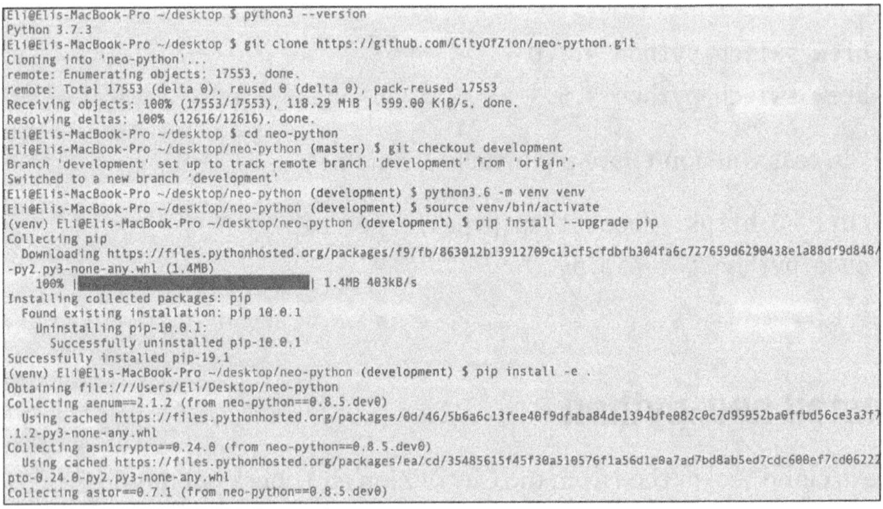

```
Eli@Elis-MacBook-Pro ~/desktop $ python3 --version
Python 3.7.3
Eli@Elis-MacBook-Pro ~/desktop $ git clone https://github.com/CityOfZion/neo-python.git
Cloning into 'neo-python'...
remote: Enumerating objects: 17553, done.
remote: Total 17553 (delta 0), reused 0 (delta 0), pack-reused 17553
Receiving objects: 100% (17553/17553), 118.29 MiB | 599.00 KiB/s, done.
Resolving deltas: 100% (12616/12616), done.
Eli@Elis-MacBook-Pro ~/desktop $ cd neo-python
Eli@Elis-MacBook-Pro ~/desktop/neo-python (master) $ git checkout development
Branch 'development' set up to track remote branch 'development' from 'origin'.
Switched to a new branch 'development'
Eli@Elis-MacBook-Pro ~/desktop/neo-python (development) $ python3.6 -m venv venv
Eli@Elis-MacBook-Pro ~/desktop/neo-python (development) $ source venv/bin/activate
(venv) Eli@Elis-MacBook-Pro ~/desktop/neo-python (development) $ pip install --upgrade pip
Collecting pip
  Downloading https://files.pythonhosted.org/packages/f9/fb/863012b13912709c13cf5cfdbfb304fa6c727659d6290438e1a88df9d848/
-py2.py3-none-any.whl (1.4MB)
    100% |████████████████████████████████| 1.4MB 403kB/s
Installing collected packages: pip
  Found existing installation: pip 10.0.1
    Uninstalling pip-10.0.1:
      Successfully uninstalled pip-10.0.1
Successfully installed pip-19.1
(venv) Eli@Elis-MacBook-Pro ~/desktop/neo-python (development) $ pip install -e .
Obtaining file:///Users/Eli/Desktop/neo-python
Collecting aenum==2.1.2 (from neo-python==0.8.5.dev0)
  Using cached https://files.pythonhosted.org/packages/0d/46/5b6a6c13fee40f9dfaba84de1394bfe082c0c7d95952ba0ffbd56ce3a3f7
.1.2-py3-none-any.whl
Collecting asn1crypto==0.24.0 (from neo-python==0.8.5.dev0)
  Using cached https://files.pythonhosted.org/packages/ea/cd/35485615f45f30a510576f1a56d1e0a7ad7bd8ab5ed7cdc600ef7cd06222
pto-0.24.0-py2.py3-none-any.whl
Collecting astor==0.7.1 (from neo-python==0.8.5.dev0)
```

Figure 7-6. *neo-python installation output*

To confirm the installation went well, run the `--version` command. At the time of writing, it outputs version 0.8.3.

```
> np-prompt --version
neo-python v0.8.3-dev
```

Now you can open a NEO bash with the `np-prompt` command. To exit bash, run the `exit` command.

```
> np-prompt
neo>exit
```

Install neo-privatenet-docker

You already installed Docker, so now you can create a Docker container that will create four NEO nodes to create a private testnet. Go ahead and install the Docker container on your desktop and build the files, as shown here:

```
> cd ~/Desktop
> git clone https://github.com/CityOfZion/neo-privatenet-
  docker.git
> cd neo-privatenet-docker
>./docker_build.sh
```

After the image is built, you can start a private network like this:

```
>./docker_build.sh
Successfully built #build number
```

Note   If Docker needs to be restarted or is not running, run the following command:

```
> ./docker_run.sh
```

Start a Network and Claim Initial NEO and Gas

Next, you will start your private network, create your wallet, and claim the initial NEO and 40 gas. This is done by running the docker_run_and_create_wallet.sh script. You can see the output in Figure 7-7.

```
> ./docker_run_and_create_wallet.sh
```

```
Waiting for tx 803ec81b9ddb7dec5c914793a9e61bf556deafb561216473ad7a8ee7a91979cc to show up on blockchain..
[I 190107 08:55:46 LevelDBBlockchain:383] Could not find transaction for hash b'803ec81b9ddb7dec5c914793a9
Waiting for tx 803ec81b9ddb7dec5c914793a9e61bf556deafb561216473ad7a8ee7a91979cc to show up on blockchain..
[I 190107 08:55:49 LevelDBBlockchain:383] Could not find transaction for hash b'803ec81b9ddb7dec5c914793a9
Waiting for tx 803ec81b9ddb7dec5c914793a9e61bf556deafb561216473ad7a8ee7a91979cc to show up on blockchain..
[I 190107 08:55:52 LevelDBBlockchain:383] Could not find transaction for hash b'803ec81b9ddb7dec5c914793a9
Waiting for tx 803ec81b9ddb7dec5c914793a9e61bf556deafb561216473ad7a8ee7a91979cc to show up on blockchain..
[I 190107 08:55:55 LevelDBBlockchain:383] Could not find transaction for hash b'803ec81b9ddb7dec5c914793a9
Waiting for tx 803ec81b9ddb7dec5c914793a9e61bf556deafb561216473ad7a8ee7a91979cc to show up on blockchain..

All done!
- Wallet file: /tmp/wallet
- Wallet pwd: coz
Shutting down.  This may take a bit...

Copying wallet file and wif key out of Docker container...

-------------------

All done! You now have 2 files in the current directory:

  neo-privnet.wallet .. a wallet you can use with neo-python (pwd: coz)
  neo-privnet.wif ..... a wif private key you can import into other clients

Enjoy!
```

Figure 7-7. *docker_run_and_create_wallet script output*

Once the process is completed, you can get a confirmation of the two files that were created (see Figure 7-7).

- *neo-privnet.wallet*: This file is a wallet that you can use with `neo-python`.
- *neo-privnet.wif*: This file is a WIF private key you can import into other clients, such as `neo-gui`.

These files give you access to the wallet containing the NEO and gas for your private network. The script automatically claimed the NEO and gas for you.

You can check Docker and see the `neo-privnet` container running, as shown in Figure 7-8.

```
> docker ps
```

```
Eli@Elis-MacBook-Pro ~/Desktop/neo-privatenet-docker (master) $ docker ps
CONTAINER ID        IMAGE               COMMAND                  CREATED             STATUS              PORTS
                                                                  NAMES
fea7270d705e        neo-privnet         "/bin/bash /opt/ru..."   41 seconds ago      Up 44 seconds       0.0.0.0:203
33-20336->20333-20336/tcp, 0.0.0.0:30333-30336->30333-30336/tcp   neo-privnet
```

Figure 7-8. *neo-privnet Docker container running*

Bootstrapping the Testnet

Now that you have a private testnet running, you need to bootstrap the testnet blockchain database. This synchronizes the network and is done by running np-bootstrap. This can take a while; once completed, you will get confirmation.

```
> np-bootstrap -n
confirm
Successfully downloaded bootstrap chain!
```

Notice that you use the –n flag to get database notifications.

Start NEO Bash

Now that you have your private testnet container running with four nodes and you bootstrap your testnet database, you can start a neo-cli bash by calling the prompt.py command.

```
> cd ~/Desktop/neo-python/neo/bin
> python3.6 prompt.py –p
```

Once you run this command, the NEO bash opens, and you can use the state command to view information about the blockchain, as shown in Figure 7-9.

```
neo> state
```

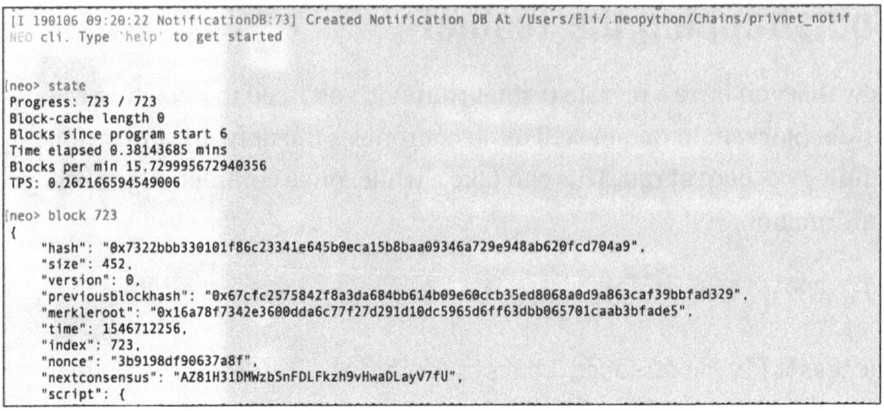

```
[I 190106 09:20:22 NotificationDB:73] Created Notification DB At /Users/Eli/.neopython/Chains/privnet_notif
NEO cli. Type 'help' to get started

[neo> state
Progress: 723 / 723
Block-cache length 0
Blocks since program start 6
Time elapsed 0.38143685 mins
Blocks per min 15.729995672940356
TPS: 0.262166594549006

[neo> block 723
{
    "hash": "0x7322bbb330101f86c23341e645b0eca15b8baa09346a729e948ab620fcd704a9",
    "size": 452,
    "version": 0,
    "previousblockhash": "0x67cfc2575842f8a3da684bb614b09e60ccb35ed8068a0d9a863caf39bbfad329",
    "merkleroot": "0x16a78f7342e3600dda6c77f27d291d10dc5965d6ff63dbb065701caab3bfade5",
    "time": 1546712256,
    "index": 723,
    "nonce": "3b9198df90637a8f",
    "nextconsensus": "AZ81H31DMWzb5nFDLFkzh9vHwaDLayV7fU",
    "script": {
```

Figure 7-9. *Information about your blockchain via the state command*

neo-cli offers access to many RPC calls via the NEO API; however, the wallet needs to be open to run these commands. You can open your wallet with the wallet command and the file location. This command will ask for the wallet's password. For the password, use coz.

neo> wallet open ~/Desktop/neo-privatenet-docker/neo-privnet.
wallet
password: coz

Next, rebuild the wallet and call the wallet command. You will see the NEO and NeoGas fake testnet coins available (see Figure 7-10).

neo> wallet rebuild
neo> wallet

```
Wallet {
    "path": "/Users/Eli/Desktop/neo-privatenet-docker/neo-privnet.wallet",
    "addresses": [
        {
            "version": 0,
            "address": "AK2nJJpJr6o664CWJKi1QRXjqeic2zRp8y",
            "script_hash": "e9eed8dc39332032dc22e5d6e86332c50327ba23",
            "frozen": false,
            "votes": [],
            "balances": [
                {
                    "asset": "0xc56f33fc6ecfcd0c225c4ab356fee59390af8560be0e930faebe74a6daff7c9b",
                    "value": "100000000.0"
                },
                {
                    "asset": "0x602c79718b16e442de58778e148d0b1084e3b2dffd5de6b7b16cee7969282de7",
                    "value": "40.0"
                }
            ],
            "is_watch_only": false
        }
    ],
    "height": 241,
    "percent_synced": 100,
    "synced_balances": [
        "[NEO]: 100000000.0 ",
        "[NEOGas]: 40.0 "
    ],
    "public_keys": [
        {
            "Address": "AK2nJJpJr6o664CWJKi1QRXjqeic2zRp8y",
            "Public Key": "031a6c6fbbdf02ca351745fa86b9ba5a9452d785ac4f7fc2b7548ca2a46c4fcf4a"
        }
    ],
```

Figure 7-10. *neo-privnet wallet showing claimed coins*

To close the wallet and exit bash, use the `wallet close` command and exit.

```
neo> wallet close
neo> exit
```

You have succeeded in creating a private NEO blockchain running on a testnet with 100 million NEO and 40.0 NeoGas claimed coins that you can use for development.

Potential Problems During Installation

NEO feels like chasing a moving target at times. In fact, it's likely that by the time you are utilizing the instructions in this book, the code won't work as expected because of changes in NEO. Moreover, during installation, there are some potential problems that you can encounter. I suggest you check the latest information here:

```
https://github.com/CityOfZion/neo-python#getting-started
```

Clean Database

If you need to clean the neo-python database to bootstrap and sync again, run the following command:

```
> rm -rf ~/.neopython/Chains/privnet*
```

b'Corruption Message

If you are getting a "b'Corruption: corrupted compressed block contents" message, you need to re-install LevelDB.

```
> brew reinstall leveldb
```

Restart Docker

It's good to know how to restart Docker in case you need to restart your computer, upgrade the Docker version, or upgrade the container files. To restart Docker, select Docker from the top menu and click Restart (see Figure 7-11).

The state is deleted (the whole "old" blockchain will be gone), and you should also remove Chains/privnet from neo-python and any privnet wallets you created.

```
> rm ~/Desktop/neo-privatenet-docker/*.wallet
> rm ~/Desktop/neo-privatenet-docker/*.wif
> rm -rf ~/.neopython/Chains/privnet*
> docker ps
```

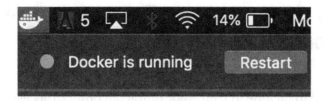

Figure 7-11. *Docker top menu icon restart button*

NEO "Hello, World"

You have your local private testnet environment and NEO tools set up on your machine, so now you are ready for the development of your NeoContract project. You can develop in different languages, and the process is similar. I will show you the code in C# as well as Python. I have kept the code to a simple working "Hello, World" example, but once you are able to get to this point, you can experiment with the different features NEO has to offer. Follow these steps to create and publish your code:

1. *Building the NeoContract framework*: Generate a Neo.SmartContract.Framework.dll file.

2. *Create a NEO "Hello, World" Project*: Create your #C contract project.

3. *Code a NEO "Hello, World" smart contract in C#*: Code your minimalistic example in C#.

4. *Code a NEO "Hello, World" smart contract in Python*: Code your minimalistic example in Python.

5. *Publish*: Publish your contract to your private testnet chain.

Building the NeoContract Framework: Neo. SmartContract.Framework.dll

The first step is to create a file that holds the NeoContract framework code that you need to include in your NeoContract in order to access the NEO features.

To build your NeoContract, you will be downloading and installing the NEO Development Pack. You will place these tools on your desktop for easy access. Note that you can always move the files to a better location later. Navigate to the desktop and clone the neo-devpack-dotnet project.

```
> cd ~/Desktop
> git clone https://github.com/neo-project/neo-devpack-dotnet
```

Next, run the neo-devpack-dotnet.sln file by double-clicking it or run the Terminal open command.

```
> open neo-devpack-dotnet.sln
```

VS opens, and you should expect to get three error messages. Click OK to dismiss these messages, as these errors will not affect building your project.

In the left window, you can see the Solution tab, as shown in Figure 7-12. Expand "neo-devpack-dotnet (master)" if it's not expanded.

Next, right-click Neo.Smartcontract.Framework and choose Build Neo. Smartcontract.Framework. See Figure 7-12.

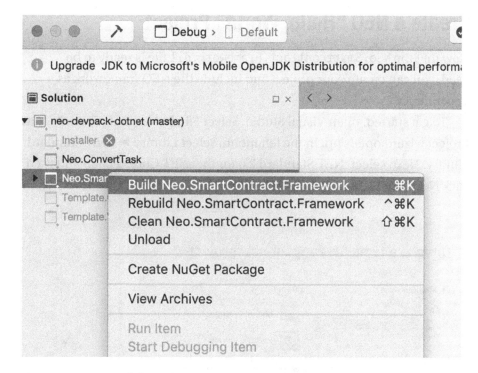

Figure 7-12. *Building the Neo.SmartContract.Framework project*

Once the build is completed, you will get a "Build successful"
message in the VS output's top middle window. You can also find the Neo.
Smartcontract.Framework.dll file here:

```
> cat ~/Desktop/neo-devpack-dotnet/Neo.SmartContract.Framework/
  bin/Debug/netstandard1.6/Neo.SmartContract.Framework.dll
```

The .dll file is a .NET Intermediate Language (IL) language file
that you will include in your library to have access to the NeoContract
framework code. Neo.SmartContract.Framework does not support the full
set of C# features because of the differences between the NeoVM and the
C# IL file.

Create a NEO "Hello, World" Project

Now that the `Neo.Smartcontract.Framework.dll` file is ready to be used, you can create your project and include the NEO framework as a dependency.

To get started, open Visual Studio. Select File ➤ New Solution... ➤ New Project wizard opens up. In the left menu, select Library ➤ .NET Standard Library. Next, select .NET Standard 2.0 for the .NET Core version and then click Next. See Figure 7-13.

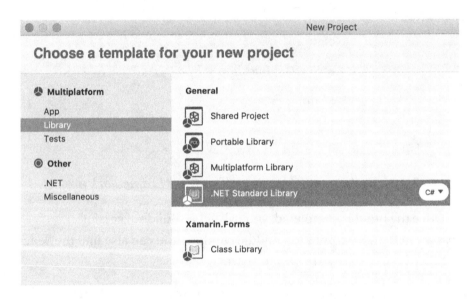

Figure 7-13. *New Project template wizard*

The configure wizard opens with a new project window. Call the project **hello_contract**, leave the default settings and click the Create button. See Figure 7-14.

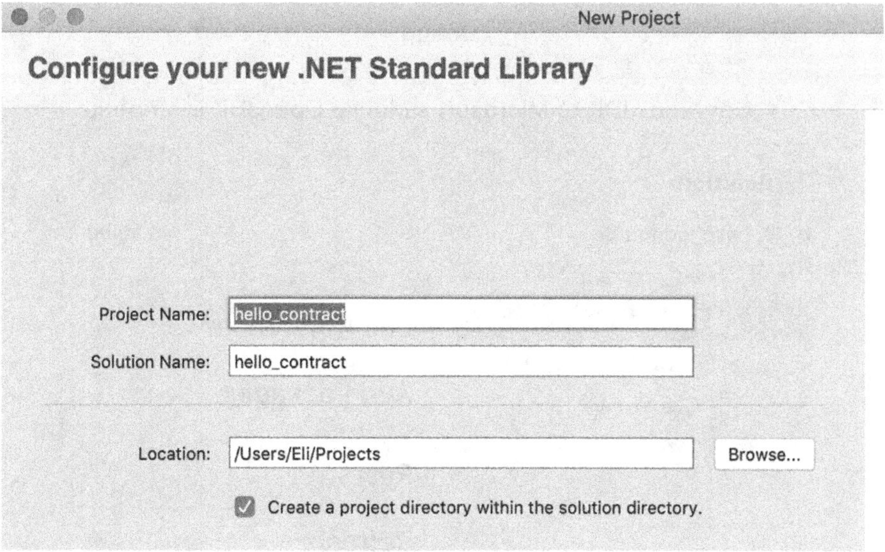

Figure 7-14. *VS create new project wizard*

Once the project is created, you need to attach the file Neo. Smartcontract.Framework.dll as a dependency. To do that, right-click the Dependencies folder in the Solution menu and then click Edit References. See Figure 7-15.

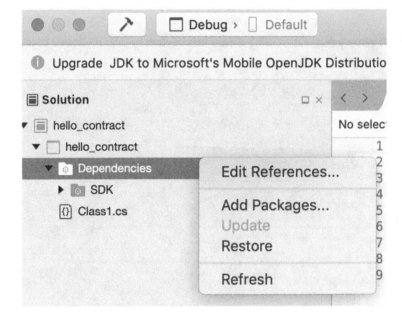

Figure 7-15. *"Hello, World" project dependencies edit reference*

In the Edit References window, go to the .NET assembly tab. Choose Browse and add the `Neo.Smartcontract.Framework.dll` file located here:

`~/Desktop/neo-devpack-dotnet/Neo.SmartContract.Framework/bin/`
`Debug/netstandard1.6/Neo.SmartContract.Framework.dll`

Next, click Open, as shown in Figure 7-16. Select the Neo. SmartContract.Framework.dll checkbox and click Ok.

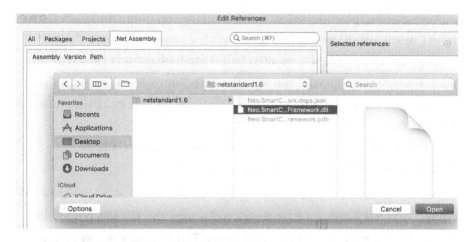

Figure 7-16. *VC edit references .NET assembly*

Coding the NEO "Hello, World" Smart Contract in C#

In this section, you will be using C# to develop your NEO "Hello, World" smart contract in .NET. The NeoVM is more compact; you can compile only limited C#/dotnet features into your AVM file. You can view the list of features available for development here: https://docs.neo.org/en-us/sc/quickstart/limitation.html.

The examples will use the "Hello, World" example provided in the NEO examples.

```
using Neo.SmartContract.Framework;
using Neo.SmartContract.Framework.Services.Neo;

public class Class1: SmartContract
{
    public static void Main()
    {
        Storage.Put(Storage.CurrentContext, "Hello", "World");
    }
}
```

After writing the code, select Build from the top menu and then Build All (or Command+B) to compile the `Class1.cs` code.

The `.dll` library file was created in the `bin/Debug/netstandard2.0/` folder. You will use this `.dll` file with the neo-compiler and convert the `.dll` file to an AVM file. After compiling the DLL file, the `hello_contract.dll` file is created here:

`~/Projects/hello_contract/hello_contract/obj/Debug/netstandard2.0/hello_contract.dll`

Note   The NeoContract framework generates the NeoVM bytecode. The code is saved in the AVM file format. The `*.avm` file can then be deployed on the NEO blockchain.

Coding the NEO "Hello, World" Smart Contract in Python

Like in #C, you can generate some minimalistic Python code to print "Hello, World." You can use the Eclipse IDE (`https://www.eclipse.org/ide/`) or any editor of your choosing. These instructions will be using vim. Create a file named `sample1.py`.

```
> vim ~/Desktop/smartContracts/sample1.py
```

Type the following code to print "Hello World."

```python
def Main():
  print("Hello World")
  return True
```

To close and save the file, type `:wq` in vim.

Compiling Your Smart Contracts to .avm

Now that you have two files named sample1.py and hello_contract.dll, the next step is to compile these files into NEO virtual machine files (.avm) that you will deploy on the NEO blockchain.

Let's start by compiling the hello_contract.dll file. Change the directory to the DLL file.

```
> cd ~/Desktop/neo-compiler/neon/bin/Debug/netcoreapp2.0/
  osx.10.11-x64/publish
```

Copy Neo.SmartContract.Framework.dll.

```
> cp ~/Projects/hello_contract/hello_contract/bin/Debug/
  netstandard2.0/Neo.SmartContract.Framework.dll ~/Projects/
  hello_contract/hello_contract/obj/Debug/netstandard2.0
```

Now, you can use the dotnet core tool to publish your DLL into an AVM file, as shown in Figure 7-17.

```
> dotnet neon.dll ~/Projects/hello_contract/hello_contract/obj/
  Debug/netstandard2.0/hello_contract.dll
```

You can see the output, as shown in Figure 7-17.

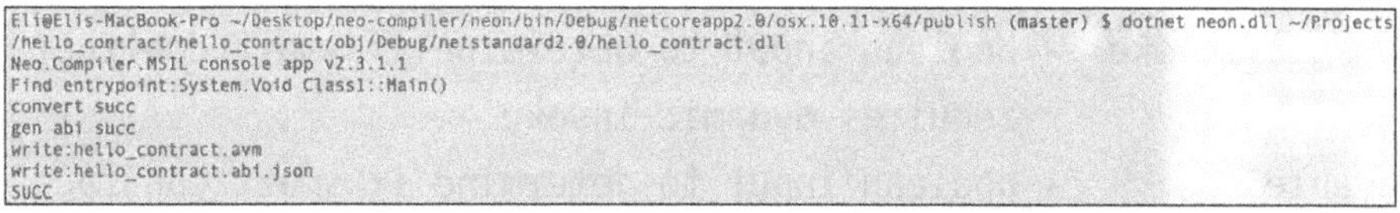

```
Eli@Elis-MacBook-Pro ~/Desktop/neo-compiler/neon/bin/Debug/netcoreapp2.0/osx.10.11-x64/publish (master) $ dotnet neon.dll ~/Projects
/hello_contract/hello_contract/obj/Debug/netstandard2.0/hello_contract.dll
Neo.Compiler.MSIL console app v2.3.1.1
Find entrypoint:System.Void Class1::Main()
convert succ
gen abi succ
write:hello_contract.avm
write:hello_contract.abi.json
SUCC
```

Figure 7-17. *Converting a DLL into AVM bytecode*

You can see the AVM bytecode file using the ls command.

```
> ls ~/Projects/hello_contract/hello_contract/obj/Debug/
  netstandard2.0/*.avm
hello_contract.avm
```

Similarly, you can compile the Python `sample1.py` file into AVM. In NEO bash, use the `sc build` command.

```
> cd ~/Desktop/neo-python/neo/bin
> python3.6 prompt.py -p
neo> sc build ~/Desktop/smartContracts/sample1.py
Saved output to ~/Desktop/smartContracts/sample1.avm
```

Publish a Smart Contract on a Private Testnet

The next step is to deploy your AVM files to the NEO private testnet chain. You don't need to remember all the options. You can call the command with the help flag to see the options.

```
neo> sc deploy help
Deploy a smart contract (.avm) file to the blockchain
Usage: sc deploy {path} {storage} {dynamic_invoke} {payable}
{params} (returntype)
path            - path to the desired Python (.py) file
storage         - boolean input to determine if smart contract
                  requires storage
dynamic_invoke  - boolean input to determine if smart contract
                  requires dynamic invoke
payable         - boolean input to determine if smart contract
                  is payable
params          - input parameter types of the smart contract
returntype      - (Optional) the return type of the smart
                  contract output
For more information about parameter types see
                  https://neo-python.readthedocs.io/en/latest/
                  data-types.html#contractparametertypes
```

Next set storage, dynamic_invoke, and payable as false, and set params and returntype as 01, as shown in Figure 7-18.

```
neo> sc deploy ~/Desktop/smartContracts/sample1.avm False False
False 01 01
```

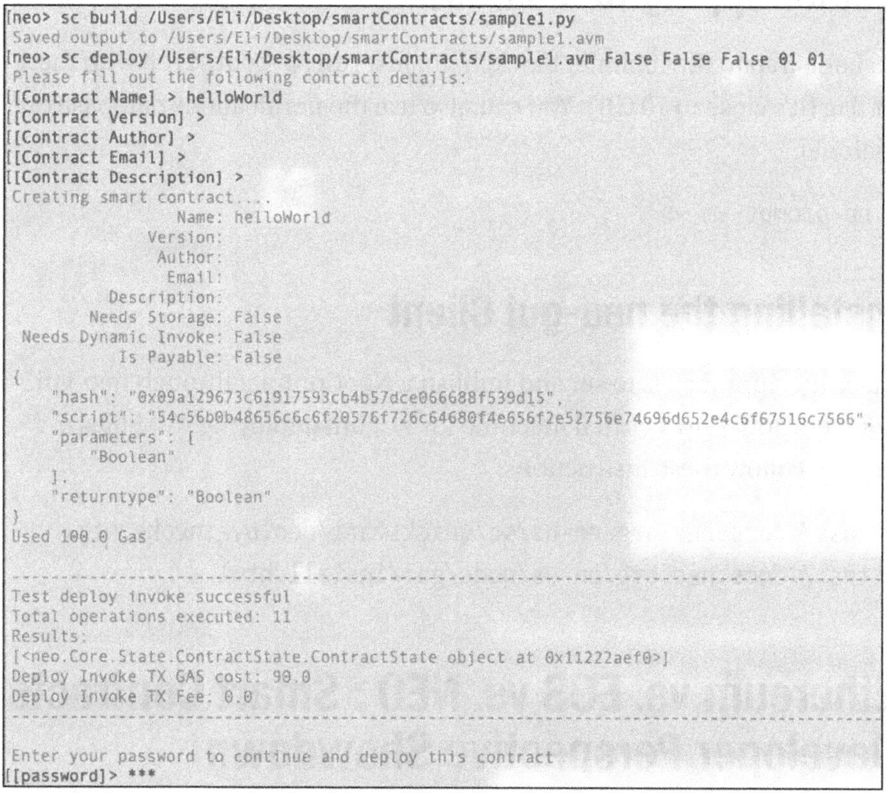

```
neo> sc build /Users/Eli/Desktop/smartContracts/sample1.py
Saved output to /Users/Eli/Desktop/smartContracts/sample1.avm
neo> sc deploy /Users/Eli/Desktop/smartContracts/sample1.avm False False False 01 01
Please fill out the following contract details:
[[Contract Name] > helloWorld
[[Contract Version] >
[[Contract Author] >
[[Contract Email] >
[[Contract Description] >
Creating smart contract....
              Name: helloWorld
           Version:
            Author:
             Email:
       Description:
     Needs Storage: False
Needs Dynamic Invoke: False
        Is Payable: False
{
    "hash": "0x09a129673c61917593cb4b57dce066688f539d15",
    "script": "54c56b0b48656c6c6f20576f726c64680f4e656f2e52756e74696d652e4c6f67516c7566",
    "parameters": [
        "Boolean"
    ],
    "returntype": "Boolean"
}
Used 100.0 Gas

---------------------------------------------------------------------------------------
Test deploy invoke successful
Total operations executed: 11
Results:
[<neo.Core.State.ContractState.ContractState object at 0x11222aef0>]
Deploy Invoke TX GAS cost: 90.0
Deploy Invoke TX Fee: 0.0
---------------------------------------------------------------------------------------

Enter your password to continue and deploy this contract
[[password]> ***
```

Figure 7-18. *Publishing an AVM file on a private testnet chain*

NEO asks for a contract name; let's call the contract helloWorld. Leave the version, author, email, and description fields blank and enter your wallet password to pay for the contract.

Publishing to Mainnet

To publish on mainnet, you can use the same process as you did with the testnet; just bootstrap to the mainnet.

Bootstrapping to Mainnet

To bootstrap to the mainnet blockchain, just run `np-bootstrap` with the -m flag (it's close to 10 GB). You can also use the notifications database on mainnet.

```
> np-prompt -m -n
```

Installing the neo-gui Client

An easier approach is to set and publish a NeoContract through neo-gui. You need to set up a virtual machine for PC, but deploying AVM files is a breeze. Follow these instructions:

```
https://docs.neo.org/en-us/sc/quickstart/deploy-invoke.html
https://docs.neo.org/en-us/node/gui/install.html
```

Ethereum vs. EOS vs. NEO : Smart Contracts Developer Perspective Showdown

At this point, I have covered three major blockchains for developing smart contracts, and it's hard not to compare them. However, there are so many factors to take into account when comparing these three blockchains. Additionally, at the time of writing, there are more than 40 blockchain projects that you can choose from for the deployment of smart contracts. Each project has pros and cons, and it's beyond the scope of this book to cover all of them. Instead, I will be focusing on specific criteria to try to help you understand what factors to consider when selecting a platform out of the three I have covered so far.

There is an organization that tries to rate these different blockchains; it's called the China Center for Information Industry Development (CCID). CCID utilizes contributions from professors and researchers at China's most prestigious educational institutions including Tsinghua and Beijing University to take into account features, adoption rates, and many other indicators to rank each blockchain. However, these ratings change often, and you should check the latest blockchain ratings on the web site: `http://special.ccidnet.com/pub-bc-eval/index.shtml`. Note that at the time of writing, EOS and Ethereum have been maintaining their dominance for the fourth consecutive time on the CCID list.

Further, determining what blockchain to utilize to publish smart contracts should take into account more factors, such as your team's ability, funding, the number of needed transactions, the number of accounts needed, wallets, exchanges, and much more.

Another major indicator to consider in determining the health of a blockchain is the user and developer adoption. You can find the current number of dapps for different smart contract platforms by checking these sites:

- *EOS*: `https://dappradar.com/eos-dapps`

- *Ethereum*: `https://dappradar.com/dapps`

- *NEO*: `http://ndapp.org/`

Looking through the list of dapps, keep in mind that although there are 6,050 dapps listed on Dappradar.com at the time of writing, there are only 106,938 users, which indicates that few dapps are being used and mass adaptation is not here yet.

Additionally, note that this comparison holds true at the time of writing and is based on my opinion. You should do your own research and due diligence before selecting the ideal blockchain to fit your smart contract needs. Table 7-1 provides the comparison.

Table 7-1. *Etherum vs. EOS vs. NEO Smart Contracts Comparison*

Category	Ethereum	EOS	NEO
Adoption	Currently holds the crown	Steady increase in adoption	Least adopted out of the three
CCID ranking	Rank #2	Rank #1	Rank #5
Consensus mechanism	PoW	DPoS	dBFT
Transactions per second	15	Millions	10,000 transactions per second
Dapp deployment cost	Minimum fee of 32,000 gas, plus 200 gas per byte of the source code	~120 EOS	Fixed cost of 100 to 1,000 gas ICO costs 5,000 gas to register digital asset; renew fee of 5,000 gas per year
Transaction cost	$0.05 to $3.5	$0 (however, creating a new account costs $1 to $4 per account paid by application developers)	Initial 10 gas execution free, fees for system calls and instruction (see white paper)
Scalability	No; await hard fork	Yes	Yes
Dev tools	Mature development tools from project and community, including tools for development frameworks, IDEs, communicating, and test tools	Dev tools could use an upgrade; debugging still done utilizing caveman debugging	Mature development tools

(continued)

Table 7-1. (*continued*)

Category	Ethereum	EOS	NEO
Docs	Well documented by both project and community	`Developers. EOS.IO` docs and community tutorials are not keeping up with EOS.IO GitHub changes; many GitHub issues regarding installation	Projects docs (`http://docs.neo.org`) and community tutorials
Community support	The Ethereum Community Fund (ECF) with organization support: Microsoft, Intel, Amazon, J.P. Morgan, and even government involvement	Committed $1 *billion* in funds focused on the growth of the EOS ecosystem	Has run and supported more than 100 community events
Development languages	Solidity, Bamboo, Vyper, LLL, Flint	C, C++	C#, VB.NET, F# Java, Kotlin, and Python; future plans to support more languages
Market cap	$14,068,553,166 USD	$2,341,702,969 USD	$488,507,580 USD
Number of dapps	*1,324*	226	Less than 100

(*continued*)

Table 7-1. (*continued*)

Category	Ethereum	EOS	NEO
Wallet	Desktop and hardware wallets, more options than EOS and NEO	Desktop and hardware wallets	Desktop and hardware wallets
Large exchange support	Available on all major exchanges	Not supported yet on many major exchanges such as Coinbase	Not supported yet on many major exchanges such as Coinbase
Turing complete	Yes	No	No

This list summarizes the Ethereum, EOS.IO, and NEO Blockchain platforms' pros and cons:

- Ethereum's biggest pro is that it was the first and most popular smart contract platform and has the most developers, third-party tools, support, documentation, and support community. The biggest downside is the Ethereum scalability issue of using PoW; there is a hard fork in the works at the time of writing to remedy this downside and move Ethereum to PoS. Another downside is the cost of 200 gas per byte for source code; this is pricey if your code is not optimized, especially as you need to constantly republish your code. Lastly, the support for less popular programming languages such as Solidity is less than ideal.

- EOS's advantage is its scalability and ability to run millions of transactions per second with no change, as well as faster code execution using WASM. EOS supports C and C++, and the actual blockchain coded in C++ gives it an advantage as C has a larger developer base than Solidity. However, EOS has a long way to go in terms of adoption, providing $1 billion funding can be useful for companies and individuals with the right idea. Its high ratings and great features are not enough to replace Ethereum in dominance it claims to be. Only time will tell.

–   NEO supports major programming languages (C#, VB.NET, Java, and Python), giving it a big advantage as a large number of developers can code with a smaller learning curve. Additionally, the efficient and inexpensive computationally execution of contracts is an advantage; however, NEO has the smallest community support out of the three platforms, and the stiff 5,000 NeoGas to register digital assets yearly may be a buzz killer for many potential projects.

Where to Go from Here

Try these resources:

- Read the NEO docs here: `http://docs.neo.org`. The site includes tutorials for sample NeoContracts, creating NEO nodes, NEO utilities, white papers, and more.

- Visit `https://neo.org/client` to find NEO wallets from third parties.

- For debugging, check Neunity.Adapter or Neo-Debugger to write test cases and run source code in the IDE: https://github.com/CityOfZion/neo-debugger-tools/releases.

- Create additional NeoContracts and include SmartContractEvent, which gets dispatched through neo.EventHub; subscribe and test your contracts.

Summary

In this chapter, I covered the NEO blockchain and NEOContracts. You looked at NEO's high-level blockchain architecture and learned about NEO's smart economy. You set your local environment and upgraded Xcode, installed Visual Studio 2017 IDE, and installed .NET Core.

You installed Docker, so you can now create containers, and you downloaded neo-compiler and generated neon.dll. Lastly, you built the neo-cli so you can manage your wallet and run other RPC operations.

Next, you created a local NEO private testnet by installing neo-python and neo-privatenet-docker. You bootstrapped the testnet and started NEO bash and were then able to start your network and claim NEO and gas.

Additionally, I covered potential problems during the installation of your NEO tools.

Next, you created two "Hello, World" projects, one in C# and one in Python, and were able to compile these projects into the NEO virtual machine's bytecode (AVM) files. You took these files and learned how to publish them on the NEO testnet blockchain as well as on the NEO mainnet.

Lastly, I compared Ethereum versus EOS versus NEO to help you better understand the differences between these platforms as well what criteria to look at when selecting a platform for your smart contracts.

CHAPTER 8

Hyperledger

In previous chapters, I covered blockchain technologies that are focused on cryptocurrency, and in fact, each project I have covered so far has included its own currency. Hyperledger is different; it does not have a currency attached, although you can create a coin if needed. Instead, Hyperledger was created with the aim of being an open source platform targeted at utilizing blockchain to fit business needs.

Hyperledger started in 2015 as an open source blockchain contributed by Digital Asset and IBM as a result of a hackathon (now the blockchain is called Hyperledger Fabric), and it extended to consists of multiple pluggable modules and the entire project is called Hyperledger aimed at improving a blockchain's performance and reliability so you can assemble modules to create your own unique platform to fit your business needs.

Note   The Hyperledger project is an umbrella strategy modular architecture consisting of a collection of pluggable components that are used to create custom blockchain solutions for businesses. The Hyperledger architecture aims to provide scalability, performance, confidentiality, resiliency, and flexibility. Note that if you visit Hyperledger's documentation, you'll often see the term *distributed ledger technology* (DLT); this term is synonymous with *blockchain*.

© Elad Elrom 2019
E. Elrom, *The Blockchain Developer*, https://doi.org/10.1007/978-1-4842-4847-8_8

Hyperledger Overview

The modular architecture allows you to adjust things like the blockchain's consensus mechanism, as well as manage storage, set services for identities, set permissions for the identities you set, and create smart contracts (in Hyperledger Fabric, smart contracts are called *chaincode*). In terms of programming languages, Hyperledger's chaincode is written in Go (Golang); however, you can utilize JavaScript with the Hyperledger Composer tool. Chaincode can then be used to implement and automate the business logic.

The Hyperledger project's managing team consists of ten members, and the executive director at the time of writing is Brian Behlendorf. In addition, 159 engineers from 27 organizations contributed to Hyperledger Fabric v1.0, according to developer.ibm.com.

> *"Hyperledger is an open source development project to benefit an ecosystem of Hyperledger based solution providers and users. It is focused on blockchain related use cases that will work under a variety of industrial sectors."*
>
> —Brian Behlendorf (executive director, Hyperledger)

Hyperledger is hosted by the Linux Foundation, and in terms of adoption, it's supported by large enterprise companies such as IBM, Intel, and SAP, as well as implemented by Oracle, Accenture, The National Association of Realtors, Deutsche Borse Group, Sony Global Education, and many others.

The Hyperledger consensus mechanism allows the network of nodes to choose between a no-op (no consensus) mechanism and an agreement protocol called Practical Byzantine Fault Tolerance (PBFT). The PBFT consensus enables two or more nodes to agree by giving the nodes full control. This precludes other nodes on the network from forcing a block, which can prevent potential double spending attacks, as you saw with PoW's 51 percent potential for mining attacks. Hyperledger gives control over the consensus mechanism, and you can restrict access to transactions. This results in improved performance and scalability as there are fewer nodes that need to agree on a block. Additionally, PBFT provides privacy for the network, which fits businesses better instead of providing full transparency as you have seen in other blockchains.

To give you an idea about Hyperledger's flexibility, you can use a dynamic consensus and enable what is called *hot swapping*, where you replace the consensus algorithms while the network is running (done with Hyperledger Sawtooth).

Blockchains focused on cryptocurrency usually provide transparency of transactions and network data, because they are dealing with funds and mostly untrusted members. However, this also limits the flexibility and how much you can modify the network and how much you can control as you are limited by the set of rules. Hyperledger is not backed by its own currency and provides more granular control.

Hyperledger project was built with basic functionality, vanilla flavor, with the intention of enabling developers to customize as much as possible, from the blockchain's consensus mechanism to the web interface identity's permissions, which provides limited data to members.

This modular architecture approach allows developers to create specific customized personalized blockchains to fit exact business needs. Hyperledger contains the following main open source frameworks and tools.

- Hyperledger frameworks:

    - *Hyperledger Fabric (contributed by IBM)*: This is a permission blockchain infrastructure with SDKs for Node.js, Java, and GoLang. Hyperledger Fabric is the heart of Hyperledger and supports chaincode in GoLang and JavaScript (utilizing Hyperledger Composer or natively). Blockchain is based on the endorser/orderer architecture. You'll learn more about this later this chapter.

- *Hyperledger Burrow*: This is an Ethereum VM built to specification.

- *Hyperledger Indy*: Think independent. This is a tool and library for running independent identities on distributed ledgers.

- *Hyperledger Iroha*: This is focused on mobile applications; the code is based on Hyperledger Fabric.

- *Hyperledger Grid*: This is a solution for a supply chain on a distributed ledger. The framework encapsulates Hyperledger implementations of data types, models, and smart contracts as well as showcases practical ways to create a supply chain business solution.

- *Hyperledger Sawtooth (contributed by Intel)*: This framework includes dynamic consensus and enables hot swapping of consensus algorithms on a running network. This is a more traditional blockchain architecture.

- Hyperledger tools:

  - *Hyperledger Caliper*: This is a blockchain benchmark tool.

  - *Hyperledger Cello*: This is an on-demand blockchain module toolkit for creating, managing, and terminating blockchains.

  - *Hyperledger Composer*: This tool has collaboration features used with Hyperledger Fabric for building blockchains aimed at businesses for chaincode and blockchain applications.

- *Hyperledger Explorer*: This is a module to view, invoke, deploy, and query blocks, transactions, and network data.

- *Hyperledger URSA*: This is a shared cryptographic library; it includes shared projects such as the implementation of several different signature schemes (base crypto libraries) and Z-mix, zero-knowledge proofs (`https://github.com/hyperledger-labs/z-mix`).

- *Hyperledger Quilt/Interledger.js*: This is an Interledger Protocol (ILP), meaning an atomic swapping between ledgers. The payments protocol enables transferring an asset (value) across distributed and nondistributed ledgers. There are two implementations: the Java one is called Quilt, and the JavaScript one is called Interledger.js.

A Hyperledger project can be built to allows transactions to be transparent as well as confidential when needed. For instance, think of the following business need: an airline wants to sell seats to another business, let's say Expedia. The airline business need is to create its own blockchain to keep track of its inventory, create transactions, set the price, and keep data confidential. The airline can benefit from blockchain, but it has no need for cryptocurrency nor does it want to share all the data publicly. The airline can utilize Hyperledger and set a private permission network, without exposing the data to the whole world, as you would on a public ledger.

The airline can then set special permissions to identities by issuing encryption keys with limited access and then give these encryption keys to specific parties only. For instance, only one organization, let's say Expedia, is able to view Expedia-related transactions, seat pricing, and flight information, while other identities such as the actual customer can view only the reservation's information related to their account and flight information.

The finance team can hold the encryption key that can provide more data such as profits and loss, cost of fuel, and other data needed for internal usage. This can be beneficial to businesses because they can run their data on a ledger instead of a centralized database, which is more prone to hacker attacks.

As you see, Hyperledger is a large project that covers six frameworks as well as five tools. It is impractical to cover all these in one chapter; in fact, it could easily take a whole book. In this chapter, I will give you a good foundation that can help you understand Hyperledger basics, and you can continue to experiment on your own with the other platforms and tools. In this chapter, you will be focusing on Hyperledger Fabric, as it's the most popular Hyperledger platform.

Understanding Hyperledger Fabric

As I pointed out, Hyperledger Fabric is an open source framework implementation, and it's intended for a private and permission-based business network.

In this chapter, you will create private network permission identities, and then you will create a chaincode to implement specific business logic.

Hyperledger Fabric is designed as the foundation for Hyperledger, and you can then use the Hyperledger's modular architecture to add specific modules depending on your business needs. A Hyperledger Fabric network consists of the following components:

– *Assets*: Assets are key-value pairs that represent a value. A value can be anything such as a document, stock, or cryptocurrency token. Each asset holds a state and ownership.

- *Shared ledger:* A shared ledger holds its own copy of the ledger with the state of the asset. This ledger is called the *world state.* The shared ledger also holds a copy of the blockchain, which stores the ownership of the asset by recording the transaction's history.

- *Smart contracts (chaincode):* Hyperledger Fabric calls smart contracts *chaincodes* that can be programmed in Go (GoLang) or JavaScript (Node.js). Chaincode can interact with the shared ledger, assets, and transactions. There's nothing new here; you saw this in other blockchains. Chaincode contains the business logic and can set an endorsement policy.

Note   In Hyperledger Fabric, users can define an asset endorsement policy for the execution of a chaincode. The endorsement policies set the node peers that are needed in order to agree on an accepted transaction to be valid and added to the shared ledger.

- *Membership services provider (MSP):* The MSP is the certificate authority that manages the digital certificate; it manages user IDs and authenticates all participants on the network. All members must be known identities in order to transact on Fabric. That's because the network is private and based on permissions. The MSP is used to authenticate and validate these members' identities and permissions. The MSP uses a certificate generation tool called *cryptogen.* To understand MSP better, visit the documentation here: `https://hyperledger-fabric.readthedocs.io/en/latest/msp.html`.

- *Peer nodes*: The Hyperledger Fabric network is built on peer nodes that are owned and contributed by members of the network. A node can be an organization or an individual. Nodes hold shared ledgers and can execute chaincode. Nodes can access ledger data; they can endorse transactions and interface with applications. Nodes can have permission to endorse peers or role for endorsers. Peer nodes receive ordered ledger state updates as part of the blocks they receive in order to maintain the ledger, or what Hyperledger calls *world state*.

- *Channel*: Channels can be created by a collection of peer nodes. A group of nodes can create a separate ledger of transactions. A channel is similar to the P2P channel you created when you formed your own blockchain in Chapter 3.

- *Organizations*: Each peer node contributes resources, and together they form the collective network. The owning organization can assign peer nodes using a digital certificate through the MSP. Additionally, peer nodes from different organizations can join a channel. Organizations with separate peer nodes are able to share the same MSPs. Best practice is to have one MSP for each organization.

- *Ordering service:* This service packages transactions into blocks. Blocks can then be broadcast to peer nodes and clients on the shared P2P channel. The channel outputs the same messages with the same logical order to all peer nodes. A consistent logical order is called *atomic delivery*.

Take a look at Figure 8-1, which is a graphical representation of the components that make up Hyperledger Fabric.

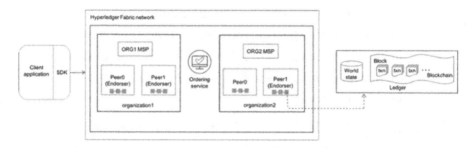

Figure 8-1. *Hyperledger Fabric graphical explanation. Photo credit: developer.ibm.com.*

Let's walk through the Fabric network using the 10,000-foot graphical overview in Figure 8-1. The Hyperledger Fabric network acts as the back-end layer for client applications.

A client application can be anything such as a dapp, portal, business activity, or web site; these types of applications are the front-end layer, and they can access chaincodes, transactions, and events through coding the Hyperledger Fabric SDK or a REST web service. The client calls a chaincode node, which uses the SDK to interact with the network. Unlike the traditional blockchains covered so far, Fabric is different because not all peer nodes have the same permissions.

Also unlike traditional blockchains, Hyperledger Fabric does not allow unknown identities to transact on the network. Organizations, which are called *members*, build the Hyperledger Fabric network, and each member can set up their node peers through the MSP. You can see in Figure 8-1 that the example has ORG1 MSP and ORG 2 MSP.

Peer nodes can be set up with different rules in the network: endorser peer, anchor peer, and orderer peer.

- *Endorser peer:* This receives a request to validate the transaction and execute chaincode. The endorser can approve or disapprove the transaction. Only the endorsing peer executes chaincode, so there's no need to install chaincode on all peer nodes.

307

- *Anchor peer:* These peers receive messages and send messages to other peers in the organization. The P2P network is made up of the different channels that can be set up with permissions so they are not visible to everyone on the network.

- *Orderer peer:* This peer handles the shared ledger and is responsible for keeping state across the network. The orderer peer generates blocks and broadcasts to all peers. The orderer peer can be set as Solo or Kafka.

  Solo: This is used for development with a single point of failure. That's what you'll set for your development environment in this chapter.

  Kafka: This is used for production. Kafka is built with fault-tolerant features.

You'll create chaincode and deploy it to the Fabric network on a Solo peer, and then you will be able to access and run functions. To send a transaction, your client application can connect to the SDK and create a transaction. The transaction is then sent to the endorsing Solo peer, which verifies the signature and sends an endorsement signature. The endorsement signature is sent out to the ordering service. In production, the ordering service will then send the transactions to all network-connected peers, which update their world state on their ledger.

I encourage you to visit the Hyperledger page to learn more and read the white papers: `https://www.hyperledger.org/projects/fabric`.

Installing Hyperledger Fabric and Composer

A good place to start with a Hyperledger network is to install Hyperledger Fabric and Composer. You will be setting up the environment by installing all the tools and libraries as well as Hyperledger Fabric and

Composer; then you will verify installation went well by starting and stopping Hyperledger Fabric and checking that Composer's libraries installed correctly.

Prerequisites

Hyperledger Fabric and Hyperledger Composer rely on many tools and libraries, and because each user uses a different machine, it is possible that this process won't be quick and easy and will probably limit the adaptation of the Hyperledger. I have broken the process down to these steps:

1) Verify the already installed prerequisites.

2) Update Git.

3) Install Node Version Manager.

4) Update Node.js.

5) Install VSCode.

6) Install Hyperledger Composer Extension.

7) Install the Hyperledger Composer Essential CLI tools.

8) Install Hyperledger Fabric.

It's recommended that you visit the Hyperledger Fabric prerequisites page as the versions and requirements may have changed: `https://hyperledger.github.io/composer/v0.19/installing/installing-prereqs.html`.

Before getting started, it's recommended that you update and upgrade Brew if you haven't done so for a while.

```
> brew update && brew upgrade
```

Verifying the Already Installed Prerequisites

There is a long list of prerequisites for installing Hyperledger Fabric; however, if you have been following along with this book's chapters, most of the prerequisites should already be installed on your computer.

For the operating system (OS), Fabric needs at least macOS 10.12. You can check your version via the top-left menu on your computer. Click the Apple icon, and click About This Mac. The Overview tab opens and shows the macOS version. If you are running an older version, then get the 10.12 update by clicking the software Update button. At the time of writing, macOS is called Mojave at version 10.14.4.

You also need Xcode and Docker. These were already installed in previous chapters, but you need to confirm they are installed and are the correct versions. Just run the `xcode-select --version` command to ensure Xcode is running. You can compare your results with mine, shown here:

```
> xcode-select -v
xcode-select version 2354.
> docker --version
Docker version 19.03.0-beta3, build c55e026
```

You need Docker-Compose version 1.8 or higher.

```
> docker-compose --version
docker-compose version 1.24.0, build 0aa59064
```

You need npm version v5.x or higher.

```
> npm --version
6.8.0
```

You need Python 2.7.x or higher.

```
> python --version
Python 2.7.10
```

Updating Git

The installation is requesting Git 2.2.x or higher. However, Mac comes with an older version of Git; you can check your version with this:

```
> git --version
git version 2.20.1 (Apple Git-117)
```

To upgrade Git, you will be installing Git via Brew and set your machine to use the Git version in Brew instead of the one that comes with Mac. First, install Git via Brew.

```
> brew install git
```

Next, you will set your path to point to the new Git location; use vim or your favorite text editor.

```
> vim ~/.bash_profile
```

Add the following to the PATH:

```
#git point to brew
PATH=/usr/local/bin:$PATH
```

Don't forget to run bash_profile after you save and quit the bash profile file to ensure the changes take effect.

```
> . ~/.bash_profile
```

Lastly, you can verify the version of Git.

```
> git --version
```

You are now pointing to the location of Git you installed with Brew, and for a future upgrade of Git, you can just run the following:

```
> brew upgrade git
git version 2.21.0
```

Installing Node Version Manager (nvm)

Node Version Manager (nvm) is needed. To download or update nvm, check the GitHub page at https://github.com/creationix/nvm/blob/master/README.md and run this command:

```
> curl -o- https://raw.githubusercontent.com/creationix/nvm/
  v0.33.0/install.sh | bash
```

Once the installation is completed, you can confirm it's installed correctly. Open a new terminal, and type the following. I have version 0.34.0 installed.

```
> nvm --version
0.34.0
```

Updating Node.js

Node needs to be version 8. To check what you are running, run this command:

```
> node --version
```

At the time of writing, the prerequisites hyperledger.github.io page stated that you should install the latest (long-term support) version of Node; however, it has been generating fatal errors and has a recorded bug on GitHub. Node.js version 9 is not supported either at the time of writing.

To get Hyperledger Composer to work, you will be installing node 8 and pointing nvm to use node 8.

```
> nvm install 8
> npm config delete prefix
> nvm use 8
```

You can confirm node 8 is installed and set correctly.

```
> node --version
v8.15.0
```

Installing VSCode with Hyperledger Composer Extension

It's recommended that you install Visual Studio Code (VSCode) with the Hyperledger Composer extension and use it as your code editor. The extension will provide code highlighting and is a professional free IDE. To get started, download VSCode from here: `https://code.visualstudio.com`. Click Download for Mac, as shown in Figure 8-2.

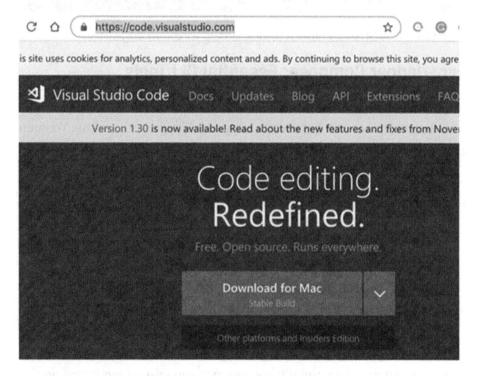

Figure 8-2. *Visual Studio Code installation page*

Once installation is complete, launch VSCode.

To install the Hyperledger Composer extension, click VSCode's left menu, select Extensions (two square icons) from the left menu bar, and type **Hyperledger Composer** in the search box. Select: Hyperledger Composer. Then click Install. Lastly, Reload to activate it. See Figure 8-3.

Figure 8-3. *VSCode Hyperledger Composer extension*

Hyperledger Composer Essential CLI Tools

You will be installing the Hyperledger Composer Essential CLI tools including `composer-rest-server`, Composer Playground, and the Yeoman generator.

To install the Composer CLI, run the following command.

```
> npm install -g composer-cli @0.19
```

Note   I am using version 0.19. There are some open bugs with Hyperledger's latest version, 0.20.6, in connection with all the tools and libraries, so I am using a previous version of Hyperledger Composer and Hyperledger Fabric. This may change, so you may want to check the documentation and install another version. Also, I assembled many potential bugs you may run into during installing and running Hyperledger Composer and Fabric; see the "Error Troubleshooting" section later in this chapter.

Next, install the Yeoman tool for generating Hyperledger Composer applications, which utilizes `generator-hyperledger-composer`. Execute the following command:

```
> npm install -g generator-hyperledger-composer@0.19
```

You can now install Composer Playground globally with npm.

```
> npm install -g composer-playground@0.19
```

Part of Composer is a tool called `composer-rest-server` that generates a loopback-based REST interface to be able to access the network you will create. To install the tool, execute this command:

```
> npm install -g composer-rest-server@0.19
> npm install -g Yeoman
```

You can verify that the installation went well by running the `--version` flag.

```
> composer --version
v0.19.20
> composer-rest-server --version
v0.15.2
> composer-playground --version
0.20.6
```

To ensure the generator tool was installed, if you run the Yeoman command, it should list Hyperledger Composer generator.

```
> Yeoman
```

It will output the following:

```
? 'Allo! What would you like to do? (Use arrow keys)
  Run a generator
□ Hyperledger Composer
```

Press Control+C to get out of the Yeoman command.

Installing Composer Playground with Docker

In addition to installing Composer tools globally with npm, you can run Hyperledger Composer Playground with Docker; just run the container and assign composer-playground as the name. You will be running it on port 8080.

```
> docker run --name composer-playground --publish 8080:8080
  hyperledger/composer-playground
```

The Docker command downloads the image, and you can see the output in Figure 8-4.

```
Eli@Elis-MacBook-Pro ~/fabric-dev-servers $ docker run --name composer-playground --publish 8080:8080 h
yperledger/composer-playground
Unable to find image 'hyperledger/composer-playground:latest' locally
latest: Pulling from hyperledger/composer-playground
cd784148e348: Pull complete
f6268ae5d1d7: Pull complete
97eb9028b14b: Pull complete
5360254f0376: Pull complete
Digest: sha256:8f29a2d18ae90af038724e62862a2ca5a98579ebbdaf36563c1b4cc7d40d9d2e
Status: Downloaded newer image for hyperledger/composer-playground:latest
2019-01-26T15:14:12: PM2 log: Launching in no daemon mode
2019-01-26T15:14:12: PM2 log: App [composer-playground:0] starting in -fork mode-
2019-01-26T15:14:12: PM2 log: App [composer-playground:0] online
WARNING: NODE_APP_INSTANCE value of '0' did not match any instance config file names.
WARNING: See https://github.com/lorenwest/node-config/wiki/Strict-Mode
2019-01-26T15:14:13.975Z INFO    :LoadModule              :loadModule()           Loading composer-
wallet-filesystem from /home/composer/.npm-global/lib/node_modules/composer-playground/node_modules/com
poser-wallet-filesystem ()$
2019-01-26T15:14:14.014Z INFO    :PlaygroundAPI           :createServer()         Playground API st
arted on port 8080 ()$
2019-01-26T15:14:27.599Z INFO    :PlaygroundAPI           :createServer()         Client with ID 'c
u12KqXWLfosbLLJAAAA' on host '::ffff:172.17.0.1' connected ()$
```

Figure 8-4. *Composer-playground docker container output*

To cancel the container, press Control+C.

Now to run Playground in the browser on port 8080, open a new Terminal window by pressing Command+T and run the open command.

```
> open http://localhost:8080
```

You can see the Hyperledger Composer playground welcome page, as shown in Figure 8-5.

Figure 8-5. *Playground welcome screen*

Keep in mind that to stop Docker, you can run the stop command.

```
> docker stop composer-playground
```

To remove the composer-playground name so you can use it again, you will need to run the following command:

```
> docker rm --force composer-playground
```

Installing Hyperledger Fabric Dev Servers

At the time of writing, Hyperledger Fabric's latest version is v1.4.1; you should visit the GitHub page to find out the latest version and documentation as this may change; see https://github.com/ hyperledger/fabric.

The Hyperledger Fabric dev servers have different versions to choose from. You will be setting up a Hyperledger Fabric v1.2 network for your development.

You then can deploy your blockchain business networks built with Hyperledger Composer and test your applications.

Create a directory to download Fabric; I picked ~/fabric-dev-servers, but you can choose any directory.

```
> mkdir ~/fabric-dev-servers && cd ~/fabric-dev-servers
```

You'll use curl to get the .tar.gz file you need to install Hyperledger Fabric, as shown here:

```
> curl -O https://raw.githubusercontent.com/hyperledger/
  composer-tools/master/packages/fabric-dev-servers/fabric-dev-
  servers.tar.gz
```

Use tar to extract the files you downloaded.

```
> tar xzf fabric-dev-servers.tar.gz
```

Once these are extracted, you have script files to help you quickly spin up a Hyperledger Fabric instance.

Run the ls command, and you can see the .sh files among other useful files.

```
> ls
startFabric.sh
teardownAllDocker.sh
stopFabric.sh
teardownFabric.sh
```

When you run the Composer -v command, you can check the version you are running. You saw that you indeed installed Hyperledger Composer v0.19, so you will need to use Hyperledger Fabric v1.1 according to the documentation, and you can also set the starting Fabric timeout to 30 seconds; that's the wait time once you run the script to ensure the network is running.

```
> export FABRIC_VERSION=hlfv11
> export FABRIC_START_TIMEOUT=30
```

Tip   If you are running a different version of Hyperledger Composer, check the GitHub page to see which version of Fabric you need to set: https://github.com/hyperledger/composer-tools/tree/master/packages/fabric-dev-servers.

To spin up your Hyperledger Fabric network, you need to first execute the download Fabric script; this can take some time, depending on your Internet connection.

```
>./downloadFabric.sh
```

That's it; you should see the output shown in Figure 8-6.

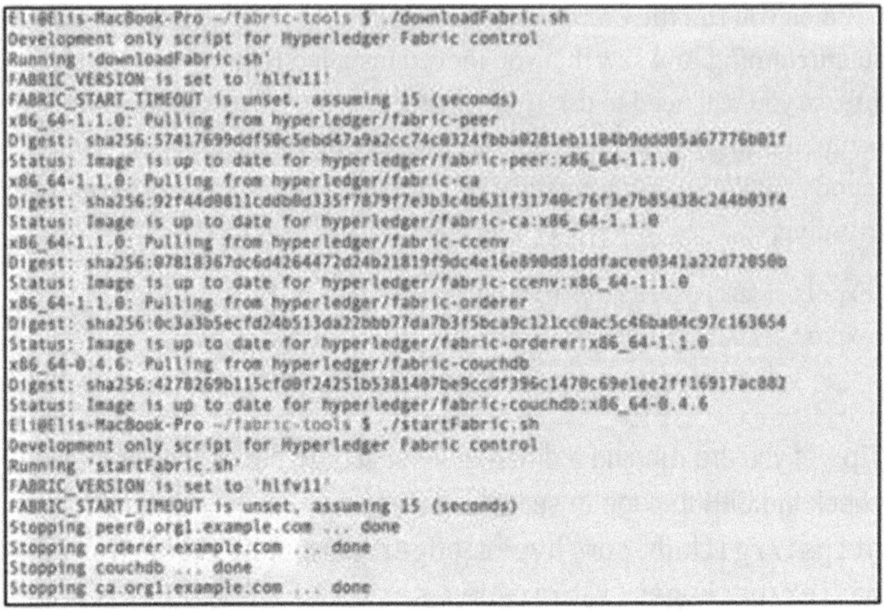

```
Eli@Elis-MacBook-Pro ~/fabric-tools $ ./downloadFabric.sh
Development only script for Hyperledger Fabric control
Running 'downloadFabric.sh'
FABRIC_VERSION is set to 'hlfv11'
FABRIC_START_TIMEOUT is unset, assuming 15 (seconds)
x86_64-1.1.0: Pulling from hyperledger/fabric-peer
Digest: sha256:57417699ddf50c5ebd47a9a2cc74c0324fbba0281eb1184b9ddd05a67776b01f
Status: Image is up to date for hyperledger/fabric-peer:x86_64-1.1.0
x86_64-1.1.0: Pulling from hyperledger/fabric-ca
Digest: sha256:92f44d0811cddb0d335f7879f7e3b3c4b631f31740c76f3e7b85438c244b03f4
Status: Image is up to date for hyperledger/fabric-ca:x86_64-1.1.0
x86_64-1.1.0: Pulling from hyperledger/fabric-ccenv
Digest: sha256:07818367dc6d4264472d24b21819f9dc4e16e890d81ddfacee0341a22d720500
Status: Image is up to date for hyperledger/fabric-ccenv:x86_64-1.1.0
x86_64-1.1.0: Pulling from hyperledger/fabric-orderer
Digest: sha256:0c3a3b5ecfd24b513da22bbb77da7b3f5bca9c121cc0ac5c46ba04c97c163654
Status: Image is up to date for hyperledger/fabric-orderer:x86_64-1.1.0
x86_64-0.4.6: Pulling from hyperledger/fabric-couchdb
Digest: sha256:4278269b115cfd0f24251b5381407be9ccdf396c1470c69elee2ff16917ac882
Status: Image is up to date for hyperledger/fabric-couchdb:x86_64-0.4.6
Eli@Elis-MacBook-Pro ~/fabric-tools $ ./startFabric.sh
Development only script for Hyperledger Fabric control
Running 'startFabric.sh'
FABRIC_VERSION is set to 'hlfv11'
FABRIC_START_TIMEOUT is unset, assuming 15 (seconds)
Stopping peer0.org1.example.com ... done
Stopping orderer.example.com ... done
Stopping couchdb ... done
Stopping ca.org1.example.com ... done
```

Figure 8-6. Downloading the Hyperledger Fabric output

Once the download is complete, you can confirm you have Docker containers.

```
> docker image ls hyperledger/*
hyperledger/fabric-ca
hyperledger/fabric-orderer
hyperledger/fabric-peer
hyperledger/fabric-ccenv
hyperledger/fabric-couchdb
```

Network Connection Profile

There is a network connection profile JSON file called DevServer_ connection.json.

In this section, you will modify the file to fit with the Docker localhost container you will create. Before you modify the file, it's a good idea to make a copy first.

```
> cd ~/fabric-tools/
> cp DevServer_connection.json DevServer_connection-backup.json
```

Change the original file's orderers, peers, and certificate authorities to point to localhost as you will be running Composer Rest Server as the Docker container in the network and will access these hostnames on the network.

Edit the DevServer_connection file with vm or your favorite editor.

```
> vim DevServer_connection.json
```

See Figure 8-7.

Figure 8-7. *Changing devServer.json to point to localhost*

You also need to edit the hosts to point to 127.0.0.1 on the local server.

```
> sudo vim /etc/hosts
# fabric
127.0.0.1 orderer.example.com peer0.org1.example.com
ca.org1.example.com
```

Spinning Off a Local Hyperledger Fabric Business Network

The first time you run Hyperledger Fabric, you need to execute commands to start a local Hyperledger Fabric instance and issue an ID card for the admin. The default admin is called PeerAdmin. To get started, run the start fabric command.

```
> ./startFabric.sh
```

The expected output is confirming your variables.

```
Development only script for Hyperledger Fabric control
Running 'startFabric.sh'
FABRIC_VERSION is set to [version number]
...
Creating network "composer_default" with the default driver
Creating ca.org1.example.com
Creating orderer.example.com
```

As part of the start script, you can see the output lines that confirm that the composer_default Docker network was created and running the containers in the created network. The containers are able to communicate using the custom hostnames: ca.org1.example.com and orderer.example.com.

Creating an Admin ID Card

Now that you have a network running, the last setup step is to create credentials.

You can use Hyperledger Composer to create what Hyperledger Fabric calls a .card file.

You can generate the admin ID card by executing the following command:

```
> ./createPeerAdminCard.sh
```

You can compare your output with mine, which is shown in Figure 8-8.

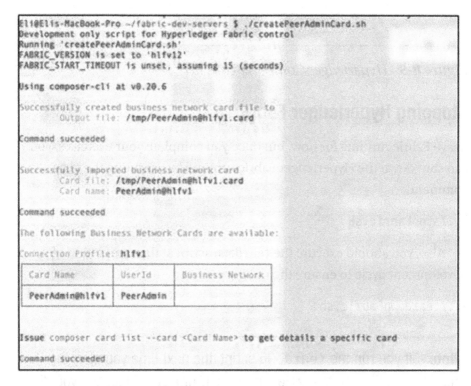

Figure 8-8. *Hyperledger Composer generate card*

To confirm the card was created correctly, execute the following command with <card name>:

```
> composer card list --card PeerAdmin@hlfv1
```

This command outputs information about the ID card. See Figure 8-9.

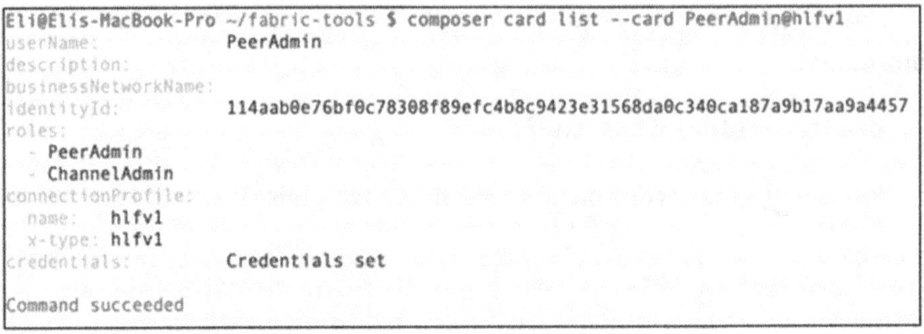

```
Eli@Elis-MacBook-Pro ~/fabric-tools $ composer card list --card PeerAdmin@hlfv1
userName:              PeerAdmin
description:
businessNetworkName:
identityId:            114aab0e76bf0c78308f89efc4b8c9423e31568da0c340ca187a9b17aa9a4457
roles:
  - PeerAdmin
  - ChannelAdmin
connectionProfile:
  name:    hlfv1
  x-type: hlfv1
credentials:           Credentials set

Command succeeded
```

Figure 8-9. *Hyperledger Composer card list*

Stopping Hyperledger Fabric

Leave Fabric running for now, but once you complete your exercises, you can shut down the Hyperledger Fabric runtime by executing the stop command.

> ./stopFabric.sh

Also, you should execute the teardown script at the completion of your development cycle to ensure the memory is freed.

> ./teardownFabric.sh

Note   If you run the teardown script, the next time you start the runtime, you'll need to create a new PeerAdmin card just like you did with the first-time startup steps. See the following steps.

Re-creating the PeerAdmin ID Card

After you stop and tear down with these commands:

> ./stopFabric.sh
> ./teardownFabric.sh

you need to re-create the admin ID card, so just follow the same commands.

```
> ./startFabric.sh
> ./createPeerAdminCard.sh
> composer card list --card PeerAdmin@hlfv1
```

It's a good idea to follow the process in Figure 8-10, which shows what you need to do in order to start a card, stop a card, create a card, and tear down.

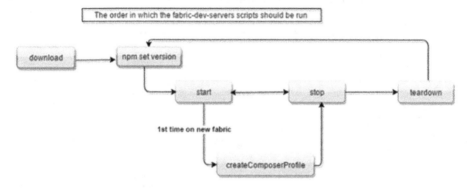

Figure 8-10.   *Fabric-dev-servers start-stop flow. Photo credit: github. com/hyperledger/composer-tools.*

Hyperledger Composer

Now that you have the Hyperledger Fabric network installed and running, the next step is to write chaincode. You can write chaincode in Hyperledger Fabric natively with Go; however, you can also utilize Hyperledger Composer to help create chaincode and blockchain applications via coding in JavaScript instead of Go. Hyperledger Composer takes definition files and generates Business Network Archive (.bna) files that you can then deploy to the Hyperledger network to run. Composer is easy to use and aimed not just at developers but at business owners.

There are three components that make up Hyperledger Composer (see Figure 8-11).

- *Business network archive (.bna)*: This consists of four files packaged together.

- *Hyperledger Composer Playground*: This is used to configure and deploy network as well as test code without rolling out a blockchain.

- *REST API support*: This exposes functions to be used by front-end clients such as dapps.

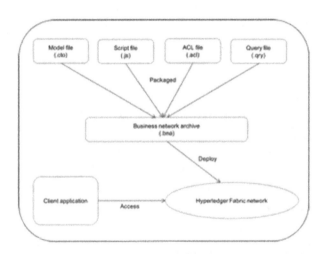

Figure 8-11. *Hyperledger Composer graphical explanation. Photo credit: developer.ibm.com.*

"Hello, World" with Playground

You will be creating a "Hello, World" application and deploying it on the network using Playground. To get started, open Playground via the command line and execute this command:

```
> composer-playground
```

Alternatively, you can use Docker. Once it's open, dismiss the welcome screen by clicking "Let's Blockchain!"

Deploying a Business Network

Next, select "Deploy a new business network." In the deploy wizard, insert the basic information, such as typing **hello-network** in the "Give your new Business Network a name" input box.

Select the middle "empty-business-network" network definition and click Deploy, as shown in Figure 8-12.

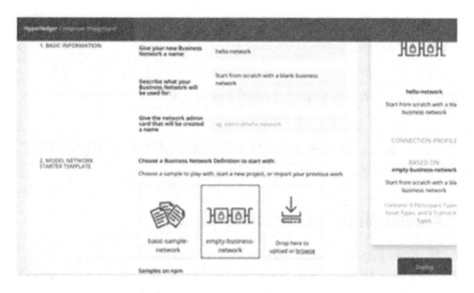

Figure 8-12.   *Hyperledger Composer Playground, deploying new business network wizard*

The ID card for an admin is created for your network. To connect to the network, click the "Connect now" link, as shown in Figure 8-13.

Figure 8-13. *Connecting to the hello-network business network definition*

You are now connected to the business network definition network, and you can define and work with the model.

Business Network Archive (.bna)

The business network model includes assets and the transactions related to these assets. Hyperledger Composer needs the following to be packaged together: a network model file, a JavaScript file (.js), an access control file (.acl), and a query file (.qry). These files are definition files that generate your network.

- – *Network model (.cto)*: This is the file that defines the assets, transactions, and participants who can interact with these assets. The file is created with a modeling language called CTO (named after the original project name, Concerto).

- *JavaScript file (.js)*: This is the file that defines the trans-action processor functions. It is the chaincode.

- *Access control (ACL) (.acl)*: This is the file that contains the access control rules that define the rights of the different participants.

- *Query (.qry)*: This is the file that defines the queries that can run in a network.

Hyperledger Composer takes these four files and creates a business network definition that is packaged as an archive (.bna) file. The .bna files can be deployed on the Hyperledger Fabric network.

You can than write a client application such as a dapp that can use Hyperledger Composer APIs to access the smart contract (.bna functions) that you write through the Hyperledger Fabric network.

Adding the Model File

To create the model file, you can add the files that make up the .bna archive. For instance, to add a model file. Click "Add a file," select Model File (.cto), and click Add, as shown in Figure 8-14.

Figure 8-14. *Adding a file to the business network model*

For the .cto file, you will define the processing function and transaction.

For the namespace, you will use a fictional company called Skynet, with an identified ID of type String. You will also create a msg string and a transaction Hello and pass the Myfunction asset that will include the message.

```
namespace org.skynet.mymodel
asset Myfunction identified by id {
  o String id
  o String msg
}
transaction Hello {
  --> Myfunction check
}
```

Adding Chaincode

Next, you will add a JS file by clicking "Add a file." Write chaincode as the logic of the transaction to print the message to the console, as shown here:

```
/**
@param {org.skynet.mymodel.Hello} hello
@transaction
*/
function hello(hello) {
  console.log("Hello " + hello.check.msg);
}
```

Transactions represent the chaincode, which is the business logic of your application. Notice that the comments state that the code is a function for a transaction and the namespace. Click "Deploy changes" to update your definition model.

Creating an Asset

Next, to test the model, you will create a new asset, extend it, and store it. To do that, click + Create New Asset at the top-right corner. The create new asset wizard opens, as shown in Figure 8-15. The model already has an ID; however, for this example, you will change it to 001 (but the string can be any string). For the message, you will pass world.

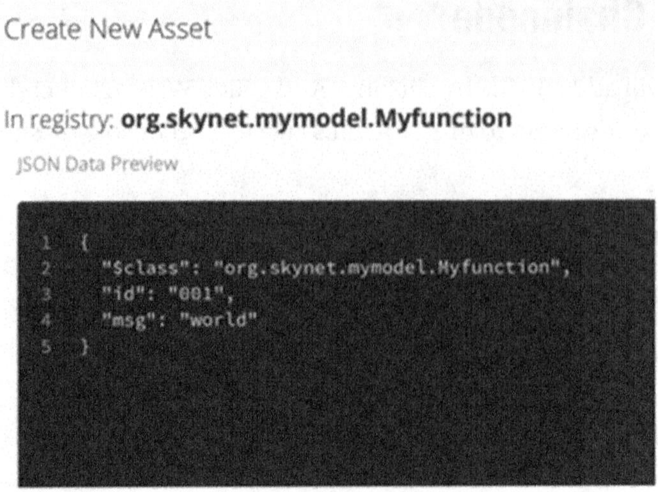

Create New Asset

In registry: **org.skynet.mymodel.Myfunction**

JSON Data Preview

```
1   {
2       "$class": "org.skynet.mymodel.Myfunction",
3       "id": "001",
4       "msg": "world"
5   }
```

Figure 8-15. *Create New Asset Wizard*

Access Control

Notice that there is an Access Control option with the `permissions.acl` file as part of the Define tab at the bottom left of the screen, as shown in Figure 8-16.

As you can see, the rules grant wide-open "allow all" access, which can be changed.

Figure 8-16. *ACL permission file on your hello-network*

Testing the Model

Now that the model instance is saved, you can submit the transaction to invoke the transaction. On the left side, click the "Submit transaction" button. The Submit Transaction Wizard opens. Set the ID to 001, as shown in Figure 8-17.

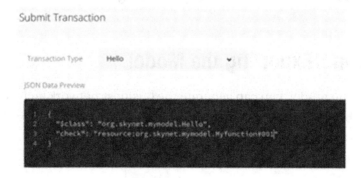

Figure 8-17. *Hyperledger Playground, Submit Transaction Wizard*

Before you test, open the developer console so you can see the JavaScript messages. For Safari, follow these instructions.

In the top menu, select Safari ➤ Preferences. Click the Advanced tab and then select the "Show Develop menu in menu bar" box.

After following these steps, you will see in the top menu Developer as an item. Select "Show JavaScript console" (or press Command+Option+C).

Next, click Submit; you will see the message "Hello world" in the JavaScript console, as shown in Figure 8-18.

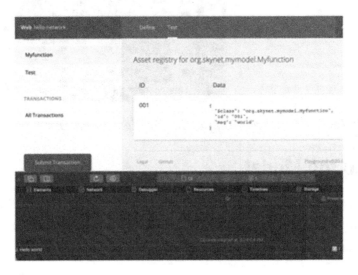

Figure 8-18. *"Hello world" message showing in the JavaScript console*

Importing/Exporting the Model

To export the model, you can generate the business network archive (.bna) file. The .bna file can then be deployed in production. All you have to do is click the Export link, as shown in Figure 8-19.

Figure 8-19. *Exporting the .bna file*

Playground generates the `hello-network.bna` file, which will be downloaded to your computer.

Similarly, you can import a `.bna` file, click the "Add a file" link, and under "Upload a file from your computer...," you can browse or drag and drop the `.bna` file.

The import/export is not just for publishing; it can be used to share models with others for testing, development, or other reasons. I included the `hello-network.bna` file with this book's code, so feel free to import it; see `https://github.com/Apress/the-blockchain-developer/chapter8/hello-network`.

The `.bna` file is nothing more than a zip folder named `bna`. In fact, you can copy the `.bna` file as `.zip` and unzip the files.

```
> cp hello-network.bna hello-network.zip
> unzip hello-network.zip
```

VSCode can be used as your IDE for your entire Hyperledger project. For instance, now that you have unzipped your files, you can open VSCode and drag and drop the model file `models/org.example.model.cto` into VSCode. You can see that the code is highlighted, as shown in Figure 8-20.

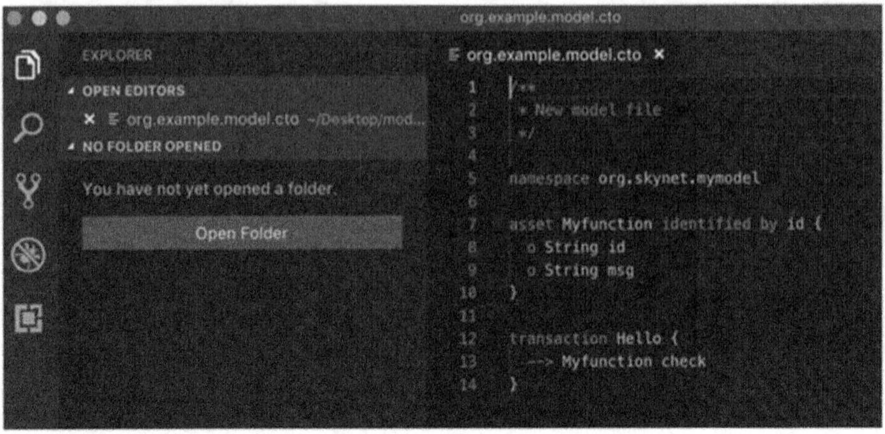

Figure 8-20. *Model CTO file in VSCode*

You wrote your files in Composer Playground using the web interface. This suite is a less developer savvy approach; however, a larger project can include complex business logic, events, many transactions, and testing, so it is advisable to create your project and manage files with VSCode and then upload those files into Playground for deployment.

Playground Online

Hyperledger Composer Playground has an online version available at `https://composer-playground.mybluemix.net/`. You can use the same steps you used before to create your network and files. See Figure 8-21.

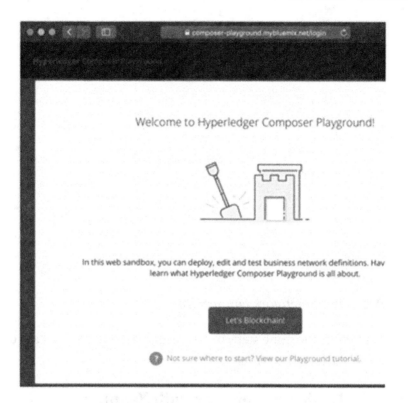

Figure 8-21. Composer Playground

To test Playground Online, you can import the `hello-network.bna` file
you created previously. To do so, first click "Let's Blockchain!" and under
"2. MODEL NETWORK STARTER TEMPLATE" select "Drop here to upload
or browse" and upload the `hello-network.bna` file. Click the Deploy
button at the bottom-right corner. You can see the network created. Click
the "Connect now" link to connect to the new network. See Figure 8-22.

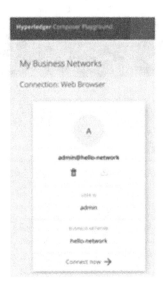

Figure 8-22. *hello-network connect link*

You can repeat the same steps to create an asset and test, just as you have done on the local playground.

Creating a Business Network with Yeoman

You used Hyperledger Playground to generate your business network. Hyperledger Playground is aimed not just for developers but also at business owners because of its simplicity; however, you can also create a network in Terminal.

Yeoman provides a wizard you can use. If you are unfamiliar with Yeoman, it provides a wizard generator through the command line. You can either run Yeoman and select Hyperledger Composer and the Business Network generator or run the following:

```
> Yeoman hyperledger-composer:businessnetwork
```

Keep in mind that Hyperledger Composer can be used for more than just generating the business network; it can be used for Angular, LoopBack, and Model as well. See Figure 8-23.

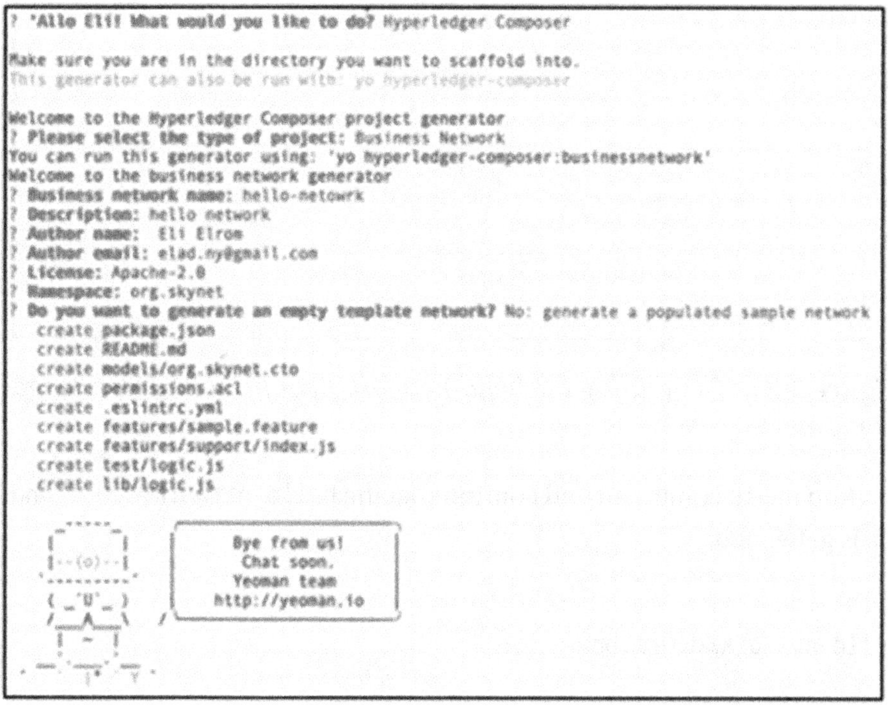

```
? 'Allo Eli! What would you like to do? Hyperledger Composer

Make sure you are in the directory you want to scaffold into.
This generator can also be run with: yo hyperledger-composer

Welcome to the Hyperledger Composer project generator
? Please select the type of project: Business Network
You can run this generator using: 'yo hyperledger-composer:businessnetwork'
Welcome to the business network generator
? Business network name: hello-netowrk
? Description: hello network
? Author name:  Eli Elrom
? Author email: elad.ny@gmail.com
? License: Apache-2.0
? Namespace: org.skynet
? Do you want to generate an empty template network? No: generate a populated sample network
   create package.json
   create README.md
   create models/org.skynet.cto
   create permissions.acl
   create .eslintrc.yml
   create features/sample.feature
   create features/support/index.js
   create test/logic.js
   create lib/logic.js


    .-----.
   {       }               .----------------.
   |--(o)--|               |  Bye from us!  |
   .---------.             |   Chat soon.   |
  {  _'U'_  }              |  Yeoman team   |
  /___A___\   /            |http://yeoman.io|
   |  ~  |                 '----------------'
 .--'---'--.
'    ' ' '  '
```

Figure 8-23. *Generating hello-network with the Yeoman wizard*

The hello-network folder is generated and includes permissions.acl, models, features, test, and lib. Next, to create the .bna file, you can use Hyperledger Composer. See Figure 8-24.

```
> cd hello-network
> composer archive create -t dir -n .
```

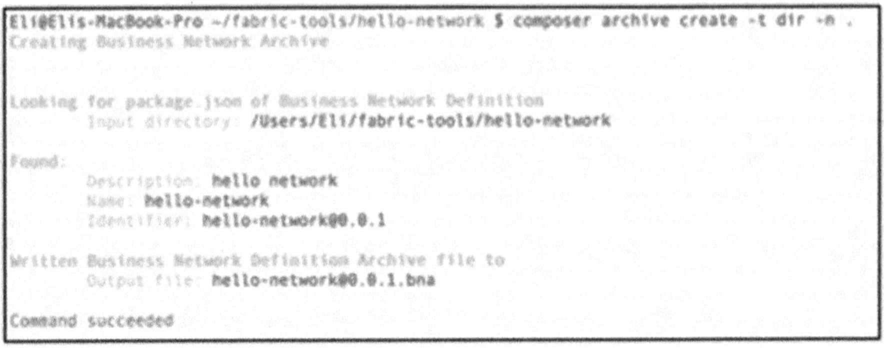

```
Eli@Elis-MacBook-Pro ~/fabric-tools/hello-network $ composer archive create -t dir -n .
Creating Business Network Archive

Looking for package.json of Business Network Definition
        Input directory: /Users/Eli/fabric-tools/hello-network

Found:
        Description: hello network
        Name: hello-network
        Identifier: hello-network@0.0.1

Written Business Network Definition Archive file to
        Output file: hello-network@0.0.1.bna

Command succeeded
```

Figure 8-24. *Generating the hello-network BNA file with Hyperledger Composer*

Run the ls command and confirm that the hello-network@0.0.1.bna file is generated.

```
> ls *.bna
hello-network@0.0.1.bna
```

Deploying on a Local Hyperledger Fabric Network

To deploy the .bna file to a local Hyperledger Fabric network, run the composer network install command and point to the .bna file while specifying the identity card.

```
> cd ~/fabric-dev-servers/
> composer network install --archiveFile ~/Desktop/hello-
  network.bna --card PeerAdmin@hlfv1
```

This will result in the successful output shown in Figure 8-25.

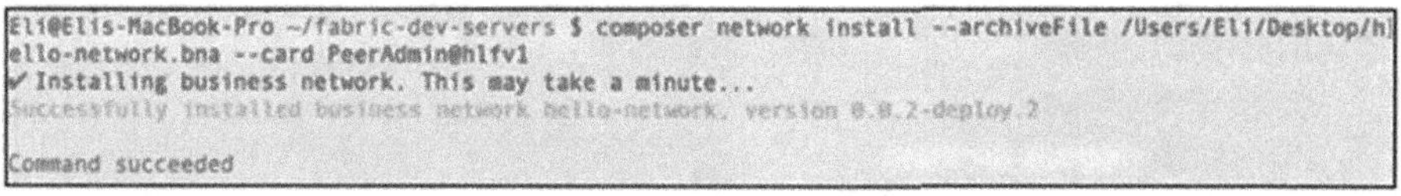

```
Eli@Elis-MacBook-Pro ~/fabric-dev-servers $ composer network install --archiveFile /Users/Eli/Desktop/h]
ello-network.bna --card PeerAdmin@hlfv1
✔ Installing business network. This may take a minute...
Successfully installed business network hello-network, version 0.0.2-deploy.2

Command succeeded
```

Figure 8-25. *Installing local Hyperledger Fabric command output*

Running the "hello-network" Network

Hyperledger Composer is the application development framework for building blockchain applications based on Hyperledger Fabric.

Hyperledger Composer generates REST APIs based on the business network definition you created. This is done using what is called a LoopBack connector. You can take these REST APIs to be used by a) a client such as a dapp b) integrate with non-blockchain clients such as a web site. That allows you to use the blockchain ledger just as you would use any other database with a middleware. That is powerful.

Hyperledger Composer can generate a REST interface. You can run Hyperledger Fabric on your computer and generate a GUI that you can then use to interact with the network running on your computer just like it would be on a real production server.

Starting the "hello-network" Business Network and Admin Card

To run your "hello-network" network, run the following command, and see the output in Figure 8-26:

```
> composer network start --networkName hello-network
  --networkVersion 0.0.2-deploy.3 -A admin -S adminpw -c
  PeerAdmin@hlfv1 --file networkadmin.card
```

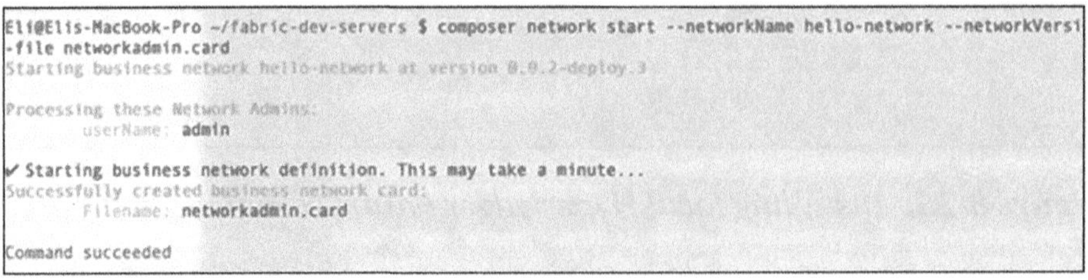

```
Eli@Elis-MacBook-Pro ~/fabric-dev-servers $ composer network start --networkName hello-network --networkVersi
-file networkadmin.card
Starting business network hello-network at version 0.0.2-deploy.3

Processing these Network Admins:
        userName: admin

✓ Starting business network definition. This may take a minute...
Successfully created business network card:
        Filename: networkadmin.card

Command succeeded
```

Figure 8-26. *Starting the business network*

To confirm this worked, you can run the docker ps command. You should see the dev-peer0.org1.example.com-hello-network-0.0.2-deploy.3-0 image created, as shown in Figure 8-27.

```
> docker ps
```

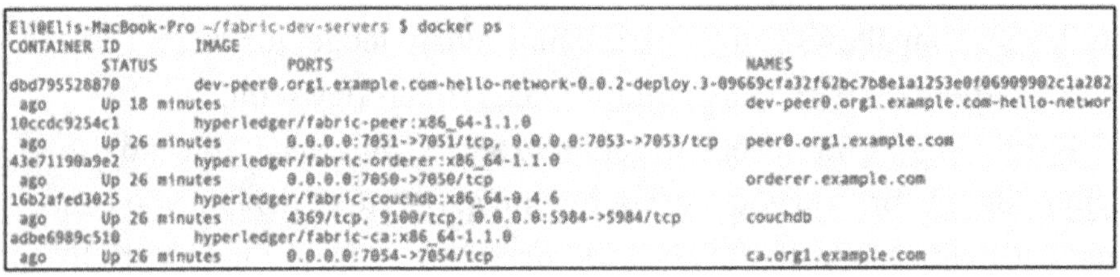

```
Eli@Elis-MacBook-Pro ~/fabric-dev-servers $ docker ps
CONTAINER ID        IMAGE
        STATUS              PORTS                                               NAMES
dbd795528870        dev-peer0.org1.example.com-hello-network-0.0.2-deploy.3-09669cfa32f62bc7b8e1a1253e0f06909902c1a282
ago     Up 18 minutes                                                           dev-peer0.org1.example.com-hello-networ
10ccdc9254c1        hyperledger/fabric-peer:x86_64-1.1.0
ago     Up 26 minutes       0.0.0.0:7051->7051/tcp, 0.0.0.0:7053->7053/tcp      peer0.org1.example.com
43e71190a9e2        hyperledger/fabric-orderer:x86_64-1.1.0
ago     Up 26 minutes       0.0.0.0:7050->7050/tcp                              orderer.example.com
16b2afed3025        hyperledger/fabric-couchdb:x86_64-0.4.6
ago     Up 26 minutes       4369/tcp, 9100/tcp, 0.0.0.0:5984->5984/tcp          couchdb
adbe6989c510        hyperledger/fabric-ca:x86_64-1.1.0
ago     Up 26 minutes       0.0.0.0:7054->7054/tcp                              ca.org1.example.com
```

Figure 8-27. *Docker container hello-network*

Importing a Business Card

Next, import a new network admin card so you can use admin@hello-network in the business network you started.

```
> composer card import --file networkadmin.card
```

This command imports the network admin card, which will include admin@hello-network.

```
> composer network ping --card admin@hello-network
```

You can compare your output with mine, which is shown in Figure 8-28.

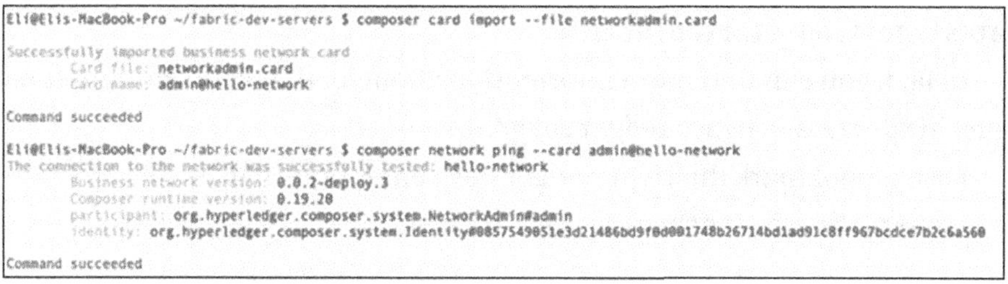

```
Eli@Elis-MacBook-Pro ~/fabric-dev-servers $ composer card import --file networkadmin.card

Successfully imported business network card
        Card file: networkadmin.card
        Card name: admin@hello-network

Command succeeded

Eli@Elis-MacBook-Pro ~/fabric-dev-servers $ composer network ping --card admin@hello-network
The connection to the network was successfully tested: hello-network
        Business network version: 0.0.2-deploy.3
        Composer runtime version: 0.19.28
        participant: org.hyperledger.composer.system.NetworkAdmin#admin
        identity: org.hyperledger.composer.system.Identity#0857549051e3d21486bd9f0d001748b26714bd1ad91c8ff967bcdce7b2c6a560

Command succeeded
```

Figure 8-28. *Importing the business network card*

Where to Go from Here

From here you can choose from many passport strategies for your users. For example, you can use Google OAUTH2.0, SAML, Passport-JWT, or LDAP, depending on what your organization is using.

Then you will be able to run a REST server in multiuser mode and test the interaction with a client application such as the one you created.

Here are couple of articles that can help you with the process of setting up your app for authenticating multiple users:

- *Passport-JWT*: `https://hyperledger.github.io/composer/latest/tutorials/google_oauth2_rest`

- *Google OAUTH2.0*: `hyperledger/fabric-ca docker hyperledger/fabric-orderer hyperledger/fabric-peer hyperledger/fabric-ccenv hyperledger/fabric-couchdb`

Hyperledger is a large project, and it consists of five major platforms as well as five major tools. This chapter focused only on Hyperledger Fabric. However, you are encouraged to continue experimenting with other Hyperledger platforms and tools such as Hyperledger Sawtooth, including setting up an environment, creating an account, writing a more complex chaincode, and deploying as well as connecting your chaincode to a dapp.

To get more information on getting started, visit the official web site here: `https://sawtooth.hyperledger.org/docs/seth/releases/latest/getting_started.html`.

In fact, you can find more information about all the platforms and tools here: `https://www.hyperledger.org/`.

Lastly, bookmark the Hyperledger dev center here: `https://developer.ibm.com/technologies/blockchain/`.

Error Troubleshooting

Hyperledger was built to be plain and allows you to stitch together modules on many different machines, but not without problems. Hyperledger is set up for more advanced users and may request system admin privileges to set up servers. You may have encountered a few errors, so here I have compiled them into this section.

Composer Runtime Install Error or Card Not Found

If you get errors such as these:

- "composer runtime install error card not found peerAdmin"

- "Error: Card not found: PeerAdmin@hlfv1"

it's because the admin ID card was not created successfully or the correct process wasn't followed; all you need to do is remove the ID card and re-create it. You need to remove the `composer` folder, create a new folder, and run the command again.

```
> rm -rf ~/.composer
> mkdir ~/.composer
> ./createPeerAdminCard.sh
```

Docker Unauthorized Authentication Required Error

You may get the following error while downloading Hyperledger Fabric:

- "unauthorized: authentication required"

There are issues with authenticating or proxying to Docker Hub and not Hyperledger Fabric.

To try to fix this, set your computer time to match UTC time zone: https://www.timeanddate.com/worldclock/timezone/utc.

Create an account with Docker at https://hub.docker.com, and then log in.

```
> docker login
```

Alternatively, try again after you logged out.

```
> docker logout
```

Docker Container Conflicting Errors

When you are using the Docker container for a project, you might need to re-create a container or stop a container; otherwise, you may get conflicting errors.

All you need to do is stop and remove the container.

```
> docker stop [container id]
> docker rm [container id]
```

Tip   If you already created a Mongo-Docker container or any other Docker container that creates a conflict, you will get the following conflict error when you try to create a new one: "The container name is already in use by container [container id]." All you need to do is stop the container and remove it.

```
> docker stop [container id]
> docker rm [container id]
```

Mismatch and Cleanup

If you have a mismatch between Hyperledger Composer and Hyperledger Fabric versions, you may get the following error:

- "Starting business network definition. This may take a minute... Error: Error trying to start business network. Error: Failed to connect to any peer event hubs. It is required that at least 1 event hub has been connected to receive the commit event Command failed."

This error is also generated on Hyperledger Fabric 1.2 with Hyperledger Composer 0.20.6 because there is an open bug. To fix this, you need to check your Hyperledger Composer and uninstall through npm, as well as re-install Hyperledger Fabric.

Additionally, if you need to completely clean up, you need to stop and tear down Fabric. To remove the Docker images, remove `fabric-dev-servers`, and lastly remove Composer, follow this process:

```
> cd ~/fabric-tools
> ./stopFabric.sh
> ./teardownFabric.sh
```

Next, stop the Docker containers, remove them, and also remove all the Docker images by running these commands:

```
> docker kill $(docker ps -q)
> docker rm $(docker ps -a -q) -f
> docker rmi $(docker images -q) -f
```

You can now completely remove fabric-dev-servers.

```
> rm -rf ~/fabric-dev-servers
```

To remove Composer and admin ID card, run these commands:

```
> sudo rm -rf ~/.composer
> npm uninstall -g composer-cli
```

The npm uninstall command will output a confirmation that the library was uninstalled.

Summary

In this chapter, I introduced Hyperledger to help you get started and understand the power of it. I covered the Hyperledger ecosystem and terminology and gave you a good understanding of the pieces that make up the network as well as the major Hyperledger platforms and tools available. You installed Hyperledger Fabric and Hyperledger Composer, ensuring the prerequisite libraries are installed. You created "Hello, World" application with Playground as well as create a .bna file you deployed on a local network. I mentioned Hyperledger Playground Online as well as explained how to generate a network with Yeoman generator. I covered the different pieces that make up the .bna archive file including handling ID cards. I also covered potential errors and troubleshooting to ensure your installation went well. Lastly, I covered a few recommendations on where to go from here to continue with Hyperledger.

In the next chapter, you will learn how to build a dapp with Angular. Dapps can interact with the smart contracts you have developed in the past three chapters and are an important ingredient in the blockchain ecosystem.

CHAPTER 9

Build Dapps with Angular: Part I

In previous chapters, I covered different blockchains, and you learned how to create smart contracts that can interact with a blockchain. You created smart contracts in Ethereum, NEO, EOS, and Hyperledger. In Chapter 1, I broke down the process into five layers: consensus layer, miner or booking layer, propagation layer, semantic layer, and application layer. Smart contracts are part of the application layer in the development cycle; however, the application layer is incomplete without having a front-end interface that enables an end user to interact with the blockchain.

Tip   Many times you will hear decentralized applications (dapps) referred to as smart contracts. Smart contracts are self-executing contracts. Dapps use smart contracts but run on a P2P network and not on a single system.

Developers and more savvy users can interact with the smart contracts you created via the command-line interface and tools mentioned in previous chapters, but developing a front-end application that is able to interact with a blockchain is essential for all other users. You do this by creating a decentralized application (dapp). In this chapter and the next, you will be creating a decentralized application with the help of Angular so that users can interact with a smart contract using a friendly and intuitive user interface (UI). I broke down the process into two parts.

Part I, covered in this chapter, contains the following topics:

- Developing the dapp, including its benefits and classification

- Using Angular, including its architecture, benefits, prerequisites, and creating an Angular skeleton app

- Creating and styling Angular custom components

Part II, covered in Chapter 10, contains the following topics:

- Creating the dapp's smart contract with Truffle

- Integrating the smart contract with the dapp

- Linking and connecting your dapp to the Ethereum network

Let's get started.

What Is a Dapp?

A *decentralized application* (shortened as ÐApp, dapp, Dapp, dApp, or DApp and pronounced as "dee-app") is a web application that is able to interact with a smart contract. Dapps run on the blockchain and utilize the distributed ledger. The Ethereum blockchain is currently the most popular platform to run dapps; however, other distributed ledger technologies (DLTs) you have seen also provide the ability to create dapps. I covered NEO, EOS, and Hyperledger in previous chapters; others include ICON, Cardano, and Hashgraph (Hedera).

"Everything that can be decentralized will be decentralized."

—David Johnston, CEO of the DApp Fund
`https://github.com/DavidJohnstonCEO/`
`DecentralizedApplications`

If you have ever developed a standard desktop, web, or mobile application, you will find that dapps are similar but also very different.

A dapp is built using the same tools and languages you use to build any other app, but for an app to be categorized as a dapp, it needs to meet the following criteria:

- *Open source*: Its code is published as open source and should not be governed by one entity (centralized). Keep in mind that the application may adapt its own protocol in response to proposed improvements and market feedback; however, the consensus of its users drives all changes.

- *Decentralized*: Dapps utilize a blockchain or a P2P network.

- *Incentive*: Dapps use digital assets for funding.

- *Algorithm/protocol*: Dapps often generate tokens and include a consensus mechanism such as PoW, PoS, or even their own.

These criteria ensure dapps don't have downtime like other apps you download from marketplaces such as iTunes or Google Play; dapps also give control to a community instead of one entity. These criteria can be significant. For instance, Apple and Google often reject apps for not meeting their arbitrary or monetary-based policies. These policies do not always make sense and are not always in the best interest of the end user; they often are there to block usage of a competitor or for monetary gain.

Dapps that are based on open source code implemented on decentralized blockchains and funded by tokens generated using a specific consensus mechanism are believed by many to be the future of all businesses. Only time will tell.

Additionally, open source software is an advantage because it allows users to view the source code and potentially contribute. Decentralizing using a blockchain harnesses the advantages of blockchain as DLT and serves as a replacement to the traditional one-server database.

Finally, adding records/transactions to ledgers is usually done utilizing tokens, and the consensus mechanism of a token is also an agreement between all the users of the dapp.

Dapp Classification

In addition to the previous criteria, dapps can be categorized. The classification is based on the infrastructure the dapp is utilizing and can be broken down to these three categories:

- *Dedicated blockchain dapps*: These are dapps that use a dedicated blockchain directly; examples are bitcoin, Ethereum, EOS, and NEO.

- *Dapps relying on another blockchain*: For instance, the Omni Layer Protocol (formerly called Mastercoin) is a digital currency and communications protocol that is built on top of the bitcoin blockchain.

- *Dapps relying on another protocol that built on top of another blockchain*: These dapps use a protocol that is built on top of another blockchain. An example is the safe network using the Omni Layer Protocol.

A good example to help understand the classification concept is the USDT (Tether) token. This token was issued twice based on two blockchains: bitcoin and Ethereum. In this case, there are two types of USDT. The original, which is based on bitcoin, is done by using the Omni Layer Protocol to generate the token, and the Ethereum-based USDT is compatible with the Ethereum's ERC20 standard. Take a look at Figure 9-1.

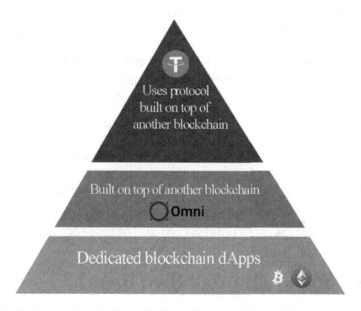

Figure 9-1. *Representation of clasisification for USDT*

Dapp Projects

Most dapps are built directly on top of the Ethereum blockchain or use a blockchain for their tokens. However, there are some dapps that even build their own dedicated blockchain. Take a look at Table 9-1 for a sample of different dapps and their classifications.

Table 9-1. *Example of Dapps and Classifications*

Dapp	Description	Classification	Token	Blockchain
Ethlance	Marketplace for job postings and hiring freelancers. 0 percent fees.	Uses Ethereum directly	No token	Ethereum blockchain
Golem	Global market for idle computer power.	Token based on Ethereum	GNT	Ethereum blockchain
The SAFE Network	Data storage and communications network.	Implementation relying on another protocol (Omni protocol) that is built on top of another blockchain (bitcoin)	SFE	Bitcoin

In addition to the information in Table 9-1, there are many resources to find more dapps; these two web sites provide a list of dapps that you can check: `https://dapps.ethercasts.com/` and `https://coinsutra.com`.

How Do You Create Your Own Dapp?

The success of bitcoin and blockchain have brought an explosion of dapps. Developers and business owners have created a basic process to follow for developing dapps. You don't need to follow this exactly, and it may change by the time of writing; however, many of the published dapps out there have followed this process. The process consists of these five steps:

1. Write a white paper.

2. Launch an initial coin offering (ICO).

3. Develop the dapp.

4. Launch your dapp.

5. Market your dapp.

Let's review these steps.

Write a White Paper

The white paper is similar to a company's business plan aimed at investors. However, it targets more than just investors; it's the technical blueprint. The white paper is the technical document as well as the business plan and should explain the problem being solved and the concept, features, and technical aspects of the dapp.

Just like in a business plan, it's a good idea to include your unique selling proposition (USP), road map, members' résumés, capabilities, and history to help establish credibility.

Note   The unique selling proposition (USP) is the problem your dapp is aiming to solve.

Once the white paper is published, it is good to get feedback from peers and the community in the early stages and prior to development. Social media, forms, and publications are often used to promote dapps and help create credibility.

Launch an Initial Coin Offering

Once the white paper is published, the next step is to launch an ICO and sell coins or tokens to fund and support your dapp. The coin should have a reason for existence, rather than be the same as another coin/token out there, so you should explain how and why your dapp needs its own token or coin.

You also need to decide on the type of classification for your dapp, which will determine whether you will need any or all of the following: 1) issue token 2) set usage fees. 3) have a dedicated blockchain. 4) have a mining mechanism 5) set the allocation of fees 6) rewards investors 7) allocate fees to pay for different departments of your business: support, development, marketing, and business.

Develop the Dapp

Development should be open source, and GitHub is usually used for repos for the development effort. On every release, it's a good idea to let investors and others know of a release to build users and a developer community around your project. Many dapps have tried to get funds and delivered no usable products; set yourself apart and avoid potential problems with regulators. (I will cover regulators in Chapter 11.)

Launch Your Dapp

Launch your dapp and include your release notes, documentation, road map, and maintenance plan. It's crucial to meet the promised launch date.

Market Your Dapp

The last step is marketing. In addition to traditional marketing, dapps often hire or work with prompters during early phases or after release to get the word out. Another unique marketing aspect for a dapp is to get the coin/ token listed on exchanges. This is the final stamp of recognition. Some exchanges have a voting system put in place to select the next coin/token to be listed. Some exchanges have been abusing this process and charging hefty fees to list a token or coin. For instance, a utility token listing on Binance exchange can cost from $0.5 million to $3 million.

Many early investors including dapp owners have been able to "cash out" if a token is listed on major exchanges as its price often goes up high because of the listing; however, it has become more and more difficult for a dapp to be listed, and it needs to provide real value. Fraudsters are often exposed, and coins/tokens get de-listed as quickly as they are listed.

Why Angular?

With dapps, just like with any traditional app, you can write your application natively to the device you publish your app to (in the supported language of your device such as Xcode for iOS); however, it has been proven that using a framework can speed up development. For instance, if you want to utilize the same code and deploy your application on multiple devices with different screen sizes, that can become a challenge for a small team. Angular helps you build cross-platform modern applications for web, mobile, and desktop at the same time. The Angular CLI and Component Dev Kit (CDK) can help accelerate the development of apps.

Using Angular can be beneficial because of the following factors:

– Large community support

– Enterprise architecture and scaling

– Cross-platform support

– Documentation

Angular is a structural framework and enables you to create front-end client-side applications. The pieces are loosely coupled and structured in a modular fashion, resulting in less code to write, added flexibility, easier-to-read code, and quicker development time.

Angular allows the developer to put together a toolset for building a framework that will fit your exact application's needs. You can use HTML as your template language and extend HTML's syntax so the application's components can be read easily. Other than HTML, the coding is done with TypeScript, which turns JavaScript into an object-oriented programming language and gives you an enterprise-level environment.

Additionally, Angular is well structured and built to be fully accessible, in accordance with accessible rich Internet applications (ARIAs), so your app or site can be built correctly for people with disabilities.

Angular also gets along well with other JavaScript libraries so you can install libraries such as the Ethereum JavaScript API web3.js with npm manager. Lastly, Angular's features can be easily modified or replaced to fit your exact needs.

Note   The word *angular* means having multiple angles or measured by an angle. Angular is a structural framework and enables you to create front-end client-side applications for the Web, mobile, and desktop. It is an open source, front-end framework for dynamic app development.

Angular's most significant features are data binding and dependency injection. These can help decrease code. Also, Angular has been around for years; it's on its seventh release.

Note   Dependency injection is a design pattern technique. As the name suggests, it means using one object as a dependency to another object by injecting the code.

Angular 2 was a complete rewrite of AngularJS and offered a major change; however, there are no major differences between Angular 2 up to version 8.

The latest release version of Angular at the time of writing is 7.3.1, and in this version, a few features were added such as the following:

- *Dependencies*: The dependencies were upgraded, and support for Typescript 3.1, RxJS 6.3, and Node 10 was added.

- *Bundle budget*: You can set a warning for the size of the application to ensure you don't exceed the limit (the default is 2 MB).

- *Angular CLI*: By running the CLI wizard, you can add components such as routing and decide on the format of the CSS.

- *Component Dev Kit (CDK) of Angular Material*: Add new features such as out-of-the-box virtual scrolling, drag and drop, and "mat-form-field" support for native select fields. (I'll cover Material later in this chapter.)

Angular 8 is at release candidate 2 (rc.2), and the features expected are mostly to improve performance. It will include an improved view engine called Angular Ivy, improved upload of JavaScript for modern browsers that support ES2015+, support for web workers to use hardware for heavy lifting, support for TypeScript, a benchmarks tool, and more.

Tip   I selected Angular, but Angular is not the only framework that can help expedite development. You can use other frameworks such as React (`https://reactjs.org`) and achieve similar benefits. This decision is really a matter of personal taste and your team's skill set. You could easily convert this project to a React project mostly by copying your project's files over to the React project.

Creating an Angular Dapp

In this section, you will be creating an actual dapp that will connect to the Ethereum network and transfer funds from one account to another. This is often the core feature of any dapp out there. For instance, you can build a dapp that sells products, provides services, or pays users to take quizzes, and all these types would need to have a mechanism in place to transfer coins/tokens. In this section of this chapter, you will be creating a dapp utilizing Angular.

In terms of environment and deployment, you will be using the Truffle web framework you used in Chapter 5, as it offers benefits for quickly creating a smart contract. Truffle is able to do more than just help compile your smart contract; it does everything you need to inject your smart contract into a web app and can run the test suite. You are also going to utilize MetaMask again to get a secure blockchain account in the browser. Lastly, you will use and run Ganache to create a local blockchain RPC server to test and develop against.

Prerequisites

Most of what you need is already installed. Angular needs Node and npm manager, which you have installed previously. Confirm the correct version is installed by running the libraries with the v flag, just as you have done in previous chapters.

```
> node -v
> npm -v
```

In case you do not have npm and node, just run the following command:

```
> brew install node
```

Give npm ownership for your user so you won't need to use sudo to install libraries.

```
> sudo chown -R $USER:$GROUP ~/.npm
> sudo chown -R $USER:$GROUP ~/.config
```

It's recommended that you upgrade npm to ensure you are using the latest version; at the time of writing, it's 6.9.0.

```
> [sudo] npm install -g npm
+npm@6.9.0
```

Angular CLI

Next, you need to install the Angular command-line interface (CLI). For Angular CLI, it's recommended (but not required) to install Angular CLI with sudo and allow-root and ensure Angular CLI will have the correct privileges. You will be installing version 7.3.9, which is the latest stable release version of Angular.

```
> sudo npm install -g @angular/cli@7.3.9 --unsafe-perm=true
  --allow-root
+ @angular/cli@7.3.9
added 363 packages from 197 contributors in 13.691s
You could also install the latest version of Angular but your
example code may break, with newer versions of Angular.
> sudo npm install -g @angular/cli --unsafe-perm=true --allow-root
```

To verify installation went well, run the version flag, and you should see version 7.3.9; Figure 9-2 shows the expected output.

```
> ng version
```

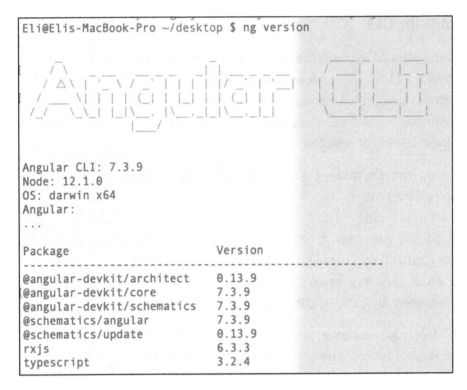

```
Eli@Elis-MacBook-Pro ~/desktop $ ng version


  /  \   _ __   __ _ _   _| | __ _ _ __      / ___| |   |_ _|
 / /\ \ | '_ \ / _` | | | | |/ _` | '__|    | |   | |    | |
/ ____ \| | | | (_| | |_| | | (_| | |       | |___| |___ | |
\_/    \_\_| |_|\__, |\__,_|_|\__,_|_|        \____|_____|___|
              |___/


Angular CLI: 7.3.9
Node: 12.1.0
OS: darwin x64
Angular:
...

Package                           Version
------------------------------------------------------------
@angular-devkit/architect         0.13.9
@angular-devkit/core              7.3.9
@angular-devkit/schematics        7.3.9
@schematics/angular               7.3.9
@schematics/update                0.13.9
rxjs                              6.3.3
typescript                        3.2.4
```

Figure 9-2. *Angular CLI installation verification*

Create an Angular Project

Now that you have the main tools and libraries installed, you can proceed
and create your project from scratch by downloading other needed
libraries, test libraries, and build scripts, as well as make your own folder
structure; however, to expedite this process, you can use the Angular seed
project that includes a skeleton project to quickly bootstrap your project.

Using the Angular seed project can help you start development quickly
and efficiently, following Angular's best practices. There are pros and cons
of using boilerplate skeleton code. You can decide on your own if you want
to use this skeleton for future projects, but for this demo app, it is ideal.

There are many ways you can create your project using the Angular seed skeleton. I will be showing you two options here: using the Angular CLI and using WebStorm.

The ng new command will run a script that will create your app. You can run the CLI new command and give the name ethdapp as your app name.

```
> cd ~/desktop
> ng new ethdapp
Would you like to add Angular routing? (y/N) y
Which stylesheet format would you like to use? CSS
```

Notice that I added routing here and decided to use CSS for styles. I will get more into these later in the chapter.

Once installation is complete, it will output all the files that are created.

```
CREATE ethdapp/README.md (1024 bytes)
CREATE ethdapp/angular.json (3557 bytes)
CREATE ethdapp/package.json (1313 bytes)
...
```

Change directories to the newly created folder and confirm you have the initial files and directories.

```
> cd ethdapp
```

Running the following command will analyze your package.json config file with recommendations:

```
> ng update
```

You can run the following command to follow the recommendations:

```
> ng update --all
```

Next, install Bower globally. Bower is a package manager that is used often with Angular. At the time of writing, it's at version 1.8.8.

```
> npm install -g bower
> bower -v
1.8.8
```

Let's do a walk-through of what was created in a workspace and the starter project files (see Figure 9-3).

```
drwx------+  29 Eli   staff      928 May 11 12:54 ..
-rw-r--r--    1 Eli   staff     1024 May 11 12:54 README.md
-rw-r--r--    1 Eli   staff      246 May 11 12:54 .editorconfig
-rw-r--r--    1 Eli   staff      629 May 11 12:54 .gitignore
-rw-r--r--    1 Eli   staff     3816 May 11 12:54 angular.json
-rw-r--r--    1 Eli   staff     1306 May 11 12:54 package.json
-rw-r--r--    1 Eli   staff      435 May 11 12:54 tsconfig.json
-rw-r--r--    1 Eli   staff     1621 May 11 12:54 tslint.json
drwxr-xr-x   16 Eli   staff      512 May 11 12:54 src
drwxr-xr-x    5 Eli   staff      160 May 11 12:54 e2e
drwxr-xr-x  776 Eli   staff    24832 May 11 12:55 node_modules
-rw-r--r--    1 Eli   staff   375785 May 11 12:55 package-lock.json
drwxr-xr-x   14 Eli   staff      448 May 11 12:55 .
drwxr-xr-x   12 Eli   staff      384 May 11 12:55 .git
```

Figure 9-3. *Ethdapp files created by Angular CLI*

- *A new workspace*: This is the root folder named ethdapp.

- *e2e folder*: This contains an end-to-end test project, located here: ethdapp/e2e. The testing folder includes the Jasmin library's JSON configuration file.

- *src folder*: This is your project folder, which includes all the files of your project.

  - An initial skeleton app project, located here: ethdapp/src/app

  - The assets folder with the entry file index.html

  - Other configuration files

- *.gitignore*: Here you list any files and folders that you would like to ignore when you upload your project to Git.

- *angular.json*: This is your project configuration file and includes information about your project.

- *package.json*: This is the npm manager configuration file and includes all the libraries you will be using in your project.

- *README.MD*: This is documentation about your project; this will be the "home page" document of your project and the first file developers will read to get instructions on how to get the project running.

- *tsconfig.json*: This is the TypeScript config file.

- *tslint.json*: This is the Lint config file used to set your best-practice formatting, spacing, and the like.

Serve the Application

To see your actual dapps, you will be using the ng serve command, which builds the app, starts the development server, watches the source files, and rebuilds the app as you make changes to those files. The --open flag opens the app in a browser on port 4200 here: http://localhost:4200/. Run the ng serve command with the open flag.

```
> ng serve --open
```

You should see the dapp running in your browser, as shown in Figure 9-4.

Welcome to ethdapp!

Here are some links to help you start:

- <u>**Tour of Heroes**</u>
- <u>**CLI Documentation**</u>
- <u>**Angular blog**</u>

Figure 9-4. *Angular seed app running in the browser*

The skeleton app includes links to a tour, documentation, and an Angular blog. By going through the "Tour of Heroes" and the CLI documentation, you can get a good understanding of how Angular works, and bookmarking the Angular blog can give you updates on future releases and announcements.

To stop the application from serving, press Command+C in Terminal.

Angular Project with WebStorm

Another option for firing up the Angular seed project is utilizing the WebStorm IDE, which you have been using in previous chapters. WebStorm allows you to either import the seed project you created or create a new seed project.

To import the ethdapp project you created with the Angular CLI ng new command, open WebStorm, select File ➤ Open, and navigate to the ethdapp directory. That's it; WebStorm will automatically import the project.

Alternatively, to start a new Angular seed project in WebStorm, select File ➤ New ➤ Project from the top menu. Next, select Angular CLI and name your project **ethdapp**. Use the drop-down menu to select the version of the Angular CLI, as shown in Figure 9-5.

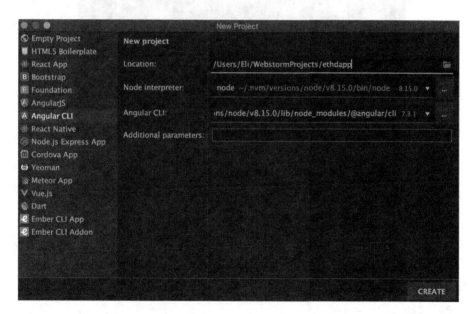

Figure 9-5. *Generating the Angular seed project in WebStorm*

Now that the project is created, you can run the same command, utilizing the Terminal tab in the bottom menu of WebStorm, as shown in Figure 9-6.

```
> ng serve -open
```

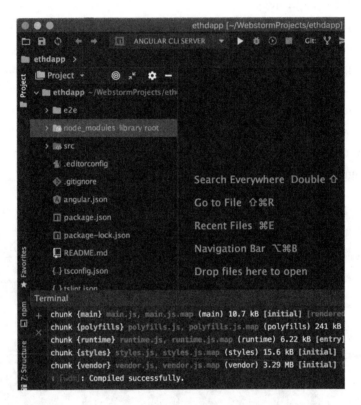

Figure 9-6. Serving ethdapp in WebStorm's Terminal

You can download the skeleton application from the book repository: https://github.com/Apress/the-blockchain-developer/chapter9/step1.zip.

When you download your steps, make sure you run npm install because I stripped out the node module to decrease the size of the project.

```
> npm install
```

Note   I excluded node_modules, which holds all the project's dependencies, from the project. It's common not to include it with a project because of its size; you can install it with the npm install command.

Ensure No Mismatch with Angular CLI Version

You can create your Angular seed project either with WebStorm or through the ng command, and you need to check that there is no mismatch of the global Angular CLI with the local project Angular CLI. This can happen when setting files pointing to a previous version, or you may have used Angular in the past with an older version. What happens is that your local project Angular shows an older version than the global Angular installed on your computer.

To ensure this is not the case, run any ng command, and if this issue exists, you will see the following error message:

```
> ng
Your global Angular CLI version (7.3.9) is greater than your local
version (6.2.9). The local Angular CLI version is used.
```

If you continue with these settings, you will be running version 6.x instead of 7.x. To fix this, what you need to do is uninstall the Angular CLI from your dev environment and then install version 7.x.

```
> npm uninstall --save-dev angular-cli
> npm install --save-dev @angular/cli@7.3.9
```

Notice that you use the --save-dev flag so the new version will be saved in your package.json project file. Now if you run the version command again, you should see the correct version with no warning messages.

```
> ng --version
Angular CLI: 7.3.2
```

Now that you have ensured you are running the correct version of Angular CLI, you are ready to continue development and make changes to the seed starter app.

Angular Components

An Angular best practice is to use a Model View Controller (MVC)–style architecture. Angular supports coding with a separation of concerns just like any other mature framework.

The Angular MVC includes the following three elements:

- *Model*: This contains the application's data and Angular data binding, which allows reflection of data.

Note   reflection in relation to data binding, elements bound to a data and any data change is automatically reflected. For instance, you bind price change to multiple view elements and once the price change data is updated all the view elements are updated automatically.

- *View*: This contains the HTML or a template and directives.

- *Controller*: This is the glue holding the model and the view together. The controller takes the data, applies business logic, and sends the results to the view.

As you probably recall, Angular's welcome page opened when you were running the serve command. The welcome component is the application shell. The shell is controlled by an Angular component named AppComponent.

Components are the fundamental building blocks of an Angular application. They display data on the screen, listen for user input, and take action based on that input.

You will be creating a component called `transfer` that you will be using to transfer coins to another address. To create the `transfer` component, run the `ng generate component` command.

```
> ng g c components/transfer
```

Notice that you used the shortcuts g and c that stand for "generate" and "component," respectively, but you can also use the full name instead of the abbreviation.

The ng command generated the four following files for you:

- `transfer.component.css`: Component's specific CSS styles

- `transfer.component.html`: Component template, written in HTML

- `transfer.component.spec.ts`: Testing file

- `transfer.component.ts`: Component class code, written in TypeScript

These four files together act as the implementation of the `transfer` component. You can see the folder structure in Figure 9-7.

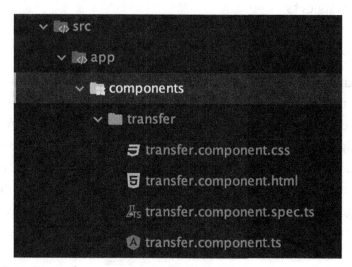

Figure 9-7. Transfer component file structure

An application's structure is usually created with a header, a footer, and a navigation menu so you can navigate to different partial views.

Using this architecture of header and footer components can help you create different views and split the page view into separate files. Think of each piece as a stand-alone reusable UI module. Angular Seed promotes this type of architecture and comes with the welcome component already created. Let's create a start component, a header, and footer components.

```
> ng g c components/start
> ng g c components/header
> ng g c components/footer
```

You can see in the output that each component generated the following files:

```
CREATE src/app/components/[component-name]/[component-name].
component.css
CREATE src/app/components/[component-name]/[component-name].
component.html
CREATE src/app/components/[component-name]/[component-name].
component.spec.ts
CREATE src/app/components/[component-name]/[component-name].
component.ts
```

In addition to these files, you can open `ethdapp/src/app/app.module.ts` and notice that the `app.module.ts` file was modified every time you created a component. The `app.module.ts` file is one of the most important files in Angular; it's the app controller written in TypeScript. The controller is a global file that will tie your components together, so every component you want to use in your app needs to be defined in that file. If you did not use the `ng` script, you will need to modify `app.module.ts` yourself to link to the new component.

Since you used the CLI, these imports are included automatically for you:

```
import { TransferComponent } from './components/transfer/
transfer.component';
import { StartComponent } from './components/start/start.
component';
import { HeaderComponent } from './components/header/header.
component';
import { FooterComponent } from './components/footer/footer.
component';
```

Routing Module

Another important file and a good practice to create is an app-routing module. This file acts as a controller to instruct Angular how to navigate to different views in your app.

Normally to generate a route for your app, you do not need to manually do so, since during the creation of your app, you decided to create the routing file called app-routing.

If you need to create the app-routing file, you can run the following the module command:

```
> ng generate module app-routing --flat --module=app
CREATE src/app/app-routing.module.ts
UPDATE src/app/app.module.ts
```

Notice that this time in your command you are using the full name generate module instead of just the first letters of g and m. Both options work the same way.

The generate module command creates the initial code shown in Listing 9-1 for src/app/app-routing.module.ts.

Listing 9-1. app-routing Initial Startup Code

```
import { NgModule } from '@angular/core';
import { Routes, RouterModule } from '@angular/router';

const routes: Routes = [];

@NgModule({
  imports: [RouterModule.forRoot(routes)],
  exports: [RouterModule]
})
export class AppRoutingModule { }
```

The initial code includes an `import` statement to Angular code and module tag. Next, replace the pre-populated code of app-routing. module.ts file with the code in Listing 9-2.

Listing 9-2. app-routing Code to Route Views

```
import { NgModule } from '@angular/core';
import { CommonModule } from '@angular/common';
import { RouterModule, Routes } from '@angular/router';
import { StartComponent } from './components/start/start.
component';
import { TransferComponent } from './components/transfer/
transfer.component';
const routes: Routes = [
  { path: '', redirectTo: '/start', pathMatch: 'full' },
  { path: 'start', component: StartComponent },
  { path: 'transfer', component: TransferComponent }
];
@NgModule({
  declarations: [],
  imports: [ RouterModule.forRoot(routes), CommonModule ],
```

```
  exports: [ RouterModule ]
})
export class AppRoutingModule { }
```

In Listing 9-2, you imported the view components you will be using; these are start and transfer. They will act as web pages on a web site or partial views on a mobile app. The route tells your app what view to match with what keyword, and lastly you set import statements to tell Angular who can access this module.

Now that the routing is set, you can get the footer, header, and body of the page to display. All you have to do is open src/app/app.component. html and update from the welcome page's HTML code to the following three lines:

```
<app-header></app-header>
<router-outlet></router-outlet>
<app-footer></app-footer>
```

To test the changes you made to your application, you don't need to publish your app again or run any scripts; just save the files and run the same serve command you ran before in Terminal.

```
> ng serve
[wdm]: Compiled successfully.
```

The serve script includes scripts to watch for changes in files and update your app automatically, so all you have to do when you make a change to your files is go back to the browser. Most of the time you won't even need to refresh your web page; the changes will be there automatically. Navigate to http://localhost:4200 to see the changes.

If you would like to go directly to the transfer page, all you have to do is add the keyword you selected at the end of the URL as you set up the routing mechanism: http://localhost:4200/transfer. See Figure 9-8.

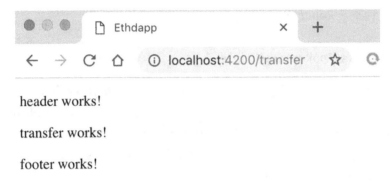

Figure 9-8. *Ethdapp header, footer, and transfer page*

You can download this step here: `https://github.com/Apress/the-blockchain-developer/chapter9/step2.zip`.

Styling an Angular App

Your app at this point is not styled and only shows text with a header, the page, and a footer; however, before you start styling, it's helpful to understand the Angular style architecture to ensure you don't end up with a Cascading Style Sheets (CSS) file that is too big to manage. You can style your app on a global level with styles that you need across your entire app as well as a specific style unique to only one component.

Additionally, it would be neat to sprint from zero to a styled app quickly. This can be done with Angular Material. Angular Material gives you a shortcut to get a consistent "look" to your app without all the hassle of thinking about cross-browser, cross-device programming. Let's take a look.

Angular-Style Architecture

Angular is set up to have a global CSS file. That CSS file is called `style.css`, and you can find it in the root of the project. `src/style.css` holds the styles that you want to use for your entire app, such as fonts, themes, styles for all the components, and so on.

As you have seen, each component also includes a private CSS file. The specific component CSS file is where you put styles that are unique and used only for that component.

For instance, /src/app/components/footer/footer.component.css holds the styles specific for the footer component.

Angular Material

Right now, your starter application is fast because it includes minimal code; however, there is a potential performance issue as you add more and more components, assets, and style to your app. You can get your app bloated easily, and every millisecond dealy counts.

The other potential issue is testing. All the different browsers, versions of browsers, screen sizes, and devices need to be tested, and creating your pages from scratch will require rigid testing and a quality assurance (QA) team to ensure it works consistency across devices.

Angular Material solves all these issues plus provides accessibility and internationalization. That is because Angular Material is optimized for Angular and built by the Angular team, so it integrates seamlessly with Angular. It has already passed all these compatibility tests.

For more information, check the Angular Material getting started page: https://material.angular.io/guide/getting-started.

Install Angular Material

There are a few ways to install Material. Because you have installed the Angular DevKit, you are able to just run the ng add command to get the Angular Material library. You need to first install cdk because it's a dependency.

```
> ng add @angular/cdk
```

Next, install Material.

```
> ng add @angular/material
```

Notice that the output asks you which theme color you would like with links. I will cover themes in the next section of this chapter, but for now, select the first or any color you prefer.

```
? Choose a prebuilt theme name, or "custom" for a custom theme:
(Use arrow keys)
□ Indigo/Pink        [ Preview: https://material.angular.
                       io?theme=indigo-pink ]
  Deep Purple/Amber  [ Preview: https://material.angular.
                       io?theme=deeppurple-amber ]
  Pink/Blue Grey     [ Preview: https://material.angular.
                       io?theme=pink-bluegrey ]
  Purple/Green       [ Preview: https://material.angular.
                       io?theme=purple-green ]
```

You can also set up gesture recognitions and animations.

```
? Set up HammerJS for gesture recognition? Yes
? Set up browser animations for Angular Material? Yes
```

The expected output should be showing the files that were updated:

```
UPDATE package.json
UPDATE angular.json
UPDATE src/app/app.module.ts
UPDATE src/index.html
UPDATE src/styles.css
```

Import Angular Material Modules

Next, you want to modify your app to have Angular Material include animations, Material icons, gesture support, and component modules.

In your project, you will only be using component modules and not all the features that Angular Material has to offer; what you need to do is import NgModule for each component you want to use. Open src/app/app.module.ts and add the import statements.

```
import {
  MatButtonModule,
  MatCheckboxModule,
  MatInputModule,
  MatSelectModule,
  MatDatepickerModule,
  MatNativeDateModule
} from '@angular/material';
```

Next, update the import statements of @NgModule to include the Material modules you imported.

```
imports: [
    BrowserModule,
    AppRoutingModule,
    BrowserAnimationsModule,
    MatButtonModule,
    MatInputModule,
    MatDatepickerModule,
    MatNativeDateModule,
    MatCheckboxModule,
    MatSelectModule
  ]
```

That's it. You can now have access to the Angular Material components you included.

Theme Your Angular Material App

Now that you have access to the Angular Material components, you can use themes to style them. A *theme* is a set of colors that will be used on your Angular Material components.

In Angular Material, a theme is created by creating multiple palettes.

- *Primary palette*: These are the colors most used across all screens and components.

- *Accent palette*: These are the colors used for the button and interactive elements.

- *Warn palette*: These are the colors for errors.

- *Foreground palette*: These are the colors for text and icons.

- *Background palette*: These are the colors for an element's backgrounds.

In Angular Material, all theme styles are generated statically at build time to avoid slowing the app on startup.

Angular Material comes prepackaged with several prebuilt theme CSS files. As you probably recall, you had an option of selecting a theme to use when you installed Material.

These theme files also include all of the styles for the core (styles common to all components), so you have to include only a single CSS file for Angular Material in your app. You can include a theme file directly into your application from @angular/material/prebuilt-themes.

These are the available prebuilt themes:

- deeppurple-amber.css

- indigo-pink.css

- pink-bluegrey.css

- purple-green.css

You are using Angular CLI here, so you can simply include the style you want in the global `src/styles.css` file.

Originally it has this initial precode:

```
html, body { height: 100%; }
body { margin: 0; font-family: 'Roboto', sans-serif; }
```

Add the following `import` statement at the top of the document:

```
@import "~@angular/material/prebuilt-themes/indigo-pink.css";
```

While you have the `src/style.css` file open, you can also create a style for a container, a paragraph, and a button that you can use across your app for your pages.

```
p {
  padding-left: 20px;
  font-size: 12px;
}
.container {
  margin-right: auto;
  margin-left: auto;
  padding: 20px 15px 30px;
  width: 750px;
}
button {
  color: #ffffff;
  background-color: #611BBD;
  border-color: #130269;
  display: inline-block;
  margin-bottom: 0;
  font-weight: normal;
  text-align: center;
  vertical-align: middle;
```

```
  touch-action: manipulation;
  cursor: pointer;
  white-space: nowrap;
  padding: 6px 12px;
  font-size: 12px;
  line-height: 1.42857143;
  border-radius: 4px;
  -webkit-user-select: none;
  -moz-user-select: none;
  -ms-user-select: none;
  user-select: none;
}
```

You can compare your files with mine: https://github.com/Apress/
the-blockchain-developer/chapter9/step3.zip.

Creating Content

At this point, you have a skeleton app with a header, body, and footer.
The body can be switched between your start page and transfer page by
changing the URL in the browser. You also imported and injected Material
modules and set up global styles for your app. The next step is to create
actual content to replace the temporary text message you placed in your
header, footer, and start components.

Footer Component

For the footer component, you will just replace the message for your
company copyright. To do so, all you need to do is open src/app/components/
footer/footer.component.html and replace the default code.

```
<p>
  footer works!
</p>
```

Replace the code by creating a div container with the style you added to the global CSS file.

```
<div class="ng-scope">
  <div class="container">
    <p>Copyright (c) 2019 Company Name. All Rights Reserved.</p>
  </div>
</div>
```

You are also going to create a specific style for the footer component, so every time you use the p tag, your font will be size 12px with no padding on the left. Open src/app/components/footer/footer.component.css and insert the following:

```
p {
  padding-left: 0;
  font-size: 11px;
}
```

Notice that you defined the <p> tag twice, once in the global CSS file and one at the component level. What's going to happen is that the global <p> tag will be overwritten by the component <p>, so you can use the <p> tag for your footer and a different <p> tag for other components such as the start and transfer pages while keeping your HTML code free of CSS code.

Header Component

For the header component, you will create a navigation menu to be able to switch between the start page and the transfer page. For styles specific to the header component, open src/app/components/header/header. component.css and add the nav list styles.

```
.nav {
  margin-bottom: 0;
  padding-left: 0;
  list-style: none;
}
li {
  display: block;
  float: left;
  width: 100px;
  height: 25px;
  padding: 5px;
}
.nav>li>a {
  margin-bottom: 0;
  padding-left: 0;
  font-weight: 500;
  font-size: 12px;
  text-transform: uppercase;
  position: relative;
}
```

For src/app/components/header/header.component.html, you create a container and a list of the two links to the pages start and transfer. To do so replace the initial code:

```
<p>
  header works!
</p>
```

with the following;

```
<div class="ng-scope">
  <div class="container">
    <ul class="nav">
```

```
<li>
  <a routerLink='/start'>home</a>
</li>
<li>
  <a routerLink='/transfer'>transfer</a>
</li>
  </ul>
 </div>
</div>
```

The working dapp now includes basic styling and functional navigation, as shown in Figure 9-9.

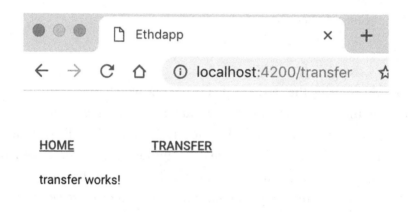

Figure 9-9. *Ethdapp with basic styling and working navigation*

You can download this step here: https://github.com/Apress/the-blockchain-developer/chapter9/step4.zip.

Transfer Component

The transfer component will hold a form that you will submit to transfer Ethereum coins from one account address to another. You will be using the forms module to expedite creating your form. To do so, you need to include the Material FormsModule and ReactiveFormsModule form modules in app.module.ts just as you did with other Material modules.

Open src/app/app.module.ts and add the following import statement:

```
import { FormsModule, ReactiveFormsModule } from '@angular/forms';
```

You also want to update the import statement.

```
imports: [
  FormsModule,
  ReactiveFormsModule,
  ..
]
```

You will be using the <mat-form-field> tag, which represents a component that wraps several Angular Material components together and applies common text field styles such as the underline, floating label, and hint messages. This will expedite development as you won't need to implement all of these and test them on multiple devices/browsers.

The form field is the wrapper component named <mat-form-field>. You can use any of the form field controls (such as input, textarea, list, etc.).

You can find information about mat-forms here: https://material. angular.io/components/form-field/overview.

For src/app/components/transfer/transfer.component.ts, you will update the initial code. First you need to import the components you will be using; in this case, you need to initialize the class and use form, form control, and validators.

```
import {FormBuilder, FormControl, FormGroup, Validators} from '@angular/forms';
```

Then you need to update the component definition to implement the OnInit method.

```
export class TransferComponent implements OnInit {
```

You will be using a flag to indicate whether the form was submitted and to create an instance of a form group, as well as an object called user, to hold the user's information.

```
formSubmitted: Boolean = false;
userForm: FormGroup;
user: any;
```

To validate your form, you will define the messages in case the form is not filled in correctly. Each form control needs to be defined with the required fields and messages.

```
account_validation_messages = {
  'transferAddress': [
    { type: 'required', message: 'Transfer Address is required' },
    { type: 'minLength', message: 'Transfer Address must be
      42 characters long' },
    { type: 'maxLength', message: 'Transfer Address must be
      42 characters long' }
  ],
  'amount': [
    { type: 'required', message: 'Amount is required' },
    { type: 'pattern', message: 'Amount must be a positive
      number' }
  ],
  'remarks': [
    { type: 'required', message: 'Remarks are required' }
  ]
};
```

When you create the constructor, you need to include the FormBuilder component to be able to generate the form.

```
constructor(private fb: FormBuilder) { }
```

When your component gets init, you will set the formSubmitted flag to false and set default values for the user's information. You then will call a method to go fetch the user's account and balance, which you will implement later. Lastly, you will call the createForms method that will generate the form.

```
ngOnInit() {
  this.formSubmitted = false;
  this.user = {address: '', transferAddress: '', balance: '',
               amount: '', remarks: ''};
  this.getAccountAndBalance();
  this.createForms();
}
```

The createForms method will generate the form controls by passing the validators and data.

```
createForms() {
  this.userForm = this.fb.group({
    transferAddress: new FormControl(this.user.transferAddress,
    Validators.compose([
      Validators.required,
      Validators.minLength(42),
      Validators.maxLength(42)
    ])),
    amount: new FormControl(this.user.amount, Validators.
    compose([
      Validators.required,
      Validators.pattern('^[+]?([.]\\d+|\\d+[.]?\\d*)$')
```

```
      ])),
      remarks: new FormControl(this.user.remarks, Validators.
      compose([
        Validators.required
      ]))
    });
  }
```

The getAccountAndBalance method will set the user account's address and balance; for now you are using dummy data, but you will implement the actual service later in this chapter.

```
getAccountAndBalance = () => {
  const that = this;
  that.user.address = '0xd8d0101f83e79fb4e8d21134f5325e64816b
                       d6a0';
  that.user.balance = 0;
  // TODO: fetch data
}
```

Lastly, once you submit your form, you need a method to handle the data and call the service. submitForm will be used by checking whether the form is valid, and then later you will call the service component you will create.

```
submitForm() {
  if (this.userForm.invalid) {
    alert('transfer.components :: submitForm :: Form invalid');
    return;
  } else {
    console.log('transfer.components :: submitForm :: this.
    userForm.value');
    console.log(this.userForm.value);
```

```
    // TODO: service call
  }
 }
}
```

For `transfer.component.html`, you will set the form tag to call the `submitForm` method once the form is submitted.

```
<form [formGroup]="userForm" (ngSubmit)="submitForm()"
    novalidate autocomplete="off">
```

Next, you will create the wrapping `divs` and use data binding to display the user's account address and balance.

```
<div class="container">
  <div class="transfer-container">
    <div>
      Address: {{user.address}} <br/>
      Balance: {{user.balance}} Eth
    </div>
```

Notice that you have used the `transfer-container` style, which you have not yet defined; you will define it in your CSS file, and it will be used to format your form.

For form controls, you need input boxes for the account you are transferring the funds to, the amount, and a message. You also need to set up your validations.

```
    <mat-form-field>
      <input matInput placeholder="Transfer Address"
        name="transferAddress" formControlName="transferAddress"
            maxlength="42" minlength="42" required>
      <mat-error *ngFor="let validation of account_
        validation_messages.transferAddress">
```

```
      <mat-error *ngIf="userForm.get('transferAddress').
      hasError(validation.type) && (userForm.
      get('transferAddress').dirty || userForm.
      get('transferAddress').touched)">{{validation.
      message}}</mat-error>
    </mat-error>
  </mat-form-field>
  <mat-form-field>
    <input matInput placeholder="Amount" name="amount"
     formControlName="amount" required>
    <mat-error *ngFor="let validation of account_
     validation_messages.amount">
      <mat-error *ngIf="userForm.get('amount').
      hasError(validation.type) && (userForm.
      get('amount').dirty || userForm.get('amount').
      touched)">{{validation.message}}</mat-error>
    </mat-error>
  </mat-form-field>
  <mat-form-field>
    <input matInput placeholder="Remarks" name="remarks"
     formControlName="remarks"
          maxlength="42" required>
    <mat-error *ngFor="let validation of account_
     validation_messages.remarks">
      <mat-error *ngIf="userForm.get('remarks').
      hasError(validation.type) && (userForm.
      get('remarks').dirty || userForm.get('remarks').
      touched)">{{validation.message}}</mat-error>
    </mat-error>
  </mat-form-field>
```

Lastly, remember to close the `divs` and form, as well as include a submit button.

```
<div style="width: 100px">
  <button type="submit">Transfer Ether</button>
</div>
    </div>
  </div>
</form>
```

For `transfer.component.css`, you will be using the `transfer-container` div to format your form horizontally.

```
.transfer-container {
  display: flex;
  flex-direction: column;
}
.transfer-container > * {
  width: 100%;
}
```

That's it. Now you can check your dapp in the browser, and you should be able to see the user's default data, test the form, validate it, and submit the form. See Figure 9-10.

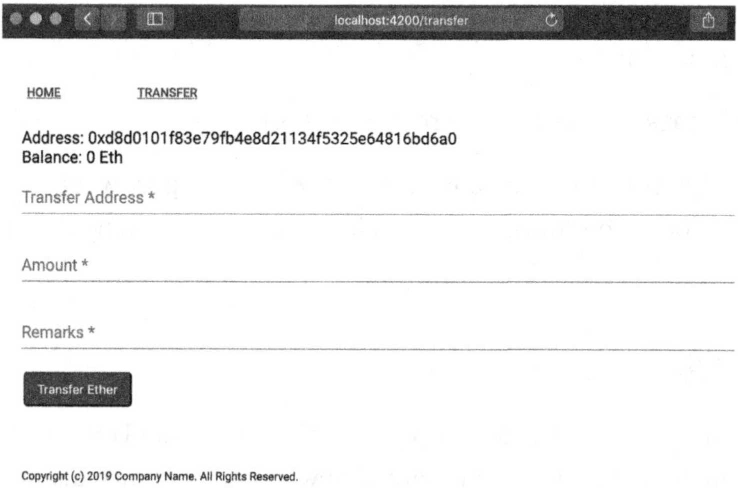
localhost:4200/transfer
HOME
TRANSFER
Address: 0xd8d0101f83e79fb4e8d21134f5325e64816bd6a0
Balance: 0 Eth
Transfer Address *
Amount *
Remarks *
Transfer Ether
Copyright (c) 2019 Company Name. All Rights Reserved.

Figure 9-10. *Ethdapp transfer page including user's info, validators, and submit button*

You can download this step here: `https://github.com/Apress/the-blockchain-developer/chapter9/step5.zip`.

Angular Directives

Creating directives in Angular gives you the ability to create your own custom HTML tags with just a few lines of code, just as you saw in the Material form. You were able to include custom tags that wrap many components. At a high level, directives are markers on a DOM element.

These markers can point to any DOM component, from an attribute to an element name or even a comment or CSS class. These markers then tell the AngularJS's HTML compiler to attach a specified behavior or to transform the entire DOM element and its children based on specific logic.

Angular comes with many of these directives built-in. However, during development, it's a good chance you will be creating your own directives. Your dapp is simple now, so you don't need to create any directive, and it's beyond the scope of this chapter to explain this. When you do need to generate a skeleton directive, use the Angular CLI just as you generated other components.

```
> ng generate directive {directive-name}
```

Although you are not creating a directive in your app, I wanted to introduce you to the concept as it's an integral part of creating an Angular project.

Summary

In this chapter, you took a deep dive into what a dapp is and looked at dapp classifications and projects. You learned how to start your own dapp project by breaking the process into five steps: writing a white paper, launching an ICO, developing the dapp, launching it, and marketing your dapp.

You then looked at why to use Angular. Next, you created an Angular dapp, first ensuring the prerequisites were installed and installing the Angular CLI. Then you created an Angular project and served the application.

Next, you learned how to import your Angular project to WebStorm or create a new project. You looked at the pieces that make Angular such as components, modules, and directives. You also learned how to style the dapp by understanding Angular-style architecture and working with Angular Material.

You started building components and created content; you split your app into a footer, header, and body and created a custom component called transfer that includes a form to be able to later transfer tokens.

In the next chapter, you will create a transfer smart contract and a Truffle development project as well as connect to the Ganache development network. You will learn how to work with the Ethereum network via Truffle and test your smart contract. You also will link your dapp with the Ethereum Network's web3 library and connect via MetaMask.

CHAPTER 10

Build Dapps with Angular: Part II

In the previous chapter, you started developing your dapp. Specifically, you learned about dapp classifications and projects and that you can break your own dapp project into five steps. You then looked at why to use Angular and its benefits. Next, you created an Angular project, first ensuring the prerequisites were installed and then installing the Angular CLI. You looked at the pieces that make up Angular such as components, modules, and directives. You also learned how to style a dapp by understanding Angular-style architecture and working with Angular Material. You started building your own custom components and creating content; you split your app into a footer, header, and body and created a custom transfer component that you will be using in this chapter.

In this chapter, I will cover the following:

- Creating the dapp's smart contract with Truffle

- Integrating a smart contract in your dapp's Angular project

- Linking and connecting your dapp to the Ethereum network

© Elad Elrom 2019
E. Elrom, *The Blockchain Developer*, https://doi.org/10.1007/978-1-4842-4847-8_10

You will be utilizing the tools I have been covering so far: the Angular CLI, Truffle, ganache-cli, and MetaMask. You will create a smart contract that you will use for your dapp with Truffle, and then you'll use the web3 library to connect to the Ethereum local network and call the smart contract's functions and events. MetaMask will be used to manage and connect to your account.

Tip   It's recommended that you complete the previous chapter and Chapter 5 prior to going through this chapter in order to fully understand the examples here, which build on the concepts, tools, and installed libraries from Chapters 9 and 5.

Transfer a Smart Contract

You already have the front-end logic to transfer tokens in your app from the previous chapter; however, you don't have a smart contract to interact with the blockchain. Smart contracts can be created before the front-end portion, after, or in parallel (if you work with a team of developers).

You already created an Ethereum smart contract in Chapter 5, so the steps in this section should be familiar to you. Feel free to revisit Chapter 5 to refresh your memory, as I won't go into much detail regarding the tools and commands used in this chapter.

To get started, you will create a new folder in your ethdapp project to hold the Truffle project. You can download the latest step, where you left off from, here: https://github.com/Apress/the-blockchain-developer/chapter9/step5.zip.

In real-life projects with multiple developers, the smart contract could be a separate project. For simplicity, you will be including it in your project so you can utilize the WebStorm Terminal window's bottom tab to run commands.

Start by creating a folder called truffle inside your project and
initialize Truffle to create the project. You can see the expected output in
Figure 10-1.

```
> mkdir ethdapp/truffle
> cd truffle
> truffle init
```

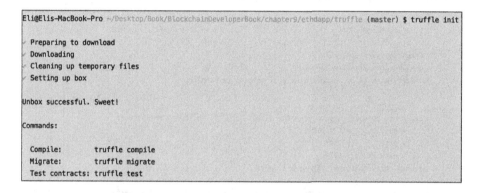

Figure 10-1. *Output of creating a Truffle project*

Tip   If you get errors such as "Error: Truffle Box," uninstall Truffle,
and then re-install it and try again.

To re-install truffle in case of error messages, remove truffle
globally and install it again.

```
> npm uninstall -g truffle
```

If you do not have Truffle installed or need to re-install Truffle globally,
run the install command.

```
> npm install -g truffle
```

After re-installing or performing a fresh install, run the `truffle init` command again and make sure you run the test in a new Terminal window to ensure the changes were applied.

```
> truffle compile
> truffle migrate
> truffle test
```

You can compare your results with mine, shown in Figure 10-2.

```
Eli@Elis-MacBook-Pro ~/Desktop/ethdapp/truffle (master) $ truffle migrate

Compiling your contracts...
===========================
> Everything is up to date, there is nothing to compile.


Could not connect to your Ethereum client with the following parameters:
    - host       > 127.0.0.1
    - port       > 7545
    - network_id > 5777
Please check that your Ethereum client:
    - is running
    - is accepting RPC connections (i.e., "--rpc" option is used in geth)
    - is accessible over the network
    - is properly configured in your Truffle configuration file (truffle-config.js)

Truffle v5.0.17 (core: 5.0.16)
Node v12.1.0
Eli@Elis-MacBook-Pro ~/Desktop/ethdapp/truffle (master) $ truffle test
Using network 'test'.
```

Figure 10-2. *Truffle compiling, migrating, and testing your project*

Create a Smart Contract

You'll create a smart contract and call it `Transfer.sol`; put it here: `truffle/contracts/Transfer.sol`. The contract will allow you to transfer funds from one account to another. First navigate to the location of the contracts in Truffle and use an editor to create a new file.

```
> cd ethapp/truffle/contracts
> vim Transfer.sol
```

The complete `Transfer.sol` code is listed here:

```solidity
pragma solidity ^0.5.0;

contract Transfer {
  address payable from;
  address payable to;

  constructor() public {
    from = msg.sender;
  }

  event Pay(address _to, address _from, uint amt);

  function pay( address payable _to ) public payable returns
  (bool) {
      to = _to;
      to.transfer(msg.value);
      emit Pay(to, from, msg.value);
      return true;
  }
}
```

Let's walk through the code. First you need to define the solidity version you will be using and the contract name.

```solidity
pragma solidity ^0.5.0;
contract Transfer {
```

Next, define the from and to addresses and the constructor.

```solidity
  address payable from;
  address payable to;
  constructor() public {
    from = msg.sender;
  }
```

You will be using a Pay event that will be dispatched once the pay function is used.

```
event Pay(address _to, address _from, uint amt);
```

The pay function uses the Pay event to interact with the network and do the actual transfer.

```
function pay( address payable _to ) public payable returns
(bool) {
    to = _to;
    to.transfer(msg.value);
    emit Pay(to, from, msg.value);
    return true;
  }
}
```

That's it. You kept it basic and simple with only one event and one function. You can download this step from here: `https://github.com/Apress/the-blockchain-developer/chapter10/step1.zip`.

Create the Truffle Development Network

The next step is to replace the `truffle/truffle-config.js` file with the following configuration:

```
module.exports = {
  networks: {
    development: {
      host: "127.0.0.1",
      port: 8545,
      network_id: "*",
      gas: 5000000,
```

```
    gasPrice: 100000000000
  }
 }
};
```

Notice that you point to port 8545, which will help you when you run MetaMask later in this chapter.

Deploy the Smart Contract

The other configuration file you need is the deploy contract file. Create a deployment file and call it truffle/migrations/2_deploy_contracts.js. In this config file all you do is point to the Transfer smart contract SOL code you created.

```
var Transfer = artifacts.require("./Transfer.sol");
module.exports = function(deployer) {
  deployer.deploy(Transfer);
};
```

Now you are ready to create your network on port 8545 with Ganache, so navigate to the Truffle project, and run this command:

```
> cd ethdapp/truffle
> ganache-cli -p 8545
```

Tip   If you get any errors such as "NODE_MODULE_VERSION mismatch," uninstall and re-install ganache-cli. Then open a new Terminal window and ensure it's running correctly.

To re-install ganache-cli if needed, run this:

```
> npm uninstall -g ganache-cli
> npm install -g ganache-cli
```

To ensure it's running correctly, run this:

```
> ganache-cli help
```

Next, in a new Terminal window, let's compile and deploy your contract while ganache is still running.

```
> truffle compile
```

The compile output should provide success, creating your contract in the Contract folder.

```
Compiling ./contracts/Transfer.sol...
Writing artifacts to ./build/contracts
```

The file that was created is Transfer.json, which you will be using in your dapp to interact with the network. Next, you will deploy your contract with the migrate command.

```
> truffle migrate --network development
```

The output should confirm the contract was migrated to the network, as shown in Figure 10-3.

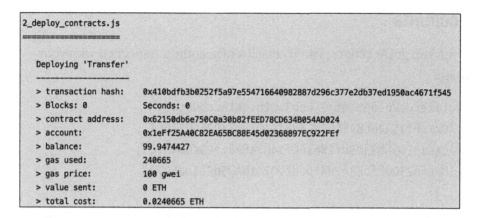

```
2_deploy_contracts.js
=====================

  Deploying 'Transfer'
  --------------------
  > transaction hash:    0x410bdfb3b0252f5a97e554716640982887d296c377e2db37ed1950ac4671f545
  > Blocks: 0            Seconds: 0
  > contract address:    0x62150db6e750C0a30b82fEED78CD634B054AD024
  > account:             0x1eFf25A40C82EA65BC88E45d02368897EC922FEf
  > balance:             99.9474427
  > gas used:            240665
  > gas price:           100 gwei
  > value sent:          0 ETH
  > total cost:          0.0240665 ETH
```

***Figure 10-3.** Truffle migrate project*

The output summary should also show that the deployment went well and a charge.

```
Summary
=======
> Total deployments:   2
> Final cost:          0.0525573 ETH
```

Truffle Console

Now that you have the contract compiled and deployed, to interact with the network, start a console, as shown here:

```
> truffle console --network development
```

A good resource for the commands you can run against the Truffle CLI is at the Ethereum JavaScript API wiki page here: https://github.com/ethereum/wiki/wiki/JavaScript-API.

Accounts

If you run getAccounts, you'll get a list of accounts associated with your wallet.

```
truffle(development)> web3.eth.getAccounts()
[ '0x1eFf25A40C82EA65BC88E45d02368897EC922FEf',
  '0xC135058b33d5df78636Cf14b74F281f95c4a407c',
  '0xe682300Ef633F7d4f0d8Cb07c1bAD5d9B4eaE974'
....]
```

You can then define address1 and address2 as the first and second accounts.

```
truffle(development)> web3.eth.getAccounts().then( function(a)
{address1=a[0]})
undefined
truffle(development)> web3.eth.getAccounts().then( function(a)
{address2=a[1]})
undefined
```

Now that they are defined, you can call them and get the first and second accounts in the output.

```
truffle(development)> address1
'0x1eFf25A40C82EA65BC88E45d02368897EC922FEf'
truffle(development)> address2
'0xC135058b33d5df78636Cf14b74F281f95c4a407c'
```

You can also use getBalance to get the balance you have in these addresses.

```
truffle(development)> web3.eth.getBalance(address1)
'99942134400000000000'
truffle(development)> web3.eth.getBalance(address2)
'100000000000000000000'
```

Test the Transfer of a Smart Contract

Now that you have defined two addresses and you know the balance in these accounts, you can define your contract and pass some funds between the accounts. To do so, first define the contract and call it transferSmartContract.

```
truffle(development)> Transfer.deployed().
then(function(instance){transferSmartContract = instance;})
undefined
```

Next, run the transferSmartContract variable you defined to ensure it worked and show the object value.

```
> transferSmartContract
```

Now you can transfer funds with your smart contract between the two accounts. Account 2 holds a nice round number, so you will transfer 5 eth.

```
> transferSmartContract.pay(address2, {from: address1, value: 5});
```

The command output shows information about the transaction and mining. Now you are able to see the balance updated.

```
> web3.eth.getBalance(address1);
'99942134399999999995'
> web3.eth.getBalance(address2);
'100000000000000000005'
```

As you can see, the balance changed, and you were able to transfer tokens between two addresses.

Link with the Ethereum Network

You got your contract working in Terminal; the next step is for your dapp to interact with the contract. This is done via web3.js, which is a collection of libraries allowing you to interact with a local or remote Ethereum node using an HTTP or IPC connection. First navigate back into your Angular project folder and then install web3.js with the flag --save to save the library you are installing.

```
> cd ethdapp/
> npm install web3 –save
+ web3@1.0.0-beta.55
```

If installation went well, you will see in the output that the version did install. At the time of writing, web3 is at version 1.0.0-beta55.

You also need to install truffle-contract, which provides wrapper code that makes interaction with your contract easier. At the time of writing, the latest is version 4.0.7 but will probably change by the time you are reading this book.

```
>  npm install truffle-contract –save
+ truffle-contract@4.0.15
```

Tip   web3 version 1.0.0 beta and truffle-contract version 4.0.15 are the latest versions and compatible with Angular 7.3.x. However, this can change, so watch the version you are installing to ensure it's compatible and to avoid errors. Re-install with exact @[version], for instance @4.0.15, if you run into compatibility issues.

Transfer Service

Now that you have your libraries installed, you can continue. In this section, you will create and write a service class. A service class is going to be your front-end middle layer to interact with web3. To get started, you can utilize the ng s flag, which stands for "service."

```
> ng g s services/transfer --module=app.module
CREATE src/app/services/transfer.service.spec.ts
CREATE src/app/services/ transfer.service.ts
```

You will replace the service class's initial code with logic to interact with web3. First you will define the libraries you will be using, which are the Angular core and the truffle-contract and web3 libraries you installed.

```
import { Injectable } from '@angular/core';
const Web3 = require('web3');
import * as TruffleContract from 'truffle-contract';
```

Next, you will define three variables you will be using later: require, window, and tokenAbi. Notice that tokenAbi points to the ABI file you compiled from the contract SOL file.

```
declare let require: any;
declare let window: any;
const tokenAbi = require('../../../truffle/build/contracts/
Transfer.json');
```

You need access to root to interact with web3, so you need to inject it into your project.

```
@Injectable({
  providedIn: 'root'
})
```

Next, define the class definition, the account and web3 variables, and init web3.

```
export class TransferService {
  private _account: any = null;
  private readonly _web3: any;
  constructor() {
    if (typeof window.web3 !== 'undefined') {
      this._web3 = window.web3.currentProvider;
    } else {
      this._web3 = new Web3.providers.HttpProvider('http://
      localhost:8545');
    }
    window.web3 = new Web3(this._web3);
    console.log('transfer.service :: this._web3');
    console.log(this._web3);
  }
```

Notice that you wrapped console.log messages around the code so you can see the messages in the browser console messages section under developer tool mode to help you understand what's happening. To do so open the browser in a developer tool mode. For Chrome, select View Developer View ➤ Developer ➤ Developer Tools.

You need an async method to get the account address and balance, so you can use a promise function. If your account was not retrieved previously, you'll call web3.eth.getAccounts just as you did in Terminal to retrieve the data. You also need error code if something goes wrong.

```
private async getAccount(): Promise<any> {
    console.log('transfer.service :: getAccount :: start');
    if (this._account == null) {
```

```
this._account = await new Promise((resolve, reject) => {
  console.log('transfer.service :: getAccount :: eth');
  console.log(window.web3.eth);
  window.web3.eth.getAccounts((err, retAccount) => {
    console.log('transfer.service :: getAccount: retAccount');
    console.log(retAccount);
    if (retAccount.length > 0) {
      this._account = retAccount[0];
      resolve(this._account);
    } else {
      alert('transfer.service :: getAccount :: no
      accounts found.');
      reject('No accounts found.');
    }
    if (err != null) {
      alert('transfer.service :: getAccount :: error
      retrieving account');
      reject('Error retrieving account');
    }
  });
}) as Promise<any>;
}
return Promise.resolve(this._account);
}
```

Similarly, you need a service method to interact with and get the balance of the account. You use web3.eth.getBalance just as you did in Terminal and wrap some error checking. You also set this as a promise. The reason you need a promise is that these calls are async, and JavaScript is not.

```
public async getUserBalance(): Promise<any> {
  const account = await this.getAccount();
  console.log('transfer.service :: getUserBalance :: account');
  console.log(account);
  return new Promise((resolve, reject) => {
    window.web3.eth.getBalance(account, function(err, balance) {
      console.log('transfer.service :: getUserBalance ::
      getBalance');
      console.log(balance);
      if (!err) {
        const retVal = {account: account, balance: balance};
        console.log('transfer.service :: getUserBalance ::
        getBalance :: retVal');
        console.log(retVal);
        resolve(retVal);
      } else {
        reject({account: 'error', balance: 0});
      }
    });
  }) as Promise<any>;
}
```

Last, you need a method to pass the values from your form and transfer payment from one account to another. Use the contract pay method and wrap some error checking.

```
transferEther(value) {
  const that = this;
  console.log('transfer.service :: transferEther to: ' +
  value.transferAddress + ', from: ' + that._account + ',
  amount: ' + value.amount);
  return new Promise((resolve, reject) => {
    console.log('transfer.service :: transferEther :: tokenAbi');
```

```
console.log(tokenAbi);
const transferContract = TruffleContract(tokenAbi);
transferContract.setProvider(that._web3);
console.log('transfer.service :: transferEther ::
transferContract');
console.log(transferContract);
transferContract.deployed().then(function(instance) {
  return instance.pay(
    value.transferAddress,
    {
      from: that._account,
      value: value.amount
    });
}).then(function(status) {
  if (status) {
    return resolve({status: true});
  }
}).catch(function(error) {
  console.log(error);
  return reject('transfer.service error');
  });
  });
  }
}
```

Now that you have the transfer service complete, you can connect
transfer.component to get the user's account address and balance and be
able to transfer funds once the form is filled in.

First you need to define the service component you created. Open src/
app/component/transfer/transfer.component.ts and add the import
statement at the top of the document.

```
import {TransferService} from '../../services/transfer.service';
```

For the component definition, add TransferService as a provider.

```
@Component({
..
  providers: [TransferService]
})
```

Also, add TransferService to the constructor so you can use it in your class.

```
constructor(private fb: FormBuilder,
            private transferService: TransferService) { }
```

Next, update the getAccountAndBalance method to include a call to the service class and retrieve the user actual account and balance.

```
  getAccountAndBalance = () => {
    const that = this;
    this.transferService.getUserBalance().
    then(function(retAccount: any) {
      that.user.address = retAccount.account;
      that.user.balance = retAccount.balance;
      console.log('transfer.components :: getAccountAndBalance
      :: that.user');
      console.log(that.user);
    }).catch(function(error) {
      console.log(error);
    });
  }
```

Lastly, update submitForm to call transferEther to transfer and pay. Replace the submitForm TODO comments shown here with the call to the service calls:

```
// TODO: service call
```

Then pass the data the user submitted:

```
this.transferService.transferEther(this.userForm.value).
then(function() {
    }).catch(function(error) {
      console.log(error);
    });
});
```

You can download the complete step from here: `https://github.com/Apress/the-blockchain-developer/chapter10/step2.zip`.

Connect to MetaMask

At this point, your dapp code is complete. However, if you test your dapp now, `web3` won't be able to connect to an account. What you need to do is connect to MetaMask. There is a privacy issue related to dapps where malicious web sites are able to inject code to view users' activities and Ethereum addresses and then find the balance, transaction history, and personal information.

These malicious sites are then able to initiate unwanted transactions on a user's behalf, and the user accidentally may approve an unauthorized transaction and lose funds.

To avoid these issues and to connect your Angular service, you will connect the browser to the network via MetaMask.

You have already used MetaMask, so you should have it installed.

Let's back up for a second. As you'll recall, you started a network via `ganache-cli` on port 8545.

```
> ganache-cli -p 8545
```

And you connected Truffle to the network.

```
> truffle migrate --network development
```

Then you were able to connect on port 8545 and run commands in Terminal.

You can now connect MetaMask in a browser. To connect, select MetaMask and select Localhost 8545 in the drop-down menu. See Figure 10-4.

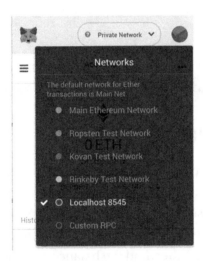

Figure 10-4. *Connecting MetaMask to a private network on port 8545*

Notice that you picked port 8545 earlier in this chapter. It's the default port on MetaMask, so it's easy to connect to on your private network by selecting the drop-down menu item instead of pointing to a custom port.

However, when you check the list of accounts, you don't see any accounts. The reason you don't see accounts is that every time you start your network, you need to update the accounts. There are two ways to update MetaMask with the list of accounts.

Option 1: When you run Ganache, use the m flag to pass the mnemonic that represents the private keys you had in Ganache. For instance, the command will look like this:

```
> ganache-cli -p 8545 -m 'journey badge medal slender behind
  junk develop produce spy enemy transfer room'
```

Option 2: When you run `ganache-cli`, you will see the list of accounts, private keys, and mnemonics.

```
> ganache-cli -p 8545
```

Look for this output and copy the mnemonic.

```
HD Wallet
==================
Mnemonic: journey badge medal slender behind junk develop
produce spy enemy transfer room
Base HD Path:  m/44'/60'/0'/0/{account_index}
```

Then, log out of MetaMask and paste the mnemonic manually. Click the right button and select "Log out," as shown in Figure 10-5.

Figure 10-5. *MetaMask logout of account*

After logging out, the welcome screen comes back with a link under it that says, "Import using account seed phrase." Click that link, as shown in Figure 10-6.

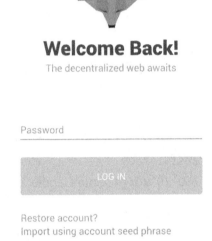

Welcome Back!

The decentralized web awaits

Password

LOG IN

Restore account?
Import using account seed phrase

Figure 10-6. *MetaMask welcome page*

Now you can paste the mnemonic by selecting a password and clicking Restore, as shown in Figure 10-7.

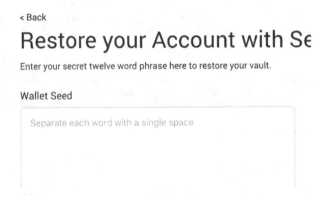

< Back

Restore your Account with Se

Enter your secret twelve word phrase here to restore your vault.

Wallet Seed

Separate each word with a single space

Figure 10-7. *Restoring MetaMask account using a mnemonic*

Test Your Dapp Functionality

Now you are finally ready to test your dapp. Once the browser gets refreshed, you will see the address and balance.

Next, fill in the form and initialize a transfer. Notice that MetaMask opens to confirm the transfer. This is an extra measurement of security to ensure only authorized transfers get approved.

See Figure 10-8.

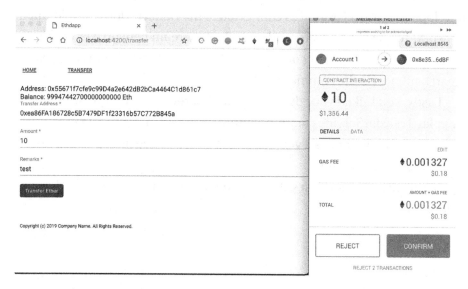

Figure 10-8. *MetaMask notification to complete a transfer*

Where to Go from Here

Continue working and improving the dapp you created. For instance, you could do the following:

- Create a user service class and a shared service class to hold users' information and shared information

- Create a login/logout service

- Create an option to switch between accounts

- Create a side menu to better navigate the app

- Update the smart contract and add more methods and events

Summary

In this chapter, you created a transfer smart contract and Truffle development project as well as connected to the Ganache local development network. You learned how to work with the Ethereum network via Truffle and how to test your smart contract. You test the transfer of funds using your smart contract via the command line.

Lastly, you linked your dapp with the Ethereum network using an Angular TransferService component that you created. Using the web3 library, you made some service calls. Lastly, you connected to MetaMask to manage your accounts.

In the next chapter, you will learn about blockchain security and compliance.

CHAPTER 11

Security and Compliance

As you have seen, most blockchains are decentralized, and the identity of each party is normally protected; however, most blockchain-related code involves storing some confidential data such as a user's personal information, passwords, cryptocurrency, and wallets.

Blockchain-related code has characteristics that make it a magnet for hackers.

- The code is usually open source for transparency and to promote contributors.

- Much of the code out there is not mature enough to be considered release grade.

- In cryptocurrency-related blockchains, losing data can mean more than just a mere privacy breach. Once funds are transferred, it's not easy to track them, and the transfer is likely to be irreversible.

These concerns have been magnified as blockchain technology has become more popular and more people are invested in blockchain. In fact, there have been increasing reports regarding blockchain-related losses, and new attacks are being published on news outlet almost daily. For instance, during the writing of this book, $40 million was stolen from the

© Elad Elrom 2019
E. Elrom, *The Blockchain Developer*, https://doi.org/10.1007/978-1-4842-4847-8_11

Binance exchange. Additionally, in the past 12 months, an estimated $23 million was stolen in double spending attacks. Similarly, a staggering $1.5 billion was stolen from crypto exchanges.

Postmortem reports sometimes show a sophisticated heist method that you would need to be a genius to prevent. However, most attacks can be prevented easily and are nothing more than a simple oversight or the result of not using tools capable of revealing vulnerabilities.

"Intellectuals solve problems; geniuses prevent them."

—Albert Einstein

As professionals, it is your responsibility to your customers who place their trust in you, as well as your reputation and fiduciary responsibility, to mitigate these risks and ensure data is protected. Security measures should be considered during all stages of the development cycle; in fact, security should be the most important aspect of your development. However, it is unrealistic to presume that I will be able to cover all aspects of security in just one chapter, as there are thousands of specific known attacks.

In addition to security, another aspect that needs to be addressed is regulation. Regulators have been shaping technology in general and the blockchain industry in particular, and there are multiple regulations to abide by in each geographic location.

Because new attacks are invented daily, regulatory laws are revised often. Understanding common attacks, security, privacy, compliance, and regulations can be a challenging task.

In this chapter, I will give you insights into the security mind-set and help you become more aware of security, privacy, and compliance. This chapter is split into three parts.

- *Security readiness*: I will cover areas you should be taking into account before and while developing your platform.

- *Common blockchain attacks*: I will cover some of the most famous and common blockchain attacks.

- *Development cycle*: I will provide you with a recommended development cycle so you can take into account security and compliance.

Specifically, I will cover security testing, privacy, and compliance requirements to ensure your code takes into account as many scenarios as possible to help secure your users' data. I will cover common blockchain-related cyber attacks that caused large losses, as well as blockchain network–specific attacks. I will cover how these attacks could have been prevented as a user and as a developer. Lastly, I will introduce a recommended development cycle that you can employ to reduce the risks of losses and your platform shutting down.

Security and Compliance Readiness

In this section, I will cover what the general areas are that you need to consider in regard to security testing and what it means to achieve security readiness. Additionally, you will understand what it means to achieve compliance readiness by looking at the regulations in Europe and the United States as examples. Lastly, I will highlight recommendations you should be considering during the development cycle and prior to releasing your code.

Security Readiness

In a traditional coding environment, you need to consider security testing to find security defects in your code to ensure it functions correctly, as intended, and that the data is protected.

Note   *Security testing* is a process aimed at finding security defects in code to ensure that both the code and the data are functioning as intended.

Security testing includes the following measures:

- *Confidentiality*: Ensuring a user's information is protected. An example is implementing a members-only area behind a Secure Sockets Layer (SSL) connection, which uses encryption for data sent via the Internet.

- *The integrity of information*: Protecting information from being changed. An example is encrypting and decrypting data as it passes between different layers of your system.

- *Authentication*: Confirming a user's identity, as well as ensuring the system is trusted. An example is a login system.

- *Availability*: Ensuring your system is up and running. An example is to install a firewall to prevent an attack.

- *Authorization*: Ensuring the requester is allowed to receive a service or perform an action. An example is creating a Hyperledger-permissioned blockchain that limits access to a specific entity.

- *Nonrepudiation*: Ensuring that there is a confirmation system in place when sending and receiving messages so parties cannot deny receiving a message. An example is an e-mail notification sent to confirm a transfer of digital assets.

Compliance Readiness

In addition to these traditional security testing considerations, you need to also consider blockchain-specific security and local compliance to ensure your platform is in compliance with regulatory requirements.

Note   *Security compliance* is a legal concern for entities. It is a regulatory standard for providing recommendations for privacy as well as improving security.

Being in compliance doesn't directly focus on security; however, many of the local compliance requirements take into account security and ensuring both the user and the data are protected, so indirectly they are intertwined. Many large companies employ both security and compliance experts to ensure both are met.

You may be wondering, why do I even need to take regulations into account anyway? Wasn't blockchain intended to be decentralized?

That is true; however, in recent years, regulations have been taken against blockchain's operators because of constant frauds and attacks, which resulted in significant losses, and privacy policies and security measures have been put in place in many countries. As a result, you need to check compliance and security regulations to ensure you are not breaching any laws.

In fact, many institutions and authorities have published research papers to analyze the relationship between blockchain and data protection regulations and how to prepare to achieve "compliance readiness."

Note   Compliance readiness ensures that the implementation meets governance requirements. Blockchain is not excluded from any applicable laws and regulations in many locations around the world.

For instance, in Europe and the United States, there are compliance legislation and policies tied to the Data Protection Impact Assessment (DPIA) and the General Data Protection Regulation (GDPR) that describe specifically what information is not allowed to be stored on a blockchain.

It's not just what data can and cannot be stored, though; many countries have implemented privacy laws that restrict the type of data that can be transferred across geographical boundaries.

Unlike many in the blockchain community who believe that compliance laws are put in place only to restrict and control blockchain technologies from replacing traditional institutions, many of the rules are to protect investors from losses, as well as to protect a user's privacy. Additionally, in some countries there are laws and regulations that require that you do record-keeping and store users' data to help prevent fraud, money laundering, and terrorism.

For instance, in 2013 in the United States the Bank Secrecy Act of 1970 (BSA) and FinCEN issued guidance to exchanges and ICOs, categorizing them as money service businesses (MSBs) that require registration, reporting, and record-keeping regulations. What this means is that in the United States, exchanges and ICOs are required to register to FinCEN as MSBs.

Ignoring compliance can lead to subpoenas, financial penalties, shutdown, and even criminal charges. For instance, in Europe, the GDPR set a deadline to comply with specific compliance. Companies that are unable to comply risk getting a hefty fine. This applies to mobile devices, TV apps, web portals, web sites, APIs, and cloud storage. In fact, in 2019, CNIL fined Google 50 million euros. Another example is the stable coin tether that at the time of writing was ordered to freeze transfers of its coin on the Bitfinex exchange by the New York Supreme Court.

Each geographical location is subject to a specific requirement regarding dealing with blockchain technology, so it's important to be aware of the law, security, and privacy rules put in place prior to developing your software.

In fact, each geographical boundary regulators can set their own rules. If you take the United States and Europe as an example, each has different rules regarding blockchain, and in case you have even one visitor from these countries, you should be complying with these regulations. In this chapter, you will take a look at the United States and Europe as an example; however, you need to check each specific geographical boundary for the specific rules that apply locally.

United States Compliance

The United States has security regulations and money transfer laws that require that you comply with specific state laws, and you may even need to apply for a state license if you transfer crypto. The bodies that deal with blockchain-related technologies in the United States are the Securities and Exchange Commission (SEC) and Alternative Trading Systems (ATS).

At the time of writing, the SEC views both initial coin offerings (ICOs) and security token offerings (STOs) as securities. As such, they are under the regulations of the Securities Exchange Act of 1934, which outlines how to transfer securities between entities. For instance, the SEC requires exchanges to register with the national securities exchange and/or ATS.

Tip   STO and ICO are both considered securities in the United States; however, STOs are more fashionable among investors than ICOs, as many ICOs were forced to refund investors in 2018 and 2019.

Exchanges also bind to specific regulations; for instance, exchanges that deal with the derivative need to register with the Commodity Futures Trading Commission (CFTC) as a CFTC Exchange or Designated Commodity Market (DCM) because of the Commodity Exchange Act of 1936 (CEA).

Note   To better understand how to become compliant in the United States, read the following report by NIST: `https://nvlpubs.nist.gov/nistpubs/ir/2018/NIST.IR.8202.pdf`.

Europe Union Compliance

The European Union is in the process of implementing specific requirements for blockchain and crypto markets; these requirements will take into account a protocol known as Know Your Client (KYC) and antimoney laundering (AML) laws.

In regard to digital assets, the European Union's regulation currently doesn't oppose crypto-fiat and fiat-crypto exchanges. Most of the concerns are to make sure that crypto is not used to finance illicit activities, such as money laundering and terrorism.

To take these concerns into account, crypto platforms need to do due diligence on customers and report any suspicious transactions according to KYC.

To better understand how to become compliant in Europe, read these EUBOF and CNIL report:

- `https://www.eublockchainforum.eu/sites/default/files/reports/eu_observatory_blockchain_in_government_services_v1_2018-12-07.pdf`.

- `https://www.cnil.fr/sites/default/files/atoms/files/blockchain.pdf`

Tip   Regulations change often; keep an eye out for news and information released by the SEC, EUBOF, and other organizations where your platform is published. If you are on social media, follow those organizations' accounts or add news updates to your reading list.

Readiness Recommendations

By having awareness, you can achieve both compliance and security readiness to ensure your platform is ready for production and help prevent shutdown by attackers or governments.

There isn't an exact set of rules you can use globally to ensure readiness because compliance is different between geographical boundaries; however, there are certain key elements that are good practice and can help you be security and compliance ready. In the next sections, I will cover specific attacks; these general recommendations are basic recommendations to take into account while you're still developing your app.

- *Geographical location*: If you intend to have even one user registered on your platform, you need to be compliant ready at that user's location and be aware of the rules and regulations there.

- *Solve a problem*: Ensure you are actually solving a problem. Ask yourself, what is my unique selling proposition (USP)? Don't just utilize the blockchain to get in on the hype. The 2017 ICOs party is over as many coins got de-listed and ICOs have been forced to refund investors.

- *Permission-based blockchain*: If you are building a permission-based blockchain, you should define the roles of members such as admin, publishers, users, and so on.

- *Privacy*: Regarding providing user information, the more the better. Inform your users as much as possible concerning privacy matters. When you gather data, the less is better; capture only what you need. The following are some specific recommendations in regard to privacy.

Tip   Based on reports from CNIL, NIST, and EUBOF, implement your code following the General Data Protection Regulation (GDPR).

- *Privacy policy*: Set a privacy policy and let the user know what information is stored and what information is shared with third parties. For example, inform users of logging data into an analytics tool in your privacy policy.

- *Unsubscribe*: Publish a form or an e-mail address for consent, withdrawal, and complaints related to the privacy policy on your platform.

- *Policy changes*: Inform the user of any privacy policy change.

- *Gathering users' data*: Take a minimalistic approach when gathering all users' information; store only what's needed.

- *Data collected*: Split data into the data you need in order to operate your platform and the other data collected.

- *Anonymization*: Consider implementing your platform with full anonymization.

- *Geographical location*: When storing data, ensure the data is collected according to the guidelines in that geographical location.

- *Permission*: Request permission from the user when storing any data, such as in cookies, in a local database, or in the cloud.

- *Clear everything*: Clear cookies, sessions, and other storage once the user has logged out. Allow the user to clear data from any third-party tools used on your platform.

- *Clean*: Allow the user to delete data and clean history.

- *Export*: Allow the user to export data.

- *Inform*: Inform users of any data breach.

  – Here are general security recommendations:

  - *Secure Sockets Layer (SSL)*: HTTPS should be used throughout web applications and especially when requesting and exporting data.

  - *Zero knowledge proof (ZKP)*: For blockchains, use zero knowledge proof (ZKP); see `https://github.com/topics/zero-knowledge-proofs`.

Note   ZKP is a method where one party proves to the verifier that they know the value of, let's say, x. A real-life analogy would be knocking on a door and providing a secret word to get access to a private, members-only club.

- *Encryption*: Use homomorphic encryption or secure multiparty computation.

- *Secure authentication system*: Use a secure authentication system such as OAuth 2.0 standards. Example: `https://developer.github.com/apps/building-oauth-apps/`.

- *Service timeout and restrictions*: Set up a timeout mechanism on services for delayed responses to ensure not to cause services to choke (slow down). Implement throttling login attempts. Set up secured handshake everywhere.

- *Common security vulnerabilities*: Protect against common security vulnerabilities such as distributed denial-of-service (DDoS) and cross-origin resource sharing (CORS).

Note   CORS uses additional HTTP headers to give an application running on one domain access to resources on a server at a different domain.

- *Sensitive information*: Save passwords and any other sensitive information as hashed data using an encrypted method.

- *IP restriction*: Restrict IPs that can access your ports. For example, don't have root and FTP access to any IP addresses, just to your IP address.

- *Security measurement*: Include security measures into the development cycle (see the "Development Cycle" section later in this chapter).

To summarize, I reviewed what it means to be security ready, what security testing is, and how to be compliance ready. You looked at the United States and Europe Union compliance regulations regarding blockchain technology, and lastly, I covered security readiness recommendations you should take into account in the early stages of your development cycle. In the next section of this chapter, you will be looking at specific crypto wallet attacks that can cause significant losses and how to prevent them.

Common Blockchain Attacks

In this section, I will be covering some of the most famous and common blockchain attacks. I have broken these attacks into three categories.

- *Wallet cyberattacks*: Directed at crypto wallets.

- *Blockchain network attacks*: Aimed at the blockchain P2P network.

- *Platform attacks*: Aimed at platforms that support blockchain, such as exchanges, web sites, and lending platforms.

Keep in mind that although I have broken the process down into three categories, most of these attacks use different techniques and different targets but have the same goal of capturing crypto private keys.

Wallet Cyberattacks

In this section, I will review specific cyber attacks directed at crypto wallets. As I highlighted at the beginning of this chapter, once crypto funds are transferred, it's not easy to track them down as they can be transferred from one wallet to another, and the transfer is irreversible, unless the majority of peers on the network agree to change the block.

> *"For every lock, there is someone out there trying pick it or break in."*

> —David Bernstein

Common wallet attacks can come in many shapes and forms by producing the same result of the user losing their private keys. The attacker often starts as a "phishing attack" resulting in a user's confidential information being compromised, and then the perpetrator is able to transfer funds out of the account.

Note   A *phishing attack* (think fishing for information) is an attempt
to fraudulently capture a user's confidential information such as
usernames, passwords, account numbers, and so on. This is done
by using electronic communication such as e-mail to disguise the
attacker as a trustworthy entity.

In fact, other than crypto scams such as Bitconnect and iFan, wallet-
related theft has resulted in the second biggest losses in crypto assets,
amounting to close to $5 billion (see Figure 11-1).

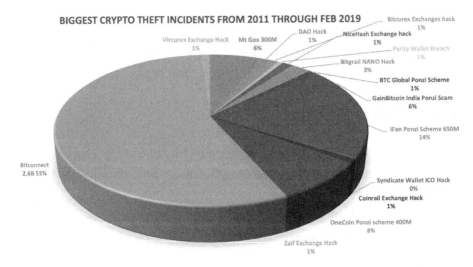

BIGGEST CRYPTO THEFT INCIDENTS FROM 2011 THROUGH FEB 2019

Figure 11-1. Biggest crypto theft incidents

The best solution against a wallet attack is removing cryptocurrency
from exchanges altogether when not in use and placing these cryptos in
your own "cold wallet" centralized storage. This can be achieved with
hardware wallets such as Nano, Trezor, KeepKey, and so on. Moving
crypto to a cold wallet gives you the highest level of protection and avoids
exchange losses such as the Mt. Gox incidents where the admin's password
was cracked and many users lost their wallet keys.

Note   *Cold storage* is a method of keeping crypto's private keys on a USB drive, paper wallet, or other data storage medium in a safe location. Think of it as being your own bank.

In the next section, you will be looking at common wallet attacks. I will provide a postmortem analysis to help ensure you don't repeat the same mistakes others did, both as a developer and as a user.

Online Wallet Phishing-Malware Attacks

Online wallets are more prone to attacks than offline wallets as they are connected to the Internet. For instance, a phishing-malware attack was carried out recently against Electrum's wallet and caused more than $1 million in losses.

Note   Malware comes from a mashup of the words *malicious* and *software*. The software is built to disrupt, damage, or gain access to the victim computer.

This was done by the hacker setting up malicious servers; then when a user wallet got connected to one of those servers and tried to send a BTC transaction, the attacker's code showed an official-looking message telling the user they needed to update their Electrum wallet, along with a false URL to download a fake version of Electrum's wallet with malware.

Once the user used the attacker URL and downloaded the new fake version of Electrum, the wallet requested the user to re-enter their passwords, which was then sent to the hacker. Then the hacker was equipped with the login information of the user and was able to log into the real Electrum's wallet and transfer the user's private keys into their own wallet.

Postmortem

As a user, besides avoiding online wallets altogether and using cold storage, you can reduce the risk by doing the following:

- *Download only official software*: Do not download online wallets or upgrade from any other source other than the wallet's official web site. Check URLs by hovering over links but not clicking them. Especially check for small misspelling; see if you can notice the little misspellings here: paypaI.com, Electrom.com.

- *Protect your information*: Be careful with information shared via e-mail. E-mails requesting that you confirm your account credentials need to be sent from the business you recognize and by you initiating the request.

- *Ensure authentication*: Download the wallet's software and check the GPG signature. Never give away your crypto assets' private keys to any "official" representative.

- *Recognize false support phone number*: Often companies that are phishing for your information use a fake support number. Many do a Google search to find the phone number of companies and fall victim of this attack.

As a developer, you should do the following:

- *Use GPG signature verification*: Implement GPG signature verification.

Tip   GPG/GNU is a suite of cryptographic software used in encryption to ensure authenticity by checking signatures against the downloaded files. To ensure the prevention of wallet attacks, implement GPG or GNU Privacy Guard. As a user, don't forget to also check that the actual GPG/GNU itself is authenticated and from the developer.

- *Educate your users*: Set pages, video tutorials, and blog posts to educate your users and prevent users from making common mistakes.

Keylogger Malware

Most malware software intends to harm your computer. Popular malware software that can be used to extract your cryptos is a keylogger or screen scraper. This software records everything you type as well as takes screenshots of your computer in an attempt to capture passwords and personal information. These types of attacks are less likely to happen at home, as the attacker needs to attach an actual Universal Serial Bus (USB) key to your computer to record the key log; however, this can happen when you use a public computer, for example, at a hotel lobby or a library.

Postmortem

As mentioned, at home you are less likely to be attacked by a keylogger; however, when logging into a public computer, be cautious, check if there is a USB key attached to that computer, and avoid accessing your important accounts. At your own computer, on a Mac, check Activity Monitor to ensure you recognize all the services that are running in the background. If needed, do a web search to find any services you don't recognize, and if anything looks odd, stop and remove the service and app. Install antivirus software and re-install your OS if in doubt.

Dust Attack

A dust attack is done by the attacker sending a tiny (dust) transaction that the hackers use either to spam the blockchain network and take up a block space or to mark the targeted addresses in hopes that the user transacts these cryptos, which can help the attacker identify a user's personal information by tracing the transaction history.

Postmortem

As a user, do not spend unrecognized transactions.

As a developer, implement a coin control feature so unrecognized transactions can be marked as "Do Not Spend" and not be included with your transactions.

Read the privacy document regarding bitcoin, which provides valuable information regarding protecting privacy that can apply to many scenarios: `https://en.bitcoin.it/wiki/Privacy`.

Hot Wallet Attack

In a hot wallet attack, the attacker retrieves the wallet's private keys from a "hot wallet" where the private keys are stored online by way of phishing, password cracking, or any other method. Once the private keys are pulled from an online network, attackers can transfer these keys to their own wallet.

Note   Exchanges store the user's crypto private keys online in what is called *hot wallets*, or operational wallets. The reason these private keys are stored online is to allow real-time withdrawals from wallets.

Postmortem

As a user, the best way to avoid these losses is to keep your crypto under your own control in a cold wallet and not on centralized exchanges.

As a developer, do the following:

- *Keep a cold wallet*: Store a user's keys in cold storage and avoid hot wallets as much as possible. For instance, Coinbase.com claims that it stores 98 percent of its users' funds on paper backups distributed geographically to safe deposit boxes.

- *Encrypt private keys*: If you need to store private keys on storage connected to an online network, at least encrypt the keys with a strong encryption key.

- *Watch for unusual activity*: For instance, many exchanges approve large withdrawals manually.

Blockchain Network Attacks

In this section, I will cover common attacks that target the blockchain network.

Sybil Attacks

The name Sybil is synonymous with someone who has a multiple personality disorder.

Note   A blockchain Sybil attack is an entity attempting to influence the P2P network by way of creating multiple identities and controlling multiple nodes.

A Sybil attack creates multiple fake accounts in order to control a network. The entity that controls these multiple accounts can then influence the network as they have additional voting power in a democratic network.

An easy way to understand this is the 2017 United States election where one entity, Russia, influenced an election process by creating multiple social media accounts and controlling the content of them.

A blockchain example would be attackers attempting to out-vote honest nodes on the P2P network by creating multiple Sybil identities. By having a majority vote, the attackers can refuse to receive blocks or transmit fake blocks.

If the Sybil attacks carry out a large enough attack, they are able to control the majority of the P2P network's hash rate and change blocks, which is then a double spending attack.

Postmortem

As a developer, you can discourage Sybil attacks by making them impractical. If there is a cost associated with launching a Sybil attack such as costs to create an account, run servers, have electricity, etc., this can discourage or make attacks impractical. However, make sure you take into account legitimate users who need to create multiple accounts.

In fact, popular blockchains have been taking Sybil attacks into consideration. For instance, the bitcoin PoW census algorithm needs a lot of processing power, so creating a block is proportional to the total processing power. This discourages attackers, because miners would rather do actual mining than risk losing on a failed Sybil attack. Similarly, the PoS census algorithm requires staking coins, so attackers will risk losing these coins.

In addition, as you have seen in previous chapters, Ethereum, EOS, and NEO include a large cost associated with the deployment of dapps. Ethereum has a minimum fee of 32,000 gas and 200 gas per byte, EOS is around 120 coins, and NEO has a fixed cost of 100 to 1,000 gas. On top of that, many blockchains such as bitcoin, Ethereum, and NEO charge a transaction fee, which helps discourage attackers. Similarly, EOS does not charge transaction fees, but it is using a "chain of trust" to combat attackers.

Note   A *chain of trust* is a way to combat Sybil attacks by requiring trust before allowing new identities to join a network. A version of the chain of trust can include allowing a user to create a new account but not giving it full privileges for a certain time.

EOS charges $1 to $4 per new account to developers; obviously, developers will be reluctant to create accounts and put in place mitigation to get an account approved.

Another way to combat a Sybil attack is by changing the hierarchy from a democracy to a meritocracy (governed by selected people). Users who were created a long time ago and have a good reputation would have more weight than new accounts. Think of the Stackoverflow.com or Wikipedia. com reputation system; see `https://stackoverflow.com/help/whats-reputation`.

Double Spending or 51 Percent Attack

Previously in this book, I talked about potential double spending attacks against cryptocurrencies, where a malicious node gains control of more than 50 percent of a blockchain network's hash rate and is able to alter and manipulate blocks. Large blockchains like bitcoin and Ethereum are not easy to overtake by a 51 percent attack due to the miner competition, which demands a high level of resources. For instance, according to `https://www.crypto51.app`, the theoretical cost of attacking bitcoin would be $257,472 at the time of writing; see Figure 11-2.

PoW 51% Attack Cost

This is a collection of coins and the theoretical cost of a 51% attack on each network.

[Learn More] [⚡ Tip]

Name	Symbol	Market Cap	Algorithm	Hash Rate	1h Attack Cost	NiceHash-able
Bitcoin	BTC	$69.07 B	SHA-256	39,513 PH/s	$257,472	0%
Ethereum	ETH	$14.64 B	Ethash	147 TH/s	$78,446	4%
Litecoin	LTC	$3.43 B	Scrypt	259 TH/s	$34,892	5%

Figure 11-2. *Theoretical cost of a 51 percent attack on various blockchains*

However, smaller blockchains have been the target of the 51 percent attack. This happened to the Verge blockchain, which lost almost $3 million in two attacks. Bitcoin gold suffered the biggest loss of $18 million, and Ethereum Classic lost $1.1 million. In fact, there was a total of $23 million in losses in less than a year during 2018 and 2019; see Figure 11-3.

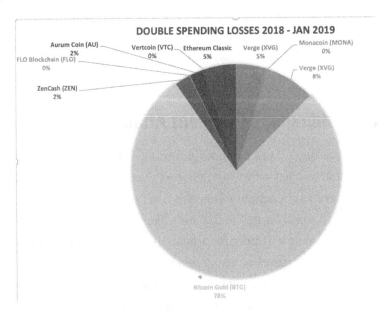

Figure 11-3. *Double spending losses from 2018, to January 2019*

Postmortem

As an investor, you should check the cost to attack the blockchain you are interested in investing in and whether there is a safety net mechanism in place for the blockchain.

Blockchain developers should create some sort of a safety net mechanism, for instance, creating a hash that holds a snapshot of all transactions and balances of each of your blocks and then storing that hash into a larger blockchain. For instance, you could utilize bitcoin's OP_ RETURN, just as you did in Chapter 4, and store the hash as a backup in case there is a 51 percent attack.

In fact, `http://komodoplatform.com` was able to solve the double spending problem by creating a delayed proof of work (dPoW) security mechanism.

Miner Ransomware

As I mentioned, bitcoin has been unaffected by these 51 percent attacks so far; however, hackers have found a new way to affect blockchains by attacking miners with ransomware.

Note   Ransomware is a type of malicious software aimed at blocking a computer until money is paid. The name is a mashup of the words *ransom* and *software*.

Hackers lock up mining rigs using similar techniques that ransomware is using on personal computers. On personal computers, malware, such as the NotPetya ransomware, gets downloaded and installed and then is able to lock the user's computer until a ransom is paid to a wallet address.

Up until now, ransomware targeted only personal computers; however, new ransomware such as hAnt is taking aim at miners. How hAnt is installed is not known, but it is estimated that it is probably downloaded with a version of the mining rig firmware. Then the ransomware has access to the firmware of the miner and can control the miner.

The attacker displays a message once the admin login threatens to overheat and destroy the miner. This can be achieved by turning off the fans if the victims don't infect other devices or pay a bitcoin ransom, as shown in Figure 11-4. So far, only bitcoin and litecoin miners manufactured by Antminer and Avalon have been affected, but this attack can be potentially done to any miner.

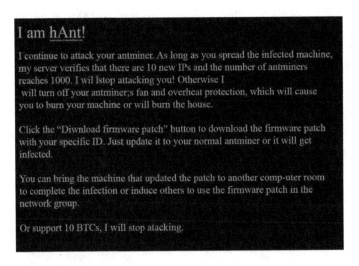

Figure 11-4. *hAnt ransomware message. Image credit: sensorstechforum.com.*

Postmortem

Getting rid of the ransomware is not easy. The software may be built with a "tripwire" script that can damage the miner if the miner disconnects from the Internet. To solve this problem, you need to first remove the ransomware surgically from the miner's Secure Digital (SD) cards. Additionally, a mining farm going offline for a period of time is costly.

The best approach is to avoid this attack altogether by not downloading a firmware upgrade from any source than the official vendor's web site.

Eclipse Attack on the P2P Network

An informational eclipse attack can be conducted on its own or as part of a different attack, such as a 51 percent attack. The attackers gain control over a peer's access to information in the P2P network by manipulating the network so that nodes communicate only with malicious nodes. The attacker can then manipulate the mining and the consensus mechanism.

Postmortem

Run analysis, simulations, and experiments to find countermeasures to avoid an eclipse attack. Good research with potential countermeasures to increase bitcoin's security countermeasures against an eclipse attack can be found here (and can be applied to many other blockchain networks): https://hackernoon.com/eclipse-attacks-on-blockchains-peer-to-peer-network-26a62f85f11.

Routing Attacks

Internet routing attacks include BGP hijacks, and malicious attacks against Internet service providers (ISPs) can be also executed against blockchains.

Note   A BGP hijack is a maliciously rerouted Internet traffic attack. This is done by falsely announcing ownership of groups of IP addresses (IP prefixes).

Large mining farms are centralized in a few geographical locations, which makes them ideal for an ISP type of attack. Attackers can commit the following:

- **Partition attack**: An ISP can partition the P2P network by hijacking a few IP prefixes.

- **Delay attack**: An ISP delays traffic to and from a blockchain node, which results in a delay in the block propagation, slowing transactions.

These types of attacks could reduce a node's revenue as well as turn into a 50 percent attack as fewer nodes influence the network. Additionally, these attacks can also prevent the transaction from being sent by large entities such as exchanges.

Postmortem

Create a custom script or install hardware to monitor the network. Many ISPs provide a paid solution to monitor the network and prevent an attack. Refer to the "DoS and DDoS Attacks" postmortem section for more solutions that can help mitigate this attack.

Platform Attack

Bitcoin's blockchain network is by design a secure network and has proven reliable. Bitcoin was released in 2009, and there has not been a successful attack on bitcoin's blockchain network at the time of writing.

The reason bitcoin's blockchain has a high level of security is that the data is distributed between nodes. Additionally, mining bitcoin is energy expensive, so attacking bitcoin's network could cost more than mining itself, and attackers risk losing money just attempting an attack. However, that's not the only reason; a big contributing factor to bitcoin withstanding the test of time is that it's open source and enables developers to quickly implement changes based on research and recommendations by security experts.

With that being said, that does not keep other platforms safe that provide services built on top of safe blockchains, such as exchanges, lending platforms, wallet-based services, and dapps that store private keys.

For instance, exchanges hold billions in deposits and make a perfect target for hackers. As mentioned, exchanges store the user's crypto in the form of private keys, and some of these keys are kept online in a hot wallet to allow real-time withdrawals and trading. Not handling these private keys with care can cause losses.

Mt. Gox's 2011 security breach is a good example. This attack happened because a hacker was able to crack the password of a Mt. Gox auditor and was able to transfer 800,000 bitcoins to himself. Besides Mt. Gox, there is a constant stream of news about exchanges shutting down due to loss of crypto.

As you can see from Figure 11-5, the biggest loss of close to $1 billion was by Mt. Gox in two attacks, and the largest theft in crypto history was caused by an attack on the Coincheck exchange network in 2018.

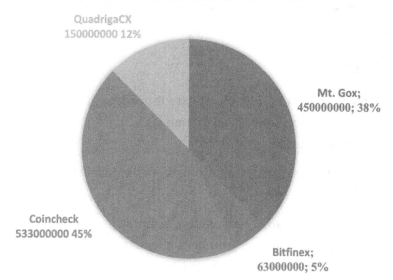

Figure 11-5. *Biggest exchanges losses of BTC*

In the next section, I will review some of the largest attacks and give you recommendations for how these attacks could be prevented.

Credential Attacks

Authentication-related attacks such as password cracking caused losses in the millions.

- *Direct attack on exchanges*: As mentioned, Mt. Gox's 51 percent attack in 2011 caused two separated losses: 2,609 BTC and over 750,000 BTC. Hackers were able to get an auditor's credentials and transferred these bitcoins to the hacker's address.

- *Attack on users*: Millions in losses occurred because of taking over users' accounts. For instance, phone companies enabled the takeover of cell phone numbers by providing simple billing information. Hackers can port a number to a new provider and can then approve a reset password of accounts on exchanges using SMS verifications.

Postmortem

As a user, the best way to avoid these losses is to keep your crypto assets in a cold wallet and not on centralized exchanges.

On your own computer:

- *SSL*: Don't register on sites that don't have an SSL certificate.

- *Strong passwords*: Use unique and strong passwords long in length and include numbers, characters, and special characters.

- *Unique passwords*: Don't reuse the same password on different platforms.

- *Layers of security*: Set up all recommended layers of security such as SMS, 2FA enabled, e-mail confirmation, and so on.

- *Antivirus*: Install paid or free virus-scanning software. On personal computers, Avast security has a free version used by 435 million people: `https://www.avast.com`. It includes a plugin for Chrome that warns against phishing sites.

- *VPN*: Use VPN connection as much as possible especially on a network that is public and isn't secured.

- *Avoid malware and ransomware*: Be mindful of software you install and ensure it's from a reputable vendor. Read all messages during the installation; don't just agree to all messages. Install software that prevents ransomware.

Tip   Keep your crypto assets under your own control in a cold wallet and not on centralized exchanges. Set up more layers than just SMS verifications on important accounts. Security layers can be 2FA authentication, e-mail verifications, and IP restriction.

As a developer, password cracking is the most common way of gaining access to a web app. Implement a security tester that ensures the system demands a strong encrypted password.

A good example of such a solution is the John the Ripper password cracker: `https://github.com/magnumripper/JohnTheRipper`.

In addition, implement the following:

- *Protect credentials*: Protect your users' credentials using multiple layers.

  - *Strong password*: Enforce strong passwords on account creation and reset passwords.

  - *2FA enabled*: Set up a two-factor authentication (aka 2FA enabled); a popular example is Google Authenticator.

  - *Confirmation*: Require both SMS confirmation and an e-mail verification on important operations such as transfers.

- *Storage*: Store users' sensitive data (such as private keys) encrypted and on servers that are disconnected from the Internet.

- *Encryption*: Use SSL on all pages. Use AES-256 encryption. Hash passwords with a cost factor of 12.

- *Lock account*: Limit login attempts and lock an account once multiple failed attempts occur.

- On your development personal computer:

  - *Remote connection*: Use strong login passwords especially if you connect remotely to your machine.

  - *Encrypt data*: Encrypt your hard drive to turn encryption on. Go to System Preferences and select Privacy & Security. Click Turn On FileVault.

  - *Lock on inactive*: On the General tab under Advanced, set it up to log out after five minutes of inactivity and enable screen locking by selecting "require an admin password to access system-wide preference."

- *Firewall*: Set up a firewall on your computer; on the Firewall tab, turn on the firewall.

- *VPN*: Use a VPN when working on a none-secure network.

- *Software*: Be mindful of software you are installing and ensure it is from a reputable vendor.

- *Libraries*: Avoid installing code libraries with root access if possible.

Faulty Code

Faulty code is one of the biggest reasons for losses. It has become so significant that many large companies set bounties for white-hat hackers to discover bugs, making it profitable for hackers to point out flaws instead of steal.

Note   A white-hat hacker is a moral person who gains unauthorized access to data to point out flaws in a system.

For example, hackers exploited a faulty withdrawal code in Poloniex in 2014. The exact number of bitcoin stolen was not shared by the company.

Postmortem

As developers:

- *SQL injections*: Avoid SQL injections by testing and implementing SQL injection filters. You can find more information here: http://sqlmap.org/.

Note   A SQL injection is an attack where a hacker passes illegal SQL statements through a text entry input box to gain access to content. The hackers can then use this vulnerability to add, change, or delete data from a SQL database.

- *CSRF attack*: The hacker exploits service requests to modify and retrieve data and verify the authenticity of POST, PUT, and DELETE requests. To avoid this, follow these recommendations:

  - *Restrict IPs*: Set services to respond to certain IPs only.

  - *Set tools and libraries*: Find tools to avoid CSRF attacks here: `https://github.com/0xInfection/XSRFProbe`.

- *Cross-site scripting (XSS)*: Avoid XSS by using tools and libraries such as these:

  - `https://pentest-tools.com/website-vulnerability-scanning/xss-scanner-online`

  - `https://github.com/topics/xss-scanner`

Note   XSS attacks are executed by an injection of malicious code into a trusted website.

Dependency Backdoor Attack

A dependency backdoor attack starts as a social engineering attack and includes the injection of malicious code.

> **Note**   A social engineering attack, the engineer is a conman.
> The attacker conceals his true identity and motives to gain access
> or data. For instance, you get an email that seem legit from your
> manager asking for a specific information.

For instance, in late 2018, a hacker was able to successfully insert malicious code into `event-stream`, an npm JavaScript library (`https://www.npmjs.com/package/event-stream`). The library is used by millions and targets a company called Bitpay, which has a Git library called `copay`. `copay` is an open source wallet hosted on GitHub (`https://github.com/bitpay/copay`).

Like many open source libraries, the developer was not being paid for the work on `event-stream` and lost interest in the project before giving it away to a new maintainer. The new maintainer injected malicious code that targets `copay`. The code captures account details and private keys from accounts having a balance of more than 100 bitcoin or 1,000 bitcoin cash. `copay` then updated its dependency library on versions 5.0.2 and included the attacker code, which resulted in a loss of millions.

The code captured the victims' account data and private keys and then, using a service call, sent the data to the attacker server undetected.

The complete detail and analysis of this attack can be found here:

- `https://blog.npmjs.org/post/180565383195/details-about-the-event-stream-incident`

- `https://snyk.io/blog/a-post-mortem-of-the-malicious-event-stream-backdoor/`

Postmortem

As a user, as recommended throughout this chapter, place crypto in a cold wallet. As a developer, be cautious when handling open source libraries. The open source model relies on many packages, but few developers support the libraries, which could enable a malicious takeover. To help avoid this, run npm audit to detect any vulnerable dependency.

```
> npm audit
```

Check and test your code for any reported vulnerabilities on a vulnerability database, such as the snyk.io site: https://snyk.io/vuln.

Do not set your package.json file to include an automatic update of libraries.

```
"dependencies": { "some-library": "latest" }
```

Instead, check pull requests on the libraries you want to update and check changes manually for the dependencies you use. Use a library-specific version.

```
"dependencies": { "some-library": "1.0.0" }
```

It's the same with npm install. Install specific libraries, especially on less known libraries.

```
> npm install -g some-library@1.0.0
```

DoS and DDoS Attacks

A *denial-of-service* (DoS) attack is a common attack intended to prevent users from accessing a service. A *distributed denial-of-service* (DDoS) attack is similar to DoS, but instead of the attacker utilizing a single machine to attack, the attacker uses multiple machines all attacking at the same time. Because of the usage of multiple machines, the chances of a successful attack increases, and it's harder to pinpoint the attacker's exact location.

Exchanges and web sites are popular targets for DoS and DDoS attacks. For instance, when bitcoin gold officially launched, it was targeted by a DDoS attack that ended up crashing the web site for hours.

Popular blockchain networks have a simple built-in DoS prevention mechanism; however, many networks are not protected against more sophisticated attacks.

The most common types of attacks are as follows:

- *Buffer overflow*: This attack sends more traffic to the target service than the service is able to handle. This attack can give the attacker the ability to crash and even control the targeted service.

- *ICMP flood*: Also known as "the ping of death" or a "smurf attack," this attack is intended to overload the network by forcing a node to distribute bogus packets to all nodes, which results in an overload on the network.

- *SYN flood*: A request to connect is sent, but it never gets fully authenticated. The requester then attacks all the open ports on the server until the server crashes.

- *NTP/DNS amplification*: This is an attack on NTP servers, where the attacker sends a large number of UDP packets and spoofs the source IP address, making the NTP server believe that these packets are legit traffic from the intended target. The overload causes the NTP server to crash.

Postmortem

As a developer, you need to take Dos/DDoS attacks into account and implement countermeasures against them. See the following examples:

- *Filter bad traffic*:

    • *Script*: One way to prevent is to implement a script to check for DOS/DDOS attacks. Check out the GitHub DDOS protection libraries: `https://github.com/topics/ddos-protection`. `http://vddos.voduy.com/` is a popular one.

    • *Firewall*: Use a firewall to block bad traffic. See Figure 11-6.

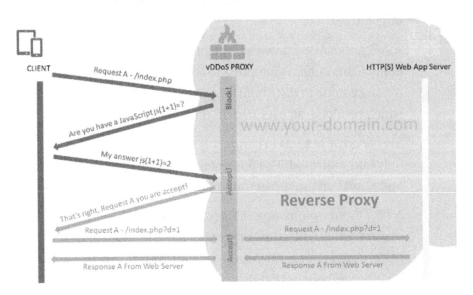

Figure 11-6. *DDoS protection reverse proxy explained. Photo credit: vddos.voduy.com.*

- *Dedicated hardware*: Purchase and deploy dedicated hardware to handle mitigations of DDoS attacks. The hardware sits in a data center in front of the servers and routers and can detect and filter malicious traffic. An example of such hardware is FortiDDoS from `www.fortinet.com`.

- *ISP*: ISPs provide DDoS mitigation solutions to customers. For instance, Amazon provides a shield where all AWS customers benefit from automatic protections and provides a higher-tier levels of protection against attacks; see `https://aws.amazon.com/shield`.

- *Cloud mitigation*: Some cloud services provide DoS/DDoS mitigation. These services scrub the traffic to eliminate any malicious traffic. A popular provider is `cloudflare.com`, which provides a free standard version and paid enterprise solution.

In terms of a blockchain network DoS/DDoS attack, examine existing blockchain prevention implementations such as the bitcoin satoshi client protection, which was implemented in version 0.7.0; see `https://en.bitcoin.it/wiki/Weaknesses`.

To summarize, I reviewed common attacks on platforms. You looked at credential attacks, faulty code, dependency backdoor attacks, and DoS/DDoS attacks. Additionally, I reviewed ways to help you reduce the risk and prevent these attacks. In the next section, I will give you a suggested development cycle you can employ to help reduce the risks and to use a methodological approach to prevent attacks.

Development Cycle

As you saw throughout this chapter, your platform needs to be secure and protected against potential attacks. You cannot rely on luck and need to ensure you use all the available measures to reduce the risk of an attack on your platform as well as ensure you implement all the latest regulations related to your locale.

The process can be broken into the following phases:

- *Design and coding*

- *Discover, audit, and test*

- *Readiness assessment*

- *Release*

As you can see from Figure 11-7, each phase can result in going back to the design and coding phase as the findings can result in a security risk or a showstopper.

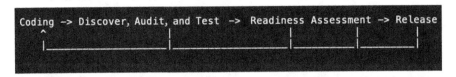

Figure 11-7. *Suggested development cycle to reduce security and compliance risks*

Tip   This development is a basic approach for a development cycle. Feel free to employ your own approach or a different approach that fits your platform and needs better.

Design and Coding

Prior to and during the design and coding phase, you should incorporate all the security, privacy, and compliance elements discussed in the early part of this chapter. These should be taken into account for all the elements of your platform, including the pages, login system, privacy page, integrations with third-party plugins, the creation of services, setting up servers, and so on.

It is a good idea for you to create your own checklist of everything that needs to be incorporated and taken into account that specifically applies to your unique platform. It's not possible to get one list that fits everything. Every platform should have a unique checklist. Additionally, as you start a new development cycle, you may need to update the requirements. For instance, let's say you want your platform to be supported in a new locale; this will require a new checklist.

Discovery, Audit, and Test

This step can be broken into three steps. The steps are intertwined and rely on one another, so you should consider these steps as one phase. These steps are as follows:

- *Discovery*: Find out the versions used in your platforms such as versions of libraries, firmware, software, third-party SDKs, and so on.

- *Audit*: Audit your code and platform to find common problems, accessibility of your services, and performance issues that can degrade and make your platform inaccessible.

- *Test*: This is when you run actual tests against your platform. The purpose is to identify the systems and services that your platform is using and potential security vulnerabilities.

Discovery

The discovery is all about discovering what versions are used in your platform. For instance, you need to run a discovery phase to find out the firmware you are using. Knowledge of the version provides valuable information in case a version of something was marked with security vulnerability or has been deprecated. The discovery phase can then be used to audit and test and provide an indication of potential vulnerabilities in your platform.

You may find out during the discovery check that you need to go back to the coding and design phase because of versioning issues. For instance, once you change the version of a library or firmware, your code may break, and you may need to refactor your code.

Audit

For the auditing phase, you should conduct a systematic review of specific potential issues.

Just as an accountant audit financial aspect of a company and even this book was audited by a team, your platform needs auditing and testing to ensure your code follows best practices to improve performance, accessibility, and compliance with security and regulatory requirements.

An audit inspection can be done by your own platform team but is often done by an independent entity. It's important to recognize that audits can't be expected to detect all the issues that need to be addressed. A blockchain-based platform should take into account security and compliance audits as well.

Security Audit

The security audit can utilize a complete manual approach or utilize automated tools to do vulnerability assessments, security assessments, and penetration tests to determine what needs to be addressed. There are more than 1,500 exploits, so it's a good idea to rely at least to some degree on automated audit tools as an integral part of your development cycle and ensure your platform passes common problems. Even when hiring a third-party auditor, it's better to first check for common problems before starting a more vigorous audit.

Compliance Audit

In blockchain, you need to check beyond just the security aspects; you need to also conduct a compliance audit to ensure privacy and regulations are implemented according to the law.

Just like a security audit, a compliance audit can be done by a third-party auditor or in-house. As you saw previously in this chapter, many of the problems that concern lawmakers in different locales relate to security vulnerabilities. As I pointed out, the compliance regulations can change often and different between locales, so the compliance assessment is often better done in a manual manner than an automatic one.

Test

The discovery and audit rely on testing to make recommendations on how to fix problems in your platform. In terms of testing, there are three types.

- *Dynamic testing*: Test vulnerabilities that an attacker may target. An attacker trying to exploit your platform would not have access to your code and platform, so the tests are run without access to your source code.

- *Static testing*: This is an inside-out approach, testing for vulnerabilities in the source code of your platform. This testing offers a more in-depth real-time snapshot of your platform and the libraries that make up your platform.

> — *Penetration test*: This simulates an actual malicious attack. The penetration test can rely on found vulnerabilities to gain further access to your platform. This can help you understand what access an attacker can gain over confidential information.

Tests can be conducted by automated tools, but it's recommended you also include a manual test by an actual tester, who can rely on his experience and knowledge to find vulnerabilities not found by automated tools.

Automated Tools

There are many testing tools that can assist you in doing the three types of testing. For instance, for the static testing of libraries, I already mentioned the npm audit, which helps detect any vulnerable in a dependency's version.

```
> npm audit
```

For a web app, the Google Chrome developer tools provide built-in audit tools, as shown in Figure 11-8.

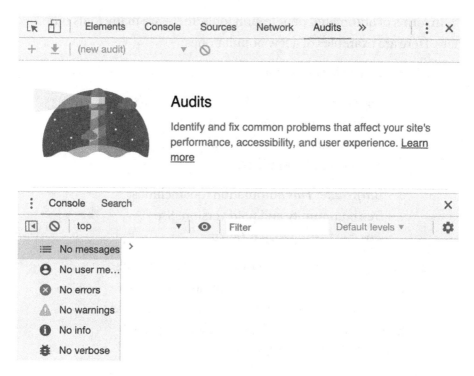

Figure 11-8. *Google Chrome developer tool audit report*

A browser's developer tools provide a simple web proxy network tool; however, these tools don't have many of features you may need, such as exporting data, running simulations, and filtering data. You may find it useful to utilize a third-party web proxy tool during the audit phase. The web proxy tool is mainly a network protocol analyzer, which can provide details of your network protocols, packet information, decryption, and so on. The two popular tools are Charlesproxy and Wireshark.

- `https://www.charlesproxy.com/`

- `https://www.wireshark.org/`

In terms of automated penetration tools, there are many tools out there. Here are examples of a few popular ones:

1. *Security automation tools*

    a. *The OWASP Zed Attack Proxy (ZAP)*: *This includes p*opular free security tools. *See* `www.owasp.org/index.php/OWASP_Zed_ Attack_Proxy_Project`.

    b. *Burp Suite*: *This a*utomation tool includes free community and paid version. *See* `www.portswigger.net/burp`.

2. *Metasploit*: This tool is based on `exploit`, which tries to overtake the security measures of your platform. You can run it from a GUI or command line. See `https://www.rapid7.com/products/ metasploit/download/editions/`.

3. *CORE Impact*: Core Impact Pro tests mobile device penetration, password identification, cracking, and so on. It also has a GUI and a command-line interface but has high price tag. See `https://www. coresecurity.com/core-impact/`.

4. *Netsparker*: This includes a web application scanner that can help identify vulnerabilities such as accessing sensitive data and suggesting solutions. It includes SQL injection and local file induction (LFI). The penetration test fabricates an internal or external unauthorized attack. See `https://www. netsparker.com/`.

5. *Free Security tool from Google (ratproxy)*: *See* `https://code.google.com/archive/p/ratproxy/`.

6. *Kali Linux operating system (OS)*: This tool is for
    hackers, with many hacking tools pre-installed already.
    The OS sits as a virtual machine on your Mac/PC.

7. SQL injections:

    a. *Sqlmap*: This is an open source penetration
        automated testing tool to detect and exploiting
        SQL injections. See `https://sqlmap.org`.

    b. *SQLNinja*: This tool checks for SQL injection
        vulnerabilities aimed at Microsoft SQL Server.
        See `https://sqlninja.sourceforge.net`.

    c. *Firefox add-on called Hackbar*: This test helps you
        test site security including SQL injections and
        XSS holes. See `https://www.addons.mozilla.`
        `org/en-US/firefox/addon/hackbartool/`.

Note   File inclusion allows an attacker to insert a file by exploiting
dynamic file inclusion (such as jQuery's `$.getScript`), which is
implemented in the application to include another file. The file is then
uploaded by user input and where there isn't proper validation to
check the file. The solution is to implement validation for dynamic file
inclusion to ensure the origin and content.

There are security testing automated tools to list; however, you can
check a few curated lists of security testing automated tools online that fit the
exact test you want to run:

- `https://github.com/topics/testing-tools`

- `https://github.com/atinfo/awesome-test-automation`

- `https://forum.bugcrowd.com/t/researcher-`
  `resources-tools/167`

Follow the OWASP IoT testing guide and OWASP IoT testing handout recommendations:

- Print and follow: https://www.owasp.org/ images/2/2d/Iot_testing_methodology.JPG

- Follow this checklist: www.owasp.org/index.php/ IoT_Testing_Guides

During the discover, audit, and test phases, you most likely will find small to major vulnerabilities that may require you to go back to the coding phase and rinse and repeat this process until your platform passes all the tests.

Readiness Assessment

Once your platform passes the discover, audit, and test phases, you are ready to take an in-depth look at the technical aspects of the blockchain application to ensure security and compliance have been implemented. That is done by running a security and compliance assessment manually.

Security and Compliance Assessment

This assessment builds upon the vulnerability assessments you did in previous phases. Prior to release, it's recommended that you add a manual verification step to confirm that industry and/or internal security standards have been applied to your platform and assess the risks and exposure. This phase should also include the security readiness concerns I discussed in the first part of this chapter.

In addition, verification could examine the following:

- Checking authorized access to your platform and confirming system settings

- Examining platform and server logs

- Ensuring compliance with current regulations

- Checking and tracking error codes and messages

- Examining the latest privacy and laws

- Examining the design and architecture documents to ensure the code meets these requirements

- Performing a code review

Keep in mind that the security and compliance assessment is the bigger picture, and you shouldn't be looking at specific exposure of just one vulnerability. Instead, look at the platform as a whole. The assessments may find additional risks and exposures that are not acceptable, which will require you to go back to the design and coding phase and start this process all over again.

Release

Once your platform has passed the readiness assessment phase, publish your platform. It's advised to run the same tests and checks again on the actual production code to ensure the platform is still passing the tests and assessments. Once you have completed this cycle, you can rinse and repeat this process for your new development cycle.

Where to Go from Here

- A good resource with links related to blockchain security is available online: `https://github.com/1522402210/BlockChain-Security-List`.

- Create a compliance and security checklist, taking into account your specific platform and locale.

- If you have a platform/site, run the audit and automated testing tool on your existing platform or site.

Summary

In this chapter, I broke down the security and compliance of the blockchain process into three parts: security readiness, common blockchain attacks, and a recommended development cycle.

The first part served as an introduction so you could better understand the terms and mind-set of building a secure platform. I covered security testing and compliance readiness, looking specifically at the United States and the Europe Union compliance requirements as examples. I covered security readiness recommendations to take into account during the design and coding phase. Then I covered common blockchain attacks that resulted in billions of dollars in losses. These attacks were targeting mostly crypto wallets, but also blockchain networks and blockchain-based platforms. Lastly, I gave you a recommended development cycle to ensure you take into account all the needed security and compliance issues.

In the next and last chapter, you will explore blockchain beyond just crypto. I will cover the power of blockchain and how it can be harnessed, as well as the decentralization of specific industries, examining a few industries being disrupted by blockchain and specific case studies.

CHAPTER 12

Blockchain Beyond Crypto

As you are approaching the last pages of this book, I wanted to inspire you and help you see what's possible in the coming years from the blockchain technology. Crypto paved the way by providing an alternative to fiat currency with the introduction of bitcoin. Although the invention of bitcoin was more than a decade ago (it was introduced in 2008), blockchain is still in its infancy. However, it's poised to potentially become one the most useful technological innovations of the 21st century.

With that said, the road for technological integration and adoption by the masses is still long and bumpy, and blockchain has already experienced multiple ups and downs, driven by financial speculation, security, performance, trust, scalability, and regulation (not to mention crypto attacks from charlatans and hackers). These concerns have caused many to become skeptics. Despite all this, blockchain cannot be ignored. It has the potential to improve all industries and become as big of a globalized technological innovation as the Internet or the fax machine.

The potential of blockchain has been recognized by many, and in fact, in 2019 alone, companies are expected to invest more than $3 billion in blockchain technologies. By examining the current projects in development, the bigger picture shows that cryptocurrency is not the final frontier but just the beginning, because many blockchain projects are expanding beyond just cryptocurrency and disrupting more than just fiat currencies.

© Elad Elrom 2019
E. Elrom, *The Blockchain Developer*, https://doi.org/10.1007/978-1-4842-4847-8_12

In fact, many large corporations are incorporating blockchain technologies into their systems in one way or another. Hundreds of startups are slowly entering the mainstream, the potential utilization of blockchain technology seems limitless, and in many cases, blockchain opens up new potential revenue streams and new business models.

> *"We'll all look back in 20 years and conclude that bitcoin was an influential platform for innovation as the Internet itself was."*
>
> —Marc Andreessen

This chapter is broken into two parts. First I will cover how blockchain can be harnessed and expand on what's possible when utilizing elements of blockchain technologies. Then I will cover the decentralization of industries by discussing a few industries being disrupted by blockchain and by showing specific case studies.

Understanding the power and capabilities of blockchain technology and the technological innovations can give you insight into how you can harness the blockchain technological innovations for your own new greenfield project or an existing project and industry.

Harnessing Blockchain

Before discussing the decentralization of industries, let's quickly review the specific elements of blockchain that are readily available to implement now. Although I already covered everything in this section in previous chapters, here I will expand on these elements in the context of how they can be used in a project. I'll discuss the following:

- Coins

- Tokens

- Ledgers

- Smart contracts and dapps

These blockchain elements can then be used on their own, mashed together, or used as a hybrid of a blockchain and none-blockchain project to implement a unique application.

Coins

Blockchain technology started with bitcoin and expanded to more than 2,000 listed cryptocurrencies with a market cap of billions of dollars. Many of these coins listed through ICOs are not providing much value other than attempting to enrich the publishers and investors of these coins. However, the capabilities of creating coins and using blockchain as a cryptocurrency to make payments globally quickly and for low costs have inspired many. The crypto use cases highlight blockchain reliability as it's able to replace fiat currency.

"The future of money is digital currency."

—Bill Gates

At the time of writing, a large portion of the population in certain countries have heard of crypto, but it is not considered mainstream just yet. But in this section you'll see there are projects in the works that can push the usage of coins into mainstream use. For instance, in December 2018, media outlets reported that Facebook is developing a "stablecoin" for its WhatsApp users and is holding talks with exchanges about listing its stablecoin, which will be tied "to a basket of different foreign currencies, rather than just the dollar." Adoption by Facebook, which is used by a large portion of the population, will raise more awareness of crypto.

Note   *Stablecoins* are crypto designed to minimize the volatility of price because they are tied to a more "stable" asset (or a basket of stable assets), such as a currency or exchange-traded commodities such as gold.

In addition, you saw examples of how coins themselves can offer more value than just the face value of the coin.

- *Bitcoin cash (BCH) colored coins*: These use the BCH protocol to create tokenized assets, which allows you to add tokens to BCH.

- *Bitcoin*: This uses bitcoin's `OP_RETURN` param to allow you to store data with the transaction.

These examples highlight the potential of coins as they can be used to transfer value more than just the digital currency.

Tokens

Cryptographic tokens are accounting units that can be used to represent the digital balance of a certain asset. For instance, bitcoin is a cryptographic token because it uses a digital signature in conjunction with ownership; however, not all cryptographic tokens are cryptocurrencies.

Tokens can be created with unique data and are called *nonfungible tokens* (NFTs) to represent something completely unique. These NFTs are not interchangeable as there is only one token with that exact data.

Note   In contrast to crypto digital asset coins or many utility tokens that are fungible in nature, NFT is a special cryptographic token that represents something unique. These tokens are not interchangeable because they cannot be replaced.

Both NFT and utility tokens use a tokenization process that allows you to create a *security*. The security takes the digital asset and fractionalizes its ownership by creating digital tokens. Each token then represents a percentage of ownership in the asset. The use of blockchain makes the chain of custody and proof of ownership immutable, which gives an advantage to certain applications as the information cannot be altered like in a regular database.

Note   Chain of custody in this context is the "paper trail" that records the sequence of transfer or analysis of the data.

In practice, this can be done with both digital assets and physical assets. For instance, the Kik messaging app (`https://www.kik.com`) turned its company into a digital asset and started selling tokens that represent a fraction of ownership in its company. Kik was able to raise $100 million that can now be used to grow its platform. What it has done is a reverse ICO; instead of raising funds prior to creating the company, it is selling a portion of the company after it's already up and running, just as a company can "go public" in the stock market.

Tip   Keep in mind that there are many other industries, not mentioned in this chapter, that have the potential to gain by utilizing blockchain technology. I picked a few to get you inspired; however, you should do your own research to investigate and find more industries.

Additionally, tokens can take old ideas and revive them. For instance, some pay phones and trains used tokens; these token have no value other than the context of using them in a pay phone or the train station but not anywhere else. The dollar also used to be tied to the amount of gold that the government kept in vaults, so when you held dollars prior to 1971, you used to own a token in the gold the U.S. government kept in its vaults. Similarly, today, stablecoin tokens represent fiat currency such as DAI, GUSD, TUSD, USDC, and USDT tokens created with the use of Ethereum. These tokens are based on companies placing fiat currency in an escrow account and registering their company with regulators.

Tokens can then represent any digital or physical value such as the following:

- Stocks

- Options

- Digital obligations

- Fiat currencies

- Ownership rights

- Rights for a service

Tokens can also combine a few assets. For instance, a token can represent a basket of different stocks or a basket of different fiat currencies.

The possibilities are unlimited, and as you have seen in previous chapters, there are many blockchains such as Ethereum, EOS, Hyperledger, and NEO that can provide an easy mechanism to create tokens.

Ledgers

A blockchain ledger can be used as a decentralized data storage for more than just crypto. Traditional cloud storage services are centralized, and you need to place your trust in a single entity with your valuable information or digital assets.

With blockchain, the data storage itself can become decentralized. P2P networks such as PirateBay, Limelight, and others have proven capable of stitching pieces of data together from different computers around the globe to store digital assets such as video, music, images, and software. Although many of these P2P networks are in violation of copyright Material and considered illegal in many countries, a blockchain P2P network can share files by legitimate publishers while limiting access to authorized customers. Blockchain works in a similar way to these P2P networks and can be used to store any data. In fact, Storj (`https://storj.io/`) and Sai (`https://sia.tech`) are examples of cloud storages based on blockchain aimed at improving security, reducing costs, and decreasing dependency. Users can rent out their storage capacity when not in usage, creating a whole new marketplace that never existed.

Utilizing blockchain as decentralized data storage combined with other elements of blockchains such as coins and tokens can create interesting new possibilities.

Smart Contracts and Dapps

As you have seen, smart contracts are the programming of the cloud; they allow you to code against a blockchain. Smart contracts are created to be legally binding, programmable, digital documents. Just like traditional agreements, smart contracts create a set of rules to which two or more parties agree.

When the contractual obligations are met, funds can be automatically released, eliminating the need for a third party to be involved in the arrangement. Utilizing smart contracts for legal concerns can potentially become a better alternative to paper as they are stable, honest, and less prone to human errors. Using a smart contract, the middleman is not needed (middlemen can be attorneys, escrow agents, notaries, bankers, loan officers, and so on).

In this book, you created smart contracts on multiple blockchain platforms. Using these smart contracts, you were able to create a dapp's front-end interface to utilize the smart contract and publish the dapp.

In fact, companies are using smart contracts to automate many services. For instance, Slock.it created payments for renting usable devices; these devices can be any object such as bikes, cars, or even toolboxes. Similarly, Fizzy (`https://fizzy.axa/`) tracks flight delays and automatically refunds passengers when flights are delayed. These services are done automatically; you don't need to stand in lines or be passed along by phone representatives from one department to another. Additionally, these refunds can occur automatically. These contracts are saving the user and the businesses time, effort, and money. Additionally, customer service is improved, and as these services are automated, this can reduce the number of employees you need.

To summarize, in this section, I covered what's readily available from a business point of view that you can implement utilizing blockchain technology. I covered what you can do with coins beyond crypto, including using tokens to represent any value, using the blockchain ledger as a decentralized database, and writing code in the cloud utilizing smart contracts and dapps. By combining these elements, you get expedited services that are more reliable and cut out the middleman.

Decentralization of Industries and Verticals

In this section, I will show you examples from a few industries and how blockchain is utilized or can be utilized vertically and horizontally across different industries. The industries I am covering can serve as inspiration when implementing blockchain into an existing industry or for a new greenfield project.

Note   In this context, *vertical* means specifically in a particular field, and *horizontal* can be adopted by everyone or any field.

I will be covering the following industries:

- Financial

- Cybersecurity

- Real estate

- Mobile

- Supply chain improvement

- Encrypted messaging platforms

- Elections and voting

- Marketing

- Healthcare

- Gaming

In today's world, many industries rely on one another, and there is much crossover between technology and brick-and-mortar businesses. For instance, real estate relies on the financial industry. The financial industry relies on security as there is a need to be able to verify documents and identities. Marketing relies on collecting data and forecasting. These crossovers and a mashup of services have the potential to create a seamless user experience that expedites the security, reliability, and globalization of blockchain; increases the speed of executing transactions; and offers lower costs to everyone involved.

Financial

In terms of the financial industry, you can split the actors into two groups: small financial groups and major financial institutions. Small financial groups can be startups, retailers, small banks, and individually owned companies. Major institutions include investment groups, large banks, and Fortune 500 companies.

Small financial groups have been experimenting with crypto and blockchain for years now. In regard to major financial institutions, it has been a love-hate relationship in regard to crypto; many financial CEOs and gurus have been criticizing crypto, with J.P. Morgan leading the way by calling any employee caught trading bitcoin "stupid" and with financial guru Warren Buffett calling bitcoin "delusion" and "attracts charlatans." However, when it comes to the blockchain technology itself, it's a different story. J.P. Morgan announced this year the creation of its own blockchain called Quorum and its own coin called JPM Coin.

Many other major financial companies are also starting to slowly warm up to the blockchain technology. Crypto exchanges have already passed through the Nasdaq's vetting process. NASDAQ, Citi, and Visa have invested $30 million in the blockchain-based startup Chain.com. NASDAQ also recognized Overstock.com's full support of a bitcoin payment option as well as the not-yet-published platform Roobee (`https://roobee.io`), an investment platform developed for retail investors.

In general, there are many areas in which both small and major financial groups can benefit from blockchain. I will be covering three: currency, infrastructure, and digital assets.

- *Currency:* This replaces fiat with crypto as an electronic cash system. Anyone can hold coins and pay quickly and inexpensive, cutting out the middle man (such as banks and credit cards). The current concerns around crypto replacing fiat currency are the volatility of price (because of the fluctuations of many coins), trust, and knowledge of how to create and accept a transfer and manage a wallet. These concerns can make many uneasy, especially ones who are not technology savvy. The large financial institutions can benefit from crypto by formalizing the transfer of crypto funds to the mainstream by creating their own cryptocurrency and/or accepting transfers of existing crypto. Sure, there will probably be a fee involved as the middleman is getting involved again; however, crypto can potentially be used by the mainstream as a payment method just like other methods such as Visa, fiat currency, automated clearinghouses (ACHs), exchange-traded funds (ETFs), and so on. Users can then send funds around the globe while dealing with a trusted party. Here are some case studies:

- Coinpayments (https://www.coinpayments.net), BitPay (https://bitpay.com/), and Abra (https://www.abra.com/) are just a few examples of merchants that accept crypto payments.

- Bank-backed coins are another example. J.P. Morgan announced that the bank was starting a trial by transforming a trillion dollars that the bank lends to corporations to JPM Coin. This represents the first coin from a major bank.

- *Infrastructure*: Companies can replace existing infrastructure such as a centralized database with blockchain to replace to achieve better security and reduce costs. One of the concerns with a crypto transfer is that the user needs to understand what they are doing or risk losing funds. Here are some case studies:

  - *Transferring funds*: Western Union *is* testing Ripple (XRP) to see *whether it* can optimize the existing settlement system to expedit*e the* transfer of funds with blockchain. For the time being, Western Union claims it *has* not proved that *using* XRP can expedite transfer*s*. "We tested with Mexico, one of our biggest corridors...*an*d with the efficiency that

477

we have currently, we didn't find the efficiency with Ripple yet," *according to* Western Union CEO Hikmet Ersek.

- *Bookkeeping*: J.P. Morgan's Quorum blockchain (`https://www.jpmorgan.com/global/Quorum`) is being used by institutions to keep track of financial data.

- *Digital assets*: As I mentioned, blockchain can be used to create digital assets using tokens. These assets can be any financial vehicle. Here are some case studies:

  - *Chain (`https://chain.com/`)*: This offers what is called a *sequence*. It uses blockchain infrastructure to let organizations build financial services from the ground up with open source code on GitHub; see `https://github.com/chain`.

  - *Openchain (`https://www.openchain.org`)*: This is a startup focused on issuing and managing digital assets.

  - *Symbiont.io (`https://symbiont.io/solutions`)*: This brings mass adoption of blockchain to financial services. Additionally, NASDAQ has invested in Symbiont.io.

Cybersecurity

As you saw in the previous chapter when I covered security, phishing-malware and other hacker attacks aimed at identity theft have become a common practice. Many identity thefts are due to a hacker cracking a user's password. Instead of relying on a password to authenticate a user, blockchain has the potential to revolutionize digital identities by using cryptography to secure them. This is done by assigning each user private keys in the same way blockchain attaches private/public keys and then uses these keys to authenticate a user and find transactions that belong to a user.

In addition, verifying data can be an agonizing process and a major pain point for many people. Think about when you need to get a passport, notarize a document, or renew your driver's license. These processes involve a lot of effort and time. Blockchain can help ensure and verify the document's ownership and authenticity while expediting the time it takes, and you can do it all from the comfort of your home instead of waiting in a line or filling out a complex form.

These techniques can be applied to the following:

- Passports

- Digital identity

- Driver's license and ID

- E-residency

- Birth certificates

- Wedding/divorce certificates

- Notary of documents

- Online account login

Some use cases include the following:

- *Verifying identity*: Companies that offer blockchain IDs can be used to sign in on apps and web sites, digitally sign documents, and so on, reducing the risk of *identity theft*. Here are some case studies:

  - *Guardtime (https://guardtime.com)*: This is a blockchain company that has enhanced data authentication protocols by using Keyless Signature Infrastructure (KSI) transactions. The code either grants or denies access to the network based on the command received instead of a password. A prominent client of Guardtime is Verizon.

- *Keybase (https://keybase.io)*: Keybase holds an encryption key directory to map social media identities. Users can then use encrypt chat and cloud storage.

- *Onename (https://onename.com)*: This company provides you with an .id namespace on its Blockstack network.

- *ShoCard (https://shocard.com)*: This identity service is aimed at providing banks and financial institutions with a way to authenticate users.

- *Verifying data*: You can use blockchain to create a verifiable record of any data, file, business process, or just about anything on the blockchain. Here are some case studies:

  - *Factom (https://www.factom.com)*: This provides a REST API to read, write, and search its Factom blockchain entries and platform, which includes SDKs, documentation, and a blockchain explorer to verify and debug entries.

  - *Proof of Existence (https://proofofexistence. com)*: This company verifies the existence of files via the transaction's timestamped property.

  - *Tierion (https://tierion.com)*: This is similar to Proof of Existence. Tierion offers proof and chainpoint. Chainpoint protects data by anchoring it to the bitcoin's blockchain, and the proof is using blockchain's timestamp property as a notary. This service is used by companies such as Dell and Xero. It also has a developer portal: https://chainpoint.org.

Real Estate

The real estate industry can potentially benefit from utilizing blockchain technology vertically and horizontally. If you have ever been involved in a real estate transaction, you know they are often complex and nontransparent and include a lot of paperwork and hard-to-follow moving pieces such as dealing with agents, property checks, deeds, financing, notaries, and in many cases attorneys. There are many pain points in the process. Blockchain can help reduce the costs, increase security, increase privacy, and expedite the process.

Combined with some of the elements discussed previously, these solutions can provide value such as identity, verify documents, and financial:

- Confirming identity

  - Securely identifying both buyer and sellers

  - Ensuring ownership

  - Keeping information private and on a need-to-know basis

- Verifying documents

  - Due diligence on property

- Conducting financial transactions

  - Transferring funds

  - Distributing funds between parties such as agents and sellers

  - Paying bills

Blockchain services addressing these elements can speed up the process and at the same time reduce paperwork and decrease costs.

Here are some case studies:

- *Harbor (https://goharbor.io)*: This provides an Ethereum ERC-20 token that allows for the resale of currency as security. It's a platform for digital securities such as funds, private equity, and commercial real estate.

- *Ubitquity (https://www.ubitquity.io)*: This offers a real estate SaaS platform utilizing the blockchain platform aimed at mortgage, title, and financial companies. It works with entities around the globe to gather property information and documents. Ubitquity offers an API for integration with its blockchain platform (https://www.ubitquity.io/).

- *Propy (https://propy.com/browse/)*: This company raised an ICO of more than $15 million and claims it can save people up to 25 percent in fees when buying property as well as avoid wire and fraud. Propy processes payments in any currency, including crypto.

- *Silentnotary (https://silentnotary.com), Dnote (www.dnote.online), and Blocknotary (https://www.blocknotary.com)*: These are just a few examples of companies that offer a decentralized notary. The concept is similar to Proof of Existence. The company verifies identity, and using blockchain's timestamp property it can verify documents. Blockchain captures the hash at a specific point in time, which can then be utilized to confirm the existence of something at that time. The timestamp can be used in a court of law and in the same way as a traditional notary. These services can eliminate the need for a physical notary. In fact, many states such as Arizona, Florida, Kentucky, Louisiana, Nebraska, and Nevada are already accepting e-notaries of deeds.

- *ShelterZoom (https://www.shelterzoom.com)*: This
  company is aimed at buyers, sellers, and renters. Sales are
  done using Ethereum's smart contracts.

- *StreetWire (http://www.streetwire.net/)*: This
  company tokenized physical real estate assets as well as
  providing data management services.

Mobile

Blockchain-based services can benefit users and help pain points related
to mobile devices. Here are some examples:

- *Privacy*: Users around the globe are getting fed up with
  the lack of privacy as social media, telecommunications,
  and Internet companies are taking advantage of them by
  holding users' data and sharing the data for profit.

- *Dapps*: Supporting dapps can provide access to large
  numbers of new services without being censored by the
  mobile app's store.

- *Income*: Mobile phones can generate income via mining,
  leaving reviews for coins, etc., reducing the monthly bills
  for the user.

In fact, the mobile industry has recognized the potential and is
harnessing blockchain to provide the user with more control, value, and
privacy, with many big names making headlines this year.

*"Telecommunications and Internet companies have derived
tremendous value from controlling data. By decentralizing
apps, we can put this data onto a smart contract, effectively
giving control back to creators and to users," and "Much of
what we call peer-to-peer or 'decentralized' services continue
to be built upon centralized networks. We are changing that."*

—Pundi X founder and CEO Zac Cheah

483

Here are some case studies:

- *Electroneum (https://electroneum.com/m1/)*: This is a new phone from a company called Electroneum. It has the following features:

  - *ETN cloud mining*: Users can mine up to $3 worth of ETN per month by running the cloud mining application.

  - *Low price*: It has a low price tag of $80.

  - *Hardware/software*: It is an Android device running version 8.1 Go, powered by a quad-core 1.3GHz CPU and supports 4G broadband cellular network technology and dual SIM cards.

- *HTC (https://www.htc.com/)*: This supports multiple dapps.

- *Pundi X (https://pundix.com)*: This company has redesigned its XPhone, estimated to be released for purchase in late 2019. It will include the following:

  - *Blockchain mode*: Services can operate independently of centralized carriers. Users can route phone calls, messages, and data via blockchain nodes without a centralized service provider.

  - *X button*: This allows users to switch to blockchain mode.

- *Samsung Galaxy S10 (https://www.samsung.com/us/mobile/galaxy-s10/)*: This includes the following:

- *Built-in crypto wallet*: This has private key storage with support for bitcoin, Ethereum, Cosmo Coin, and Enjin Coin, a gaming cryptocurrency.

- *Dapps*: It has out-of-the-box support for dapps.

- *Cosmo coin (COSM)*: It has support for the cosmo token, which powers the South Korean blockchain.

- *Earn coins*: Users can earn cosmo tokens in exchange for leaving reviews in the app.

- *Payment*: It has support for contactless payments with crypto.

Supply Chain

Companies can benefit greatly by utilizing blockchain as a private decentralized ledger to better store and use their own data globally. As you have seen, blockchain can store, monitor, and optimize data in an immutable and honest way that can be applied to supply chains. The supply chain can be broken down into these elements:

- *Chain of custody*: You can trace the chain of ownership of an asset.

- *Product identity*: You can store serial numbers or other product identification information on a blockchain allowing all parties (manufacturers, distributors, retailers, and consumers) to verify an item's authenticity. Keeping track of supply chains can help in many ways such as eliminating counterfeit products.

- *Monitor*: You can trace in real time supply chains, from raw Materials to a finished good.

Here are some case studies:

- *Blockverify (www.blockverify.io)*: This company uses blockchain for anticounterfeit measures by identifying counterfeits, preventing the duplication of products, and enabling companies to verify their products and monitor their supply chains.

- *British Airways (https://www.britishairways.com)*: This company uses blockchain to ensure that flight information is correct. It is also testing VChain (https://www.vchain.tech), a verification system to replace security checks.

- *Inxeption (https://www.inxeption.com)*: UPS has teamed up with the Inxeption platform to improve merchant supply chains.

- *Maersk (https://maersk.com/)*: The world's largest shipping company has teamed up with IBM to create a Hyperledger blockchain to monitor the cargo of ships.

- *Tracr (https://www.tracr.com)*: This is used by De Beers, the largest diamond producer utilizing blockchain technology, to create an immutable and permanent digital record for registered diamonds to cut down on conflict ("blood") diamonds.

- *Walmart*: This company is using blockchain to allow its employees to scan goods in the store's app and monitor the product from manufacturing to the store's floor.

Encrypted Messaging

In Chapter 1, I covered cryptography and how the Enigma machines were used to encrypt and decrypt messages in military communication. Blockchain is derived from messaging, and it can be used to send reliable encrypted messaging.

Blockchain can be used to update traditional solutions for end-to-end messaging encryption by leveraging a decentralization ledger to send messages anonymously and without a private user's data being sent, even masking the user's IP address.

Here are some case studies:

- *ADAMANT (https://adamant.im)*: This is an open source private messenger with a crypto payment option. See `https://github.com/adamant-im`.

- *Crypviser (https://crypviser.network)*: This is a private message platform.

- *Matrix (https://matrix.org/blog/home/)*: This is a chat ecosystem with open source code; see `https://github.com/matrix-org/matrix.org`.

Elections and Voting

Voting manipulation and electoral integrity are real problems; attackers have been known to use techniques such as Sybil attack to manipulate elections. Not surprisingly, many times there are recounts, accusations of fraud, and distrust as the whole process is often vague.

Voting requires the authentication of the voters' identities and secure record keeping, vote tracking, and tallying. Blockchain has the potential to revolutionize how voters cast their votes and could expedite the speed of completing this process in an honest and open way.

Blockchain tools could be used together as the infrastructure from start to finish. This could potentially eliminate the need for recounts and could build public trust in elections.

Voatz and Votem both point to a few potential advantages of utilizing blockchain for voting.

- *Verification*: Voters can verify that a vote was cast as intended and detect false results.

- *Transparency*: Governments and independent outside parties can confirm a vote's results as they are transparent when stored on a public blockchain.

- *Security*: Instead of one centralized computer on a traditional server system, voting data on the blockchain is distributed on many nodes, making it harder to alter results like when hacking into a single system.

Here are some case studies:

- *FollowMyVote (`https://followmyvote.com`)*: This is an election platform in beta.

- *Voatz (`https://voatz.com/`)*: This company wants to make voting safer and more accessible. It has already teamed up with the City of Denver and West Virginia to offer a mobile voting pilot.

- *Votem (`https://votem.com`)*: This voting platform is focused on mobile to secure votes in elections across the globe.

Marketing

Traditional analysts combine data from different sources in a nontransparent way and then use the data in many ways such as to monetize data, make a prediction, make businesses decisions, and so on. However, if the data is false, the cost is high. False data gathering is estimated to cost more than $1 billion in losses every year.

As you have seen, the blockchain ledger can include other data with the transactions in a precise and immutable manner. The data can then be used to support planning, analysis, and forecasting, as well as follow supply chains. Data can be captured more accurately with a blockchain decentralized ledger because it reduces human error and data alteration. Once marketing data is captured, it can be analyzed by many industries such as entertainment, sports, music, and finance as well as by machine learning algorithms.

Using blockchain as an immutable database, where you can follow the chain of custody, is already is use in many of the blockchain industries covered in this chapter. In this section, I will highlight companies that focus on just the data aspect. The data can then be used for forecasting, leads, and decision-making.

Online advertisers rely on pay-per-click rates, followers on social media, and analytics, and it can become a challenging task to verify the accuracy of statistics and ensure companies are billed correctly for advertisements. There have been many tracking and measurement miscalculations, causing businesses to overpay. The reason for the miscalculations is that the traffic sent can come from bots, artificially bolstering stats, or fake followers in security attacks such as a Sybil attack. These miscalculations have resulted in billions of dollars in losses in the advertising industry.

Blockchain can record an encrypted and transparent chain of traffic (like chain of custody) to help determine whether the ads clicked and followers are coming from real audiences in a transparent way.

Additionally, blockchain can help connect brands with influencers and reach consumers easier by offering an agreement based on a smart contract and immediate crypto payment.

Here are some case studies:

- *AdChain (https://metax.io/en/products/adchain_ registry/)*: This is a community-curated list of ad-supported web sites to provide advertisers with a stamp of approval on the web sites best suited for serving their ads.

- *Augur (https://www.augur.net)*: This is a prediction market protocol based on Ethereum, allowing users to forecast events. The platform incorporates a reward system for accurate predictions, enabling users to bet on everything including stocks, sports, presidential predictions, and more.

- *BOOSTO (https://boosto.io/)*: This is a decentralized app store, where brands can ensure that partners are reaching the consumers that the brand requests. Smart contracts are used for agreements, and payment are made once the terms decided on by the parties involved have been met utilizing its own crypto.

- *SWIPECrypto (https://www.swipecrypto.com/)*: This data monetization platform includes a privacy and data sharing protocol, as well as governance layers that reward data entry.

- *Wilbson (https://wibson.org)*: This allows users to sell their private information for profit, while protecting privacy.

Healthcare

There are many specific pain points in the healthcare industry that blockchain can help solve. For instance, just as with high-end brands, drug counterfeiting is a major problem in the pharmaceutical industry as 10 percent to 30 percent of all the drugs sold in developing countries are counterfeit. These counterfeits amount to a loss to healthcare companies of billions of dollars. Most of the counterfeit drugs are manufactured in either India or China. Additionally, many of the counterfeit drugs contain the wrong ingredients or wrong dose, putting patients' health at risk.

Private blockchains controlled by a pharmaceutical company can register drugs and ensure that fake drugs get discovered as they won't be registered on their ledger.

According to Bisresearch, the blockchain market is expected to grow and reach more than $5 billion by 2025: `https://bisresearch.com/industry-report/global-blockchain-in-healthcare-market-2025.html`.

> *"A global blockchain in the healthcare market is expected grow at a CAGR of 63.85% from 2018 to 2025, to reach a value of $5.61 billion by 2025. The use of blockchain for healthcare data exchange will contribute the largest market share throughout the forecast period, reaching a value of $1.89 billion by 2025, owing to the use of blockchain to solve the most widespread problem in healthcare information systems related to interoperability and nonstandardization that has created data silos in the industry."*

—Bisresearch

In addition, the healthcare industry can utilize blockchain to benefit from storing all kinds of important information about drugs as well as analyzing and processing information better.

- *Identifying patients*: Organizations such as CHIME and HIMSS have been pushing to create patient identity cards for almost two decades. The creation of a unique patient identifier can be easily solved with blockchain and ensure there are no mismatched patient electronic health records (EHRs), which leads to errors in patient care.

- *Tracing drugs*: As I mentioned, counterfeits can hold the wrong ingredients and cause harm to patients. Internet sales of counterfeit drugs account for $75 billion of the total market. Blockchain can be utilized to register all the authentic drugs' serial numbers.

- *Tracking drug results*: Blockchain can make it possible create a public ledger of patients to report the results of a specific drug. The system can validate that the user actually purchased the drug and the patient's condition. Using this data can provide valuable information to the pharmaceutical company or any related entity.

Here are some case studies:

- *Ambrosus (https://ambrosus.com/#mission)*: This blockchain system is aimed at following the chain of custody of clinical trials and pharmaceuticals. Food and pharmaceutical enterprises can use the platform to optimize supply chain visibility and QA.

- *ConnectingCare (https://www.simplyvitalhealth. com/)*: Here, patients and providers can share health data. It allows all kinds of unique applications, from calculating costs to the patient's ability to control their privacy to even allowing users to sell their data for research.

- *FarmaTrust (https://www.farmatrust.com)*: This is aimed at stopping counterfeit drugs with the usage of blockchain as a ledger.

- *Hashed Health (https://hashedhealth.com)*: This is aimed at solving credential problem by making data more transparent and easily accessible. The platform has a professional credentials exchange, where members can verify the credentials of and track records of various health professionals. This can expedite the hiring process and provide an unalterable history of a professional's healthcare career history.

- *MedicalChain (https://medicalchain.com/en/)*: This enables patient–doctor interactions through the usage of blockchain. The project is funded through MedTokens. Patients have full access and control over their own personal health data and can grant doctors access to their health record via their mobile devices, while data is secure on the blockchain or via wristbands on patients, which medical professionals can scan to access a person's medical history if they are unconscious.

- *MedRec (https://medrec.media.mit.edu/)*: This provides EHRs on the blockchain via an Ethereum smart contract.

- *MTBC (https://www.mtbc.com)*: This is a large player aimed at improving EHR with the usage of blockchain. A patient will have the ability to allow the transfer of records from one doctor to another. The blockchain API runs on the Hyperledger platform.

- *Phros (https://phros.io/#home)*: This was released by Taipei Medical University Hospital and Digital Treasury Corporation (DTCO) to share health data while ensuring data privacy. The goal is to place all of a patient's medical information on the blockchain.

- *U.S. Department of Defense, U.S. Defense Logistics Agency*: These organizations are experimenting with a block-chain-based system that would allow data to be added and tracked through a blockchain ledger, providing a live feed of multiple agencies' relief efforts in order to help save lives and reduce costs. See `https://www.dla.mil/AboutDLA/News/NewsArticleView/Article/1720207/troop-support-event-poses-question-how-and-where-can-blockchain-help/`.

Gaming

Games can benefit from blockchain by utilizing a blockchain ledger to store information as well as implement hybrid games that use a crypto marketplace for NFT transactions to purchase game-related items.

This usage of blockchain is already in motion. Sony is utilizing blockchain to record who owns what on the PlayStation Network. Fortnite creator Epic Games has partnered with a blockchain firm, Microsoft is using blockchain to handle Xbox Live royalty payments to developers, and many other companies are experimenting with blockchain usage.

Additionally, there is a Blockchain Game Alliance (BGA), which includes companies such as Ubisoft, ConsenSys, Everdreamsoft, and Enjin. The goal of BGA is to combine blockchain and gaming to develop solutions and develop standards and best practices.

Here are case studies:

- *Beyond the Void (`https://beyond-the-void.net/`)*: This is a game that utilizes Ethereum's blockchain to allow players to buy, sell, and trade "cosmetic in-game items" using NFT transactions.

- *Crypto card games*: These are similar to traditional card games, but instead of being physical cards, the cards are nonfungible. The cards are created using ERC-721 Ethereum tokens. Trading cards can be exchanged or played arcade-battle style. These cards can get expensive.

For instance, in 2018, CryptoKitties sold one cat for $111,000, and Gods Unchained sold a single card for $60,000. Examples are CryptoKitties (`https://www.cryptokitties.co`), Gods Unchained (`https://godsunchained.com`), and Spells of Genesis (`https://spellsofgenesis.com`).

— *HashCraft by Ubisoft*: This was built as an unreleased prototype that incorporates blockchain as the core gameplay, enabling players to be the builders of the game by utilizing a blockchain ledger as a database.

— *Plague Hunters (`https://store.steampowered.com/app/746530/Plague_hunter/`)*: This is a free-to-play strategy game with a built-in, Ethereum marketplace using NFT transactions for buying and selling weapons and "hunters." Plague Hunters passed Sony's review process and is scheduled to be released on PlayStation 4. It is the first blockchain-enabled game that provides NFT token trading on a major console.

In addition to these case studies, there is a dedicated web site just to keep track of advancements in blockchain technology related to games: `https://blockchaingamer.net/`. This resource can provide valuable information regarding current trends and news.

Music

In the current marketplace, many music industry artists, producers, fans, and consumers are frustrated, and blockchain has appeared to be a breath of fresh air to them because it has the potential to solve many pain points.

For instance, many artists and producers spend a lot of time and resources to infiltrate the market, publish work, and access the top music streaming platforms. Once an artist reaches the large streaming platforms such as Pandora, Spotify, and so on, they can access 250 million customers; however, many artists are unhappy with the payment structure and the time it takes to get paid. For instance, a song on Spotify would need more than 152,000 playbacks from premium users to be able to generate a mere revenue of $100 to the artist. The majority of the money goes to a long list of intermediary middlemen. Not only do artists get paid very little, it sometimes takes years to get these payouts.

By utilizing blockchain, artists can benefit in the following ways:

- *Increase the artist's revenues*: Blockchain can offer transparent and fair payouts. The content provider's revenue share can be split in a fair and transparent manner.

- *Streamline revenues*: Blockchain can provide a quicker way to pay artist royalties right away using crypto globally.

- *Split revenues automatically*: Smart contracts can be used to set up a payment structure for each individual involved in content creation such as songwriter.

- *Better connect with customers*: Fans can invest and connect with artists directly.

- *Store data*: Blockchain can be used to store information on the public ledger for digital right management (DRM), artists, assets, events, artists, venues, and so on.

- *Provide a streaming service*: A blockchain's P2P network can be used to stream music. Current music streaming services cost a lot or include too many ads.

The integration of music platforms needs to account for music formats and industry standards such as the following:

- *Common Works Registration (CWR) (www.cmrra.ca/)*: This is the standard format for registering and revising musical works.

- *DDEX (http://ddex.net)*: Provide a digital supply chain consortium by receiving data from leading media companies, music licensing organizations, digital service providers, and technical intermediaries and creating a standard.

Just like the gaming BGA Alliance, the music industry has created an organization to keep up with blockchain developments. The Open Music Initiative (open-music.org) explores the use of blockchain to help identify the rightful music rights holders and originators so they can modernize and streamline royalty payment and so artists can receive fair royalties. This can be done by utilizing blockchain for transparency and analyzing data better. Prominent members are Soundcloud, Red Bull Media and Netflix, Sony, YouTube, and Spotify.

Similar to hackathon competitions, Smackathon (https://www. smackathon.co) is an annual competition for interesting blockchain-based ideas in the music industry. For instance, in 2018, a blockchain platform was invented to pay listeners for every second they listened to a song, as well as providing fan engagement tools.

Looking at some of the more prominent projects, you will see that there are duplications of similar ideas. This reinforces how there are real pain points that need to be resolved in the music industry. The following are some case studies:

- *Audius (https://audius.co/)*: This uses a blockchain P2P network as a streaming service. Audius also uses blockchain for payment via smart contracts to send artists their payments immediately.

- *BitSong (https://bitsong.io/en)*: This company claims to be the first to use blockchain's P2P network for music streaming. Artists can upload songs and attach advertisements. For each advertisement listened to, the artist and the listeners get up to 90 percent of the profits that were invested by the advertiser. The platform includes a token called $BTSG to donate to indie artists and to purchase music.

- *Blokur (https://www.blokur.com)*: The Blokur platform combines AI and blockchain. Blockchain is used as the database to allow publishers to catalog their music, and then the community can approve or reject it. An AI algorithm resolves data conflicts automatically, such as rights disputes, to ensure the original artists get paid. There are already 50,000 songwriters and 7,000 publishers that have published their work.

- *Choon (https://choon.co)*: This uses blockchain for music streaming as well as digital payments to expedite the artists' payment. Artists can use Ethereum's smart contracts with each song to split the contributors' revenue. Other features are crowdfunding for new artists and rewards for users who create playlists.

- *eMusic (https://www.emusic.com)*: This uses blockchain and Ethereum smart contracts for music distribution of royalty payouts using a crypto token called eMusic.

- *Inmusik (https://inmusik.co)*: This has a crypto token called $OUND. Sounds are classified as "securitized music," and fans can "invest" in an artist to share earnings. Fans can also earn tokens for finding new songs, voting for best artists, and supporting the community. Artists can create an "army," get investors, and earn more than $20,000 per million streams.

– *MediaChain (www.mediachain.io)*: Acquired by Spotify, MediaChain utilizes blockchain's ledger for sharing information across different applications and organizations by issuing unique identifiers for each piece of information. MediaChain also works with artists to get them paid fairly using smart contracts.

– *Mycelia (myceliaformusic.org)*: This uses a blockchain ledger to hold a "creative passport," which contains information about a song, including IDs, acknowledgments, business partners, and payment mechanisms. Artists can create a smart contract payment system to split pay among all contributors.

– *MusicLife (https://www.musiclife.io)*: MusicLife created a media app called Echo (www.app-echo.com/index/download) with millions of users. The platform uses blockchain to process transactions quickly and do the bookkeeping. It created its own ecosystem and issued a token called $MITC. The algorithm allows an artist to claim music rights and get paid. Users can earn tokens as well as make purchases.

– *Musicoin (https://musicoin.org)*: This is a music blockchain streaming platform. Musicoin created a coin called $MUSIC to trade music-related purchases. Royalty earnings and tips go to artists immediately.

– *Ujo Music (https://www.ujomusic.com)*: This blockchain is used as a database to hold music ownership rights of an artist. Smart contracts and crypto are used to automate royalty payments to the artist and enable fans to tip artists directly. Artists can upload songs, control licensing, and manage distributions for free. Fans are charged a small fee of $1 for every 100 streams.

- *Viberate (https://www.viberate.com/fan)*: This uses a blockchain ledger. Viberate claims to be the world's largest live music database, which holds at the time of writing 460,000 artists and 500,000 events at 100,000 venues in 230 countries. Instead of hiring data entry people to keep insert and update artists, events, and venues, Viberate pays contributors with a $VIB crypto token.

- *VOISE (https://www.voise.com)*: This is a blockchain-powered app with an Ethereum token called $VOISE. Artists can upload content. Users' royalty pay goes almost entirely to the artists, cutting out the middleman.

Where to Go from Here

Blockchain already is in usage by many industries as well as has the potential to alter and improve many industries horizontally and vertically. I have covered only a few in this chapter; other industries include gambling, insurance, entertainment, and many others. I encourage you to do your own research regarding the relevant industry you are interested in as well as check the latest news, trends, and updates regarding current blockchain projects.

Summary

This book has been a journey into understanding blockchain technology. This chapter served as a 10,000-foot big picture of what's possible and I hope has inspired you on ways you can harness the blockchain technology.

As I pointed out, there are many use cases where replacing a centralized service with blockchain would not bring much value; however, there are many specific usages where blockchain platforms are benefiting industries already. Blockchain helps remove the long list of middlemen, closes the gap between users and entities, automates payments, improves data integrity, expedites services, globalizes transactions, improves security, lowers costs, and increases reliability.

In the first section of this chapter, I covered how to harness blockchain by examining what's readily available for you right now. I identified coins, tokens, ledgers, smart contracts, and dapps as the main elements that can be utilized to quickly tap into blockchain to potentially improve an existing platform. In the second part of this chapter, I covered many specific industries that can and have benefited from blockchain technology as well as listed case studies of specific blockchain-related ideas that being developed or have already been published.

Blockchain technology shows great promise, and the use cases, as well as the functionalities, are still unfolding. Over the next few years, blockchain usage is expected to increase and result in more widespread experimentation in many industries and verticals. Knowledgeable blockchain developers are believed to be a valuable commodity.

I would like to thank you, the reader, for purchasing this book and congratulate you for completing this chapter and this book. I hope that this book has provided you with valuable information, good coding examples, and a point of reference that will inspire you to create blockchain technology. Good luck in any new project you may take on.

Index

A

Accessible rich Internet
applications (ARIAs), 358
Alternative Trading Systems
(ATS), 425
Anchor peer, 308
Angular 2, 358
Angular app
benefits, 357
content
directives, 393, 394
footer component, 382, 383
header component, 383–385
transfer component (*see*
Transfer component,
Angular app)
dapp (*see* Decentralized
application (dapp),
Angular)
features, 358, 359
styling, 376
architecture, 376
import Material
modules, 378, 379
install Material, 377, 378
Material, 377
theme, 380, 381
Angular CLI, 359

Angular CLI and Component Dev
Kit (CDK), 357
Angular Ivy, 359
Angular project, dapp, 362
ensure no mismatch, 369
ethdapp files, 364
ng new command, 363
serve application, 365, 366
WebStorm, 367, 368
Application binary interface
(ABI), 203
Application layer, 29
Application program interface
(API), 109
creating, 110
getDBBlock service, 111
getWallet service, 111
initHttpServer, 110
retrieving blocks, 112
Application-specific integrated
circuit (ASIC), 33

B

Bitcoin, 7
HTTP JSON-RPC server, 121
Bitcoin core API
bitcoin wallet, 71, 72
block header, 63, 64

Printed in the United States
By Bookmasters